# CONSUMER LAW
# IN SCOTLAND

**AUSTRALIA**
LBC Information Services
Sydney

**CANADA and USA**
Carswell
Toronto

**NEW ZEALAND**
Brooker's
Auckland

**SINGAPORE and MALAYSIA**
Sweet & Maxwell Asia
Singapore and Kuala Lumpar

# CONSUMER LAW IN SCOTLAND

By

W.C.H. Ervine
*Senior Lecturer in Law, University of Dundee*

EDINBURGH
W. GREEN/Sweet & Maxwell Ltd
2000

First Edition 1995
Second Edition 2000


Published in 2000 by W. Green & Son Ltd
21 Alva Street
Edinburgh EH2 4PS

Typeset by YHT, London
Printed and bound in Great Britain by MPG Books Ltd,
Bodmin, Cornwall

A CIP catalogue record for this book is available from the
British Library

ISBN 0 414 013549

© 2000 W. Green and Son Ltd

*For*
*Carol and Jonathan*

# PREFACE TO THE SECOND EDITION

In the five years since the first edition there have been a number of developments in the field of consumer protection which have made it worth producing a new edition. Inevitably there have been more judicial decisions and legislation. In the latter area probably the most significant has been the revised Unfair Terms in Consumer Contracts Regulations 1999 which widen the range of organisations which can seek interdicts to prevent the use of unfair terms. Local government has been reorganised thereby altering the organisation of enforcement. Potentially the most significant development is the White Paper, *Modern markets: Confident consumers* published in 1999. This is the first White Paper to deal with consumer protection and to find any other official document of similar importance in this field one must go back to the Molony Report of 1962. The White Paper promises much, how much will be delivered remains to be seen.

Once again it is a pleasure to thank all those who have helped me. These include officials at various government departments, especially the Office of Fair Trading, and many trading standards officers. I am also indebted to colleagues in the Department of Law at the University of Dundee and the staff of the Law Library who have been unfailingly helpful. I am also grateful for the help and encouragement of the staff at W. Green.

I have tried to state the law as at April 6, 2000 though it has been possible to add some references to developments after that date.

W.C.H. Ervine
Dundee
June 2000

# PREFACE TO THE FIRST EDITION

This book attempts to set out the law relating to consumer protection in Scotland. Consumer protection is a recent development and much of the law originates in statutes having application throughout the United Kingdom. While there are a number of good books on the subject they approach the area from the point of view of English practitioners. It seemed to me that there was scope for a book which stated the law in Scotland. Where the law is statutory there are often Scottish decisions interpreting it; and the common law still has an important role to play. In addition, the separateness of the Scottish legal system also has an impact.

The term consumer protection is not a precise one and there can be legitimate difference of opinion as to what material should be covered in such a work. My approach has been to deal with the protection afforded to private consumers of goods and services. It could be objected that even within that definition of the subject there are gaps. This is particularly true when considering the area of services where very little is said, for example, about the important topic of financial services. The answer to this criticism is purely pragmatic: space does not allow everything to be covered; and, in any event, there are excellent specialist works in this area.

Consumer principles are increasingly being applied to areas not normally associated with consumer protection such as the provision of services by the State. Consumer organisations have for some time been dealing with the operation of the courts, the social security system and education. A tentative look at this new aspect of consumer protection has been taken but once again constraints of space have dictated that it should be brief.

I am indebted to numerous people for their help. Over many years staff at the National and Scottish Consumer Councils and trading standards officers have been ready to answer my queries as have officials in various government departments, notably the Office of Fair Trading. My colleagues in the Department of Law at the University of Dundee, and in other departments, have been extremely helpful. Although, with the passage of time, there have been many changes in relation to advertising, trade practices and the institutions of consumer protection, it would not be right to omit mention of my debt to the editors of the *Stair Memorial Encyclopaedia of the Laws of Scotland*, especially Mr Hamish McN. Henderson. Their assistance with my articles on consumer protection and advertising made work in those areas for this book much easier. Judith Pearson of the University of Aberdeen was good enough to read a draft of Chapter 9, and saved me from a number of errors. Needless to say, the errors in the work are solely my responsibility.

I have endeavoured to state the law as at January 5, 1995, though I have anticipated the coming into force on July 1, of the Unfair Terms in Consumer Contracts Regulations 1994, and it has been possible to incorporate some changes which took place after that date.

W.C.H. Ervine
Dundee
July 1995

# CONTENTS

# CONTENTS

# TABLE OF CASES

# TABLE OF STATUTES

xxxii *Consumer Law in Scotland*

# TABLE OF STATUTORY INSTRUMENTS

# TABLE OF TREATIES

CHAPTER 1

# BACKGROUND AND INSTITUTIONS OF CONSUMER PROTECTION

Consumer protection is essentially a modern topic. Indeed it is   **1–01**
tempting to say that it is a topic that dates only from the 1960s.
Even in 1968 it was not sufficiently well developed to merit a
chapter in one of the leading Scottish legal textbooks.[1] As in
many other countries in Europe, North America and elsewhere,
the 1960s were certainly the beginning of a period of substantial
development in Britain in the field of consumer protection.[2]

It would be misleading, however, to give the impression that   **1–02**
consumer protection does not have a lengthy history. One of the
oldest forms of consumer protection is what would now be
described as weights and measures legislation. There are numerous examples of such legislation by the Scottish Parliament
dating from the Middle Ages. The Weights Act 1425 defined the
standard stone at 15 lb. Troy, 16 lb. Scots, and under the Weights
Act 1540 burghs were required to keep one set of weights for
buying and selling, implying that there was a widespread practice
of using one set of weights when buying and another when
selling. In the same year standard measures for barrels of salmon
and herring were instituted by the Measures Act 1540. The
Measures and Weights Act 1587 appointed a commission to
prepare a universal standard of weights and measures. The
results of its efforts appear as the second Measures and Weights
Act 1587 which set out the "Mesuris and wechtis and the just
quantitie thereof", while in the Justices of the Peace Act 1661 it
was laid down that all measures were to conform with the
measure of Linlithgow.

The Measures Act 1685 defined three barleycorns set length-   **1–03**
ways as an inch, 12 inches as a foot, 36 inches as a yard, 37 inches

---

[1]   See Gloag and Henderson, *Introduction to the Law of Scotland* (7th ed.,
1968). Succeeding editions have had such a chapter.
[2]   Borrie, *The Development of Consumer Law and Policy – Bold Spirits and
Timorous Souls* (Stevens, 1984), p. 2.

as a Scots eln and 1760 yards as a mile. The purpose of this Act is stated as being "that there should be a fixed standard for measuring and computation of Myles [*sic*] and that the whole Isle of Britain should be under one certain kind of commensuration". The foot so calculated was to be "the only foot by which all workmen, especially Masons, Wrights, Glasiers, and others are ordained to measure their work in all time coming, under the pain of ane hundreth pounds *toties quoties*".[3] The importance of weights and measures was demonstrated by reference to them in the Act of Union, which provided that English weights and measures were to be used throughout the United Kingdom.[4]

**1–04**     The purity of goods is of cardinal importance to the consumer, and since the nineteenth century, legislation on this topic has continued to expand. In 1860 the "Act for Preventing the Adulteration of Articles of Food or Drink" was a mere 14 sections long.[5] This has gradually grown into a vast corpus of law of which the Food Safety Act 1990 is but the tip of a veritable iceberg of legislation, mostly to be found in statutory instruments.

**1–05**     The merchandise marks legislation, dating originally from 1862,[6] was the ancestor of the Trade Descriptions Act 1968, and was intended to control misleading claims about goods.

**1–06**     The legislation mentioned above has in common the fact that it invokes the criminal law as a means of consumer protection. Civil law had a much more limited role to play in protecting the consumer. It is sometimes said that the Sale of Goods Act 1893[7] was the first consumer protection statute of this type. Leaving aside the argument that in Scotland it may actually have weakened the consumer's position by importing alien concepts, it is difficult to see it in this light. True, it could be said to have benefited consumers in the sense that it clarified the law and made it more accessible, but as one might expect in the age of laissez-faire it left much scope to the parties to a contract to make their own bargain.

**1–07**     The role of the courts must not be forgotten. Theirs has not, on the whole, been a prominent role in protecting the consumer. However, *Donoghue v. Stevenson*[8] has had immense importance for consumers, as for many other groups, and its reverberations

---

3     I am indebted to Mr H. McN. Henderson, Deputy General Editor of the *Stair Memorial Encyclopaedia,* for drawing my attention to this material. For a comprehensive list of old statutes, see the General Index to the Act of the Parliaments of Scotland, Weights and Measures, APS xii 1232,1233.
4     See the Treaty of Union between Scotland and England 1707, art. XVII.
5     *i.e.* the Adulteration of Food and Drink Act 1860 (repealed).
6     See the Merchandise Marks Act 1862 (repealed).
7     Although the Sale of Goods Act 1893 was passed in 1894 it describes itself as the Sale of Goods Act 1893: see s. 64 (repealed).
8     1932 S.C. (H.L.) 31; 1932 S.L.T. 317.

continue to be felt. One might also regret that consumers or their advisers have not been more adventurous in invoking the principles of Scots law. On occasion clear invitations to do so seem to have been thoughtlessly ignored. For example in *McKay v. Scottish Airways Ltd*[9] Lord President Cooper seemed clearly to be pointing to the adoption of a reasonableness test for exclusion clauses, but this never seems to have been taken up by counsel in any later case.

While one must not ignore the ancient origins of some aspects    **1–08** of consumer protection, it was only in the 1960s that it came to have such prominence. If one were seeking an arbitrary point to use as the beginning of the modern era for consumer protection, July 1962, the date of publication of the *Molony Report*,[10] would be appropriate. This report reviewed a wide range of consumer issues and advocated reform in many areas. The Trade Descriptions Act 1968 can be traced directly to its recommendations and many other legislative reforms were given an initial impetus by its conclusions.

In the four decades since the publication of the *Molony Report*    **1–09** much has been achieved. Legislation on consumer safety, exclusion clauses, consumer credit and various marketing practices has been enacted. Perhaps of more importance, an institutional structure has been erected with the creation by the Fair Trading Act 1973 of the Office of Fair Trading, and the formation of the National Consumer Council which has a vigorous committee, the Scottish Consumer Council.[11]

In the same three decades the voluntary organisations which    **1–10** play such an important role have increased in importance and effectiveness. The Consumers' Association was barely eight years old when the *Molony Report* was published. It has developed into a dynamic organisation not only providing valuable information on products and services but also effectively lobbying for changes in the law. The Citizens' Advice Bureaux have expanded their network; and in a number of cities consumer groups have been set up under the aegis of the National Federation of Consumer Groups.

The last two decades have seen important changes in the    **1–11** techniques employed to achieve the ends of consumer protection. Administrative control has become more prominent and, perhaps somewhat paradoxically, self-regulation has expanded. The advertising industry is the most striking example of control by self-regulation, but self-regulation has come to play a

---

[9] 1948 S.C. 254; 1948 S.L.T. 402.
[10] *Final Report of the Committee on Consumer Protection* (the Molony Report) Cmnd. 1781 (1962).
[11] See paras. 1-39–1-42.

significant part in other areas such as package holidays, servicing
and repair of electrical goods and the car trade. In the consumer
white paper *Modern Markets: Confident Consumers* published in
July 1999, the Government has indicated that they intend to
place more emphasis on codes of practice as a way of improving
trading standards.[12] There are still many reforms that are necessary as the following pages will, at least, imply. At present the
prospects for reform are good following the publication of the
white paper. This is the first thorough review of consumer
protection since the *Molony Report* over 30 years ago and
promises a number of reforms.

**1–12**     As pointed out above, one of the most important developments in the protection of the consumer in recent years has been
the creation of a structure of organisations dealing with the
subject. To properly understand the operation of consumer
protection requires some knowledge of this structure and the
next section of this chapter therefore deals with this.

## INSTITUTIONS OF CONSUMER PROTECTION

### CENTRAL GOVERNMENT AND THE SCOTTISH EXECUTIVE

**1–13**  On May 12, 1999 for the first time for almost three hundred years
a Scottish Parliament met in Edinburgh. This devolved Parliament was created by the Scotland Act 1998 and has wide
legislative competence. It can legislate within Scotland on all
matters except those that have been reserved to the Westminster
Parliament. However, many areas of consumer protection are
among these reserved matters. The precise list is set out in
Schedule 5, sections C7 to C9. Most of these are topics which
have been the subject of United Kingdom-wide legislation. Section C7 is entitled "Consumer Protection" and covers the
regulation of the sale and supply of goods and services and fair
trading. Section C8 covers product safety and liability as well as
product labelling except in relation to food, agricultural and
horticultural produce and fish. Section C9 covers weights and
measures, units and standards of weight and measurement.
Important as these issues are it should be noted that there are
several important areas related to consumer protection which
are within the competence of the Edinburgh Parliament. The
exclusion of food, agricultural and horticultural produce and fish
from the reserved matters in C8 has just been noted. It must also
be remembered that the Scottish Parliament can legislate con-

[12] *Modern markets: confident consumers*, Cm. 4410 (1999), Chap. 4.

cerning the courts, and civil and criminal procedure. These areas impinge directly upon consumer protection. One has only to think of the importance of small claims procedure and the legislation on compensation orders for victims of crime in relation to consumer redress. Also, as we shall see later in this chapter, local government is a devolved matter. As much important enforcement work is carried out by local authorities, the Scottish Parliament and Executive could have an important, if indirect, influence on consumer protection.

While the role of the Scottish Parliament and Executive in **1-14** consumer protection should not be overlooked, the government department with the greatest responsibility for consumer protection is the Westminster Department of Trade and Industry (DTI) many of whose functions are carried out on a United Kingdom basis. The DTI is responsible for policy and legislation on trading standards, weights and measures, consumer credit — and consumer safety. It is also the sponsoring department for the National Consumer Council, including the Scottish Consumer Council, the Nationalised Industry Consumer Councils, and the British Standards Institution. Competition policy, which is also relevant to consumer protection, is the responsibility of this department. These issues are dealt with by the Department's Consumer and Corporate Affairs Division which is headed by a junior minister. Where Scottish issues are involved the DTI will liaise with the Scottish Executive.

### The Office of Fair Trading

One of the most interesting of the organisations with consumer **1-15** protection functions is the Office of Fair Trading, created by the Fair Trading Act 1973.[13] The office has similarities to the American Federal Trade Commission and similarly it has both consumer protection and competition functions. The government spokesman said in moving the second reading of the Fair Trading Bill that "[i]n the Office of the Director General of Fair Trading, the Bill creates machinery whereby a continuing watch can be kept on new developments which are likely to damage the consumer's economic interests".[14] The fact that the Director General not only has consumer protection functions but also important duties in relation to competition policy was regarded as an important aspect of this new office. The two roles were described as complementary. "Consumer sovereignty requires that the consumer should be adequately and accurately informed and adequately protected against unfair or misleading marketing

[13] See the Fair Trading Act 1973, s.1.
[14] 848 HC Official Report (5th series), col. 457.

techniques, and adequately protected, finally, against abuse of market power, monopoly or aspects of imperfect competition".[15]

**1–16**     The Director General of Fair Trading holds office for a five-year period and can be reappointed, as a previous Director General, Sir Gordon Borrie, was on two occasions. The current Director General is Mr John Bridgeman, though he will not be reappointed when his present term ends in August 2000. The Director General can be dismissed only for misbehaviour or incapacity and holds office on the terms set out in the Fair Trading Act 1973. He is permitted to appoint such staff as he thinks fit, subject to the approval of the Treasury to numbers and terms and conditions of service. The Director's office is in London. For several years a Scottish Office was maintained in Edinburgh, but this was closed as an economy measure. In 1998 the average number of permanent staff employed by the Office of Fair Trading was 416 of whom approximately 180 were employed in consumer protection work.[16] The original functions of the Director General are set out in section 2 of the Fair Trading Act. He is required to keep himself informed about commercial activities carried on in the United Kingdom relating to the production and supply of goods and the supply of services. He is to obtain this information in order to become aware of practices which may adversely affect the interests of consumers with respect to health, safety or other matters. In addition, such information may be obtained with a view to his becoming aware of monopoly situations and uncompetitive practices.

**1–17**     To this general remit the Fair Trading Act and later legislation adds certain specific functions. The Fair Trading Act permits him, the Secretary of State or other ministers to refer to the Consumer Protection Advisory Committee consumer trade practices"[17] which are considered adversely to affect the economic interests of consumers."[18] This function is now in abeyance as the members of the committee have not been reappointed on the expiry of their terms of office.[19] The procedure appears not to have worked as

[15]   848 HC official Report (5th series), col. 454.
[16]   *Annual Report of the Director General of Fair Trading 1998,* H.C. 524, London Stationery Office, p.92 and *The Office of Fair Trading: Protecting the Consumer from Unfair Trading Practices,* Report by the Comptroller and Auditor General, p. 14, H.C. 57 Session 1999-00, London, the Stationery Office.
[17]   For the meaning of "consumer trade practice" see the Fair Trading Act 1973, s.13.
[18]   Fair Trading Act 1973, s.14.
[19]   See Department of Trade and Industry Press Notice, Sept. 24, 1982, printed in the Annual Report of the Director General of Fair Trading for 1982 (198384 H.C. 20), p.45. Para. 7.06 of the White Paper appears to indicate that this part of the Act will be amended to make it effective.

effectively as had been hoped. A number of references were made to the committee and resulted in statutory instruments proscribing trade practices. A good example is the Business Advertisements (Disclosure) Order 1977[20] which makes it a criminal offence for someone who sells goods in the course of a business to fail to reveal this fact in an advertisement indicating that the goods are for sale. This issue was referred to the committee when it was revealed that it was not uncommon for traders, particularly in the second hand car trade, to masquerade as private sellers. The point of this is that in private sales the purchaser does not have the benefit of the implied terms relating to quality and fitness for purpose."[21]

Under Part III of the Fair Trading Act the Director General **1–18** has important powers to discipline traders who persist in a course of conduct which is detrimental to the interests of consumers. These are discussed in detail in the chapter on trading practices. The Consumer Credit Act 1974 introduced a general licensing system for the credit industry and the Director General operates it.[22]

The Director General has acquired further functions under **1–19** the Estate Agents Act 1979 which gives him wide powers to control the activities of estate agents. The keystone of this is what may be termed negative licensing. Unlike the credit industry where entry is conditional on having a licence, anyone may set up in business as an estate agent. The Director General, however, has power to prevent a person continuing to carry on such a business in certain circumstances. Section 4 of the Act provides that he may issue warning notices where an estate agent has failed to comply with his obligations under the Act. These included compliance with the rules relating to interest on clients' accounts, informing clients of his charging methods and observing the prohibition on taking pre-contractual deposits or having a personal interest in a transaction. A warning notice states that failure to comply with the statutory requirements will render the agent unfit to carry on estate agency work and further failure to observe these requirements may result in a banning order being made under section 23. Such an order may also be made by the Director General where an estate agent has been convicted of offences involving fraud, dishonesty or breaches of the Estate Agents Act or has committed discrimination in the course of estate agency work.

---

[20] S.I. 1977 No. 1918.
[21] Other examples are to be found in the Consumer Transactions (Restrictions on Statements) Order 1976 (S.I. 1976 No. 1813) and the Mail Order Transactions (Information) Order 1976 (S.I. 1976 No. 1812).
[22] For details see Chap. 9.

**1–20**     The Office of Fair Trading has a duty under section 124(3) of the Fair Trading Act to negotiation codes of conduct with appropriate trade associations and so far about 30 codes have been drawn up with trades as diverse as laundering and dry-cleaning, funeral undertaking, double glazing, the car trade and the travel industry. It is hoped that codes of conduct will raise standards in a trade or industry and bring benefits to consumers which it would be difficult to secure by legislation. As the previous Director General, Sir Gordon Borrie, put it in his Hamlyn lectures "codes are meant to refresh those parts of business life that laws cannot reach".[23]

**1–21**     Two examples illustrate achievements of this approach. Several codes of practice ban certain types of contractual term that have given rise to consumer complaint in the past, thus helping to make standard form contracts less one-sided than before. The Association of British Travel Agents have agreed that booking conditions shall not include clauses purporting to exclude or limit responsibility for the tour operator's contractual duty to exercise diligence in making arrangements for his clients or for consequential loss following from breach of his duty.

**1–22**     The Association of Manufacturers of Domestic Electrical Appliances has a code entitled Principles for Domestic Electrical Appliance Servicing. This contains good examples of attempts to improve levels of service which it would be difficult, if not impossible, to achieve by legislation. It provides that where a home repair service is required, the first visit should (wherever possible) be made within three working days from receipt of the request. The availability of spare parts has been a cause of concern but the Law Commissions have rejected statutory regulation as impracticable.[24] The code addresses this issue by stating that functional parts should be available for certain minimum periods after the date on which production of the appliance ceases. These range from five years for some small appliances to 15 years for thermal storage space heating.

**1–23**     The recent white paper indicates that the Government thinks that codes of practice can have an important role to play in improving trading standards. The white paper announced ambitious plans to alter the Fair Trading Act 1973 to permit the Office of Fair Trading to promote core principles of codes and to approve and publicise codes in individual market sectors which meet these principles. Given that the limited research into the

---

[23]  Borrie, *The Development of Consumer Law and Policy — Bold Spirits and Timorous Souls* (Stevens, 1984), p.74.

[24]  The Law Commission and the Scottish Law Commission, *Sale and Supply of Goods* (Law Com. No. 160, Scot. Law Com. No. 104), (Cmnd. 137), para. 3.66.

effectiveness of codes as a method of improving consumer welfare is equivocal this seems a questionable step.[25] Further doubt about the value of the proposed codes arises from the fact that some of the core principles requiring truthful advertisements and clear and fair contracts go no further than the law already requires.[26]

To implement its duties the Office is divided into three divisions — consumer affairs, competition policy and legal supported by administration, economics and information branches. In the report on Consumer Strategy[27] the Office set out its strategy for protecting the economic interests of consumers. This grouped the work of the consumer affairs division into three areas of regulation, consumer policy and information. The regulatory work involves credit licensing and enforcement of credit law, misleading advertising, control of unfair terms and dealing with problem traders. To make this work more effective teams with regional responsibilities have been set up. The policy work involves monitoring the market and producing reports recommending changes in the law or the behaviour of traders. The information function is one, which has always had a high priority and comprises information and advice for consumers, consumer education and advice and guidance on credit and estate agency for businesses. The report on the Office of Fair Trading's consumer protection work by the National Audit Office[28] presents a generally favourable picture. The quality of its information leaflets is praised and it is noted that its work in removing unfair terms in mobile telephone contracts alone is estimated to have saved consumers up to £80 million. Suggestions are made about improving the consumer licensing work and the Part III procedures for dealing with rogue traders. To ensure that the Office continues to operate effectively, the white paper announced at page 59 a fundamental review of its consumer affairs functions, and this is being carried out by the Director General.

**1–24**

---

[25] Pickering and Cousins, *The Economic Implications of Codes of Practice*, UMIST, 1980.
[26] See the White Paper, Chap. 4.
[27] OFT (1991).
[28] *The Office of Fair Trading: Protecting the Consumer from Unfair Trading Practices*, Report by the Controller and Auditor General, p. 14, H.C. 57 Session 1999-00, London, Stationery Office.

**Public Utility Schemes**[29]

**1-25** Public utilities, many of which have recently been privatised, create special problems of regulation. The solution adopted has been to create in the statute authorising privatisation a public official with the title of Director General whose role is to act as the industry regulator. The Director General of Telecommunications and the Office of Telecommunications (OFTEL), the Director General of Gas Supply and the Office of Gas Supply (OFGAS) are examples as is the Office of Electricity Regulation (OFFER). OFGAS and OFFER were amalgamated in June 1999 to form the Office of Gas and Electricity Markets (OFGEM). These industries have also had consumer organisations such as the Gas Consumers' Council and the regional Electricity Consumer Councils. The white paper announced that the government intend to replace the telecommunications consumer body with an independent consumer council and the gas and electricity bodies with a single energy consumer council.[30] One of the functions of the utility regulators is, in conjunction with other bodies, to protect the interests of consumers.

**1-26** The new arrangements for the Scottish water industry following the reorganisation of local government follow a different pattern. As this is not privatisation it was not thought appropriate to have a regulator in addition to the water authorities. To protect the interests of consumers, however, the Scottish Water and Sewerage Customers Council has been set up.[31]

**Local Government**

**1-27** Much of the day-to-day enforcement of consumer protection measures is carried out by local government. The reorganisation of local government carried out by the Local Government (Scotland) Act 1994 created 29 single purpose district councils in place of the two-tier structure of regions and district councils. The three island authorities also remain in existence. As the weights and measures authorities for their areas, these new councils have statutory responsibility for the enforcement of much consumer protection legislation. They are responsible for the enforcement of weights and measures legislation, labelling and standards requirements of food and drugs, the Trade Descriptions Act 1968 and the Consumer Credit Act 1974. This list includes only the better known pieces of consumer legislation which contain provisions impinging directly on everyday concerns. The

[29] For further details see Chap. 8.
[30] White Paper, p.56.
[31] Local Government (Scotland) Act 1994, s.68.

enforcement of weights and measures legislation, for example, helps to ensure that the customer receives a kilogramme when he or she requests that amount, or a pint of beer or a quarter gill as appropriate. They also enforce many other pieces of legislation as diverse as the Agriculture Act 1970, dealing with fertilisers and animal feeding stuffs, the Poisons Act 1972 and the Video Recordings Act 1984, to say nothing of many pieces of subordinate legislation often made under the European Communities Act 1972. One advantage of reorganisation has been that it has resulted in all the consumer protection functions of local government being carried out by one council. Previously, the regions were the weights and measures authorities and carried out the bulk of consumer protection work, while the former district councils had responsibilities in the field of food hygiene and the licensing of dealers in second-hand goods under the Civic Government (Scotland) Act 1982.

To carry out these duties the district councils have set up    **1–28** trading standards or consumer protection services. These are almost invariably located in larger departments often termed environmental health and consumer protection departments, or even protective services departments. The use of the term trading standards service indicates the modern approach to the task which is seen as being neutral between traders and consumers. It recognises that the function of a trading standards department in ensuring fair trading is important not only to consumers but also to those traders who meet their legal obligations. Those who do not trade fairly harm not only consumers but also those traders who act honestly.

The size of the larger Scottish regions meant that a service of    **1–29** considerable sophistication could often be provided. Strathclyde Region was probably the largest regional consumer protection department in Europe. It was able to build up an impressive unit dealing with unlicensed moneylending. Lothian Region's department had considerable success with specialist task forces such as the Vehicle Enquiry Team. As many authorities are now much smaller than the old regional authorities there must be concern about their ability to deal as effectively with some aspects of their functions as the regions were able to do. However, section 58 of the Local Government (Scotland) Act 1994 permits two or more councils to combine in providing services and it may be that trading standards functions could be provided on a joint basis.

In addition to their statutory duties, trading standards services    **1–30** provide advice to traders on how to comply with legislation. Most also provide advice to consumers. Some have shop front premises where consumers can obtain shopping advice as well as advice about their legal rights. With the creation in the sheriff

court of the small claims procedure which permits lay representation, several services have been accompanying consumers
to court and acting as their advocates.

## Local Authority Co-ordinating Body on Trading Standards

**1–31**    In 1976 local authorities in the United Kingdom set up the Local
Authority Co-ordinating Body on Trading Standards
(LACOTS). It provides machinery for trading standards departments to liaise with the Government and industry on technical
matters; co-ordinate local practice to ensure uniform enforcement of legislation; and to advise local authorities on the
interpretation and enforcement of legislation. A central feature
of the work of LACOTS is the "home authority principle" which
was relaunched on April 1, 1994 to announce its general extension to food hygiene.

**1–32**    The home authority principle is designed to avoid businesses
which may have offices and factories in several different parts of
the country receiving conflicting advice or being subject to
differing interpretations of the law from various local authorities. The main feature of the principle is to prevent
infringements by offering advice at source and by encouraging
enforcement authorities and enterprises to work in liaison with a
particular authority called "the home authority". This is the
authority where the decision making base of the enterprise is
located and can be the head office, the factory, a service centre or
the place of importation. The role of the home authority is to
provide advice on policy issues, compliance with the law and
adherence to standards and codes of practice. It is the link
between enforcement authorities and originating authorities
with whom they must liaise. Originating authorities are only
relevant where an enterprise operates a decentralised structure
and decisions may be made at a number of different places. It
will monitor premises within its area at which goods or services
are produced. It keeps the home authority informed about
significant findings and, if there are problems, it will liaise with it
to solve them.

**1–33**    Each local authority enforces the law in its area. Under the
home authority principle when enforcement authorities detect
breaches of the law they should consider consultation with the
home or originating authority before embarking on detailed
investigations or legal action. They should also routinely inform
the home authority of enforcement action which they have
taken.

**The National Consumer Council**

The National Consumer Council (NCC) was set up in 1975 as a   **1–34**
non-departmental public body (or Quango) following the White
Paper, *A National Consumers' Agency*.[32] It replaced the Consumer Council which, on the recommendation of the Molony
Committee,[33] had been set up by the Government in 1963 but
abolished in 1971. Technically, it is a company limited by guarantee and its Memorandum of Association states that its purpose
is:

> "to promote action for furthering and safeguarding the inter-
> ests of consumers, to ensure that those who take decisions
> which will affect the consumer can have a balanced and
> authoritative view of the interests of consumers before them
> and to insist that the interests of all consumers including the
> inarticulate and disadvantaged are taken into account."

The memorandum then goes into more detail about how these   **1–35**
purposes are to be achieved. The Council shall make representations of the views of consumers to central and local government
and industry (including the nationalised industries). It may also
represent consumers on appropriate government and other
organisations including international organisations. While it
does not give advice or information to individual consumers, one
of the Council's functions is to provide information and advice to
consumers in general and to comment on the adequacy of
consumer advice services and support facilities.

This work is directed by a Council of 19 members chaired by a   **1–36**
part-time chairman. Members of the Council, who are appointed
by the Secretary of State for Trade and Industry, come from a
geographically wide range of places and diverse backgrounds.
The chairmen of the associate councils, the Scottish and Welsh
Consumer Councils, and the General Consumer Council of
Northern Ireland are members. There are usually members with
backgrounds in trading standards, the legal profession, industry
and commerce and other consumer organisations. The full-time
staff of 31, including professional and secretarial staff, are
located in central London.

Given the distinctive socio-economic, geographic and cultural   **1–37**
issues as well as the separate legal, administrative and educational

[32] Cmnd. 5726 (1975).
[33] *Final Report of the Committee on Consumer Protection*, Cmnd. 1781 (1962), Chap. 20.

system in Scotland, it was appropriate that a Scottish Consumer Council should have been set up. There is also a similar Welsh Council. The Scottish Consumer Council (SCC), which has offices in Glasgow, is technically a sub-committee of the NCC. Its structure is similar to the parent body. There is a chairman and 13 members, who are appointed by the Secretary of State for Trade and Industry in consultation with the Secretary of State for Scotland. All are part-time and they have a similar range of backgrounds to the members of the NCC.

**1–38**     Funding comes mainly from a modest grant-in-aid from the Department of Trade and Industry which provided 80 per cent of the NCC's income in 1998–99. The other 20 per cent came from research projects carried out for various organisations; mostly in the public sector. In the case of the SCC only half of its income comes in the form of a grant-in-aid channelled through the NCC.[34] In 1998–99 it raised the other half from research projects. In the first edition of this book the fear was expressed that pressure from the Government to generate more income from non-government sources might compromise the independence of the SCC and deflect them from their main role. Happily, this does not seem to have happened.

**1–39**     The NCC and its associate councils adopt the same strategy for carrying out their task. As they have no statutory powers they can only achieve their objectives by persuasion. They have built up a formidable record of achievement based on thorough research and effective lobbying and campaigning. They have also been instrumental in assisting other consumer organisations. For example, the NCC has played a central role in the creation and growth of the Consumer Congress.

**1–40**     Since its creation the Scottish Consumer Council has come to play a prominent part in public affairs in Scotland. Much of its work involves responding to proposals of the Government but it has also, where possible, attempted to set its own agenda. Good examples of this have occurred in legal reform where the SCC was prominent in the campaign for a small claims procedure and the inclusion of Scotland in the Unfair Contract Terms Act 1977. More recently, it has argued strongly for a review of the civil justice system in Scotland and has supported the creation of the Scottish Sheriff Court Users' Group. It has not confined itself to a narrow definition of consumer issues. Over the years it has done a good deal of work on education and was one of the few organisations to argue strongly for the introduction of school boards. It has also built up a strong reputation in health issues and food matters. Given the geography of Scotland it has also paid particular attention to the problems of consumers living in

[34]  SCC, *Annual Report 1998–99*, p.34.

rural areas, as its report *Consumer Problems in Rural Areas* demonstrates.

**Consumers in the European Community Group**

Consumers in the European Community Group (CECG) is   **1–41**
constitutionally separate from the NCC, though its funding is
included in the NCC's grant-in-aid and its staff are formally
employed by the NCC. It addresses similar issues to those of the
NCC but within the context of the European Union. It is a
membership organisation with a constituency of 32 supporting
bodies.

**Nationalised Industry Consumer Councils**

A diminishing range of goods and services is provided for   **1–42**
consumers by nationalised industries. These industries are statutory corporations invested with monopoly, or near monopoly,
powers, and this makes it especially important that there should
be scrutiny of their activities in the consumer interest. As the
Molony Report noted, "the evils of monopolistic control are not
the exclusive prerogative of private enterprise".[35] The consumer
interest in many of these industries has been represented by the
creation of consumer or consultative councils. The Coal Industry
Nationalisation Act 1946 set up the Domestic Coal Consumers'
Council to consider any matter affecting the sale or supply of
coal, coke or manufactured fuel. The consumer bodies associated with the railways are the Central Rail Users' Consultative
Committee and local Rail Users Consultative Committees; one
of which covers Scotland. They were created by the Railways
Act 1993.[36] The interests of users of postal services are protected
by the Post Office Users' National Council and "country councils", one of which is the Post Office Users' Council for
Scotland.

**Consumer Congress**

Consumer Congress exists to help United Kingdom consumer   **1–43**
groups to work together for the benefit of all consumers. It aims
to facilitate United Kingdom consumer organisations to develop
cohesive policies on matters of concern to consumers, including
those who are disadvantaged, and to encourage, facilitate and
inform joint and co-operative action to promote these policies. It

---

[35] *Final Report of the Committee on Consumer Protection*, Cmnd. 1781 (1962),
p.296.
[36] ss. 2 and 3.

encourages and assists communication and consultation between consumer organisations, the Government, industry and regulators on matters of concern to consumers. Congress was established in 1975 by the NCC and became an independent organisation in 1997. Although still funded primarily by the NCC with a guarantee of support until September 2000, Congress employs its own staff and has an office at 20 Grosvenor Gardens in London. It currently enjoys support from some 200 members, and these organisations represent a very wide range of consumer interests. Members include organisations with particular interest in specific issues such as disabilities and utility services; others such as the Scottish Consumer Council will have a much wider remit. Many local and health authorities hold "observer" membership so as to remain in contact with developments and to hear the views of consumer groups with whom they will have contact. Membership subscriptions account for approximately 20 per cent of income. Whilst the Congress is expecting to develop its communication and networking facilities (with plans for use of the Internet) its present main means of communication is by way of a directory, a monthly newsletter and its annual Conference which is used to provide information, to allow debate on current issues and formulate views that can be supplied to others.

**Consumers' Association**

1–44    The Consumers' Association, best known as the publisher of *Which?* magazine, was founded in 1957. In 1987 it became a charity and changed its name to the Association for Consumer Research, a private company limited by guarantee which is entitled to omit the word "limited" from its name. With effect from April 1, 1995 the name again became the Consumers' Association. This company carries on research and charitable functions and, since April 1, 1995 also carries on campaigning functions. A subsidiary, Which? Ltd now carries on the trading functions which consist primarily of publishing both books and magazines. The Consumers' Association is financed by members' subscriptions, donations and fees for advisory services which it undertakes and the trading profits of its subsidiary. In 1999 the Consumers' Association had 670,000 members, and 982,000 subscribers to its magazines.[37]

1–45    While the Consumers' Association is best known for *Which?*, it also publishes other magazines such as *Holiday Which?*, *Gardening Which?*, *Which? Way to Health*, *Drugs and Therapeutics Bulletin* and *Legal Services*. These contain reports of comparative tests of products and services which have been

37    Annual Report 1998–99, p.26.

carried out completely independently. Consumers' Associations' publications carry no advertising and tests are carried out on products purchased anonymously. It also publishes a wide range of books such as *What to Do When Someone Dies* and *The Which? Hotel Guide.* In addition to this work, the Consumers' Association has increasingly been involved in campaigning. It was prominent in the campaigns for the Unfair Contract Terms Act 1977 and has vigorously campaigned on safety issues.

**National Federation of Consumer Groups**

The National Federation of Consumer Groups is a body which **1–46** co-ordinates the activities of local consumer groups, of which there are 13 in the United Kingdom, including groups in Aberdeen and Edinburgh. It receives grants from the Consumers' Association and the Department of Trade and Industry. Local groups encourage interest in consumer affairs and campaign for better local shops and services. At national level it puts forward its views to the Government and has produced guides on consumer matters.

**The British Standards Institution**

The British Standards Institution, incorporated by royal charter **1–47** in 1929, is an independent, non-profitmaking body which exists to co-ordinate the production of goods by devising, where possible, national standards. A "British Standard" sets out testing requirements, specifications or measurements with which a product should comply. Such standards are devised after consultation with representatives of manufacturers, distributors and users. Of particular relevance to consumers is the Consumer Standards Advisory Committee, which includes representatives of consumer organisations.

**The Advertising Standards Association**

The Advertising Standards Association Ltd (ASA) administers **1–48** the system of self-regulatory control in the print, cinema and poster media. It is a company limited by guarantee whose directors are its chairman and council members. The chairman, currently Lord Rodgers of Quarry Bank, is appointed by the Advertising Standards Board of Finance Ltd (ASBOF); an independent body created by the advertising industry. ASBOF is obliged by its articles of association, before making any appointment, to consult with the Department of Trade and Industry, and the appointment is also made in consultation with, and subject to the agreement of, the existing members of the ASA Council. The

ASA articles provide that the chairman is not to be engaged in the business of advertising. It is the chairman who chooses the members of the council, normally totalling 12, of whom at least half must be independent. It is present policy to ensure that the proportion of independent to industry members remains at the maximum permissible level of two to one.

**1–49** The functions of the ASA are to oversee the work of the Code of Advertising Practice (CAP) Committee in drafting and amending the British Code of Advertising Practice; to act as an appeal tribunal from the CAP Committee from within the industry; to maintain a procedure for investigating complaints from members of the public; and to publicise the existence of the self-regulatory system of control. The ASA has been funded since 1974 by a surcharge of 0.1 per cent on the cost to the advertiser of advertisements other than those appearing in the classified columns of the press. The surcharge is collected by ASBOF.

## EUROPE
### The European Union

**1–50** As with so many areas of law, consumer protection is influenced by the United Kingdom's membership of the European Union. Our accession to the E.U. (or the European Communities as it was then known) coincided with the development of its consumer policy and the creation of its consumer institutions. These institutions are described in Chapter 2 (see paragraphs 2–11 to 2–13).

### Bureau Europeen des Union de Consommateurs

**1–51** To try to ensure that the consumer voice is heard in the councils of the European Union, Europe's consumer organisations set up the Bureau Europeen des Union de Consommateurs (BEUC). It is a lobbying organisation with a small staff and is based in Brussels. Its methods are similar to those of the National Consumer Council.

CHAPTER 2

# THE EUROPEAN DIMENSION

An English judge once said memorably that E.C. law was like an **2–01**
"incoming tide. It flows into the estuaries and up the rivers. It
cannot be held back. Parliament has decreed that the Treaty [of
Rome] is henceforward to be part of our law."[1] Like other areas
of law, consumer protection is subject to this process and it is
important to appreciate its impact. For the E.C. has had an
impact on the development of consumer protection law and
policy in the United Kingdom. It is an impact which has produced benefits but can also be argued to have had disadvantages.
In this chapter the origins and implementation of this policy are
considered as well as its benefits and disadvantages.

In an economic community it is a remarkable irony that **2–02**
consumer protection has not had a high profile. There were only
four references to consumers in the original treaty and, with one
exception, the translation is probably not accurate. "End user"
rather than "consumer" would probably be more appropriate.
This, no doubt, is explained by the fact that the Communities
were the result of negotiations which took place in the 1950s,
well before consumer protection became the conspicuous issue
that it did in the mid-1960s and 1970s.

The term "consumer protection" first appeared in Article 100a **2–03**
of the Treaty of Rome, as a result of the Single European Act.
This Act did not accord consumer protection the status of a
separate policy of the E.C. in the way that environmental policy
was recognised. That, however, was achieved by the Maastricht
Treaty on European Union, signed in 1992, which added a Title
XI on consumer protection to the original Treaty. This now
appears in a slightly modified form in Article 153 of the Treaty as
modified by the Amsterdam Treaty.

[1] *per* Lord Denning, *H.P. Bulmer Ltd and Showerings Ltd v. 1. Bollinger SA
and Champagne Lanson Pére et Fils* [19741 2 All E.R. 1226, at p. 1231.

## THE LEGAL COMPETENCE OF THE E.C.

**2–04**    When looking at any legislative action of the E.C. it must always
be borne in mind that the E.C. is not a sovereign state, and so one
must always be able to point to some power in the E.C. treaties
permitting the action taken. In the field of consumer protection
there have, in the past, been some doubts on this score. However, it has long been accepted that where the interests of
consumers in health and safety have been at stake the E.C. has
competence.[2] This could be justified by arguments based on the
original Article 30 (now Article 28) which are implicitly accepted
in the series of cases starting with the *Cassis de Dijon* judgment
discussed below. There had been a little more doubt about
legislation dealing with the protection of the economic interests
of consumers but, legally, it could be justified by pointing to
Article 2 of the original Treaty of Rome which sets out the
objectives of the treaty to create a common market and improve
living standards. It was argued that differing national laws on
advertising, contract terms and marketing practices impede the
attainment of a truly common market, and that the improvement
of the protection of the consumer is an aspect of a better
standard of living. As Professor Bourgoignie has pointed out,
"[i]mproving the standard of living . . could no longer be understood only in a quantitative way (increase in income and
purchasing power of individuals) but also qualitatively, aiming to
improve, in the widest sense of the term, the living conditions of
European citizens."[3]

**2–05**    With the amendments made to the original treaty by the Single
European Act and the Maastricht and Amsterdam Treaties the
situation is now clearer. The starting point is Article 3 of the
Treaty which sets out the activities which the E.C. may carry out.
Paragraph (h) provides that these include "the approximation of
the laws of Member States to the extent required for the func-
tioning of the common market" and paragraph (t) provides that
these may include "a contribution to the strengthening of consumer protection". One then turns to Article 153 (using the new
numbering following Amsterdam) which contains the title on
consumer protection. This amends this title which was originally
inserted by the Maastricht Treaty. It provides in paragraph 1
that:

---

[2]    See Close, *The Legal Basis of the Consumer Protection Programme of the
EEC and Priorities for Action,* in *Consumer Law in the EEC* (Woodroffe,
1984).
[3]    Bourgoignie, "Euorpean Community Consumer Law and Policy: from Rome
to Amsterdam", 1998 Cons. L.J. 443 at p. 444.

"In order to promote the interests of consumers and to ensure a high level of consumer protection, the Community shall contribute to protecting the health, safety and economic interests of consumers, as well as to promoting their right to information, education and to organise themselves in order to safeguard their interests."

These objectives are to be achieved by two means. The first is by **2–06** Article 95 (formerly 100a) measures relating to the internal market. Such measures can be adopted using the qualified majority voting procedures of the Treaty and must "take as a base a high level of protection". In addition, they will be attained by measures which support, supplement and monitor the policy pursued by the Member States. A further important paragraph of Article 153 provides that " [c]onsumer protection requirements shall be taken into account in defining and implementing other Community policies and activities". The reference in Article 153 to supporting and supplementing measures taken by Member States is a reminder that all of this is subject to the principle of subsidiarity. This is now found in Article 5 of the EC Treaty.

This clause, which has been the subject of intense debate, is **2–07** one of those provisions which can be used by opposing sides in an argument to justify their position. Lord Mackenzie-Stuart, a former President of the European Court of Justice, went so far as to call it "gobbledygook" in a letter to *The Times*.[4]

As has been pointed out: **2–08**

"The quest for a definition of subsidiarity is doomed to failure. It has become an intrinsic part of the debate on greater social, political and economic integration, and as such, will be subject to constant evolution, adapting to shifts in policy and opinion. It is a flexible but elusive concept, with the potential both to act as a dynamic for change and as a bulwark of the status quo. The priority for consumers is to ensure that it does not serve as a pretext to block proposals to improve consumer protection at Community level which might otherwise be neglected at national level."[5]

The important point to grasp, which Article 153 supports, is that **2–09** consumer protection is not just an optional extra for the Community. It is an essential feature of a single market. Such a market can be exploited by the unscrupulous who engage in fraudulent practices across national boundaries. This calls for

---

4 Dec. 11, 1992.
5 Gibson, "Subsidiarity: The Implications for Consumer Policy" (1993)16 J.C.P 323 at p. 336.

action at E.C. level both in the interests of honest traders, who should be protected from such unfair competition, and consumers, who are entitled to protection of their interests. A failure to provide effective protection is bound to weaken consumer confidence and thus the success of the single market.

**2–10**     A difficult question is how to decide when action should be taken at Community level and when it should be left to Member States. In a communication to the Council and the European Parliament in October 1992, the Commission proposed three tests to assist in the application of the subsidiarity principle. These were "comparative efficiency", "value added", and "proportionality". In deciding whether there should be Community action the first two would involve the use of a number of criteria, such as whether there was a significant cross-border dimension, the effects on trade and competition, and the costs of taking action. The proportionality test would be used to ensure that action taken would be no more than necessary to achieve the desired aim. This would require consideration to be given to self-regulatory measures as well as legislation.

## THE INSTITUTIONAL ARRANGEMENTS

**2–11**     The low status of consumer protection has often been reflected in the institutional arrangements in Brussels. As a result of a heads of state meeting in Paris in 1972 a directorate-general for environment and consumer protection was, for the first time, created in the Commission. After various changes of title the consumer protection functions were moved to a separate Consumer Protection Service with the intention that this service would influence the policies of all directorates which have implications for consumers. In 1995 consumer protection once again became the responsibility of a directorate-general (DG XXIV). In 1998 the mad cow crisis and other health concerns resulted in it being renamed the Directorate General for Health and Consumer Protection; now commonly referred to as DG Sanco.[6] This reflected the fact that its responsibilities and manpower have been considerably increased as a result of the decision of the Commission to separate the services deciding policy on food and health from those responsible for questions of control which have been transferred to DG XXIV.

**2–12**     As Professor Bourgoignie notes, while there is reason for pleasure at this increase in the resources and responsibilities for consumer protection there is also cause for caution. The frequent reorganisations of DG XXIV have not been conducive to

[6]   This acronmymn derives from the French name of the directorate — Santé et Protection des Consommateurs.

the creation of an effective and coherent service. He also observes "[t]hat one would also hope that a balance is observed between the new tasks of DG XXIV and its more traditional responsibilities".[7] At least, as a result of these changes the financial stringency that has bedevilled E.C. consumer protection activities seems to have been eased.

At the same time as what is now the Consumer Protection **2–13** Directorate was set up, a Consumers Consultative Committee (CCC) was created. The idea was that this body, consisting of representatives of national consumer organisations and trade union representatives, would be consulted by the Commission on its consumer programme. It has recently been renamed the Consumer Consultative Council. In practice consultation is sporadic and the CCC, in any event, does not have the resources to be an effective commentator on policy issues.

### THE CONSUMER PROTECTION PROGRAMMES

It was in 1975 that the Community adopted its first programme **2–14** for consumer protection[8] which set out to guarantee five basic consumer rights:

(1) protection of the consumer against health and safety risks.
(2) protection of consumers' economic interests.
(3) improvement of the consumers' legal position through advice, assistance, and the right to seek a legal remedy.
(4) improvement of consumer education and information.
(5) appropriate consultation and representation of consumers in the taking of decisions affecting their interests.

In May 1981 a second programme along the same lines was **2–15** adopted,[9] and ever since at regular intervals further programmes have been published. It cannot be said that a great deal was achieved by these early programmes. However, it must be remembered that there were considerable obstacles in the way of this. Until the Single European European Act and the Maastricht Treaty there were doubts about the legal basis for consumer protection measures. Another formidable hurdle in the early years was the need for unanimity amongst the member states before a measure could be implemented.

The more recent consumer programmes have shown a change **2–16** of emphasis in part brought about by the treaty changes that have established the legitimacy of consumer protection as a

[7] *op. cit.* note 3 at p. 457.
[8] [1975] O.J. C92/1.
[9] [1981] O.J. C133/1.

community policy. The Commission's Consumer Action Plan 1996-1998[10] included new priorities. These were the protection of consumers' interests with regard to public services and financial services as well as in relation to the information society. It also alluded to the importance of sustainable consumption, assistance to the countries of central and eastern Europe to develop consumer protection policies and to Third World countries in order to improve conditions in relation to basic products.

**2–17**     The current plan[11] identifies three areas as the main tasks for consumer policy. These are: a more powerful voice for consumers throughout the E.U.; a high level of health and safety for the E.U. consumers; and full respect for the economic interests of E.U. consumers. The more powerful voice for consumers will involve assistance to national consumer associations on specific prjects which improve their capacity to represent, inform and advise consumers. Preference in this area is to be given to collaborative projects. Given consumer concerns about food safety it is no suprise to find that the task of ensuring a high level of health and safety for consumers involves more coherent risk analysis using the best scientific advice and the restoration of consumer confidence in food. It is also proposed to give continuing attention to existing laws on the safety of consumer products, to examine the need to reinforce the safety of services and ensure that there is better enforcement, monitoring and response to emergencies. Under the heading of respect for the economic interests of E.U. consumers, the Commission observes that "over the next three years the critical taks will be to make legislation work in practice". It is intended to implement the action programme on financial services and to monitor the implementation of the Commission's recommendations on the introduction of the Euro.

## ACHIEVEMENTS SO FAR

**2–18**     As this recital of the various Community programmes shows, there has been no shortage of good intentions towards consumers. To what extent have there been concrete achievements? In pursuance of its aim of promoting consumer protection the Commission has encouraged debate on the subject, an aspect of their work which should not be underestimated. The Commission organises or funds conferences and research projects throughout Europe for this purpose. This is probably of more importance in those parts of Europe where consumer protection

[10]   COM (98) 696.
[11]   COM(98)0696 -C4-0035/99.

is less well developed. It must be remembered that consumer protection has, until fairly recently, been more prominent in northern Europe. However, there have been, and continue to be, benefits from this aspect of the Commission's work in the United Kingdom in general, and in Scotland in particular. The interest of the Commission in consumer redress influenced the creation of the small claims procedure in the sheriff court through both financial and moral support to the Dundee small claims experiment. Similar encouragement has been given to pilot projects in Belgium and Milan. More recently the Commission gave financial support for joint Scottish and Irish projects on in-court advice. The Scottish part of this project (which is still running) provides an adviser based in Edinburgh Sheriff Court.

Its interest in consumer redress has most recently been indi-      **2–19**
cated in its thought-provoking Green Paper on Access to Justice,[12] which has stimulated discussion on a wide range of issues. Apart from the development of small claims procedures it raises the question of the use of group actions, which is a notable lacuna in the Scottish legal system. There are no practical methods by which those who are the victims of a common misfortune or fraud can band together to sue the perpetrator.

Another type of group action is sometimes referred to as the      **2–20**
public interest action. This permits an organisation to take action in the public interest to stop some activity inimical to consumers. While available in some European jurisdictions, it is not available in the Scottish, or indeed the English, legal system. European influence may be beneficial here. Provision for such means of redress is contained in individual pieces of European legislation. As a result of the provisions of the Misleading Advertising Directive and the Unfair Contract Terms Directive it has been necessary to provide a version of this type of action. Initially, the Office of Fair Trading was given powers to take action in some circumstances under these directives. As we shall see later, in the case of unfair terms these powers have been extended to a range of other organisations. With the implementation of the Injunctions Directive there will be a further extension of this type of action. This directive addresses the problem of obtaining redress across national boundaries. This is a start and may accustom lawyers and administrators to a new idea. In time, it may be possible to develop a fully-fledged group action.

As part of their concern for safety the Commission has pro-      **2–21**
moted RAPEX, the Rapid Information Exchange System. Under this system Member States notify the Commission's Consumer Protection Service when they discover a dangerous product on

---

[12] COM (93) 378.

their market, and the Commission in turn notifies other Member States. EHLASS, the European Home and Leisure Accident Surveillance System has also been promoted by the Commission. Under it Member States provide the Commission with statistics on home and leisure accidents involving products, to help identify areas where common action is needed.

**2–22**     In discussion of the achievements of E.C. consumer protection policy most attention tends to centre on its legislative achievements. Over the years a considerable number of measures have emanated from Brussels. In the early years progress was slow but it should not be forgotten that even in the very early years legislation which benefited consumers was passed. Various directives whose primary aim was harmonisation of the common market also had the effect of improving consumer protection. Examples from this early period include legislation on the harmonisation of laws on classification, denomination, packaging and labelling of consumer goods as well as those on foodstuffs, animal health, pharmaceutical products, cosmetics and electrical home appliances. In the 1970s and 1980s more overtly consumer protection measures were adopted although the uncertainty over the legal competence of the E.C. in the area of consumer protection undoubtedly retarded progress. However, it is possible to point to a number of directives from this period directly concerning consumers. Examples are those on the labelling of foodstuffs in 1978, the Misleading Advertising Directive of 1984, the Product Liability Directive and the Door to Door Sales Directives of 1985, and the Consumer Credit Directive of 1986.

**2–23**     As Professor Bourgoignie has observed,[13] most of these measures related to improving consumer information. It was only with the recognition in the E.C. Treaty itself of consumer protection as a community policy that more fundamental initiatives have been taken in the last 10 years. To quote Professor Bourgoignie: "[b]eyond solutions of an informational nature which aim to improved the quality of the consent which a consumer gives to his actions, the provisions of the Directives most recently adopted or proposed, seek to alter the very nature of consumer relationships by imposing new obligations, by confirming new rights and by prohibiting certain practices or beaviour". Examples of such new directives are those on package travel, general product safety, unfair contract terms, timeshare, distance contracts, comparative advertising, consumer sales and guarantees, and the Injunctions Directive.

**2–24**     As has been suggested above, E.C. proposals can have a beneficial effect on domestic policy. Small claims is an example that has been cited. Added to that might be the control of unfair

[13] *op. cit.* note 3 at p.449.

contract terms. Regulation of such terms has, since the passing of the Unfair Contract Terms Act 1977, been quite effective. In many respects the E.C. Directive on Unfair Contract Terms duplicates that legislation. The importance of the Directive lies in the extensions which it makes to our law. This is discussed in more detail in the chapter on Unfair Contract Terms and at this stage it is sufficient to point out two salient features. As mentioned above, the Directive requires organisations to be permitted to take action on behalf of consumers. Not only is this important in itself but, as has been argued above, it may lead to the recognition of a wider right to act in this way. The other point is more specific. The Directive applies more widely than the 1977 Act and, with its concept of good faith, introduces a potentially revolutionary tool into our armoury of legal weapons.

While benefits have undoubtedly been derived from the E.C. consumer protection policy, it is also possible to argue that it has had its disadvantages. There are those who consider that E.C. initiatives can be an impediment to the achievement of desirable reforms in the United Kingdom. The example usually given in this context is product liability. The debate on the need for reform was well advanced in the United Kingdom when a draft E.C. directive was published. It may be argued that the desire to produce a detailed proposal put at risk the possibility of achieving any change at all.[14] **2–25**

In addition to concerns about the content of some of the Directives there has also been concern about the methods of implementing them and whether enforcement in this country is over-zealous as compared with that in some other Member States. The United Kingdom can be said to have a good record in implementing E.C. proposals. This is borne out by statistics in the Review of the Implementation and Enforcement of E.C. law in the United Kingdom.[15] **2–26**

It is sometimes said that the United Kingdom over-implements E.C. law, including single market directives, in that on transposition it includes additional requirements or complexities which are not required by the Directive. Combined with this assertion it is not uncommon to find allegations that other Member States do not implement properly and adopt a less rigorous approach to enforcement. **2–27**

The Review of the Implementation and Enforcement of E.C. law in the United Kingdom considered these issues. On the first point it **2–28**

---

[14] See Borrie, *The Development of Consumer Law and Policy — Bold Spirits and Timorous Souls* (Stevens, 1984), pp. 116–118. Doorstep selling might be another example.

[15] July 1993. An Efficiency Scrutiny Report commissioned by the President of the Board of Trade and available from the Department of Trade and Industry priced £10. See in particular Chap. 3.

"found little evidence to support the allegation that the United Kingdom deliberately adds requirements when transposing EC law". Where this did happen it was for two main reasons:

> "First, where EC Law has been integrated into existing United Kingdom law there is a tendency to carry over existing national provisions, [with] wider scope and tougher penalties than in other Member States . . . Second, the United Kingdom legal system is based on a tradition of precise drafting which aims to eradicate doubt in contrast with the purposive approach of continental jurisprudence on which EC law and that of other Member States is based".[16]

**2–29**    On the question of failure to implement properly in other Members States the same report found no evidence to suggest that other Member States have omitted requirements of a directive though they noted that not all the directives which they studied for the purposes of their review had been implemented in some other Member States.

**2–30**    It is not uncommon to hear complaints that enforcement is less stringent and more pragmatic in other Member States. The Review considered this issue mainly in relation to a small number of case studies that it undertook. It concluded that it found "no evidence to support the assertion that United Kingdom enforcers were more highly qualified than those in other Member States". It went on to say that "simple comparisons of enforcement practice are not helpful in understanding deep seated differences in culture".[17] The Review then goes on to consider the approach of *The Internal Market After 1992* (the Sutherland Report). While critical of some of the report's recommendations as overly bureaucratic it states:

> "Nevertheless, the basic thrust of the recommendations is sensible, and the call for a 'cooperative approach' to be taken to enforcement issues as the "single most important way of reinforcing mutual confidence between Member States and the Commission" should build on the collaboration that enforcement authorities in all Member[18] States are already developing."

---

[16]  Review of the Implementation and Enforcement of E.C. law in the U.K., at p.19, n. 1.
[17]  *ibid.*, at p.20.
[18]  Review of the Implementation and enforcement of E.C. law in the U.K., at p.20.

## THE ROLE OF THE EUROPEAN COURT

It must not be forgotten that the European Court has had a role    **2–31**
in the development of the law relating to consumers. Much of
this has been based on the exposition of Article 30 (now Article
28) of the Treaty of Rome which establishes the right of free
movement of goods. There is also an equivalent in relation to
services in Article 59 (now Article 49). The theory behind this is
that the removal of barriers to trade between Member States
benefits the consumer in permitting greater competition with the
benefits that economic theory says will follow from that.[19]

According to the court, Article 30 covers "all trading rules    **2–32**
enacted by Member States which are capable of hindering,
directly or indirectly, actually or potentially, intra-Community
trade".[20] One of the best known examples of the application of
the court's approach to Article 30 is the *Cassis de Dijon* decision[21] where regulations governing the composition of alcoholic
drinks which could be marketed in Germany were held to offend
against European law. That case also demonstrated that there
were circumstances where trade barriers could be justified. The
court pointed out that:

> "obstacles to movement in the Community resulting from
> disparities between national laws in question must be
> accepted in so far as those provisions may be recognised as
> being necessary in order to satisfy mandatory requirements
> relating in particular to the effectiveness of fiscal supervision,
> the protection of public health, the fairness of commercial
> transactions and the defence of the consumer."

The scope for taking advantage of these exceptions on the    **2–33**
ground of consumer protection is not great, as the case law
shows. The court has frequently pointed out that where there are
other ways of achieving the same end they should be used. The
*German Beer* Case[22] illustrates this point. Germany sought to
argue that its beer purity laws, dating from medieval times, were
justified on consumer protection grounds. The court pointed out
that the objectives of the laws could be secured by labelling

---

[19] For a detailed study of this area of E.U. law see Weatherhill and Beaumont,
*EU Law*, (3rd ed., Penguin, 1999).
[20] *Procureur du Roi v. Dassonville* (No. 8/74); [1974] E.C.R. 837.
[21] *Rewe-Zentrale AC v. Budesmonopolverwaltung für Brantwein* (No. 120/78);
[19791 E.C.R. 649.
[22] (No. 178/84); [1987] E.C.R. 1227.

requirements which would also allow a freer market in beer with greater consumer choice.[23]

**2–34**     In the past few years the Court of Justice has been altering its approach in this area. In a series of cases beginning with *Keck and Mithouard*,[24] and including *Hunermund*[25] and *Clinique*[26] the court appears to be using a new definition of "measures having an equivalent effect". A distinction is being drawn between rules on the composition and presentation of products, and those restricting and prohibiting certain sales methods. The former are subject to the *Cassis de Dijon* controls but the latter are not regarded as measures having an equivalent effect. One particular problem that this new distinction throws up is that it leaves it unclear into which category advertising falls.

## THE FUTURE OF EUROPEAN CONSUMER PROTECTION

**2–35**     Consumer protection policy in the European Union is at an uncertain stage. On the one hand the Maastricht and Amsterdam Treaty changes appear to have enhanced its significance. That must be balanced against the meaning given to subsidiarity by some Member States who see it as a means to limit the ability of Brussels to intervene in areas such as this. If one wished to be pessimistic one could go on to cite the abandonment by the Commission of the draft Directive on Services Liability. However, there continue to be achievements. The Unfair Contract Terms Directive is far from uncontroversial, yet it was adopted after Maastricht and, as we have just seen, a number of important directives have been agreed in the last few years.

**2–36**     There does appear to be increasing realisation of the importance of consumers to the success of the operation of the Single Market. The Sutherland Report[27] made this point forcibly in pointing out that consumer uncertainty was one of the major obstacles to the realisation of the internal market. If consumers have doubts about the quality of goods from other Member States or their legal rights are obscure, they cannot be expected to participate fully.

---

[23] For a detailed discussion of this area see Weatherhill, *The Role of the Informed Consumer in European Community Law and Policy* (1994) 2 Consum. L.J.49.

[24] Cases C-267–268/91; [1993] E.C.R. I-6097.

[25] *Hunermund v Landesapothekerkammer Baden-Wurttemberg*, Case C292/92, December 15, 1993.

[26] Case 315/92 *Verband Sozialer Wettbewerb eV v Clinique Laboratories SNC* [1994] .C.R. I-317.

[27] *The Internal Market after 1992: Meeting the Challenge* (the Sutherland Report).

One may expect consumer protection to make further prog-   **2–37**
ress at Community level. However, its future has been well
summarised recently by saying that "[t]here are grounds for
neither over-optimism nor over-pessimism; Community consumer policy continues to evolve patchily".[28]

[28] Weatherhill, *op. cit.* n. 21.

## CHAPTER 3

# ADVERTISING AND MARKETING

## INTRODUCTION

**3–01**    Much skill and expense is devoted to persuading consumers to purchase goods and services, and the role of advertising in our economic system is recognised as being important, if controversial. It is essential that advertising be accurate, and thus there is a good deal of legal regulation of this area. The major problems do not concern blatant falsehood but the more subtle issues of claims that are ambiguous or misleading — or offend against decency or good taste.

**3–02**    Much of the statutory control of advertising is of a negative character. However, there are a number of Acts which require that advertisers provide consumers, or potential consumers, with information which will assist them to make a rational purchasing decision. Examples of such provisions which are discussed below are to be found in the legislation on food and drugs, weights and measures and consumer credit legislation.

## THE ROLE OF THE COMMON LAW

**3–03**    The common law has traditionally tended to ignore advertising. The blatantly false advertisement would, almost certainly, involve criminal liability for fraud, and might give rise to a civil action for fraudulent misrepresentation. This is not, however, the usual kind of case. The common law has taken a tolerant attitude towards sellers' statements promoting their products. Its watchwords have been *simplex commendatio non obligat* (a mere recommendation does not bind). This does seem to have been taken too far on occasions.[1] However, the fact is that in some circumstances a statement will not be regarded as giving rise to legal consequences.

---

[1]   Mullins, *An Analysis of Simplex Commendation in Modern Society* (1984) 101 S.A.L.J. 515.

Despite this laxity in the law, it is possible that statements **3–04** made about the goods or services by the seller can have legal consequences. As we shall see later, if the statement is considered to have contractual effect the contractual remedies for breach will apply. If the offending statement does not form part of the contract but is what lawyers call a "mere representation" there are still remedies available to the consumer under the heading of misrepresentation.

To attract legal liability for misrepresentation a statement must **3–05** be material and made in the course of negotiations. It must also be a statement of fact and not one of opinion.[2] Generally, silence will not amount to a misrepresentation but in some circumstances the parties do owe each other a duty to disclose. One of the best known examples of these contracts, *uberrimae fidei* (of the utmost good faith), arises in insurance where it is the duty of the insured to make full disclosure when requesting insurance.[3]

The law recognises three types of misrepresentation: fraudu- **3–06** lent; negligent; and innocent. Fraudulent misrepresentation occurs where the maker of the statement was aware that his statements were untrue, or made them recklessly, heedless of whether they were true or false, or did not believe them to be true.[4] If fraud can be proved, not only is the contract void, that is, it has no effect, but also the victim may sue for damages.

Negligent misrepresentations occur where one party has failed **3–07** to take reasonable care in making a statement in circumstances where the law says that there is a duty of care to do so. This is an area of law which has developed since the House of Lords decision in *Hedley Byrne & Co. Ltd v. Heller & Partners Ltd*.[5] In Scotland, until the enactment of section 10 of the Law Reform (Miscellaneous Provisions) (Scotland) Act 1985, it was not clear whether damages were available for such misrepresentations. That provision now makes it clear that this is the case.

An innocent misrepresentation is one that is made in the belief **3–08** that it is true. The only remedy is to reduce the contract, which can only be done if action is taken without delay and it is possible to restore the parties to their original positions. In addition, the rights of third parties must not have been affected.[6]

Given the limitations on the remedies relating to misrep- **3–09** resentations, it is better to be able to show that a statement is a

---

[2] *Bisset v. Wilkinson* [1927] A.C. 177.
[3] See *H. Demetriodes & Co. v. The Northern Assurance Co. Ltd; The Spathari*, 1925 S.C. (H.L.) 6. And see the discussion of the concept of unfairness in the Unfair Terms in Consumer Contracts Regulations 1999 in Chap. 10.
[4] *Derry v. Peek* (1889) 14 App. Cas. 337.
[5] [1964] A.C. 465.
[6] See *Boyd & Forest v. The Glasgow & South-Western Railway Co.*, 1912 S.C. (H.L.) 93.

term of the contract rather than a representation that induced it. Distinguishing between terms and representations is not easy, but the test is what the parties intended. This in turn appears to depend on the stage at which the statement was made, whether an oral statement was put into writing, and whether the person who made the statement had special knowledge. In *Scott v. Steel*[7] a statement about the soundness of a horse made by the seller at the time of sale to clinch the sale was held to be a term of the contract. On the other hand, in *Malcolm v. Cross*[8] a gap of almost two months between the statement about the condition of a horse and the making of a contract for its sale resulted in the statement not being regarded as part of the contract.[9]

3–10    In England, the cases of *Oscar Chess Ltd v. Williams*[10] and *Dick Bentley Productions Ltd v. Harold Smith (Motors) Ltd*[11] have been explained on the basis that in one the maker of the statement was an innocent private individual with no specialist knowledge of cars, while in the other the statement was made by a motor dealer. The dealer's statement was a term of the contract: the private individual's was not.

## THE IMPLIED TERMS ABOUT DESCRIPTION

3–11    The implied term about description found in the Sale of Goods Act and other legislation about the supply of goods[12] is relevant to advertising. Section 13 of the Sale of Goods Act 1979 provides that where there is a sale by description there is an implied term that the goods will correspond with the description. If the sale is by sample, as well as by description, it is not sufficient that the bulk of the goods correspond with the sample if the goods do not also correspond with the description.

3–12    Sales are by description in a wide range of situations. An obvious example, in a consumer context, is provided by mail order purchasing where the buyer relies on the description in a catalogue or an advertisement in a newspaper or magazine. As section 13(3) makes clear, the fact that the goods are seen and selected by the buyer does not prevent the sale being one by description. Many goods are packaged and the buyer relies on

---

[7]    (1857) 20 D. 253.
[8]    (1898) 25 R. 1089.
[9]    See also *Matthew Paul & Co. Ltd v. Corporation of the City of Glasgow* (1900) 3 F. 119.
[10]    [1957] 1 W.L.R. 370; [1957] 1 All E.R. 325.
[11]    [1965] 1 W.L.R. 623; [1965] 2 All E.R. 65.
[12]    See Part 1A of the Supply of Goods and Services Act 1982 (inserted by the Sale and Supply of Goods Act 1994, s.6) and s.9 of the Supply of Goods (Implied Terms) Act 1973.

the label or packaging for identification of the product. *Beale v. Taylor*[13] extended this to a situation where the purchaser had examined the goods. Mr Taylor had placed an advertisement for a car in a newspaper, describing the car as "Herald, convertible, white, 1961". After examining the car, Mr Beale decided to buy it. In fact, the car was an amalgamation of a 1961 Herald and another of a different year which had been welded together and was in a very dangerous condition. As this was a private sale, Mr Beale could not rely on the quality terms in section 14, so he had to resort to section 13. The English Court of Appeal held that the words "1961 Herald" formed part of the description which had not been complied with.

The modern tendency is to draw a distinction between disputes about quality, which should be reserved for section 14, and those about the identity of the goods, which are appropriate to section 13. This has been asserted in two Scottish decisions; *Britain Steamship Co. Ltd v. Lithgows Ltd*[14] and *Border Harvesters Ltd v. Edwards Engineering (Perth) Ltd.*[15]  **3–13**

As the *Beale v. Taylor* decision demonstrates, almost any words describing the goods will be regarded as part of the description. Strict compliance with description has been enforced in some cases.[16] However, as the unusual facts of *Harlingdon and Leinster Enterprises Ltd v. Christopher Hull Fine Art Ltd*[17] demonstrate, there are limits. This case resulted from the sale of a painting which the defendants had purchased some time earlier when it had been described as being by the German artist, Munter. On the plaintiff, a specialist in German art, expressing interest in it the defendant emphasised that he did not know much about it, his particular expertise being in a different school of painting. The Court of Appeal held that it must be the intention of the parties that the description should be relied on. On the facts of this case that could not be said to have occurred.  **3–14**

## CONTRACTUAL CONSEQUENCES OF ADVERTISEMENTS AND SHOP DISPLAYS

The general rule is that advertisements, like shop displays, are regarded as invitations to treat and are not to be considered in contractual terms as offers which, when accepted, give rise to  **3–15**

---

[13] [1967] 1 W.L.R. 1193.
[14] 1975 S.C. 110.
[15] 1985 S.L.T. 128.
[16] See *Arcos v E.A. Ronaasen & Son* [1933] A.C. 470.
[17] [1990] 1 All E.R. 737.

contracts. There does not appear to be any Scottish authority on
the status of shop displays. The leading cases are two English
cases where, in criminal proceedings, this was the central issue. In
*Pharmaceutical Society of Great Britain v. Boots Cash Chemists
(Southern) Ltd*[18] certain drugs which, under the Pharmacy and
Poisons Act 1933, had to be sold by or under the supervision of a
registered pharmacist had been sold in a Boots' pharmacy which
operated a self-service system. Customers selected their purchases from shelves on which the drugs were displayed, put them
into a shopping basket supplied by Boots, and took them to a
cash desk at one of the two exits. There they paid the price and it
was at this stage that a registered pharmacist supervised the
transaction. To avoid liability under the Act, Boots had to prove
that supervision took place at the point of sale. It was held by the
English Court of Appeal that the contract was made, not when
the customer put the goods in the basket, but when the cashier
accepted the offer to buy and received the price.

3–16     *Fisher v. Bell*[19] involved a shop window display. Mr Bell displayed a "flick knife" in his shop window together with a price
ticket. He was charged with the offence of offering the knife for sale
contrary to section 1(1) of the Restriction of Offensive Weapons
Act 1959. The justices found that no offence had been committed
and the prosecutor appealed. It was held that no offence had been
committed. The phrase "offer for sale" must be interpreted in the
light of the law of contract, and a display in a shop window with a
price ticket was an invitation to treat, not an offer to sell which, if
accepted, would produce a binding contract.

3–17     There is good reason for this to be the law. Otherwise, if
a display were an offer the shop would be bound to supply anyone who offered the price. This could create problems where
the diplayed item had been reserved for someone else or its
sale was restricted in some way, as is the case with alcohol
and cigarettes.

3–18     There is a similar rationale behind the rule that advertisements are presumed to be invitations to treat. Were it otherwise,
traders who misjudged demand would find themselves in breach
of contract. However, it is quite possible for an advertisement to
constitute an offer, as Lord Kinnear acknowledged in *Hunter v.
General Accident Fire and Life Assurance Corporation Limited*;
"[i]t is suggested that this is making a contract by an advertisement, but it is none the worse for being an advertisement if it is
a distinct and definite offer unconditionally accepted."[20]

[18] [1952] 2 Q.B. 795.
[19] [1961] 1 Q.B. 394.
[20] 1909 S.C. 344. This passage was approved by Lord Shaw in A. & G. Patersoll
Ltd v. Highland Railway Co., 1927 S.C. (H.L.) 32, at p.46.

In that case the defenders had inserted a coupon in a diary, **3–19** inviting purchasers to avail themselves of accident insurance by completing and returning the coupon together with a small fee. The Inner House and the House of Lords regarded this advertisement as an offer.

The classic case of an exception from the rule that advertise- **3–20** ments are presumed to be invitations to treat is the English case of *Carlill v. Carbolic Smoke Ball Company Limited*,[21] where a manufacturer placed an advertisement in a newspaper inviting the public to purchase its product, a smoke ball, which, it asserted, would prevent influenza. The advertisement included a promise to pay £100 to anyone who contracted influenza after using the ball as instructed. The advertisement went on to emphasise the company's sincerity by stating that £1,000 had been deposited with a bank. Mrs Carlill used the smoke ball as instructed but contracted influenza. She was held to be entitled to recover £100 from the company because their promise in the advertisement was intended to be legally binding and was sufficiently precise to be enforced.

While the facts of *Carlill* may be regarded as highly unusual, **3–21** the principles underlying it do have modern applications. For example, the not uncommon situation where a retailer offers to refund part of the price if the purchaser discovers that an article could have been purchased more cheaply elsewhere would be decided on similar principles.

## STATUTORY CONTROL

Statutory regulation of advertising in the United Kingdom has, **3–22** until recently, been piecemeal. There was no general prohibition on false or misleading advertising. However, with the implementation of the European Communities' directive on misleading advertising,[22] the United Kingdom has moved towards that position. Before looking at that development it will be useful to look at the heterogeneous collection of statutes prohibiting, with varying degrees of generality, false and misleading advertising, and a limited number of provisions regarding the provision of information. Of these the best known and widest ranging is the Trade Descriptions Act 1968, which controls false and misleading statements relating to goods, services in many situations. While it is relevant to the control of advertising it is discussed in detail in Chapter 11.

[21] [1893] 1 Q.B. 256.
[22] Directive 84/450 ([1984] O.J. L250/17).

## ADVERTISING FOOD

**3–23**    Section 15 of the Food Safety Act 1990 provides that it is an offence falsely to describe, advertise or present food. The first of these three offences makes it an offence to sell, offer or expose for sale food which has a label which falsely describes the food or is likely to mislead as to its nature, substance or quality.[23] It is also an offence to publish, or to be a party to the publication of an advertisement which falsely describes any food, or is likely to mislead as to its nature, substance or quality.[24] The Act defines "advertisement" as including any notice, circular, label, wrapper, invoice or other document, and any public announcement made orally or by any means of producing or transmitting light or sound.[25]

**3–24**    In relation to both these offences it is no barrier to a conviction that the label or advertisement contains an accurate statement of the composition of the food.[26] This is intended to catch situations where a label or advertisement is literally true but the overall effect is deceptive. For the same reason section 15(3) creates a new offence of selling, offering or exposing for sale or having in one's possession for the purpose of sale, any food the presentation of which is likely to mislead as to its nature substance or quality. Presentation of the food includes its shape, appearance and packaging as well as the way it is arranged when exposed for sale and the setting in which the food is displayed with a view to sale. Section 53(1) excludes from this definition any form of labelling or advertising.

**3–25**    In addition to these general prohibitions, there is a considerable body of regulations controlling the labelling, marking or advertising of food for sale for human consumption. As has been traditional in this area, these regulations are made under powers now contained in the Food Safety Act 1990. Section 16(1)(e) gives a power to make regulations "for imposing requirements or prohibitions as to, or otherwise regulating, the labelling, marking, presenting or advertising of food, and the descriptions which may be applied to food". Numerous regulations were made under similar powers in previous legislation and these remain in force by virtue of section 59 of the Act.

---

[23]  Food Safety Act 1990, s. 15(1). See Howells, Bradgate and Griffiths, *Blackstones's Guide to the Food Safety Act 1990*, Chap. 4.
[24]  *ibid.* s. 15(2). For defences, see s. 15(4).
[25]  *ibid.* s. 53(1).
[26]  *ibid.* s. 15(4).

Part 4 of the Weights and Measures Act 1985 regulates the sale    **3-26**
of goods by quantity.[27] The Act, together with a vast corpus of
regulations, imposes requirements designed to ensure that consumers are accurately informed about the quantity of goods they
are intending to purchase.

ADVERTISING MEDICINAL PRODUCTS

Parts 5 and 6 of the Medicines Act 1968 deal with the promotion,    **3-27**
labelling and packaging of "medicinal products".[28] These are
defined as substances or articles (other than an instrument,
apparatus or appliance) which are for use wholly or mainly for
administration to human beings or animals for a medicinal
purpose or as an ingredient in the preparation of such a product.[29] It is an offence for a commercially interested party or
someone who does so at his request to issue a false or misleading
advertisement relating to medicinal products.[30] In addition,
there are wide powers to regulate advertisements and representations.[31] These have been exercised in order to control the
content of advertisements, to ensure that no advertisement is
issued unless the product has a product licence, and to prohibit
the issue of advertisements advocating the use of a medicine for
the treatment of certain diseases.[32] Part 5 of the Act contains
provisions concerning the labelling and packaging of medicines.[33] It is an offence to sell or supply, or to have in one's
possession for the purpose of sale or supply, a medicinal product
in a container or package which is falsely labelled or misleads as
to the nature, quality or uses of the product.[34] Similar provisions
apply to leaflets relating to medicines.[35] The appropriate ministers[36] are given wide powers to make regulations controlling the
labelling and packaging of medicines and the contents of leaflets
supplied with them.[37] These regulations are designed to ensure

[27] *i.e.* the Weights and Measures Act 1985, Pt 4, ss. 21–46. This area of law is
under review, see *Fair Measure: a consultation document on modernising the
law on the sale of goods sold by quantity*, DTI 1999.
[28] *i.e.* the Medicines Act 1968, Pt 5 (ss. 85–91) and Pt 6 (ss. 92–97).
[29] Medicines Act 1968, s. 130(1).
[30] *ibid.* s. 93(1). For the meaning of "commercially interested party", see s. 92(4).
For defences, see s. 93(5)(a).
[31] *ibid.* s. 95.
[32] *ibid.*
[33] *ibid.* ss. 85–91.
[34] *ibid.* ss. 85(3), 91(2).
[35] *ibid.* ss. 86 and 91(1), (2).
[36] For the meaning of "the appropriate minister" see s.1(2) of the Act.
[37] Medicines Act 1968, ss. 85(1) and 86(1).

that medicines are correctly described with adequate instructions and warnings, and also to promote safety in relation to medicines.[38]

<h2>CONSUMER CREDIT</h2>

**3–28**   Consumer credit is discussed in Chapter 9, but it is relevant to note that the Consumer Credit Act 1974 and the regulations made thereunder regulate the advertising of credit.[39] It is an offence to convey information which in a material respect is false or misleading.[40] The Secretary of State has a duty to make regulations governing the form and content of credit advertisements.

<h2>REGULATION OF PRICE MARKING</h2>

**3–29**   The Prices Act 1974 permits the Secretary of State for Trade and Industry to make orders regulating the way in which prices are indicated.[41] The powers given by section 2 of this Act were used to make regulations implementing the E.C. directives on the indication of prices of food and of non-foodstuffs. The Price Marking Order 1999[42] is intended to increase price transparency in the market, thus enabling consumers to know what the price of goods is and to make comparisons. The Order applies to a wide range of goods for retail sale but not those supplied in the course of the provision of a service, such as food sold in restaurants, hotels, and public houses; auction sales; and sales of antiques and works of art.[43] Where a trader indicates that a product is or may be for sale to a consumer its selling price must be indicated. This does not apply to goods sold from bulk or to advertisements. In certain circumstances the unit price, *i.e.* the price for one kilogram, litre, metre, square metre or cubic metre or the one item for goods sold by number, must also be indicated. This will be the case where products are sold loose from bulk, as in the case of fruit and vegetables. It also applies to pre-packaged products which are required by Weights and Measures legislation to be marked with quantity or to be made up in a prescribed quantity. These include most packaged food and drink and a wide range of non-food products such as construction and decorating products, fuel both solid and liquid, aerosol dispensers,

[38]   Medicines Act 1968, ss. 85(2) and 86(1).
[39]   See the Consumer Credit Act 1974, ss. 39–47.
[40]   *ibid.* s.46.
[41]   See the Prices Act 1974, s. 4 (amended by the Price Commission Act 1977, s.16).
[42]   S.I. 1999 No. 3042.
[43]   art. 3.

cleaning and toilet preparations, cosmetics and pet foods. The requirement to indicate unit prices does not apply to cinema and television advertisements or, in the case of pre-packaged products, to sales in small shops, by itinerant traders or from vending machines.[44] A small shop is defined in article 1 as one with a floor area of less than 280 sq. metres.

Whatever price must be indicated it must be indicated in a way that is "unambiguous, easily identifiable and clearly legible", as must any charges for postage, package or delivery. It must be placed in close proximity to the products to which it relates and in such a way as to be available to customers without the need for them to seek assistance from the trader to ascertain it.[45] The latter requirement overrules the decision in *Allen v. Redbridge London Borough Council.*[46]     **3–30**

"Selling price" includes VAT and any other taxes,[47] and must be stated in sterling. If a trader is willing to accept payment in foreign currency the price in that currency may also be displayed provided the price in the foreign currency or the conversion rate to be used is indicated together with any commission to be charged.[48]     **3–31**

Another order, the Price Marking (Food and Drink on Premises) Order 1979, requires restaurants to display clearly and legibly at or near the entrance the price of food or drinks offered there.[49] These prices must include any extra charges such as VAT and service charges.[50]     **3–32**

Although made under a different Act, the Tourism (Sleeping Accommodation Price Display) Order 1977, made under the Development of Tourism Act 1969, has a similar function to the price marking orders. It requires that hotels display in a prominent position, in the reception area or the entrance, the price (including any service charge and value added tax) of various kinds of accommodation.[51]     **3–33**

In all the above cases the sanction for non-compliance is a fine.[52]     **3–34**

[44] art. 6.
[45] art. 7
[46] [1994] 1 W.L.R. 139; [1994] 1 All E.R. 728
[47] art. 1
[48] art. 6. See the DTI guidance note on the order on their website at http://www.dti.gov.uk/CACP/ca/guidance.htm.
[49] See the Price Marking (Food and Drink on Premises) Order 1979 (S.I. 1979 No. 361), art.7.
[50] *ibid.* arts 6 and 7(4).
[51] See the Tourism (Sleeping Accommodation Price Display) Order 1977 (S.I. 1977 No. 1877).
[52] See the Prices Act 1974, s. 7, Sched. 1, para. 5 (amended by the Price Commission Act 1977, s. 13(5)), and the Tourism (Sleeping Accommodation Price Display) Order 1977, arts 4 and 5.

## PRICE COMPARISONS

**3–35**  The control of misleading claims about prices has proved to be a difficult and controversial matter. On the one hand, it is important not to impede the working of the competitive process by unnecessary restrictions but, on the other hand, it is difficult by simple methods to catch those determined to exploit the loopholes in legislation. The Trade Descriptions Act 1968[53] sought to regulate price advertising, but it proved necessary to buttress it with the Price Marking (Bargain Offers) Order 1979.[54] This proved unpopular both with traders and trading standards officers, and Part 3 of the Consumer Protection Act 1987 introduces a different approach to the regulation of price advertising.

**3–36**  Instead of attempting to prohibit specific practices, as the earlier legislation did, the Consumer Protection Act 1987 creates a wide general offence of giving to consumers a misleading indication as to the price of any goods, services, accommodation or facilities.[55] There are two main offences. Section 20(1) makes it an offence, "in the course of any business of his",[56] for someone to give an indication which is misleading. Section 20(2) on the other hand applies to a price indication "which, after it was given, has become misleading".[57] An indication of the price, or the method of determining a price, is misleading if what is conveyed, or what consumers might reasonably be expected to infer from the indication or any omission from it, includes any of a number of factors.[58] These are indications:

(1)  that the price is less than (or the method of determining it is not what) in fact it is;

(2)  that the applicability of the price or the method of determining it does not depend on facts or circumstances on which its applicability does in fact depend;

(3)  that the price or method of determining it covers matters in respect of which an additional charge is made;

(4)  that a trader has no genuine belief that a price increase or reduction (or alteration of a method of price determination) is imminent; and

[53]  *i.e.* under the Trade Descriptions Act 1968, s. 11 (now repealed).
[54]  Price Marking (Bargain Offers) Order 1979 (S.I. 1979 No. 364) (amended by S.I. 1979 No. 633 and S.I. 1979 No. 1124).
[55]  See the Consumer Protection Act 1987, s. 20(1).
[56]  *Warwickshire C.C. v. Johnson* [1993] A.C. 583; [1993] 2 W.L.R. 1; [1993] 1 All E.R. 299.
[57]  *Thomson Tour Operations Ltd v. Birch* (1999) 163 J.P. 465; *The Times*, February 24, 1999
[58]  Consumer Protection Act 1987, s. 21(1), (2).

(5) that facts or circumstances by reference to which a consumer might reasonably be expected to judge the validity of a comparison are not accurate.[59]

It is made clear that references to services do not include references to services provided to an employer under a contract of employment[60]; and that references to services or facilities do not include references to services or facilities provided by authorised persons or appointed representatives in carrying on an investment business.[61] However, it is emphasised that the provision of credit[62] or banking or insurance services, the purchase or sale of foreign currency,[63] the supply of electricity and the provision of off-street car parks and caravan sites[64] are included.[65]

This somewhat curious provision is explained by the fact that all these services have been the subject of frequent complaints on account of the quality of price advertising. Reference to accommodation or facilities does not include accommodation or facilities being made available by means of the creation or disposal of an interest in land, except where it is the creation or disposal of the *dominium utile* of land comprising a new dwelling (or a leasehold in such a dwelling) where at least 21 years remains unexpired.[66]

For the most part the defences available are similar to those applicable to offences under the Trade Descriptions Act 1968. The due diligence defence set out in the Consumer Protection Act 1987 applies.[67] This was successful in *Berkshire County*

3–37

3–38

3–39

---

[59] Consumer Protection Act 1974, s. 21(1)(a)–(e), (2)(a)–(e), (3).

[60] *ibid.* s. 22(2). By virtue of s. 22(5), "contract of employment" and "employer" have the same meaning as in the Employment Protection Consolidation) Act 1978 (see s. 153(1)).

[61] Consumer Protection Act 1987, s. 22(3). By virtue of s. 22(5), "appointed representative", "authorised person" and "investment business" have the same meaning as in the Financial Services Act 1986 (see ss. 1(2), 44, 207(1)).

[62] "Credit" has the same meaning as in the Consumer Credit Act 1974: Consumer Protection Act 1987, s. 22(5).

[63] In relation to a service consisting in the purchase or sale of foreign currency references in Consumer Protection Act 1987, Pt III, to the method by which the price of the service is determined include references to the rate of exchange: s. 22(4).

[64] "Caravan" has the same meaning as in the Caravan Sites and Control of Development Act 1960 (see s. 29(1)): Consumer Protection Act 1987, s. 22(5).

[65] Consumer Protection Act 1987, s. 22(1)(a)–(e).

[66] *ibid.* s. 23.

[67] Consumer Protection Act 1987, ss. 24(5), 39. In respect of offences under Pt 3 (ss. 20–26), s. 39 only applies to the offence of giving a misleading price indication under s. 20(1): s. 39(5).

*Council v. Olympic Holidays Ltd*[68] where the company showed
that the misleading price was generated by faulty computer
software which it had rigorously tested. It is a defence for a
person (1) to show that a price indication complied with regulations made under Part 3[69] of the Act[70]; (2) that he was a bona fide
publisher of an advertisement[71]; or (3) that he was the author of
a recommended price and did not offer goods, services, accommodation or facilities himself but reasonably assumed that the
recommended price was, for the most part, being followed.

**3–40**     A defence which gave rise to a good deal of controversy
during the parliamentary progress of the Consumer Protection
Bill is that in respect of the code of practice. The Secretary of
State, after consulting the Director General of Fair Trading and
such other persons as may be appropriate, may by order approve
a code of practice giving practical guidance about price indications.[72] Failure to comply with this code does not by itself give
rise to any criminal or civil liability. It will have evidential value[73]
in that contravention of the code may be relied on for the
purpose of establishing that an offence had been committed, or
of negativing a defence; while compliance with the code may be
relied on to show that no offence has been committed or that
there is a defence.[74]

**3–41**     Such a code has been promulgated by the Consumer Protection
(Code of Practice for Traders on Price Indications) Approval
Order 1988.[75] It gives guidance on the situations in which comparisons may be made. For example, it sets out the circumstances
in which a comparisons may be made with the trader's own
previous price. The comparison should be with the last price at
which the product was offered by that trader in the previous six
months. During that period the product should have been available for at least 28 consecutive days in the same shop where the
reduction is being made. This harks back to a repealed provision

[68] (1994) 158 J.P. 421; (1994) 13 Tr. L.R. 251.
[69] *i.e.* under the Consumer Protection Act 1987, s. 26.
[70] *ibid.* s. 24(1). This defence is only available in respect of offences under
s. 20(1),(2).
[71] *ibid.* s. 24(3). This defence is only available in respect of offences under
s. 20(1), (2). "Advertisement" includes a catalogue, a circular and a price list:
s. 24(6). In proceedings for an offence under s. 20(1), (2), in respect of an
indication published in a book, newspaper, magazine, film or radio or television broadcast or in a programme included in a cable programme service, it
is a defence to show that the indication was not contained in an advertisement: s. 24(2), (6).
[72] See *ibid.* s.25(1), (3), (4).
[73] *i.e.* in proceedings for an offence under the 1987 Act, s. 20(1), (2).
[74] *ibid.* s. 25(2).
[75] S.I. 1988 No. 2078.

in the section 11 of the Trade Descriptions Act 1968 which
proved very difficult to enforce.

Enforcement of this part of the Act is the duty of district    3–42
councils as the weights and measures authorities.[76] The penalties
for the offence of giving a misleading price indication are, on
conviction on indictment, a fine, and, on summary conviction, a
fine not exceeding the statutory maximum.[77]

### DETAILS TO BE DISPLAYED ON CARS FOR SALE

Car dealers are required to display on cars for sale a label giving    3–43
the results of officially approved tests of fuel consumption and
stating that the test results for other cars are available.[78] This
information must also be included in other promotional literature.

### DISCLOSURE IN BUSINESS ADVERTISEMENTS

In addition to the mandatory disclosure of information intended    3–44
to assist the consumer in making a rational purchasing decision,
there are some other statutory information disclosure provisions
which can be explained on the basis that they are intended to
assist consumers to assert their legal rights. A good example is
the Business Advertisements (Disclosure) Order 1977.[79] This is
designed to eradicate the practice of trade sellers placing advertisements in the classified columns of newspapers or periodicals
posing as private sellers. The purchaser from a private seller is
much less well protected than the purchaser from a trader —
hence the inclination of some traders to adopt such a practice. It
is a criminal offence to fail to indicate in an advertisement that
goods are for sale in the course of a business.[80]

### MAIL ORDER TRANSACTIONS

The Mail Order Transactions (Information) Order 1976 is    3–45
designed to assist purchasers by mail order to obtain redress

[76] See Consumer Protection Act 1987, s. 27(1).
[77] *ibid.* s. 20(4). As to the time limit for bringing prosecutions, see s. 20(5). "The
statutory maximum" means the prescribed sum as defined in the Criminal
Procedure (Scotland) Act, s. 289B. The only reported case on Pt 3 appears to
be *Clydesdale Group plc v. Normand*, 1993 S.C.C.R. 958; 1994 S.L.T. 1302.
[78] See the Passenger Car Fuel Consumption Order 1983 (S.I. 1983 No. 1486).
[79] S.I. 1977 No. 1918.
[80] See the Fair Trading Act 1973, s. 23, and the Criminal Procedure (Scotland)
Act 1975, s. 289B (added by the Criminal Law Act 1977, s. 63(1), Sched. 11,
para. 5, substituted by the Criminal Justice Act 1982, s. 55(2), and amended by
the Increase of Criminal Penalties, Etc. (Scotland) Order 1984 (S.I. 1984 No.
526), art. 3).

where a trader defaults on his obligations. Any "communication", be it an advertisement, circular or catalogue, which invites consumers to order goods by post and pay for them before they are to be dispatched, must set out the name of the person or company carrying on the business and the address at which the business is managed.[81]

<h2 style="text-align:center">BROADCAST ADVERTISING</h2>

**3–46**    Under the terms of its licence the British Broadcasting Corporation is not permitted to transmit advertisements on its radio and television services. The broadcasting services regulated by the Independent Television Commission (ITC), the successor to the Independent Broadcasting Authority (IBA), are expressly permitted to do so by the Broadcasting Act 1990.[82] Television, and to a lesser extent commercial radio stations, are an attractive medium for advertisers. Broadcast advertising is subject to a range of controls specific to it which encompass an interesting combination of statutory and self-regulatory methods. Broadcast advertising is, of course, subject to the various Acts of Parliament which regulate advertising in general.

**3–47**    The Broadcasting Act 1990 requires the Independent Television Commission to ensure that the rules about advertising and sponsorship are complied with. Most of these rules are contained in the ITC Code of Advertising Standards and Practice, the ITC Code of Programme Sponsorship and the ITC Rules on Advertising Breaks.[83] However, section 8 of the Act has general rules about advertising which prohibit advertisements by any body whose objects are wholly or mainly of a political nature or relate to an industrial dispute; provide that there should be no unreasonable discrimination between advertisers; and provide that there should be no sponsorship of programmes by the manufacturers or suppliers of products which may not be advertised.

**3–48**    The rules in the ITC Code, *inter alia*, require that the advertisements must be clearly distinguishable as such, recognisably separate from programmes, and inserted at the beginning or the end of programmes or in a natural break. They must not be excessively noisy or strident, nor should certain products be advertised in or adjacent to certain programmes. For example, advertisements for alcoholic drinks, liqueur chocolates and pipe tobacco must not be carried in or adjacent to children's programmes.

---

[81]   See the Mail Order Transactions (Information) Order 1976 (S.I. 1976 No.1812), art. 3.

[82]   See the Broadcasting Act 1990, s. 8.

[83]   These three documents are available from the Independent Television Commission, 33 Foley Street, London WIP 7LB.

Since the beginning of commercial of television there have **3–49**
been controls on the amount of advertising that may be shown.
These are now mainly to be found in the ITC Rules on Advertising breaks.[84] Many of the rules apply to both terrestrial channels
and cable and satellite channels, but special provision is made for
the latter. This is most marked in relation to home shopping
channels where up to eight "tele-shopping windows"; that is,
advertising features of from 15 minutes to three hours in length
may be shown. This compares with the rules for terrestrial
channels which permit a daily average of seven minutes advertising in each hour and no more than 12 minutes in any one hour.

An interesting feature of the regulation of broadcast advertis- **3–50**
ing is the fact that much of the detailed control derives from
codes of practice which the ITC is statutorily obliged to draw up
and enforce. The code of advertising standards and practice is
drawn up by the ITC in consultation with the Radio Authority,
commercial television companies, representatives of viewers and
advertisers, those qualified to give advice on advertising, and
such others concerned with standards in advertising as the ITC
thinks fit.[85]

The content of the code is very similar to the British Code of **3–51**
Advertising Practice which applies to print media and is discussed below. It shares with that code the same general
principles that advertising should be legal, decent, honest and
truthful and that its detailed rules are intended to be applied in
the spirit as well as the letter. It suffices at this point to draw
attention to some features peculiar to broadcasting. The code
permits the use of special techniques or substitute materials
where technical limitations can make it difficult to portray a
subject accurately. However, the resultant picture must present a
fair and reasonable impression of the product and must not use
unacceptable devices such as glass or plastic sheeting to simulate
the effects of floor or furniture polishes. Subliminal advertising is
not permitted under the code. Cigarettes may not be advertised,
nor may private investigation services or those of betting tip-
sters, fortune tellers, unlicensed employment bureaux or private
consumer advisory agencies.

## ADVISORY COMMITTEES AND PANELS

The ITC may appoint advisory committees to assist it with its **3–52**
responsibilities.[86] An Advertising Advisory Committee has been
set up to advise on advertising matters. In addition, a medical

[84] Rules on Advertising Breaks Consolidated revised text, December 1997.
[85] Broadcasting Act 1990 S 9(2).
[86] Broadcasting Act 1990, Sched. 1, para. 16.

advisory panel has been appointed to advise on advertisements for medical and related products.

**3–53**   Advertising on commercial radio is subject to a similar regulatory regime. This is overseen by the Radio Authority set up by section 83 of the Broadcasting Act 1990 which has drawn up the Radio Authority Code of Advertising Standards and Practice and Programme Sponsorship.[87] The code is similar in terms to the equivalent television codes.

## THE BRITISH CODE OF ADVERTISING PRACTICE

**3–54**   One of the distinctive features of advertising control in the United Kingdom is the role of self-regulation. It has already been noted that there is an element of this in broadcast advertising through the codes of advertising standards and practice of the ITC and the Radio Authority. It might be argued that this is not pure self-regulation as the codes are mandated by statute and drawn up not only by representatives of the advertising industry but also of government and consumers. Self-regulation has an important role to play in the control of advertising standards in media other than broadcasting. This is achieved by means of the British Codes of Advertising and Sales Promotion, the tenth edition of which came into force on October 1, 1999.

**3–55**   These codes were drawn up by the Code of Advertising Practice Committee composed of representatives of the advertising industry in consultation with the Advertising Standards Authority (ASA) and trade and consumer interests. The Advertising Standards Authority is a company limited by guarantee set up by the Advertising Association to supervise the code and its enforcement. It is composed of a chairman who, under the terms of the ASA's article of association, must "not be engaged in the business of advertising" and must be appointed only "after consultation with the Members of the Council of the Authority", a majority of whom must also be independent.

**3–56**   The Advertising Standards Authority receives complaints about advertisements from members of the public and also carries out a limited amount of monitoring of advertisements on its own initiative. Complaints by one advertiser against another are the responsibility of the Code of Advertising Practice Committee. The main sanction available to the ASA is that of adverse publicity, and details of complaints are published by the ASA. One of the criticisms of the self-regulatory system has been the inadequacy of its sanctions. Apart from adverse publicity, its

---

[87]   Available from the Radio Authority, Holbrook House, 14 Great Queen Street, London WC2B 5DG.

only other sanction is to request those companies controlling the
media and which adhere to the British Code of Advertising
Practice not to publish advertisements found to be in breach of
the code and not to accept advertisements from advertising
agencies which do not abide by the code.

The Advertising Code has four general principles: that adver-   **3–57**
tisements should be legal, decent, honest and truthful. It is also
stated that it will be "applied in the spirit as well as the letter". In
addition to these general principles the code goes into a good
deal of detail about various advertising practices and the manner
in which certain products and services may be advertised. Advertisements must be clearly distinguished as such and comparative
advertising is permissible, although this must be done fairly and
without denigrating other products.

A section of the British Code of Advertising Practice sets out   **3–58**
rules governing health claims, and there are sections devoted
specifically to advertisements directed at children, advertisements for slimming and medical products, vitamins, alcohol and
cigarettes, as well as mail order advertisements.

Proponents of the self-regulatory system argue that it provides   **3–59**
a positive approach to advertising control which can deal with
matters of taste and decency which it would be impractical to
control by statute. It is also argued that the code can be amended
more speedily than legislation and that it commands a high
degree of commitment from the business community and
encourages higher standards in advertising.[88]

Against this, the weakness of the sanctions available to the   **3–60**
Advertising Standards Authority has already been noted. It
should be added that such sanctions as there are operate only
after a breach of the code has taken place. There is no speedy
method of taking preventive action against major breaches of
the code. Also, as with all voluntary measures, the code only
applies to those advertisers and media that subscribe to it. To a
limited extent, this criticism of the code has lost some of its force
with the implementation of the E.C. Directive on Misleading
Advertising, and it is to consideration of this that we now
turn.[89]

---

[88] See *The Self-Regulatory System of Advertising Control:* Report of the
Working Party (the Burgh Report) DTI (1980), p. 3.
[89] For two views on the codes see Middleton and Rodwell, "Regulating Advertising" (1998) 8 Consumer Policy Review 88 and Crawford, "If it ain't broke,
don't fix it" (1998) 8 Consumer Policy Review 132.

## E.C. DIRECTIVE ON MISLEADING AND
## COMPARATIVE ADVERTISING

**3–61** The United Kingdom implemented the E.C. Council Directive on Misleading Advertising, adopted by the Community in 1984,[90] through the Control of Misleading Advertisements Regulations 1988.[91] The purpose of the directive was to protect consumers and those carrying on trades and professions against the effects of misleading advertising in any form.[92] It has now been amended by Directive 97/55 so as to include comparative advertising. The directive obliges Member States to ensure that adequate and effective means exist for the control of misleading advertising, and for compliance with its provisions on comparative advertising. This must take the form of legal provisions which permit persons or organisations regarded under national law as having a legitimate interest in prohibiting misleading advertising or regulating comparative advertising to take legal action, or to bring it before an impartial administrative authority competent either to decide on a complaint or to initiate appropriate proceeding, or both.[93]

**3–62** In so far as further action was required, the E.C. Directive on Misleading Advertising has been implemented in the United Kingdom by two pieces of legislation, the Financial Services Act 1986 and the Control of Misleading Advertising Regulations 1988 as amended by Control of Misleading Advertisements (Amendment) Regulations 2000.[94] The Act provides that investment advertisements may only be issued by or with the approval of "authorised persons".[95] Such persons will be members of self-regulatory bodies whose rules will require them not to disseminate misleading advertisements. To reinforce this provision the Act empowers the Secretary of State for Trade and Industry to seek interdict to prevent its breach.[96]

**3–63** The regulations deal with other types of advertising which they define in very wide terms.[97] An advertisement is misleading if in any way, including its presentation, it deceives or is likely to

---

[90] Directive 84/450 ([19841 0.J. L250/17).
[91] S.I. 1988 No. 915.
[92] *ibid.* art. 1.
[93] *ibid.* art.4, paras 1 and 3.
[94] S.I. 2000 No. 914.
[95] See the Financial Services Act 1986, s. 57. "Authorised person" means a person authorised under Pt 1, Chap. 3 (ss. 7–34): s. 207(1). As to exceptions from restrictions on advertising, see s. 58, and the Financial Services Act 1986 (Investment Advertisements)(Exemptions) Order 1988 (S.I. 1988 No. 316), and (No. 2) Order 1988 (S.I. 1988 No. 716).
[96] See the Financial Services Act 1986, s. 61.
[97] See the Control of Misleading Advertisements Regulations 1988 (S.I. 1988 No. 915), regs 2(1), 3.

deceive the persons to whom it is addressed or whom it reaches; and if, by reason of its deceptive nature, it is likely to affect their economic behaviour or, for those reasons, injures or is likely to injure a competitor of the person whose interests the advertisement seeks to promote.[98] An advertisement is comparative "if in any way, either explicitly or by implication it identifies a competitor or goods or services offered by a competitor".[99] The Director General of Fair Trading is required to consider complaints (other than frivolous or vexatious ones) about misleading or comparative advertisements except those relating to commercial broadcasting or cable television.[1] Before he considers a complaint the Director may require the complainant to satisfy him that appropriate means of dealing with the complaint have been tried and that, despite being given a reasonable opportunity to do so, those means have not dealt with the complaint adequately.[2] Such means might include a complaint to a local authority trading standards department who might take action under the Trade Descriptions Act 1968, or to a self-regulatory body such as the Advertising Standards Authority.

Where the Director does decide that it is appropriate for him to take action he is given power to bring proceedings in the Court of Session for interdict to prevent the publication or continued publication of an advertisement.[3] Should he decide not to take action he is required to give reasons for his decision.[4]    **3–64**

The new provisions contained in the regulations, to quote the government consultative paper on their implementation, were seen "essentially as a 'long-stop'" which it was hoped would "strengthen rather than diminish the authority of the self-regulatory system". That appears to have been how the system has operated, and the Director General of Fair Trading has only had to resort to court action on nine occasions. The first case, *Director General of Fair Trading v. Tobyward Ltd*,[5] was a good example of the "longstop" nature of the regulations.    **3–65**

Tobyward Ltd made a number of sweeping claims for a slimming product which led to complaints to the Advertising Standards Authority that its code had been breached. The ASA agreed and advised Tobyward on how it might comply with the code; advice which was ignored. It then referred the matter to    **3–66**

---

[98] (S.I. 1988 No. 915); reg. 2(2).
[99] *ibid.* reg. 2(2a) inserted by the Control of Misleading Advertisements (Amendment) Regulations 2000.
[1] *ibid.* reg. 4(1), (2), (4).
[2] *ibid.* reg. 4(3).
[3] *ibid.* regs 2(3), 5(1).
[4] *ibid.* reg. 5(2).
[5] [1989] 2 All E.R. 266.

the Director General of Fair Trading who sought an interlocutory injunction to stop the publication of the advertisements. In granting the injunction the judge held that "misleading" in the regulations meant "no more than that it must make it likely that [consumers] will buy the product." He went on to say that it was:

> "desirable and in accordance with the public interest to which he must have regard that the courts should support the principle of self-regulation. I think that advertisers would be more inclined to accept the rulings of their self regulatory bodies if it were generally known that in cases in which their procedures had been exhausted and the advertiser was still publishing an advertisement which appeared to the court to be prima facie misleading an injunction would ordinarily be granted."[6]

**3–67** In addition to obtaining injunctions, the Director General has accepted undertakings from traders on 30 occasions instead of taking court action. In 1992 an undertaking was given for the first time not only by a trader but also by his advertising agency.[7]

**3–68** The Independent Broadcasting Authority and the Cable Authority are placed under a similar duty to consider complaints relating to the services for which they have statutory responsibility.[8]

---

[6] The DGFT also obtained an injunction in another case in 1989, see *Annual Report of the Director General of Fair Trading* (1989), p. 53.
[7] See annual reports of the Director General for the relevant years.
[8] See the Control of Misleading Advertisements Regulations 1988 (S.I. 1988 No.915), regs 8–11.

CHAPTER 4

# ACQUIRING THE GOODS

This chapter deals with a number of issues connected by the fact    **4–01**
that they relate to problems which may arise at the inception of
the transaction. These will include questions such as: what sort of
contract is it, legally speaking. When was it concluded? Or what
are the consumer's rights if it turns out that the person from
whom the goods were bought was not the true owner? Other
issues could be included at this stage such as the point at which a
contract for the supply of goods is concluded. This topic has been
omitted because it is fully covered in textbooks on contract and
readers are likely to be familiar with the problems of distinguishing invitations to treat from offers and the rules of offer and
acceptance. Contracts for the supply of goods are, in general, no
different from other contracts and the general law of contract
applies to them.[1]

Many contracts for the supply of goods require no special    **4–02**
formalities. However, as we shall see in Chapter 9, those relating to
credit must comply with certain statutory formalities to be valid.

The law relating to the capacity of individuals was amended by    **4–03**
the Age of Legal Capacity (Scotland) Act 1991. As a result, a
person of or over the age of 16 has capacity to enter into any
transaction.[2] However, a person under the age of 21 may ask a
court to set aside a transaction which was entered into while that
person was 16 or over but under 18 years of age. The grounds on
which this can be done are that the transaction was prejudicial.
"Prejudicial"[3] means "a transaction which (a) an adult, exercising reasonable prudence, would not have entered into in the
circumstances of the applicant at the time of entering into the
transaction, and (b) has caused or is likely to cause substantial
prejudice to the applicant." This protection will be lost if the

---

[1]  For an example of the application of the general law to problems thrown up
by the supply of computer software see *Beta Computers (Europe) Ltd. v.
Adobe Systems (Europe) Ltd.* 1996 S.L.T. 604.
[2]  Age of Legal Capacity (Scotland) Act 1991, s.1(1)(b).
[3]  *ibid.* ss. 3 and 4.

other party to the transaction was induced to enter into it by a fraudulent misrepresentation as to age or other material fact.

**4–04**    Children under the age of 16 generally have no legal capacity to enter into any transaction.[4] This rule could be inconvenient as such children do purchase goods, so the Act provides that they shall have legal capacity to enter into transactions "of a kind commonly entered into by persons of their age and circumstances" as long as this is "on terms which are not unreasonable." The purchase of things like sweets and comics by children under 16 should not be open to challenge as a result. The same may be said of other purchases such as some sports equipment, computer software or recreational services. As the value of the goods or services rises and the age of the child diminishes it becomes more difficult to know what a child will be regarded as having capacity to buy.

## TYPES OF CONTRACT FOR THE SUPPLY OF GOODS

**4–05**    It is still necessary in Scotland to distinguish between the various types of legal transaction under which the property in, or the possession of, goods may pass from a supplier to a consumer. The enactment of the Sale and Supply of Goods Act 1994 has clarified and simplified the law in this area to a considerable extent. Nevertheless, it is still necessary to be clear about the legal nature of a transaction because the legal consequences vary in some circumstances.

**4–06**    One of the most common transactions involving the supply of goods is the contract of sale. This is largely governed by the Sale of Goods Act 1979 which consolidated legislation dating from the original Sale of Goods Act 1893 which had been amended by a number of subsequent Acts. A contract of sale is defined by section 2(1) of the 1979 Act as "a contract by which the seller transfers or agrees to transfer the property in goods to the buyer for a money consideration, called the price." The fact that sale must involve "a money consideration, called the price" distinguishes sale from barter.

**4–07**    Barter, or exchange as it is sometimes called, "is a contract under which one moveable object is exchanged or bartered for another".[5] In this form barter is rarely encountered[6] but it is very common, especially in the motor trade, for goods to be acquired

---

[4]    1991 Act, s.2(1).
[5]    Erskine, *Institutes III,* iii, 13.
[6]    It is not unknown as *Ballantyne v. Durant,* 1983 S.L.T. (Sh.Ct.) 38; a case involving the exchange of two cars and *Widenmeyer v. Burn, Stewart & Co. Ltd,* 1967 S.C. 85; a commercial transaction involving the exchange of stocks of whisky, demonstrate.

for a price consisting partly of cash and partly of another piece of moveable property. It is not entirely clear what the legal status of this trading-in transaction is. This is not merely of academic interest for important questions on the rights of the consumer turn on the classification.

In the most recent case where the problem arose, *Sneddon v.* **4–08** *Durant*,[7] the pursuer had purchased a van which was on display in the defenders' showroom with a price of £995 attached. He paid for the van by trading in his car which was valued at £845 and entering into a consumer credit agreement with the defender to pay the balance of £150. The sheriff disposed of the question of the type of contract by stating that where money was involved it should be regarded as one of sale. From the point of view of consumer protection there was much to be said for this result as it meant that the transaction was subject to the more satisfactory remedies of sale. An examination of the cases and the views of legal writers, however, demonstrates that this view may be an over-simplification.[8] As far as the terms about title, description, quality and sample to be implied in such contracts are concerned, the problem of classification no longer matters because of the Sale and Supply of Goods Act 1994. This has assimilated barter to sale in these respects. However, it is still possible for the exact nature of the contract to be important for other reasons. The new legislation does not apply to questions about the passing of the property. There would thus be no different result in a case such as *O'Neill v. Chief Constable of Strathclyde Police*[9] which concerned title to a car which had been bartered for another which had been stolen.

Goods are also supplied under contracts involving supply on **4–09** credit. These are discussed in Chapter 9. The legal significance of transactions under which a contractor agrees to provides goods and services is discussed in Chapter 7.

Goods are often supplied in return for vouchers, coupons or **4–10** stamps. One example of this is the trading stamp which is now not as popular as it once was. Sales promotions, especially by petrol companies, encourage brand loyalty by offering vouchers which can be exchanged for various "gifts". Trading stamps have their own legislation, the Trading Stamps Act 1964, but there is some uncertainty about the legal nature of the transactions offering "free gifts". The problem caused a good deal of dissension among the Law Lords in *Esso Petroleum Co. Ltd v. Customs and*

[7] 1982 S.L.T. (Sh.Ct.) 39.
[8] For a detailed examination of this question of classification see Forte, *A Civilian Approach to the Contract of Exchange in Modern Scots Law* (1984) 101 S.A.L.J. 691.
[9] 1994 S.C.L.R. 253.

*Excise Commissioners.*[10] During the 1970 World Cup a petrol
company offered motorists the opportunity to collect a set of
coins each bearing a picture of a member of the England football
team. The coins had little intrinsic value. The case turned on
whether or not this was a sale. Four of their Lordships agreed
that it was not a sale, two considering it to be a gift and two some
sort of contract for the supply of goods. The fifth decided that it
was a contract of sale, the motorist's payment buying both petrol
and the coins.

**4–11**     The importance of this case now, with the passage of the Sale
and Supply of Goods Act 1994, is that it supports the view that
such transactions are contracts for the supply of goods and
subject to the new Part 1A of the Supply of Goods and Services
Act 1982 which applies to Scotland.

### PRICE AND DELIVERY

**4–12**     Price does not usually give rise to problems in consumer sales. It
is usually perfectly clear what the price is because it is marked on
a ticket on the goods or on the shelf. The provisions of section 8
of the Sale of Goods Act 1979 which refer to the methods of
ascertaining the price have little relevance. Indeed, if the price
has not been explicitly agreed in a consumer sale it is probably
strong evidence that there has not been an agreement and that
negotiations are still continuing.[11] It is possible that there might
be misunderstanding about the price, perhaps in private sales.
Where there is genuine misunderstanding about the price to be
paid it may be that the contractual doctrine of error may operate
to show that there has been no agreement.[12] However, it should
be remembered that the courts are slow to allow resort to the
doctrine of error.

**4–13**     It is not uncommon, where a consumer orders goods, for the
seller to ask for a deposit. This serves two purposes: if the
purchase goes ahead it is looked upon as an advance payment,
but its principal purpose, to quote Lord Macnaghten in *Soper v.
Arnold*,[13] "is a guarantee that the purchaser means business". If
the purchaser fails to honour the contract the deposit is for-
feited.[14] Should the trader, in breach of contract, fail to provide

---

[10]  [1976] 1 W.L.R. 1.
[11]  Support for this may be seen in the judgement of Sellers L.J. in *Ingram v.
Little* [1961] 1 Q.B. 31, at p. 49, where absence of agreement even about the
method of payment was considered to indicate the lack of a concluded
bargain.
[12]  As in *Wilson v. Marquis of Breadalbane* (1859) 21 D. 957.
[13]  (1889) 14 App. Cases 429.
[14]  *Zemhunt (Holdings) Ltd v. Control Securities plc,* 1992 S.C.L.R. 151.

the goods ordered, the deposit is recovered using the restitutionary remedy *condictio causa data causa non secuta.*

## PROBLEMS ABOUT TITLE TO GOODS

Problems sometimes arise about the right of the seller to sell the **4–14** goods. Difficult questions may arise involving the buyer, the person from whom the goods were acquired, and the true owner. In contracts of sale the starting point is the implied terms about title in section 12 of the Sale of Goods Act 1979. These implied terms, as a result of the Unfair Contract Terms Act 1977,[15] cannot be excluded. Section 12(1) provides that there is an implied term that the seller has a right to sell the goods. Section 12(2) provides that there is also an implied term that the goods are free from any charge or encumbrance not disclosed or known to the buyer before the contract is made and that the buyer will enjoy quiet possession of the goods except so far as it may be disturbed by the owner or other person entitled to the benefit of any charge or encumbrance which was disclosed.

*McDonald v. Provan (of Scotland Street) Ltd*[16] provides a **4–15** bizarre example of the operation of section 12. McDonald bought a car from Provan Ltd, who in turn had bought it in good faith. Three months after the sale the car was taken from McDonald by the police because at least part of it was stolen property. It appeared that the car consisted of parts of two separate cars, one of which had been stolen, that had been welded together. McDonald sued for damages for breach of the implied term about title in section 12 and it was held that he was entitled to succeed if he could prove the assertions on which he relied.

The implied terms about title are useful provided that the **4–16** seller can still be found and is worth suing. In many cases raising problems about ownership of goods this is not the case. The facts of *MacLeod v. Kerr*[17] provide a typical example. Kerr had advertised his car for sale in a newspaper and sold it to a man who came to see it. He accepted a cheque in payment and permitted the man to take the car away together with the registration document. The man had given a false name and paid with a cheque from a stolen cheque book. On discovering that he had been tricked Kerr immediately informed the police. Meanwhile, the rogue sold the car to a Mr Gibson who knew nothing of these events. The rogue was not worth suing and the question in the case was which of two people who had been duped by him was

---

[15] s. 20(1)(a).
[16] 1960 S.L.T. 231.
[17] 1965 S.C. 253.

the legal owner of the car. This unfortunate situation can also arise in other ways as the cases discussed below will demonstrate.

**4–17**    Prior to the passing of the original Sale of Goods Act 1893, problems of this sort posed fewer problems at Scots common law. The approach of Scots law, contrasting sharply with that of England, was that, normally, someone could not become the owner of moveable property without *traditio*, which was the physical transfer of the article to the buyer. The Sale of Goods Act 1893 changed this in relation to the contract of sale by imposing on Scots law the English idea that the transfer of ownership and possession could be separated. It is this approach which increases the number of situations in which problems akin to that mentioned in the previous paragraph can arise.

## THE *NEMO DAT* RULE AND ITS EXCEPTIONS

**4–18**    It is a general principle of the law relating to moveable property that someone who buys from a person who is not the owner can get no better title than that person has. This is sometimes referred to by the Latin tag *nemo dat quod non habet* — no-one can give a better title than he himself has. While logical, this can be an extremely inconvenient and unjust rule in some circumstances, and so the Sale of Goods Act 1979 has a number of modifications of this principle. It should be noted that one of the exceptions to the rule relating to sales in market overt, that is, shops in the City of London and legally constituted markets, had no application to Scotland.[18]

### THE PERSONAL BAR EXCEPTION

**4–19**    The first of these exceptions is to be found in section 21 of the Act which first states the general principle. It reads as follows:

> "Subject to this Act, where goods are sold by a person who is not their owner, and who does not sell them under the authority or with the consent of the owner, the buyer acquires no better title to the goods than the seller had, unless the owner of the goods is by his conduct precluded from denying the seller's authority to sell."

**4–20**    There are no Scottish cases on this exception, though there are some examples of its operation in English case law. In *Eastern*

---

[18]    This was abolished by the Sale of Goods (Amendment) Act 1994.

*Distributors Ltd v. Goldring*[19] it came into play through the owner of a van signing hire-purchase forms in blank, for completion by another person, thus allowing that person to appear to be the owner of the van. Generally, the English courts have construed the exception narrowly, as *Moorgate Mercantile Co. Ltd v. Twitchings*[20] demonstrates. The parties to this case were both finance companies and both were members of Hire Purchase Information (HPI). HPI is a trade association set up by finance companies to keep a register of hire purchase agreements relating to cars, and to give information to members, the police and motoring organisations in order to try to reduce hire-purchase frauds. The plaintiffs let out a car on hire-purchase and for some reason, contrary to their normal practice, failed to register the agreement with HPI. The hirer offered to sell the car to the defendant who, after checking with HPI and finding that no agreement had been registered, bought it. By a majority of three to two the House of Lords held that the plaintiff owed no duty of care to the defendant and was not precluded by its conduct from denying the authority of the hirer to sell the car.

This decision has been subjected to much criticism and it is not **4–21** binding on the Scottish courts, who are free to come to a different decision in a similar case. It is suggested that it would be appropriate that this should be done. There would be no conflict with the approach of the Court of Session in *Mitchell v. Z. Heys & Sons*[21] where a claim that the owner was personally barred failed. There it was held that for such a claim to succeed it would have to be shown that a representation by words or conduct had been made to, and relied upon by, the person claiming now to be the owner.

## SALE UNDER A VOIDABLE TITLE

Section 23 of the Sale of Goods Act 1979 provides that when the **4–22** seller of goods has a voidable title to them, but his title has not been avoided at the time of the sale, the buyer acquires a good title to the goods, provided he buys them in good faith and without notice of the seller's defect of title. The facts of *MacLeod v. Kerr*[22] referred to above are a good example of the sort of situation in which this provision might be relied upon by the buyer. The language of the section is based on English law concepts and it may be misleading to rely on some of the English

[19] [1957] 2 Q.B. 600.
[20] [1977] A.C. 890, H.L.
[21] (1894) 21 R. 600
[22] 1965 S.C. 253.

cases which make subtle distinctions between situations where a contract is void, and therefore of no effect, and those where it is voidable, which means that it has effect until the seller has taken some action to rescind it.[23]

**4–23** The approach of Scots law, as Professor Gow has cogently argued,[24] is that a buyer taking in good faith and for value acquires a title which is unimpeachable unless the seller acquired the goods by theft. The fact that the seller's title was tainted by error or fraud is not relevant. While this reasoning may not have been explicitly adopted in *MacLeod v. Kerr*, the decision in the case is consistent with it. It is an approach which has much to commend it on policy grounds. As Professor Gow points out, why should an innocent buyer be "penalised and enmeshed in expensive litigation simply because [the true owner] was so naive, or so credulous, or so gullible as to trust the seller, or so reckless as to take a long chance on his creditworthiness."[25] Indeed, one might argue that the law should be amended to protect the buyer even where the goods have been stolen from the true owner. The true owner will probably be insured against this possibility, to which he may to some degree have contributed, whereas the buyer will not.

## SALE BY A BUYER OR SELLER IN POSSESSION

**4–24** Sections 24 and 25 of the Sale of Goods Act may protect someone who has purchased goods from a person who appears to be their owner. Section 24 deals with the situation where goods have been sold but, for some reason, they are left in the possession of the seller. Depending on the circumstances, the buyer may well have become the owner by this time. What if the seller purports to sell the goods to someone else? The answer given by section 24 is that that person becomes the owner provided that he or she acted in good faith and did not know of the previous sale.

**4–25** Similarly, goods which the seller has bought may come into his possession before he becomes the legal owner. If he sells or otherwise disposes of those goods the sale has the same effect as if the person making the delivery or transfer were a mercantile agent in possession of the goods or documents of title with the consent of the owner. This is conditional on the person to whom he sells having acted in good faith and having no knowledge of the original seller's rights. The significance of the reference to

---

[23] This view is supported by the Scottish Law Commission Memorandum No. 27, *Corporeal Moveables: Protection of a Bona Fide Acquirer of Another's Property*, para. 21.

[24] Gow, *The Mercantile and Industrial Law of Scotland* (1964), pp. 118–122.

[25] *ibid.* p.121.

the sale having the same effect as if made by a mercantile agent is that sales by such persons give good title to the buyer. The English Court of Appeal in *Newtons of Wembley Ltd v. Williams*[26] has gone so far as to say that this part of the section means that the sale does not simply have the same effect as if it had been made by such an agent but must actually have been made by such agent. This is an impossible situation and it must be open to doubt if a Scottish court would follow this case. There are dicta from Australian and New Zealand cases which take a contrary view and interpret this part of the section in a literal way.[27]

Before looking at some of the other points in relation to this provision it should be noted that a buyer under a conditional sale agreement[28] and someone who has acquired goods under a hire-purchase agreement are not "buyers" for the purpose of it.[29]   **4–26**

The protection of section 25 only applies if the buyer is in possession with the consent of the seller. However, the fact that the buyer obtained that consent by deception does not nullify consent for this purpose.[30]   **4–27**

A point of some uncertainty arises where the seller is not himself the owner of the goods and was not authorised to sell them. This arose in the English case of *National Employers Mutual General Insurance Association Ltd v. Jones*,[31] where Mr Jones had acquired a car which had originally been stolen from the plaintiff's insured and then passed through the hands of several parties who had dealt with it in ignorance of this fact. It was held that Mr Jones could not have the protection of section 25 because the person who sold to him did not have title to the car on the *nemo dat* principle. Strictly speaking, he was not a "seller" so Mr Jones could not be a "buyer". In effect, seller was being interpreted to mean "owner". It could, and it is submitted should, be argued that those in the position of Mr Jones are sellers for the purposes of section 25.   **4–28**

### DISPOSITIONS OF MOTOR VEHICLES SUBJECT TO HIRE PURCHASE OR CONDITIONAL SALE

Section 27 of the Hire Purchase Act 1964 was passed to alleviate the hardship that was caused where consumers bought cars and   **4–29**

---

[26] [1965] 1 Q.B. 560
[27] *See Langmead v. Thyer Rubber Co. Ltd* (1947) S.A.S.R. 29, at p.39; *Jeffcott v. Andrew Motors Ltd* [1960] N.Z.L.R. 721, at p.729.
[28] s. 25(2).
[29] *Helby v. Matthews* [1895] A.C. 471.
[30] *Du Jardin v. Beadman Brothers* [1952] 2 Q.B. 712.
[31] [1987] 3 All E.R. 385.

later discovered that they were subject to hire-purchase agreements. The seller had no title and so could confer none on the buyer. The finance company financing the transaction was the owner and was entitled to recover the vehicle, leaving the buyer with an action against the seller. The seller would often be untraceable or not be worth suing. Section 27 applies where a motor vehicle has been hired under a hire-purchase agreement or has been agreed to be sold under a conditional sale agreement and, before the property in the vehicle has become vested in the debtor, he has disposed of it to another person. In this situation section 27(2) provides that:

> "Where the disposition . . . is to a private purchaser, and he is a purchaser of the motor vehicle in good faith and without notice of the hire-purchase agreement or conditional sale agreement, . . . that disposition shall have effect as if the creditor's title to the vehicle has been vested in the debtor immediately before that disposition."

**4–30** Section 27(3) applies this also to the situation where the vehicle has been sold to a trade or finance purchaser who then hire-purchases or sells it to the private purchaser.

**4–31**    It is important to note that this protection only applies to hire-purchase and conditional sale agreements. It does not apply to simple hire agreements. Therefore, someone who buys a car from a person who has hired a car or leased it, as it is often termed, does not have the protection of this provisions. With the increasing popularity of leasing as a method of acquiring motor vehicles there is evidence that more innocent purchasers are falling victims to this fraud. "Motor vehicle" is defined as a mechanically propelled vehicle intended or adapted for use on roads to which the public has access."[32] It does not cover caravans or boats, both of which are commonly acquired by hire-purchase.

**4–32**    The term "private purchaser" is somewhat misleading as it includes anyone who is not a trade or finance purchaser; that is, anyone who does not carry on a business involving trading in motor vehicles or providing finance for their hire-purchase or conditional sale. This means that many businesses will also obtain the protection of section 27.

**4–33**    To obtain the protection the buyer must be able to show that he did not have actual notice of the fact that there was an existing hire-purchase agreement.[33] It is also important to note that the buyer only gets the title of the person who was described as the

[32] Hire-Purchase Act 1964, s. 29(1).
[33] *Barker v. Bell* [1971] 1 WL.R. 983.

creditor in the hire-purchase or conditional sale agreement. Suppose that a stolen car is sold to a dealer who then lets it on hire-purchase to someone who sells it before the end of the hire-purchase agreement. Even if the buyer from that person takes in good faith and without notice of the hire purchase agreement, section 27 does not come to their rescue. This is because the dealer did not have title to the car having bought from a thief who could not pass on a good title.

## PROBLEMS CONCERNING PROPERTY AND RISK

In this section the problems that arise when the goods are  **4–34** damaged or destroyed after the buyer has agreed to buy them are discussed. Here it is assumed that there is nothing wrong with the quality of the goods in the sense that at the time that the contract was made the goods were of satisfactory quality, fit for their purpose and matched any description applied to them. Similarly, it is assumed that none of the problems about title to goods discussed in the previous section has arisen.

Here we are concerned with the question of who bears the risk  **4–35** of something going wrong. For example, suppose that after the buyer and seller have entered into a contract for the sale of a piece of furniture it is destroyed in a fire at the showroom; or goods ordered by mail are lost or damaged in the post. The basic rule is to be found in the Sale of Goods Act 1979, section 20(1):

"Unless otherwise agreed, the goods remain at the seller's risk until the property in them is transferred to the buyer, but when the property therein is transferred to the buyer, the goods are at the buyer's risk whether delivery has been made or not."

However, this rule does not apply in two circumstances. First, if  **4–36** delivery has been delayed through the fault of either buyer or seller the goods are at the risk of the party at fault as regards any loss which might not have occurred but for such fault. And secondly, nothing in section 20 affects the liability of either seller or buyer as custodier of the other party's goods. So, for example, a motor dealer might have custody of a car which had been sold but not collected by a customer and under the rules discussed below was at the customer's risk. If the car was destroyed as a result of the failure of the dealer to take reasonable care of it he would be liable for the loss through his failure to observe his duty as a custodier.

To discover who bears the risk it is essential to discover when  **4–37** property passes, and to do this sections 16 to 18 of the Sale of

Goods Act 1979 must be considered. To understand these sections it is first essential to know what "specific goods" and "unascertained goods" are. Section 61 defines "specific goods" as "goods identified and agreed on at the time a contract of sale is made". In a consumer context an obvious example would be a product selected by the consumer in a shop. "Unascertained goods" are not defined in the Act but it is clear that the term is used in contradistinction to specific goods. It covers three situations. Where the goods are to be manufactured or grown by the seller they will be unascertained. While not common in a consumer context this would include a product made to special order. It also includes generic goods such as a ton of coal or a consumer product referred to by its general description; and an unidentified part of a specific whole such as a case of Beaujolais Nouveau from the shipment in a particular wine merchant's warehouse.

## SPECIFIC GOODS

**4–38**  In the case of specific goods section 17 states that the property (and hence the risk) is transferred to the buyer at such time as the parties to the contract intend it to be transferred. This intention is to be ascertained from the terms of the contract, the conduct of the parties and the circumstances of the case. In consumer transactions it will be rare for explicit consideration to have been given to the passing of the property though conditional sale agreements are an exception. In such contracts it will be expressly stated that ownership remains with the seller until the final instalment has been paid.[34]

**4–39**  Where the parties have not indicated their intentions, the four rules in section 18 of the Act come into operation. It should be noted that any intention expressed by the parties must be manifested before the property has passed in accordance with these rules. A good example *is Dennant v. Skinner and Collom*[35] where D had sold a car at an auction to a person who turned out to be a swindler. The swindler gave a false name and address and asked if he might take the car away in return for a cheque. This D permitted him to do after getting the swindler to sign a document stating that the title to the car would not pass until the cheque was honoured. The cheque bounced and, meanwhile, the swindler sold the car which eventually came into the possession of the defendants. It was held that the document was too late to oust the

---

[34]  *Romalpa* clauses which state that goods are to remain the property of the seller until payment has been received are another example but are normally only found in commercial contracts.

[35]  [1948] 2 K.B. 164.

statutory rules about the passing of the property because they had operated on the fall of the auctioneer's hammer.

A further general point of importance to consumers is that **4–40** made by Diplock L.J. when he said that "in modern times very little is needed to give rise to the inference that the property in specific goods is to pass only on delivery or payment."[36]

## Rule 1

"Where there is an unconditional contract for the sale of **4–41** specific goods in a deliverable state the property in the goods passes to the buyer when the contract is made, and it is immaterial whether the time of payment or the time of delivery, or both, be postponed."

This rule will apply in the vast majority of sales in a shop. On **4–42** the face of it, therefore, where a consumer agrees to buy a product but it is not to be removed from the store until some time later it is the consumer who bears the risk. If, for example, the store was accidentally burnt down and the goods destroyed the loss would fall on the consumer. However, Diplock L.J.'s comment must be borne in mind, and in the light of the commercial case of *Brown Brothers v. Carron*[37] it would seem that a Scottish court should not have too much difficulty in finding that there was a contrary intention in a consumer transaction. In that inadequately reported case, the Court of Session seem to have assumed that there must have been such a contrary intention. The defenders agreed to buy a crane but, not requiring it for some months, it was agreed that it would remain at the pursuers' premises. In these circumstances it was held that the parties could not have intended the property to pass. It would seem most unreasonable, were a consumer to leave goods with a shop for later collection, to assume that he or she intended the property and the risk to pass.

For this rule to apply the goods must be in what the rule calls **4–43** "a deliverable state". This is defined as being "in such a state that the buyer would under the contract be bound to take delivery of them". In *Philip Head & Sons v. Showfronts Ltd*,[38] carpeting which had been sold to the defendants, and which the plaintiffs were required to lay, had been left at the defendant's premises. It was not regarded as in a deliverable state and thus the risk had not passed when it was stolen because it was in a heavy bundle and difficult to move.

---

[36] *R.V. Ward Ltd v. Bignall* [1967] 1 Q.B. 534.
[37] (1898) 6 S.L.T. 231.
[38] (1969) 113 S.J. 978.

**Rule 2**

**4-44**    This rule provides that where the seller is bound to do something to the goods for the purpose of putting them into a deliverable state, the property does not pass until the thing is done and the buyer has notice that it has been done. If, for example, a consumer agrees to buy a car but it is part of the deal that the seller will add some accessories, the property and risk do not pass until this has been done and the consumer has received notice that it has been done.

**Rule 3**

**4-45**    This rule is less likely to apply to consumer sales. Under it property does not pass where the seller has to do something by way of measuring or weighing to ascertain the price until it has been done and the buyer has notice.

**Rule 4**

**4-46**    Rule 4 deals with situations where goods have been supplied to the buyer either on sale or return terms or on approval. A common example in a consumer context of sale or return terms occurs where someone is holding a party. Off-licences commonly provide refreshments on this basis. In these situations property passes to the buyer if he intimates acceptance or otherwise adopts the transaction, or if he retains the goods beyond the stipulated time or, if no time has been stipulated, beyond a reasonable time. Selling the goods or pledging them as security would be evidence of the buyer adopting the transaction.[39]

**4-47**      As Willmers L.J. observed *in Poole v. Smith's Car Sales (Balham) Ltd*[40] that a "really interesting question" arises where goods on sale or return are damaged without the fault of the person to whom they have been offered. It is suggested, on the strength of the English case of *Elphick v. Barnes*,[41] that the potential buyer would not be liable for the price.

**4-48**      How the above rules apply to some common situations is not altogether clear. It is well known that some retailers have sale policies that are more liberal than required by law. Marks and Spencer, for example, are prepared to give a refund to a customer without question. The catalogue trader, Argos, states that a full refund will be given without quibble where goods are returned within 16 days of purchase. In neither case, it may be

[39]   See *Liquidators of the Brechin Auction Co. Ltd v. Reid* (1895) 22 R.711; *Bryce v. Ehrmann* (1904) 7 F. 5.
[40]   [1962] 1 W.L.R. 744.
[41]   (1880) 5 C.P.D. 321.

argued, is the sale an unconditional one, and thus rule 1 is not applicable. The obvious rule is rule 4, but on further consideration it is by no means clear that these types of sale are properly to be classified as sale or return, or on approval. The ability to return the goods and obtain a refund has more to do with remedies than with the classification of the contract. Perhaps the answer to the question of when the property and risk pass is to be found by remembering that the rules in section 18 are only guides and are subsidiary to section 17 which states that the intention of the parties is the primary guide. It is not difficult to suggest that in these cases a court would be likely to find that the circumstances pointed to the property passing when the goods were paid for in the shop.

## Unascertained Goods

In a consumer context, mail order sales where the consumer orders a product by a general description from the seller's stock are good examples of sales of unascertained goods. It is even possible that at the time the order is placed the mail order company does not have stocks. Unascertained goods might also be involved where a consumer buys wine; and some difficult problems have resulted where consumers have agreed to buy cases of wine from shippers and the shippers have stored it in their cellars until the buyers wish to take delivery.   **4–49**

Section 16 makes clear that until goods have been ascertained no property in them can be transferred. An example of this in operation comes from *Re Goldcorp Exchange Ltd (in receivership)*.[42] There, many New Zealanders had been induced by a company dealing in gold and other precious metals to invest in these metals. The investors then received a certificate of ownership stating that they had the right, on giving seven days notice, to take possession of the metal purchased. In the meantime, the metal was stored by the company as part of their overall stock of bullion. When the company became hopelessly insolvent there was a dispute between the investors and various banks which had securities over the stock of bullion. The Privy Council had no difficulty on these facts in holding that the metal was unascertained and thus no property could have been transferred to the investors.   **4–50**

More fortunate were some of the customers involved in the case of *Re Stapylton Fletcher Ltd*[43] where the product concerned was wine. Various customers had purchased stocks of wine from   **4–51**

---

[42]  [1994] 2 All E.R. 806, P.C.
[43]  [1994] 1 W.L.R. 1181.

two companies who stored it for them for a fee. Dispute arose between the receivers of these companies and the customers over ownership of the stocks. On purchase, some cases of wine had been moved from the part of the warehouse holding the company's stocks to another part reserved for customers' stocks, though it was not allocated to a specific customer by marking it. The amount owned by each customer was clearly recorded in the company's record system. On these facts the English High Court found that the wine had been ascertained for the purposes of section 16 and was owned by the various customers as tenants in common, a form of joint ownership in English law.

**4–52**    Section 17, which speaks of the intention of the parties determining when property in the goods passes, must therefore, in this category of goods be less important and cannot operate until the goods have been ascertained. Here section 18, rule 5 comes into play and provides that:

"(1)  Where there is a contract for the sale of unascertained or future goods by description, and goods of that description and in a deliverable state are unconditionally appropriated to the contract, either by the seller with the assent of the buyer or by the buyer with the assent of the seller, the property in the goods then passes to the buyer; and the assent may be express or implied, and may be given either before, or after the appropriation is made.

(2)  Where, in pursuance of the contract, the seller delivers the goods to the buyer or to a carrier or other bailee or custodier (whether named by the buyer or not) for the purpose of transmission to the buyer, and does not reserve the right of disposal, he is to be taken to have unconditionally appropriated the goods to the contract."

**4–53**    The key to turning unascertained goods into specific goods in which property can pass seems to be appropriation. This seems to require more than just setting goods aside. According to an English judge:

"the parties must have had, or be reasonably supposed to have had an intention to attach the contract irrevocably to those goods so that those goods and no others are the subject of the sale and become the property of the buyer."[44]

**4–54**    However, this must be read in the light of the *Stapylton* case where moving the goods to a different warehouse and clearly

---

[44]  Pearson J. in *Carlos Federspiel & Co. SA v. Twigg (Charles) Ltd* [1957] 1 Lloyd's Rep. 240, at p. 255.

indicating in the company's records who the owner was sufficed to transfer the property.

In relation to mail order purchases it might be argued that **4–55** these rules mean that the consumer bears the risk of loss in the course of post and the case of *Badische Anilin und Soda Fabrik v. Basle Chemical Works, Bindschedler*[45] is said to support this view. Such a situation is hardly in line with consumer expectations and it is submitted that it is not the law. In the *Badische* case the point was not disputed and the case turned on a point of patent law. It could be argued that this is a situation where the intention of the parties could override the rules in section 18.

### THE RISK RULES AND FRUSTRATION

In relation to the problems which may arise where the goods are **4–56** damaged or destroyed some other points need to be referred to, though in the context of consumer sales they may not have much relevance. Section 6 of the Sale of Goods Act 1979 provides that where there is a contract for the sale of specific goods, and the goods without the knowledge of the seller have perished at the time when the contract is made, the contract is void. This might apply where the seller and buyer have agreed that the seller will sell a specific car identified by make and registration number. If, unknown to him, it was destroyed in a fire on the day before the contract was made the contract would be a nullity.

Section 7 deals with a slightly different situation. Like section **4–57** 6 it applies to a sale of specific goods, but here the destruction occurs, without any fault on the part of the seller or buyer, before risk passes to the buyer. In this situation the sale is avoided. In consumer sales, section 7 can have little scope for application when one considers the rules about the passing of risk. A possible example would be where a consumer buys a car which requires some work to be done to it before it is to be collected some days later. The effect of section 18, rule 2 is that the risk does not pass to the buyer so that if, through no fault of the seller, the car were stolen or destroyed in a fire the section would apply.

In the case of unascertained goods the scope for them to perish **4–58** in a legal sense is more limited. An agreement to sell purely generic goods cannot be frustrated by the destruction of the goods and it is of no concern to the buyer that the seller had a particular source in mind as Asquith L.J. explained in *Monkland v. Jack Barclay Ltd*[46]:

---

[45] [1898] A.C. 200.
[46] [1951] 2 K.B. 252.

"Suppose A has contracted to sell to B unascertained goods by description — for example, "a" Bentley Mark VI (not "this" Bentley Mark VI), and suppose, further, that the seller expects to acquire the goods from a particular source, which may, indeed, be the only source available, the bare fact, without more, that when the time for delivery comes that source has dried up and that the seller cannot draw on it, does not absolve the seller. He is still, in the absence of some contractual term excusing him, liable for non-delivery."

**Late delivery**

4–59  What is the position where the goods are delivered late? The starting point is section 10(2) of the Sale of Goods Act 1979 which provides that whether any stipulation, other than one about the time of payment, is of the essence of the contract depends on the terms of the contract. The buyer can make the delivery date an express term of the contract but the cases show that this must be done in the clearest terms.[47] This is rarely the case in consumer contracts. However, it may occur, as is shown by *Charles Rickard Ltd v. Oppenhaim*[48] where the defendant had ordered a car for delivery within six or seven months. Having allowed the supplier more time on several occasions, he lost patience eventually and wrote saying that he would not take delivery after a certain date. It was held that he was entitled to give reasonable notice making time the essence of the contract, and was thus not in breach of contract in not accepting the car when it was delivered after the stipulated date.

## TITLE IN OTHER CONTRACTS FOR THE SUPPLY OF GOODS

4–60  Implied terms about title following the model of the Sale of Goods Act 1979 are to be found in other contracts for the supply of goods. In the case of hire-purchase they are to be found in section 8 of the Supply of Goods (Implied Terms) Act 1973. Where goods are redeemed for trading stamps they are found in section 4(1) of the Trading Stamps Act 1964. As a result of the insertion in the Supply of Goods and Services Act 1982 of Part 1A which applies only to Scotland, the implied terms in other contracts for the supply of goods are to be found in two sections

---

[47]  See *T. & R. Duncanson v. Scottish County Investment Co. Ltd,* 1915 S.C. 1106, *per* Lord Guthrie, at p. 1118.
[48]  [1950] 1 K.B. 616.

of that 1982 Act. For contracts of hire this is achieved by section 11H; and for other contracts by section 11B.

As far as other questions concerning ownership of goods **4–61** subject to the non-sale contracts for the supply of goods are concerned the situation is simpler than with sale.[49] Legislation has not been superimposed on the common law in the way that occurred with the Sale of Goods Act. The transfer of title will normally occur through the handing over of possession. As a result, in these contracts one can generally rely on the person in possession being the owner. As Erskine put it:

"Such is the natural connection between property and possession, that in moveables, even where they have had a former owner, the law presumes the property to be in the possessor; so that till positive evidence be brought that he is not the right owner, he will be accounted such by the bare effect of his possession."[50]

Lord Cockburn suggested in *Anderson v. Buchanan*[51] that "This **4–62** is a presumption liable to be rebutted, and perhaps liable to be rebutted easily." In *Prangnell-O'Neill v. Lady Skiffington*[52] Lord Hunter observed that how easy it might be to rebut the presumption depended on the circumstances. In his view, to overcome the presumption it was necessary to show that the goods had once belonged to the person claiming them and that his or her possession was terminated in such a way that the subsequent possessor could not have acquired a right to them. Theft will fulfil the second requirement but, as was observed in the *Prangnell-O'Neill* case, so would evidence of removal by force.

The presumption can be rebutted, but it seems that where the **4–63** person in possession has acted in good faith and given value for the goods only proof of theft will be sufficient to permit the original owner to recover the property.

---

[49] For a detailed and learned discussion of the issues see Miller, *Corporeal Moveables in Scots Law* (1991); especially Chap.10.
[50] *Institutes* II.i.24. See also Stair's *Institutions* II.i.42.
[51] (1848) 11 D. 270, p.284.
[52] 1984 S.L.T. 282.

CHAPTER 5

# PRODUCT QUALITY

**5–01**   The vast majority of consumer complaints about goods are concerned with their quality. Consumers expect what they buy to be free from defects. Should their expectations be disappointed what can they do about it? This chapter explores the standards of quality that consumers are entitled to expect, concentrating on goods which are defective but have not caused physical injury. In the next chapter the way in which consumers are protected against unsafe goods is discussed. It is mainly the civil law, which is relevant in determining what the legal standard of quality is, but it should not be forgotten that the criminal law has some role to play as well. The core of the chapter is devoted to the terms implied in the various contracts under which goods are supplied. The final section deals with the role of criminal law in setting standards for products.

**5–02**   The claims made for a product by the seller may be relevant. If these claims have become terms of the contract the buyer is entitled to expect that they will be fulfilled and if they are not the normal contractual remedies will be available. If the claims are not regarded as terms it may be that they will be misrepresentations. These issues are discussed in Chapter 3.

### THE STATUTORY IMPLIED TERMS IN CONTRACTS FOR THE SUPPLY OF GOODS

**5–03**   The lynch-pin of consumer protection in relation to quality is the implication of terms into the various contracts under which goods are supplied. The nature of these contracts has been outlined in Chapter 4. The common law implied various terms relating to quality in these contracts. Starting with the original Sale of Goods Act 1893 the terms relevant to the contract of sale were put on a statutory footing and are now to be found in the Sale of Goods Act 1979. Until the Sale and Supply of Goods Act 1994 added a Part 1A to the Supply of Goods and Services Act 1982, the only other contracts where there were such statutorily implied terms were contracts of hire-purchase[1] and contracts under which trading stamps were redeemed for goods.[2] With effect from January 3, 1995 the new Part 1A of the Supply of Goods and Services Act 1982 has implied similar terms into the various other contracts under which goods are supplied. The discussion of the implied terms in this chapter concentrates on those implied in the contract of sale. The other contracts are dealt with more briefly.

The implied term about description found in section 13 is not discussed at this point but in Chapter 3. This is because the modern tendency, as pointed out in that chapter, is to reserve that term for matters relating to the identity of the goods leaving issues of quality to be decided under section 14. However, there is sometimes a fine line to be drawn between these two things as *Beale v. Taylor*[3] demonstrates. **5–04**

It hardly requires to be stated that as contractual liability is involved it is the supplier who is liable under the various contracts and that only the other party to the contract may invoke the implied terms. Whether this privity principle should be altered is under consideration and this was recommended in a discussion paper issued by the Department of Trade.[4] **5–05**

### IMPLIED TERMS IN CONTRACTS OF SALE

#### Quality and Fitness for Purpose

Section 14(1) of the Sale of Goods Act 1979 provides that: **5–06**

> "Except as provided by this section and section 15 . . . there is no implied term about the quality or fitness for any particular purpose of goods supplied under a contract of sale."

The section then goes on to set out the two terms that are implied: that goods must be of satisfactory quality, and that they must be reasonably fit for any particular purpose for which the goods are being bought. Before discussing these two terms in detail certain points that are common to both will be mentioned. **5–07**

The terms implied by section 14 only apply where the "seller sells goods in the course of a business", a term which, according to section 61 of the Act, includes "a profession and the activities of any government department . . or local or public authority". **5–08**

---

[1] Supply of Goods (Implied Terms) Act 1973, ss. 8–11.
[2] Trading Stamps Act 1964, s. 4.
[3] [1967] 1 W.L.R. 1193.
[4] See *Consumer Guarantees: A Consultation Document*, DTI, Feb. 1992.

In most cases this will cause no difficulty; but there will be some doubtful cases. Must the seller be selling something which he habitually sells, or are the implied terms imposed on every trader who happens to sell an item? The latter approach was the one preferred by the Molony Committee in 1962 and by the Scottish Law Commission in a report in 1969.[5] It has also got judicial support in Scotland in the Outer House judgement in *Buchanan-Jardine v. Hamilink*.[6] The case arose out of the sale of livestock on the retirement from farming of the pursuer. When it was alleged that two of the cattle which he had sold were not of merchantable quality (as the quality term then was) he argued that this had no application in the circumstances. Lord Dunpark stated that:

"In my opinion anyone who sells any part of his business equipment must sell that part in the course of his business. It can make no difference whether he sells only one item or the whole of the goods used by him for the purpose of a business."

5–09    There are several cases in England where the same phrase has been interpreted by the courts in the context of other statutes.[7] These have mainly been criminal statutes where there is a tendency to give a narrow construction to a penal provision. It is submitted that in the context of civil liability the interpretation of Lord Dunpark is to be preferred, in that it provides protection for consumers who are in no position, in many cases, to know what the seller's business consists of. It is also in accord with the plain meaning of the statute. The English Court of Appeal recently adopted this interpretation in *Stevenson v. Rogers*.[8]

5–10    Less reputable traders have been aware of the advantages of appearing to sell privately, and such was the scale of this practice that it proved necessary to make it a criminal offence.[9]

5–11    The provisions of section 14 can, however, apply where the seller is not selling in the course of a business in one situation set out in section 14(5). This occurs where someone arranges for a trader to act as his or her agent for the sale of goods. The fact that

---

5    *First Report on Exclusion Clauses* (1969) Law Corn. No. 24, Scot. Law Comm. No.12.
6    1981 S.L.T. (Notes) 60.
7    See *Davies v. Sumner* [1984] 1 W.L.R. 405. The same phrase used in the Unfair Contract Terms Act 1977 has not been applied to the purchase of a car by a company for the use of one of its directors. See *R. & B. Customs Brokers Co. Ltd v. United Dominions Trust Ltd* [1988] 1 WL.R. 321.
8    [1999] Q.B. 1028; [1999] 1 All E.R. 613; [1999] 2 W.L.R. 1064
9    See the Business Advertisements (Disclosure) Order 1977 (S.I. 1977 No. 1918).

the principal is not selling in the course of a business is irrelevant unless the buyer knows that this is the case or reasonable steps are taken to bring this fact to his attention before the contract is made. The buyer may sue either the principal or the agent.[10]

It is also clearly established that the liability under section 14 is strict, as was pointed out in *Randall v. Newsom*[11]:  **5–12**

"If there was a defect in fact, even though that defect was one which no reasonable skill or care could discover, the persons supplying the article should nevertheless be responsible, the policy of the law being that in a case in which neither were to blame, he, and not the person to whom they were supplied, should be liable for the defect."

*Frost v. Aylesbury Dairy Company Limited*[12] provides a good  **5–13** example of this principle in operation. The dairy had supplied Mr Frost and his family with milk which contained typhoid germs which caused the death of his wife. The evidence showed that the dairy's processes were extremely careful and that typhoid germs could only be detected by prolonged investigation. Nevertheless, it was held that there was an implied term that the milk would be reasonably fit for consumption. It was irrelevant that the defect could not have been discovered at the time of sale.

It is important to note that section 14 applies to the "goods  **5–14** supplied under a contract of sale." This means that in determining whether the goods are of the requisite quality the container or other packaging, the instructions, or foreign material inadvertently supplied with the goods contracted for may be relevant. A graphic illustration is provided by *Wilson v. Rickett, Cockerell & Co Ltd*[13] where the plaintiff, who had ordered Coalite from the defendants, found that he had also been supplied with a detonator which exploded in his living room when placed on the fire. The defendants had ingeniously argued, no doubt encouraged by the Court of Session's extraordinary decision in *Duke v. Jackson*,[14] that there was nothing wrong with the Coalite and that the detonator[15] was not ordered under the contract. The Court of Appeal held that the goods delivered were not of the requisite quality. As Denning L.J. (as he then

---

[10]  *Boyter v. Thomson* [1995] 3 All E.R. 135, H.L.
[11]  (1876) 45 L.J.Q.B. 364.
[12]  [1905] 1 K.B. 608.
[13]  [1954] Q.B.598.
[14]  1921 S.C. 362; 1921 1 S.L.T. 190.
[15]  Counsel does not seem to have had the temerity to go quite as far as to add that the detonator was a perfectly good detonator — as the damage to Mr Wilson's living room seemed to prove.

was) put it in referring to the words "goods supplied under a contract of sale":

> "In my opinion that means the goods delivered in purported pursuance of the contract. The section applies to all goods so delivered, whether they conform to the contract or not: that is, in this case, to the whole consignment, including the offending piece, and not merely to the Coalite alone. ... Coal is not bought by the lump. It is bought by the sack or by the hundred-weight or by the ton. The consignment is delivered as a whole and must be considered as a whole; not in bits. A sack of coal, which contains hidden in it a detonator, is not fit for burning, and no sophistry should lead us to believe that it is fit."

**5–15**   In *Duke v. Jackson* the Court of Session had dealt with a very similar case and had been seduced by the arguments of counsel into arriving at just this conclusion. Strictly speaking, that case is a binding precedent in Scotland which the English decision of the Court of Appeal is not. It is inconceivable that it would be followed today; and, indeed, two sheriffs principal on whom the decision was binding managed to distinguish it.[16]

**5–16**   The relevance of instructions is illustrated by *Wormell v. R.H.M. Agricultural (East) Ltd*[17] where a farmer argued that the inadequacy of the instructions on tins of weedkiller rendered it unfit for its purpose. In the English High Court it was observed that the goods included not just the weedkiller but also its packaging and instructions:

> "All of these . . are part of the goods. One must look at all of them as a whole . . .. By selling goods with such instructions the seller is warranting that the chemical, when used in accordance with those instruction, will be reasonably fit for its purpose . . . . If a retailer . . . sells the goods (that is the chemical together with its container and instructions) and those instructions make the goods not reasonably fit for their purpose, in my view there is a breach of section 14(3) of the Sale of Goods Act 1979.[18]

---

[16]   See *Fitzpatrick v. Barr*, 1948 S.L.T. (Sh. Ct.) 5 and *Lusk v. Barclay*, 1953 S.L.T. (Sh.Ct.) 23, cited by McBryde, *Scots and English Contract Laws*, in Birks, *The Frontiers of Liability* (1994), Vol. 2, p.146. See also *Gedling v. Marsh* [1920] 1 K.B. 668.

[17]   [1986] 1 All E.R. 769.

[18]   On appeal (see [1987] 1 W.L.R. 1091) the Court of Appeal reversed the decision of the High Court because they took a different view of the facts. No doubt was cast on the principle enunciated.

*The Implied Term of Satisfactory Quality*

The principal quality standard in the Sale of Goods Act is  **5–17**
contained in section 14(2) which states that:

"Where the seller sells goods in the course of a business, there
is an implied term that the goods supplied under the contract
are of satisfactory quality."

The term "satisfactory quality" is new. It replaced "merchant-  **5–18**
able quality" which had been introduced into the Scots law of
sale by the Sale of Goods Act 1893. Although a definition of
"merchantable quality" was eventually added, increasing dissatisfaction was felt with it, culminating in the recommendation of
the Scottish Law Commission that it be replaced. In their report,
*Sale and Supply of Goods*,[19] the Scottish Law Commission
observed:

"If the word 'merchantable' has any real meaning today, it
must strictly be a meaning which relates to merchants and
trade; the word must be inappropriate in the context of a
consumer transaction. The expression 'merchantable quality'
is, and always has been a commercial man's notion".

The change was effected by section 1 of the Sale and Supply of  **5–19**
Goods Act 1994 which inserted a new version of section 14(2)
and new subsections (2A), (2B) and (2C). The opportunity has
also been taken to draft the subsection in language which is
appropriate to Scots law. Its predecessor spoke of the implied
term being a "condition", a term appropriate in this context to
English law and its system of remedies. The significance of this
will be discussed in detail later when remedies are considered.

While "satisfactory quality" is a new phrase, the general struc-  **5–20**
ture of section 14 is broadly similar to that in the previous version.
Before examining the central features of "satisfactory quality" it is
necessary to note two qualifications to its operation.

Section 14(2C) repeats, in slightly different language, the two  **5–21**
qualifications found in the previous versions of the Act. First, the
term does not extend to any matter "which is specifically drawn
to the buyer's attention before the contract is made". It is
important to note that the factor must be specifically brought to
the buyer's attention. In *Turnock v. Fortune*[20] it was held by the
Sheriff Principal that a strong recommendation from a third
party not to buy a car did not amount to specifically drawing

---

[19] Law Com. No. 160; Scot Law Com. No. 104, Cm. 137 (1987).
[20] 1989 S.L.T. (Sh.Ct.) 32.

attention to its unroadworthiness, and thus did not prevent the
car from being regarded as unmerchantable.

**5–22**  Secondly, if a buyer has examined the goods before the
contract was made nothing which "that examination ought to
reveal" can be relied on to demonstrate that the goods are not of
satisfactory quality. There has been some doubt about the interpretation of this proviso as a result of *Thornett & Fehr v. Beers &
Son*[21] where the slightly different wording of the 1893 Act was
interpreted as if it read "a reasonable examination". A commercial buyer who had made a cursory examination of some glue was
held to have lost the protection of section 14 despite the fact that
his examination was insufficient to have detected the defect.
That case may have been wrongly decided, as it seems to be
inconsistent with an earlier Court of Appeal decision, *Bristol
Tramways, etc., Carriage Co. v. Fiat Motors Ltd*,[22] which was not
cited. In any event, the present wording is slightly different and
would seem to support the view that it is only defects which the
type of examination actually carried out should have revealed
that are relevant.

*Satisfactory Quality*

**5–23**  As was the case in the latter days of its predecessor, satisfactory
quality is defined. Section 14(2A) provides that:

"goods are of satisfactory quality if they meet the standard
that a reasonable person would regard as satisfactory, taking
account of any description of the goods, the price (if relevant)
and all the other relevant circumstances."

**5–24**  Section 14(2B) goes on to expand on this by saying that the
quality of goods:

"includes their state and condition and the following (among
others) are in appropriate cases aspects of the quality of
goods—

(a) fitness for all the purposes for which goods of the kind in
question are commonly supplied,
(b) appearance and finish,
(c) freedom from minor defects,
(d) safety, and
(e) durability."

[21] [1919] 1 K.B 486.
[22] [1910] 2 K.B 831.

The new definition retains several elements of the previous **5–25**
definition of merchantable quality, but what is novel about it is
that new factors are to be taken into account.

The new definition is based on the recommendations of the Law **5–26**
Commissions. They suggested "acceptable quality", but like the
Consumer Guarantees Bill 1990, the Act refers to "satisfactory quality". Moving the second reading of the bill, its sponsor
explained that it was thought that "[a] non-complaining buyer
might decide reluctantly that goods he bought were of acceptable quality, even if by objective standards the quality was not
satisfactory."[23] In practice this change probably does not matter
very much. What is important is that, as the Law Commissions
recommended, there is an objective test of quality and one that is
given content by the list of factors which are to be taken into
account in assessing what is satisfactory in a given case. It
remains a standard that can be applied to all kinds of goods
whether new or second-hand.

The definition of "satisfactory quality" is in two parts. The **5–27**
basic test appears in section 14(2A) and states the general
principle. The test is that of the reasonable person, and in
deciding if the standard has been met, any description applied to
the goods must be taken into account as well as the price, if that
is relevant, and all other relevant circumstances. These factors
were set out in the earlier definition of "merchantable quality".
A description may affect the standard that can be expected. If
goods are described as "second-hand" then it will usually not be
reasonable to expect the quality of new goods. On the other
hand, statements in advertising material suggesting that the
article is at the top end of the range might increase the standard
of quality that it would be reasonable to expect.

Similarly, price may be important, though it is an ambiguous **5–28**
signal. The price may be reduced simply to encourage faster sale
of the item without implying any diminution in quality. Taken
with other factors, such as a statement that the goods are
"seconds", or the mileage and general condition of a second-
hand car, it might well indicate that a lower standard of quality
can be expected.

In addition to the basic principle, section 14(2B) sets out a list **5–29**
of specific factors which, *in appropriate cases*, may be taken into
account in assessing satisfactory quality. The words emphasised
in the last sentence make it clear that not all the factors would be
relevant in every case; and it is also stated that the list of factors
is not exhaustive.

The first factor is that the goods are fit for all the purposes for **5–30**
which goods of the kind in question are commonly supplied. The

[23] *Hansard*, H.C., Vol. 237, col. 633 (Feb. 11, 1994).

placing of this aspect of quality is significant. As the Law Commissions noted in their report, this is almost always a very important aspect of quality, but the drafting of the previous definition had over-stressed it. In several decisions usability had been the touchstone and the fact that there were defects affecting the appearance of the product were not considered to be relevant.[24] In addition, the earlier definition had spoken of goods being fit for the purpose or purposes as "it is reasonable to expect". This, it can be argued, had lowered the standard of quality where the seller could establish that goods of the particular type, such as new cars, can reasonably be expected to possess a number of minor defects on delivery. *Millars of Falkirk Ltd v. Turpie*[25] can be used in support of this argument.

**5–31**    The new definition diminishes the importance of fitness for purpose by including it in the list of factors which may be taken into account. As the Law Commissions' report pointed out,[26] a new car should not only be capable of being driven safely and effectively on the roads, but should also do so "with the appropriate degree of comfort, ease of handling and reliability and . . . of pride in the vehicle's outward and interior appearance" to quote Mustill L.J. in *Rogers v. Parish (Scarborough) Ltd.*[27]

**5–32**    It goes further and reverses the previous law under which the test was satisfied if the goods were fit for any of the purposes for which goods of that type could be used.[28] The new version provides that goods must be suitable for "all the purposes for which goods of the kind in question are commonly supplied". If goods have more than one purpose and the seller intends his product to fulfil only one of those purposes it will be necessary to make this clear. This may be done explicitly or, in some circumstances, other factors such as the price may indicate this fact.

**5–33**    Appearance and finish, and freedom from minor defects are also to be taken into account in determining whether goods are of satisfactory quality. These characteristics are more likely to apply to new rather than second-hand goods. A major uncertainty of the old law is thus removed.[29] The result is, to quote the Law Commissions' report, that:

[24] More recent cases such as *Rogers v. Parish (Scarborough) Ltd.* [1987] Q.B. 933 have suggested a more realistic approach to fitness at least in relation to consumer goods.
[25] 1976 S.L.T. (Notes) 66.
[26] *op. cit.* n. 19, and see para. 3-31.
[27] [1987] Q.B. 933.
[28] *M/S Aswan Engineering Establishment Co. v. Lupdine Ltd* [1987] 1 W.L.R. 1.
[29] In *Bernstein v. Pamson Motors (Golders Green) Ltd* [1987] 2 All E.R. 220 certain *obiter* remarks suggested that minor defects were not relevant to merchantability, while *Rogers v. Parish (Scarborough) Ltd* [1987] Q.B. 933 considered that they were.

"dents, scratches, minor blemishes and discolorations, and small malfunctions will in appropriate cases be breaches of the implied term as to quality, provided they are not so trifling as to fall within the principle that matters which are quite negligible are not breaches of contract at all."[30]

The regrettable decision in the *Millars of Falkirk* case[31] is thus reversed and, if similar facts were to recur, it seems certain that the car would be regarded as of unsatisfactory quality. The application of this test will, of course, depend on the facts. Second-hand goods may be expected to have some minor marks or defects while, usually, new goods should not. However, certain kinds of product such as earthenware, pottery or natural products may be expected to have minor inconsistencies and blemishes and these may well not render them of unsatisfactory quality. In some cases this test will have no application at all. The Law Commissions gave as examples cars sold as scrap and loads of manure.    **5–34**

There has never been any doubt that unsafe goods were not of the quality demanded by law.[32] This is explicitly recognised in the definition. Somewhat less clear was whether goods had to be durable, though this does appear to have been the law.[33] The matter is now put beyond doubt by the new definition. It is important to realise that this term is to be satisfied at the time of delivery and not at some later date. Later events may be relevant in determining whether, at the time of sale, the goods were durable.[34] The criterion is durability not duration.    **5–35**

The Law Commissions rejected any suggestion that normal lifespans for classes of goods should in some way be required. They emphasised, and this is reflected in the new definition, that durability is to be a flexible concept requiring that goods should last a reasonable time taking into account whether they have been well or badly treated.    **5–36**

The only case to discuss the new satisfactory quality term is *Thain v. Anniesland Trade Centre*,[35] a decision of the sheriff principal of Glasgow and Strathkelvin. Ms Thain had had paid £2,995 for a secondhand Renault 19 car which had travelled about 80,000 miles and was about six years old. Two weeks after she purchased it an intermittent droning noise was noticed and this proved to be a failing differential bearing in the automatic    **5–37**

[30] *op. cit.* n. 18, and see para. 3-40.
[31] 1976 S.L.T. (Notes) 66.
[32] *Godley v. Perry* [1960] 1 WL.R. 9; *Lambert v. Lewis* [1982] A.C. 225.
[33] For a survey see Ervine, "Durability, Consumers and the Sale of Goods Act", 1984 J.R. 147.
[34] *Crowther v. Shannon Motor Co. Ltd* [1975] 1 WL.R. 30.
[35] 1997 S.L.T. (Sh. Ct.) 102; 1997 S.C.L.R. 991.

gear box. The sellers refused to replace the gear box. Eventually, after about nine to ten weeks, the car was unusable and Ms Thain rejected it. The Sheriff Principal upheld the sheriff's decision that the car was of satisfactory quality observing:

> "the sheriff's conclusion can only be described as that of the reasonable person. Even a negligible degree of durability may not represent unsatisfactory quality where the secondhand car supplied is as old and as heavily used as the Renault had been. The plain fact is that, given the Renault's age and mileage when supplied, its durability was a matter of luck. Durability, in all the circumstances, was simply not a quality that a reasonable person would demand of it".

5–38    One can only marvel at this view of reasonableness and ask how many car buyers would think it reasonable that they should take all the risk of a catastrophic breakdown almost immediately after purchase. The decision appears to make a mockery of the express inclusion of durability as one of the factors to be taken into account in assessing satisfactory quality. Perhaps emphasis should be placed on the fact that this case turns on its own somewhat special facts. There was evidence even from Ms Thain's own expert witness that there was no sign of a problem during the first two weeks that she drove the car and that the part which failed could work well and suddenly deteriorate. Given that nine to ten weeks was regarded as reasonable durability the issue of getting over the problem of when the test has to be satisfied never arose. It is sometimes said that that this is the date of the contract, at which point in this case there was no evidence of a defect. That could have been circumvented, as was done by Lord Denning in *Crowther v. Shannon Motor Co*,[36] by using the fact of a short lifespan as evidence that the car did not meet the statutory standard at the date of the contract.[37]

5–39    Where it is possible to show that the goods were unsatisfactory because they were not durable the benefits of including durability in the definition of satisfactory quality will not be as great as one might expect. This stems from the fact that while a lack of durability will render goods unsatisfactory, there is no corresponding change in the remedies available. By the time a consumer realises that the goods are not durable it is very likely that the right to reject will be lost. Damages will, therefore, be the only remedy in most of the cases where goods prove not to be durable.[38]

---

[36]  [1975] 1 W.L.R. 30.
[37]  See Ervine, "Satisfactory Quality, *Thain v. Anniesland Trade Centre*", 1998 J.R. 379.
[38]  In *Thain* the possibility that the right to reject had been lost was not discussed.

*Fitness for Purpose*

As well as being of satisfactory quality, section 14(3) states **5–40**
that:

> "Where the seller sells goods in the course of a business and
> the buyer, expressly or by necessary implication, makes
> known—
>
> (a) to the seller, or
> (b) where the purchase price or part of it is payable by
>     instalments and the goods were previously sold by a
>     credit-broker to the seller, to that credit-broker, any
>     particular purpose for which the goods are being bought,
>     there is an implied term that the goods supplied under
>     the contract are reasonably fit for that purpose, whether
>     or not that is a purpose for which such goods are com-
>     monly supplied, except where the circumstances show
>     that the buyer does not rely, or that it is unreasonable for
>     him to rely, on the skill or judgement of the seller or
>     credit-broker."

The reference to a credit-broker is necessary to take account of **5–41**
certain kinds of sales financed by a third party. The credit-broker
will often be a retailer in whose shop the goods have been
displayed and in which negotiations for their purchase have
taken place. If the retailer does not provide his own credit
facilities what next happens is that the goods are sold to a finance
company who then sell to the consumer. Examples of transactions which would be covered would be credit sale and
conditional sale.

The features which this term shares with that on satisfactory **5–42**
quality have already been commented on above. It will also be
noted that there is considerable overlap between the two, as
satisfactory quality is partially defined in terms of fitness for
purpose. There will be many situations where a product will fail
to satisfy either term. The weedkiller in *Wormell v. R.H.M.
Agricultural (East) Ltd*,[39] which had inadequate instructions, and
the defective car in *Rogers v. Parish (Scarborough) Ltd*[40] are
examples. However, there are circumstances where a product
might be of satisfactory quality but not pass the test of fitness for
purpose. Suppose that someone has a metal gate which is to be
painted. She goes to a DIY store and explains to an assistant that
paint suitable for the job is required. The paint which the

[39] [1986] 1 All E.R. 769.
[40] [1987] Q.B. 933.

assistant sells her turns out to be unsuitable, being intended only for application to wood. In this case the customer will succeed in a claim under section 14(3) for breach of the implied term about fitness for purpose. She would not succeed with a claim for unsatisfactory quality because there is nothing wrong with the paint which would be perfectly satisfactory for painting wood.

**5–43**   To avail oneself of the protection of this term it is necessary to show that one has, either expressly or by implication, indicated the particular purpose for which the goods are required. As Lord Wilberforce observed of both the section 14 implied terms, they are "readily and untechnically applied to all sorts of informal situations — such as retail sales over the counter of articles whose purpose is well known — and are applied rather more strictly to large scale transactions carried through by written contracts".[41] In many cases it will not be necessary for the customer to have referred expressly to the particular purpose. The burden of proof is on the seller to show that reliance was unreasonable, as was pointed out in *Grant v. Australian Knitting Mills Ltd*[42]:

> "The reliance will seldom be express: it will usually arise by implication from the circumstances. Thus to take a case like that in question, of a purchase from a retailer, the reliance will be in general inferred from the fact that a buyer goes to the shop in the confidence that the tradesman has selected his stock with skill and judgement: ... the main inducement to deal with a good retail shop is the expectation that the tradesman will have bought the right goods of a good make."

**5–44**   This quotation is redolent of an earlier age before the rise of modern retail methods. Nevertheless, if the customer relies on the staff of a store it will be difficult for it to assert that this was unreasonable, unless it had been made quite plain that they had no specialised knowledge.[43] As this case makes clear, it is not necessary to specify a particular purpose where the goods, such as underpants or hot water bottles,[44] have only one purpose.

**5–45**   If the customer does have a particular purpose in mind, which is not the common purpose or has some susceptibility, this must be communicated to the seller. *Baldry v. Marshall,*[45] where the customer required a car which would be comfortable and suitable

[41]   *Henry Kendall & Sons v. William Lillico & Sons* [1969] 2 A.C. 31 at 123.
[42]   [1936] A.C. 85.
[43]   A parallel might be drawn with the cases on services where the tradesman having done a poor job tried to assert that he did not have the specialised skill for the particular job. See cases discussed at paras 7-13 *et seq.*
[44]   See *Priest v. Last* [1903] 2 K.B. 148.
[45]   [1925] K.B.260.

for touring, is an example of the first issue; and *Griffiths v. Peter Conway Ltd*[46] an example of the second. In the latter case the plaintiff had developed a very severe attack of dermatitis as a result of wearing a tweed coat purchased from the defendants. Mrs Griffiths' skin was unusually sensitive and the evidence showed that there was nothing in the cloth that would have affected a normal person's skin. As Mrs Griffiths had not informed the sellers of her sensitivity they were not liable.

*Flynn v. Scott*[47] makes clear that the particular purpose must be clearly specified. There, the subject of the sale was a lorry which could have been used for a number of different functions, though the buyer intended to use it to transport furniture and livestock. A claim for breach of the implied term of fitness for purpose failed because it was not shown that the buyer had communicated his particular purpose. **5–46**

## SALE BY SAMPLE

Section 15 of the Sale of Goods Act 1979 implies various terms in sales by sample. There is a term that the bulk will correspond with the sample in quality; that the buyer will have a reasonable opportunity of comparing the bulk with the sample; and that the goods will be free of any defect rendering them of unsatisfactory quality which would not be apparent on reasonable examination of the sample. **5–47**

These terms are not limited to sales in the course of a business, no doubt because it was not thought likely that they would occur in any other context. They are not especially important in a consumer context, though carpets and wallpaper will often be sold by reference to samples. To some extent, section 15 duplicates other sections in many circumstances. Most sales by sample will attract the protection of the implied term about description and, if the goods are not of satisfactory quality under section 15, they must also fail to satisfy the implied term in section 14(2). **5–48**

## TERMS IMPLIED IN OTHER SUPPLY CONTRACTS

### Hire-Purchase

Terms in very similar language to that relating to sale, but adapted to the specialities of hire-purchase transactions, are to be found in sections 8 to 11 of the Supply of Goods (Implied Terms) Act 1973. The drafting of these terms has been amended **5–49**

---

[46] [1939] 1 All E.R. 685 approved in *Slater v. Finning Ltd* [1996] 3 All E.R. 398, H.L.; 1996 S.L.T. 912.
[47] 1949 S.C. 442; 1949 S.L.T. 399.

by the Sale and Supply of Goods Act 1994 to reflect the change from merchantable quality to satisfactory quality and to be appropriate for Scots law.[48]

**Trading Stamps**

5–50 Section 4 of the Trading Stamps Act 1964 implies terms about quality and description where goods are exchanged for trading stamps. These terms have been amended in the same way as the terms in sale and hire-purchase contracts and now use terminology appropriate to Scots law.

**Other Contracts for the Supply of Goods**

5–51 In addition to the contracts for the supply of goods already referred to, there are various other transactions which result in goods being supplied to consumers. Although it is not particularly common nowadays in its most basic form, goods are sometimes exchanged or bartered for other goods. Indeed, if trading in is legally barter, then this contract is very common, especially in the car market. There is some doubt, as we have seen in an earlier chapter, about this issue.[49]

5–52 It is common to hire goods of many kinds. Televisions and video recorders are frequently supplied on long-term hire, cars and equipment may be hired for short periods, and it is not uncommon for cars to be acquired for long-term use through a hire arrangement usually referred to as a lease. This is an alternative to purchasing on credit. Goods may also be acquired in exchange for coupons, vouchers or tokens in sales promotions.[50]

5–53 What all these transactions had in common, until the passing of the Sale and Supply of Goods Act 1994, was the absence of a regime of statutory implied terms such as were implied in contracts of sale and hire-purchase. There were, of course, implied terms, but these were implied by common law, and it was not always certain what they were, or easy to discover them. Part 1 of the Supply of Goods and Services Act 1982 had provided implied terms in such contracts in England but that Act did not then extend to Scotland. Section 6 of the Sale and Supply of Goods Act 1994 provides that a Part 1A is inserted in the 1982 Act to achieve the same thing in Scotland for contracts entered into after January 3, 1995. This new part is set out in Schedule 1 to the Act. As the terms implied are the same as those for sale, subject

[48] See the Sale and Supply of Goods Act 1994, Sched. 2, para. 4.
[49] See Chap. 4.
[50] The legal nature of this kind of transaction was examined in Chap. 4.

to necessary verbal changes, it is not necessary to discuss them again.[51]

## REMEDIES

### CONTRACTS OF SALE

Ever since the enactment of the Sale of Goods Act 1893 the law relating to the remedies of the disappointed consumer in Scotland has been in a confused state.[52] The Sale and Supply of Goods Act 1994 has effected considerable improvements. The problem stemmed from the fact that the original Sale of Goods Act was drafted with English legal concepts in mind. It was extended to Scotland only at a late stage in its parliamentary progress. The implied terms, for example, were described as "conditions" and "warranties", expressions which do not fit into the scheme of remedies in Scots contract law. An attempt was made to modify the legislation to conform to Scots law, but this was not satisfactory.[53]

**5–54**

The Sale of Goods Act 1979, which had not addressed this basic problem, has now been amended by the Sale and Supply of Goods Act 1994. As we have seen above, the implied terms have been redrafted and are simply described as "terms". The consequences of breach are then separately dealt with for England and Wales and Scotland in ways which are appropriate for each jurisdiction.

**5–55**

A new section 15B, inserted in the Sale of Goods Act 1979 by the Sale and Supply of Goods Act 1994, provides that, where the seller is in breach of any term of a contract, whether express or implied, the buyer shall be entitled to claim damages and, if the breach is material, to reject the goods and treat the contract as repudiated. This firmly places the remedies for breach of a contract of sale in the scheme of Scots contract law.[54] The section goes further in the case of consumer contracts. In these contracts, breach of the express or implied terms about the quality or fitness of goods for a purpose, and correspondence with description or sample, is deemed to be a material breach. This makes clear that the primary remedy of a consumer for the

**5–56**

---

[51] On the Act see Ervine, "The Sale and Supply of Goods Act 1994", 1995 S.L.T. 1. Note that the definition of satisfactory quality is split between s. 11J (in the case of hire) and s.11D (in other supply contracts) and s.18(1) of the Supply of Goods and Services Act 1982 as amended by the Sale and Supply of Goods Act 1994, Sched. 2, para. 6(10).

[52] See Clarke, "The Buyer's Right of Rejection", 1978 S.L.T. (News) 1.

[53] *ibid.*

[54] See, for example, *Wade v. Waldon*, 1909 S.C. 571.

common breaches of contract is rejection of the goods. It removes the uncertainty caused by *dicta* in *Millars of Falkirk Ltd v. Turpie*.[55] In that case the Lord President had suggested that a finding that goods were not of merchantable quality would not automatically confer a right to reject.

**5–57**    Section 15B does not deem breach of the implied term about title to be material. It is difficult to conceive of circumstances where this would not be so. It might be that there could be cases where such a breach was cured almost immediately after the goods were delivered which might justify not treating it as material.

### The Right to Reject

**5–58**    While it is now clear that rejection is the primary remedy for breach of the most important terms in contracts of sale, it is necessary to examine precisely when it may be exercised. It is now assumed that the breach is a material one that justifies rejection.

**5–59**    To exercise the right of rejection, consumers must demonstrate two things: that they have effectively intimated rejection to the seller; and that the goods have not been accepted. The first of these requires that the consumer has given the seller an unequivocal indication that the goods have not been accepted. In *Lee v. York Coach and Marine*[56] the consumer was held not to have indicated an intention to reject during the period when that was possible. Letters from his solicitors asking the seller to remedy the defects or offer a refund did not amount to rejection. As section 36 of the Sale of Goods Act makes clear, rejection does not necessarily require the consumer to return the goods to the seller unless it has been otherwise agreed. They would have to be stored carefully and, if the seller fails to collect them, damages may be claimed for any costs involved in storage.[57]

**5–60**    The right to reject ceases to be available when the consumer has accepted the goods in the legal sense. When goods are accepted is defined in section 35 of the Sale of Goods Act 1979. It occurs in three circumstances: where the buyer has intimated to the seller that he has accepted the goods; when, on receiving delivery, the buyer does an act inconsistent with the seller's ownership; and when, after the lapse of a reasonable time, the buyer retains the goods without intimating to the seller that he has rejected them.

**5–61**    The first two situations in which acceptance occurs are now clearly subject to the right to have a reasonable opportunity to

---

55  1976 S.L.T. (Notes) 66.
56  [1977] R.T.R. 35, C.A.
57  *Kolfor Plant Ltd v. Tilbury Plant Ltd* (1977) 121 S.J. 390, D.C.

examine the goods for the purpose of ascertaining that they are in conformity with the contract. This is now set out in the new version of section 35(2) of the Sale of Goods Act 1979. In the case of loss of the right to reject through lapse of time, section 35(4) achieves much the same result in a slightly different way. What constitutes a reasonable opportunity to examine goods depends on the circumstances. There do not appear to be any cases in a consumer context which shed any light on this issue. However, it seems that it may involve the use of the goods for a short time.[58]

*Intimation of Acceptance*

The most common situation where rejection by intimation has occurred in a consumer context has been through the signing of "acceptance notes". Consumers often sign such documents when goods are delivered, not realising that they may go further than merely evidencing receipt of the goods. It is not uncommon to find that they contain a statement indicating that the consumer has examined the goods and acknowledges that they are in good condition. Section 35(2) states that buyers who have not previously examined goods which are delivered to them must have a reasonable opportunity of examining them before they are deemed to have accepted them. Section 35(3) makes clear that this opportunity cannot be taken away "by agreement, waiver or otherwise". This means that signing an acceptance note can no longer sign away the consumer's right to reject the goods.

**5–62**

*Acceptance by An Act Inconsistent with the Ownership of the Seller*

There is little guidance in the case law on what amounts to an act inconsistent with the ownership of the seller in the context of a consumer transaction. In commercial transactions the most common situation where this arises is in the resale of goods. There appears to be only one Scottish case, *Hunter v. Albancode plc.*[59] Mrs Hunter bought a suite of furniture which proved to be defective and she purported to reject it. When it was not uplifted by Albancode Mrs Hunter continued to use it as she could not afford to replace it until she obtained a refund. The sheriff held that continuing to use the goods amounted to an act inconsistent with the seller's ownership and thus the right to reject had been

**5–63**

---

[58] *Lucy v. Mouflet* (1860) 5 H & N 229.
[59] 1989 G.W.D. 39-1843.

lost. Further guidance is to be found in the New Zealand case of *Armaghdown Motors Ltd v. Gray Motors Ltd.*[60] Gray Motors took a car which they had recently purchased to the premises of the plaintiffs and offered to sell it to them. They applied an incorrect description to the car and were in breach of the equivalent of section 13 of the Sale of Goods Act 1979. The sale took place on June 15, but the plaintiffs did not discover the misdescription until July 7, when they received the vehicle's registration certificate. Four days later they registered the car in their own name and put it on sale in their showroom. It was held that, as the defect was latent, the plaintiffs were entitled to have the period from the date of sale until July 7, to discover the true position. Their actions thereafter, in registering the car in their own name and putting it on sale, were acts inconsistent with the ownership of the seller which brought their right to reject to an end.

5–64     Incorporating goods into other goods from which they cannot easily be removed may well amount to an act inconsistent with the ownership of the seller.[61] So, for example, if someone buys parts to carry out a repair on a car and after fitting the part it becomes clear that it is defective it may not be possible to reject, though damages would still be available.

5–65     Prior to the amendments to the 1979 Act made by the Sale and Supply of Goods Act 1994 it was unclear whether requesting or agreeing to a repair amounted to an act inconsistent with the ownership of the seller. This matter is now put beyond doubt by the new version of section 35 of the Sale of Goods Act 1979, which states that the buyer is not deemed to have accepted goods merely because he asks for, or agrees to, their repair by or under an arrangement with the seller.

*Lapse of A Reasonable Time*

5–66     The third situation in which the right to reject may be lost is where the consumer retains the goods for a reasonable time after delivery without intimating to the seller that he has rejected them. What is a reasonable time is, as section 59 of the Act points out, a question of fact, "as if it could be anything else", as Rougier J. sardonically observed in *Bernstein v. Pamson Motors (Golders Green) Ltd.*[62] The new version of section 35 gives some important guidance on this point. Section 35(5) states that:

---

[60]  [1963] N.Z.L.R.. 5.
[61]  *Mechan & Sons Ltd v. Bow, McLachlan & Co. Ltd,* 1910 S.C. 758.
[62]  [1987] 2 All E.R. 220.

"The questions that are material in determining . . . whether a reasonable time has elapsed include whether the buyer has had a reasonable opportunity of examining the goods."

This is particularly important because under the previous version of the Sale of Goods Act 1979 the right to have an opportunity to examine the goods had no relevance to the loss of the right to reject through lapse of time. In the Bernstein case this was pointed out and it was said that a reasonable time in this context was:          **5–67**

"directed solely to what is a reasonable practical interval in commercial terms between a buyer receiving the goods and his ability to send them back, taking into consideration from his point of view the nature of the goods and their function, and from the point of view of the seller the commercial desirability of being able to close his ledger reasonably soon after the transaction is complete. The complexity of the intended function of the goods is clearly of prime consideration here. What is a reasonable time in relation to a bicycle would hardly suffice for a nuclear submarine."[63]

The judge accepted the submission of the defendants that this meant that there must be "a reasonable time to inspect and try out the car generally rather than with an eye to any specific defect". What it did not include was an opportunity for an examination.          **5–68**

How far the new version of section 35 alters this approach is not altogether easy to say. It cannot be intended to import the long term right to reject that consumer organisations have argued is necessary to make meaningful the inclusion of durability within the definition of satisfactory quality. The fact that there is still a reference to accepting through the lapse of time must lead to this conclusion. Its purpose is to make clear that there must be adequate opportunity for an examination to ensure that the goods conform to the implied terms and any express stipulations made about them. Consumers now have the opportunity to make a proper trial of the goods before losing the right to reject.          **5–69**

This is borne out in the debates on the bill in the House of Lords where Lord Peston asked for clarification of the phrase "lapse of a reasonable time". The Minister of State, Department of Trade and Industry, Earl Ferrers, after reviewing the background to the new section and referring to the fact that the *Bernstein* case "was unsatisfactory from the point of view of          **5–70**

---

[63] [1987] 2 All E.R. 220, p. 230.

maintaining a fair balance of rights between supplier and consumer" went on to add:

> "If the Act is recast, as it is in the Bill, the provisions which are at present in Sections 34 and 35 will be tied much more closely together. This will make it clear that a material question in determining whether a reasonable time has elapsed — and therefore whether the buyer has accepted the goods — will be whether he has had a reasonable opportunity to examine the goods in order to satisfy himself that they are in fact in conformity with the contract and are what he wanted to buy. This means examination to see whether, among other things, the implied terms of the contract are satisfied.
>
> It is clear, therefore, that the examination must be more than just an examination in general terms. The term 'examine' has to be interpreted in the context of the type of examination which it is necessary to conduct in order to ensure that the goods in question are in conformity with the contract."[64]

**5–71** The minister then went on to apply this to an example which Lord Peston had raised. He had referred to having a new kitchen installed for which he had separately bought a new cooker. The cooker had been delivered in its packaging but not opened immediately because the kitchen fitters had fallen behind schedule. When, some four months after taking delivery of the cooker, it was installed it was found to be defective. The Minister asserted that the "customer would not have examined the goods and would not therefore be deemed to have accepted them."[65]

**5–72** The new section is thus a valuable clarification of consumer rights. It may be said that it builds on Bernstein because there the judge was prepared to take into account the personal circumstances of the consumer who had been ill in the period immediately after buying the car. In computing a reasonable time the judge took this into account. With even greater certainty this can now be done. It might be important in many circumstances. For example, suppose that someone buys a lawnmower in November, in an end of season sale, and is unable to test it until the new season in April. Should the mower prove to be defective the right to reject will not have been lost. Similarly, it would seem that someone who, just before moving house, purchases a product which immediately has to go into storage while the house move is completed, will not lose the right to reject while the product is in store.

[64] *Hansard*, H.L., Vol.557, cols. 479–480 (July 22, 1994).
[65] *ibid.*

Even where there are not special circumstances, such as those **5–73** just outlined, it would appear that the new Act provides more time to carry out an examination than some of the cases under the old law allowed.[66] It will still be the case that a reasonable time will vary from product to product, a longer time being reasonable in the case of more complex goods; and it will still be advisable to reject at the earliest opportunity. It is also clear that the new Act does little for the victim of the latent defect of which the *Bernstein* case is such a good example. One might speculate that if the same circumstances were to recur Mr Bernstein would be found not to have lost his right to reject. However, if one assumes the same facts, except that the defect occurs six months after purchase, it is doubtful if, in the absence of some other factors, the right to reject would still be available.

From the fact that the new section says that asking for, or **5–74** agreeing to, a repair does not amount to acceptance it can also confidently be said that the clock will stop running so far as a reasonable time is concerned. Previous case law is also of some help. In *Munro & Co. v. Bennet & Son*[67] the time for rejection was extended because the seller had assured the buyer that the goods would be satisfactory after, adjustment.[68]

### Other Aspects of Rejection

Section 35A of the Sale of Goods Act 1979 deals with partial **5–75** rejection.[69] Where a buyer has the right to reject goods but is prepared to retain some of them and reject only the remainder, the right to reject is not lost by retaining some of them. Where goods are delivered by instalments the right to reject a non-conforming instalment is not lost by having accepted another instalment.

Where the seller delivers too few goods, or too many, there is no **5–76** longer, even in consumer contracts in Scotland, an automatic right to reject all the consignment. Section 30[70] provides that rejection is only possible where the excess or shortfall is material.

---

[66] It ought to be remembered that *Bernstein* gained an importance that was not wholly justified. As W.H. Thomas pointed out in an interesting survey of car cases several other judges had been much more liberal in construing a reasonable time. See 1989 N.L.J. 1188.

[67] 1911 S.C. 337.

[68] *Peakman v. Express Circuits Ltd* (1998), C.A. (Eng.; unreported; *Lexis* 3 Feb 1998), one of the few English cases since the reform of the Sale of Goods Act 1979 by the Sale and Supply of Goods Act 1994, to relate to novel points, where attempts to repair seem to have extended the time for rejection.

[69] Inserted by the Sale and Supply of Goods Act 1994, s.3(1).

[70] *ibid*. s.5(2).

**Damages**

5–77    Section 15A provides that damages are also a remedy where a contract of sale is breached. This may be the only remedy for the non-material breach of an express term or may be the remedy which must be used where the right to reject has been lost through acceptance. The Sale of Goods Act 1979 applies the normal contract rule that the damages should be such as result naturally from the breach in the ordinary course of events.[71] Where the breach is the failure of the seller to deliver the goods, section 51 goes on to say that where there is an available market for the goods the measure of damages is, prima facie, to be ascertained by the difference between the contract price and the market or current price of the goods at the time that they ought to have been delivered.

5–78    Where the seller delivers the goods but is in breach of one of the terms of the contract regarding quality section 53A says how the consumer's loss is to be calculated. It is "the difference between the value of the goods at the time of delivery to the buyer and the value they would have had if they had fulfilled the contract." In addition, other damage may have resulted to the consumer or his or her property. In *Godley v. Perry*[72] a defective catapult resulted in the purchaser losing an eye, and the claim for breach of contract was mainly for damages for this injury. Similarly, in *Wilson v. Rickett, Cockerell & Co. Ltd*[73] the breach of contract consisted in the delivery of defective Coalite and resulted in damage to the buyer's living room for which compensation was awarded. In the Bernstein case the consumer was awarded compensation for the cost of returning home after the car broke down, the loss of a tank of petrol, five days loss of use of the car and £150 for the spoilt day out.

5–79    As the *Bernstein* case demonstrates, it is possible to obtain damages for inconvenience or disappointment for breach of a contract of sale. This will only be possible where the seller is aware that breach is likely to have this result as in *Bernstein* or *Jackson v. Chrysler Acceptances Ltd*[74] where the sellers of a new car knew that the buyer wanted it for a foreign holiday and thus were liable for damages for the distress caused through a holiday ruined by the car breaking down frequently.

---

[71]  See ss. 51 and 53A.
[72]  [1960] 1 W.L.R. 9.
[73]  [1954] 1 Q.B.598.
[74]  [1978] R.T.R. 474.

## OTHER CONTRACTS OF SALE

In the case of the other contracts for the supply of goods the     **5–80**
policy has been to extend the same remedies to them as apply to
sale and to do so in terminology that is appropriate to Scots law.
In the case of contracts of hire-purchase, section 12A of the
Supply of Goods (Implied Terms) Act 1973[75] achieves this. It is
an almost exact replica of section 15A of the Sale of Goods Act
1979. In the contracts for the transfer of goods subject to Part IA
of the Supply of Goods and Services Act 1982 a similar provision
appears in section 11E. In applying these provisions it should be
noted that there are no rules providing that the right to reject is
lost by acceptance. When the right to reject is lost is not at all
clear in Scots law. It would appear to depend on the law of
personal bar and waiver and it will probably be the case that the
right to reject can not be lost before the consumer knows that the
goods are defective.[76]

In the case of contracts of hire, although Part 1A also sets out     **5–81**
implied terms it does not set out the remedies for breach. This is
because the Scottish Law Commission considered that the common law remedies were satisfactory. For breach of this contract
the consumer has the normal remedies of rejection and damages.

## MANUFACTURER'S LIABILITY

### DELICTUAL LIABILITY

So far the discussion has concentrated on the liability of the     **5–82**
supplier. In addition, it is possible for the manufacturer, or
someone else in the chain of production and distribution, to be
liable as well. This may be delictual liability or it may be the
result of the manufacturer having offered a guarantee.

Where goods are defective the consumer will normally find it     **5–83**
much easier to attempt to make the supplier liable for breach of
one of the implied terms under the Sale of Goods Act or the
analogous legislation discussed above. As we have seen, liability
is strict. However, there are circumstances where the consumer
will not be able to sue the supplier. The seller may have become
insolvent or the person who suffered the harm may, like Mrs

---

[75]  Inserted by the Sale and Supply of Goods Act 1994, Sched. 2, para. 4(8).
[76]  See the Law Commissions' report, paras 2.53 and 2.54. For an English hire-
purchase case where rejection was permitted although the motorcycle had
been ridden for 4,000 miles, see *Farnworth Finance Facilities Ltd v. Attryde*
[1970] 1 W.L.R. 1053.

Donoghue, in *Donoghue v. Stevenson*,[77] not be the purchaser. This may result in a delictual action and will often arise from goods being dangerous and not merely shoddy. The possible types of action in these circumstances are discussed in Chapter 6.

**5–84**     One avenue discussed in that chapter is the delictual action for breach of duty which stems from *Donoghue v. Stevenson*. That line of authority appears to have been extended in another Scottish appeal to the House of Lords, *Junior Books Ltd v. The Veitchi Co. Ltd*.[78] It was held that the owner of a factory had a claim in delict against a subcontractor who had laid a floor negligently, thus causing economic loss. There was no allegation that the floor was dangerous or had caused any physical injury. Liability was said to depend on the degree of proximity of the parties and in this case it was very close. It was expressly said, however, that the decision would not apply to consumer situations where the complaint was that the goods were of poor quality. This, it was said, was because there would not be the requisite degree of proximity between a manufacturer and the ultimate consumer. In view of the influence of mass advertising carried out mainly by manufacturers, and occasional cases where the retailer is little more than a conduit between the consumer and the manufacturer, this seems open to doubt. There may be situations where a consumer wants something made to special order and goes to a retailer who puts him in touch with the manufacturer. The ultimate sale may be routed through the retailer, but discussion about the product will have been directly between the customer and the manufacturer. There would seem to be little difference in principle between such a situation and *Junior Books*.

### MANUFACTURERS GUARANTEES

**5–85**     A useful supplement to the legal protection regarding quality is often given by manufacturers' guarantees, usually called warranties in the case of cars. These may consist of a written undertaking to the purchaser to replace or repair a faulty product, or to give a refund, should problems develop within a stated period. This is usually one year in the case of domestic appliances and, in the case of cars, it can be longer. Such guarantees can be a very useful addition to the consumer's statutory rights. It avoids the problems surrounding the standard of quality which the consumer is entitled to expect under the Sale

---

[77]  1932 S.C. (H.L.) 31.
[78]  [1983] A.C. 520; 1982 S.C.(H.L.) 244; 1982 S.L.T. 492.

of Goods Act and, in particular, can overcome the deficiencies in the legal remedies where goods do not prove to be durable.

Despite their widespread use, the legal status of guarantees is **5–86** not altogether clear.[79] It is probably the case that they are contracts. In this case the Unfair Contract Terms Act 1977 provides that a guarantee relating to goods of a type ordinarily supplied for private use or consumption given by someone other than the supplier of the goods is void in so far as it purports to exclude or restrict liability for loss or damage, including death or personal injury, arising from the goods proving to be defective as a result of a breach of duty by a manufacturer or distributor.[80]

### REFORM OF THE CIVIL LAW

The recent reforms effected by the Sale and Supply of Goods **5–87** Act 1994 are certainly welcome and have been particularly important in Scotland. Here, in addition to the important improvements in the definition of the standard of quality, the redrafting of the legislation in language appropriate to Scots law was long overdue. The provision of statutory implied terms in various contracts for the supply of goods to match Part I of the Supply of Goods and Services Act 1982 is also useful.

The next changes to consumer sales law will be those neces- **5–88** sary to implement the E.C. Directive on Sale of Consumer Goods and Associated Guarantees.[81] This directive is designed to harmonise throughout the Members States certain aspects of the law relating to sales of goods to consumers. It is important to note that it is a minimum directive and so, while its standards must be attained, it is open to Member States to offer a higher level of protection. This is important in the context of United Kingdom law as some aspects of the directive offer a level of protection which is lower than that currently available.[82]

The directive applies to sales of goods to consumers by sellers **5–89** acting in the course of their trade, business or profession. In such cases the goods sold must supply goods which comply with any description applied to them, are fit for their purpose and are of the quality that the consumer can reasonably expect. It seems unlikely that implementation of these aspects of the directive will cause much difficulty. The remedies set out in the directive give more cause for concern. The primary remedies are repair or replacement, but these do not apply if the cost would be

---

[79] For a discussion of this issue see Cusine, "Manufacturers' Guarantees and the Unfair Contract Terms Act", 1980 J.R. 185.
[80] Unfair Contract Terms Act 1977, s. 19(1), (2)(b).
[81] Directive 1999/44, 1999 OJ L 171.
[82] The DTI have stated that they will be consulting on implementation which must take place by January 1, 2002.

"disproportionate". If the consumer is entitled to neither repair
nor replacement, or if the seller has not completed the remedy
within a reasonable time, or a repair would cause the consumer
significant inconvenience, he or she may require an appropriate
reduction of the price or have the contract rescinded. However,
the consumer is not entitled to have the contract rescinded if the
lack of conformity is minor. A useful aspect of the directive is
that it creates a presumption that defects which appear with in
six months of delivery existed at that time.

**5–90**     The net effect of this part of the directive is to provide a
scheme of remedies which is inferior to that existing under the
Sale of Goods Act. The refusal of rescission as a remedy for
minor defects, in particular, would be a retrograde step. It is to
be hoped that implementation in the United Kingdom will go
well beyond the minimum requirements and preserve existing
United Kingdom law where this provides a higher standard of
protection.

**5–91**     The provisions on guarantees do not require manufacturers or
others to give them. However, where they do so they will be
legally binding on the persons offering them, a proposal which
was contained in a DTI consultation paper in 1992.[83] The guarantee must state that the consumer has legal rights under national
legislation and make clear that those rights are not affected by
the guarantee. It must be set out in plain and intelligible language and include particulars necessary for making a claim
under the guarantee.

**5–92**     When the directive is being implemented the opportunity
could also be taken to introduce a form of "lemon law" reform as
advocated in a National Consumer Council report in 1989.[84]
Such laws are common in relation to cars in most American
states.[85] They provide that the seller must put right a defect
appearing within a certain time or a certain mileage after purchase. If this cannot be, or is not done, within a certain number of
attempts, or the car is off the road for more than a stated time,
the buyer is entitled to a replacement or refund. The great merit
of such laws is that they get over the problems of the time within
which rejection is reasonable in the case of a car, or other
product, with chronic problems.

---

[83]  *Consumer Guarantees*, Feb 1992. It was also included in the Conservative
     party's election manifesto for that year.
[84]  *The Consumer Guarantee: Final report and recommendations for legislation*,
     NCC, Sept. 1989.
[85]  See Ervine, "Protecting New Car Purchasers: Recent United States and
     English Developments Compared" (1985) 34 I.C.L.Q. 342.

## CRIMINAL LAW

From the consumer's point of view the civil law relating to the **5–93** quality of goods is the most important aspect of this topic. In addition, there is a good deal of legislation sanctioned by criminal penalties which plays an important part in ensuring that the quality of goods is satisfactory. Under the Food Safety Act 1990 the quality and composition of food is controlled. The detailed control is to be found in a mass of subordinate legislation made principally under powers conferred by the Act. Similar powers in relation to drugs are given by the Medicines Act 1968. The Hallmarking Act 1973 updated one of the oldest forms of consumer protection and governs the quality of gold, silver and platinum.

## CHAPTER 6

# PRODUCT SAFETY

**6–01**  While it is irritating and can have serious financial consequences to find that a product that one has bought is shoddy, this is as nothing to the dangers posed by unsafe goods. This chapter considers the legal response to the problem of unsafe goods. Broadly speaking, this falls into two categories: attempts to provide compensation for the consequences of unsafe goods; and legislation to prevent unsafe goods reaching the market in the first place. The two categories are not exclusive, as the threat of having to compensate a victim of unsafe goods must act as an incentive to a trader to ensure that unsafe goods do not reach the market place.

**6–02**  We have already seen that goods which are dangerous will not be regarded as meeting the standard of satisfactory quality, and that damages for personal injury may be an element in the damages for breach of that term of the contract of supply. This is of limited utility as it will only benefit the purchaser. What happens if the injured person is someone other than the purchaser? Until recently the answer to that question was that the injured person could only succeed by bringing an action for breach of duty as Mrs Donoghue did in the famous case. As Lord Atkin put it in that case:

> "a manufacturer of products, which he sells in such a form as to show that he intends them to reach the ultimate consumer in the form in which they left him, with no reasonable possibility of intermediate examination, and with the knowledge that the absence of reasonable care in the preparation or putting up of the products will result in an injury to the consumer's life or property, owes a duty to the consumer to take that reasonable care."[1]

**6–03**  That principle has been applied in a wide range of situations, many of them outwith the realm of consumer protection. Within

---

[1] [1932] A.C. 562, at p. 599.

the category of consumer examples is *Grant v. Australian Knitting Mills Ltd*,[2] where a consumer contracted dermatitis from negligently manufactured underpants; and *Malfroot v. Noxal Ltd*[3] where a motorcycle manufacturer was held liable to a passenger in a side car which, as a result of the negligence of the manufacturer, parted company with the motorcycle and caused injury to her. A more recent example of a manufacturer's design defect founding this kind of liability is to be found in *Lambert v. Lewis*,[4] where a passenger in a car was killed and others injured when a trailer being towed behind a Land Rover became unhitched and collided with the car in which they were travelling.

It is not only manufacturers who can be liable, as *Fisher v. Harrods Ltd*[5] demonstrates. In that case the well-known London store was held liable for the injuries suffered by a lady who had been injured when defective packaging of jewellery cleaning fluid purchased by someone else damaged her eye. It was shown that the store had obtained the product from a small company with whom they had never dealt before and of which they knew nothing. Despite this, they had failed to have the product tested before putting it on sale. Repairers can also be liable to their customers, as *Stennett v. Hancock & Peters*[6] shows; as can those who sell reconditioned products[7] or those who hire out products.[8]    **6–04**

The difficulty with the *Donoghue v. Stevenson* principle of liability is that it depends on showing that the defender has failed to display reasonable care for the safety of the pursuer. Despite the assistance of the maxim *res ipsa loquitur* (the facts speak for themselves), this is not always easy or possible to prove, as the thalidomide tragedy[9] graphically demonstrated. This led to demands to introduce legislation imposing strict liability on manufacturers of defective products which have resulted in the enactment of Part 1 of the Consumer Protection Act 1987.    **6–05**

Before looking at that Act it is important to point out that, despite its enactment, *Donoghue v. Stevenson*[10] liability will, in some circumstances, still be relevant. This is because the Consumer Protection Act has a limitation period which may rule out claims that could still be made at common law; and there are some forms of loss which it does not cover, such as pure financial loss.    **6–06**

[2] [1936] A.C. 85.
[3] (1935) 51 T.L.R. 551.
[4] [1982] A.C. 225.
[5] [1966] 1 Lloyd's Rep. 500.
[6] [1939] 2 All E.R. 578.
[7] *Herschtal v. Stewart & Ardern Ltd* [1940] 1 K.B. 155.
[8] *Griffith v. Arch Engineering (Newport) Ltd* [1968] 3 All E.R. 217
[9] Thalidomide was a drug widely prescribed to combat morning sickness in pregnant women. In a large number of cases it caused their children to be born with serious abnormalities.
[10] 1932 S.C. (H.L.) 31.

## STRICT LIABILITY OF MANUFACTURERS IN DELICT

**6–07** The Consumer Protection Act 1987, Part 1 introduces what is often, though somewhat misleadingly, referred to as strict liability for manufacturers. Incidents such as the thalidomide tragedy had led consumer organisations to campaign for the introduction of such legislation paralleling judicial developments in the United States.[11] This was supported in a joint report by the Law Commission and the Scottish Law Commission, *Liability for Defective Products*[12] and the report of the Royal Commission on Civil Liability and Compensation for Personal Injury (The Pearson Commission).[13] Both the Council of Europe and the European Community took up the issue at European level. The immediate spur to legislative action in the United Kingdom was the E.C. Directive on Product Liability,[14] which Part 1 of the 1987 Act implements in the United Kingdom. The original directive has been amended.[15] The effect of this is to remove the exemption from the directive for unprocessed agricultural products, fish and game. This change must be implemented in United Kingdom law by December 4, 2000.

**6–08** Part 1 of the Consumer Protection Act 1987 introduces a regime of strict liability on manufacturers of products which prove to cause harm by reason of a defect.[16] It should be noted that section 1(1) of the Act refers to the origin of this part of the Act:

"This Part shall have effect for the purpose of making such provision as is necessary in order to comply with the product liability Directive and shall be construed accordingly."

**6–09** In view of the fact that there are several obscure provisions in the Act, which in some cases do not appear to conform to the directive, this provision may be of considerable importance. This

---

[11] The landmark decision in the United States was that of the California Supreme Court in *Greenman v. Yuba Power Products Inc.* (1963) 377 P. 2nd. 897.

[12] Cmnd. 6831 (1977).

[13] Cmnd. 7054 (1978), Chap. 22.

[14] Directive 85/374, July 25,1985.

[15] Directive 1999/34 (O.J. L 141; 4.6.1999).

[16] There has not yet been any reported case in the U.K. in which the Act has been discussed. It appears to be have been one of the grounds on which those harmed by a polluted water supply in the Camelford area of Cornwall were successful. See *A.B. v. South West Water Services Ltd* [1993] Q.B. 507, C.A. *Richardson v. LRC Products*, Feb. 2, 2000, English High Court, unreported, appears to be a case brought under Part I of the Act. For discussion of possible reasons for the paucity of cases see National Consumer Council, *Unsafe Products*, London, 1995.

was recognised by the European Court of Justice when the Commission challenged the implementation of the implementation of the directive.[17]

The key provision of the Act is section 2(1):  **6–10**

"Subject to the following provisions of this Part, where any damage is caused wholly or partly by a defect in a product, every person to whom subsection (2) . . . applies shall be liable for the damage."

As pointed out above, the liability under Part 1 is strict but it is  **6–11** not absolute. The pursuer must prove that he has been injured; that the defendant manufacturer was the producer of the product; and that it was the manufacturer's product that caused the injury.

As many negligence cases have shown, it is the issue of  **6–12** causation which frequently proves a stumbling block to claimants. An example is *Kay's Tutor v. Ayrshire and Arran Health Board*.[18] The causation issue can also defeat a claim where the manufacturer is able to show some other convincing reason for the pursuer's loss, as in *Evans v. Triplex Safety Glass Co. Ltd*.[19] Such cases may turn on complex scientific evidence and, like negligence actions raising similar issues, can be extremely expensive.[20]

### PRODUCTS

"Product" is given a very wide meaning for the purpose of Part I  **6–13** of the Act. The starting point is the definition in section 1(2) which defines a product as:

"any good or electricity and . . includes a product which is comprised in another product, whether by virtue of being a component part or raw material or otherwise".

The term "goods" is then amplified in section 45, the definition  **6–14** section of the Act, to include "substances, growing crops and things comprised in land by virtue of being attached to it and any ship, aircraft or vehicle". "Substance", in turn, is defined as:

---

[17] *Commission of the European Communities v. UK* Case C-300/95; [1997] All ER (EC) 481.
[18] 1987 S.C. (H.L.) 145.
[19] [1936] 1 All E.R. 283.
[20] See also *Loveday v. Renton* [1990] 1 Med. L.R. 117 and Ferguson, *Drug Injuries and the Pursuit of Compensation* (1996), Chap. 9.

"any natural or artificial substance, whether in solid, liquid or gaseous form or in the form of a vapour, and includes substances that are comprised in or mixed with other goods".

**6–15**    The effect of section 46(4) is that buildings are not products for the purposes of Part 1. However, while buildings are not within the Act, section 46(3) makes clear that products incorporated in a building are subject to it. The result seems to be that if a building collapses because of design faults the builder is not liable under the Consumer Protection Act. However, if injury is caused by a defective central heating boiler blowing up there will be liability.

**6–16**    The original directive provided in Article 2 for the exclusion of what it called "primary agricultural products" from the new product liability regime. However, Article 15(a) permitted Member States to derogate from this provision and impose liability on producers of primary agricultural products. This the United Kingdom did not chose to do. The directive has now been amended to apply the product liability regime to agricultural products, fish and game. This must be implemented by December 4, 2000.

**6–17**    As the amended directive applies only to products put on the market after December 4, 2000 it is still necessary to draw attention to difficulties with the implementation of Article 2 of the original directive. It excluded primary agricultural products up to the point where they have "undergone initial processing". Section 2(4) of the Act, however, exempts such products until they have "undergone an industrial process". "Initial processing" seems to cover a much narrower range of activities than does "industrial process". For example, it is possible that crop spraying, mechanical harvesting or the packaging of fruit or vegetables might be regarded as initial processes, though it is unlikely that any of these would be regarded as an industrial process. Similar problems arise in the context of who is a producer. Below, in discussing the meaning of "producer", the provision in section 2(2)(c) which refers to producers as those who carry out industrial or other processes which give the product what are called its "essential characteristics", we shall return to this problem.

### Persons Liable

**6–18**    For convenience it is usual to speak of product liability as the liability of the manufacturer, but it should be remembered that the range of people liable is rather wider than this. The following are potentially liable by virtue of section 2(2)–(4):

(a)    the producer

(b)  own branders
(c)  importers
(d)  suppliers

## (a)  The producer: section 2(2)(a)

The "producer" of a product is defined in section 1(2) to mean:  **6–19**

"(a)  the person who manufactured it;
 (b)  in the case of a substance which has not been manufactured
      but has been won or abstracted, the person who won or
      abstracted it;
 (c)  in the case of a product which has not been manufactured,
      won or abstracted but essential characteristics of which are
      attributable to an industrial or other process having been
      carried out (for example, in relation to agricultural pro-
      duce), the person who carried out that process".

The expression "the person who manufactured it" is not defined  **6–20**
in the Act. The directive can be helpful, as in Article 3 "Producer" is said to mean "the manufacturer of a finished product,
the producer of any raw material or the manufacturer of a
component part". The manufacturer of the finished product and
the producer of a component or raw material are both liable
where the finished product is defective by virtue of a defect in the
raw material or the component. In this context it is worth noting
section 1(3) which states:

> "For the purposes of this Part a person who supplies any
> product in which products are comprised, whether by virtue of
> being component parts or raw materials, or otherwise, shall
> not be treated by reason only of his supply of that product as
> supplying any of the products so comprised."

The provision is not intended to contradict the assertion that the  **6–21**
manufacturer of the finished product and the raw material or
component producer are both liable. The significant word is
"only". It appears that the manufacturer cannot be liable for
defects in raw material or components if, for some reason, he is
not liable for defects in the finished product.

For the most part it is not difficult to appreciate who is a  **6–22**
manufacturer. The term "producer" also includes those who
have "won or abstracted" a substance. This is the appropriate
terminology for substances, such as ores, which are mined. The
third category of producers is those who do not manufacture,
win or abstract, but who produce products, the "essential characteristics of which are attributable to an industrial or other

process". This would cover producers of petroleum products who produce their products by refining raw materials. This is uncontroversial. However this phrase is also relevant to the production of foodstuffs.

**6–23**    As was pointed out above in discussing the meaning of goods, the directive permits a limited exclusion from the new regime of strict liability for primary agricultural products. This is achieved by section 2(4), which has already been discussed, and also by section 1(2)(c). This brings within the definition of producer those who neither manufacture, win nor abstract products, but who carry out an "industrial or other process" which produces the "essential characteristics" of the product. The use of this terminology is open to the objections already made in discussing section 2(4). There is the further problem that the term "essential characteristics" may give rise to difficulties of interpretation. For example, during the Report Stage of the Bill in the House of Lords one member asked whether the freezing of peas could be said to have changed their essential characteristics. With the implementation of the amendments to the directive these issues will cease to be relevant in relation to damage occurring after December 4, 2000.

**(b) Ownbranders: section 2(2)(b)**

**6–24**    This clumsy heading is used to sum up the group of persons who are liable by section 2(2)(b):

> "any person who, by putting his name on the product or using a trade mark or other distinguishing mark in relation to the product, has held himself out to be the producer of the product".

**6–25**    It is quite common for supermarkets to arrange for the manufacturer of a product to supply them with that product labelled or wrapped. Some large multiple retailers have their own well-known brand names or logos which they attach to products sold in their stores. Many, if not all, of the products got up in this way will have been manufactured by someone else. It is to both these situations that section 2(2)(b) applies, and the supermarket will be liable under the Act. This will only increase their liability to a limited extent as they have liability without fault to purchasers under the Sale of Goods Act 1979. However, it does mean that in a case such as *Fisher v. Harrods Ltd*[21] the pursuer would be able to sue under the 1987 Act rather than having to raise an action for negligence.

[21] [1966] 1 Lloyd's Rep. 500.

## (c) Importers: section 2(2)(c)

To avoid the possibility of injured consumers having to bring **6–26**
actions in far off jurisdictions, section 2(2)(c) provides that the
term producer includes:

"any person who has imported the product into a Member
State from a place outside the Member States in order, in the
course of any business of his, to supply it to another."

A simple example of the effect of this provision would be the **6–27**
situation where a car is manufactured in Japan and imported into
Italy. The Italian importer then sells it to an English dealer who
sells it to a customer. The car proves to be defective, the brakes
fail, and injury is sustained by the customer. The injured person
does not have to sue the Japanese manufacturer; as a result of
section 2(2)(c) he or she can sue the Italian importer as the
person who imported the product into the European community.

## (d) Suppliers: section 2(3)

The first three categories of persons liable for defective products **6–28**
can be seen as primarily liable to the injured person. The final
category comprised in section 2(3) is different: persons in this
category become liable only where the person primarily liable
cannot be identified. Liability arises if three conditions are
fulfilled. The injured person must request the supplier to identify
one or more of the persons listed in categories (a) to (c) above;
that request must be made within a reasonable time after the
damage has occurred and at a time when it is not reasonably
practicable for the person making the request to identify those
persons; and the supplier must fail to supply the information
requested within a reasonable time.

An example of a situation where a supplier's liability might be **6–29**
extended occurs where a retailer's goods have injured someone
other than the purchaser. If the retailer cannot identify his
supplier then under this provision he finds himself strictly
liable.[22]

### DEFECT

A key concept in the Act is that of "defect" and this is defined in **6–30**
section 3. The principle part of the definition is contained in
section 3(1):

[22] That traders sometimes cannot identify who their suppliers were is demonstrated in *Lambert v. Lewis* [1982] A.C. 225.

"Subject to the following provisions of this section, there is a defect in a product for the purposes of this Part if the safety of the product is not such as persons generally are entitled to expect; and for those purposes 'safety', in relation to a product, shall include safety with respect to products comprised in that product and safety in the context of risks of damage to property, as well as in the context of risks of death or personal injury."

**6–31** It is clear from this definition that the strict liability regime is concerned only with safety, not with shoddiness. It provides no remedy where the product is defective in the sense that it does not work or has some other flaw (other than a safety defect) which might render it of unsatisfactory quality. In this situation the purchaser is thrown back on the existing remedies under the Sale of Goods Act, or other legislation setting standards of quality in relation to the supply of goods.

**Safety is relative**

**6–32** It is clear that section 3 is concerned with relative safety. There is probably no such thing as a completely safe product. Even such innocuous substances as cotton wool might, in the hands of an infant, prove dangerous, if the infant put large quantities into its mouth. On the other hand there are other products which are inherently dangerous: sharp knives, cars and matches are examples. The question is, to quote section 3(1), when is the degree of safety "not such as persons generally are entitled to expect"? To answer this question section 3(2) gives some further guidance. After stating that "all the circumstances shall be taken into account", it goes on to set out a number of specific circumstances which are to be taken into account. These are:

"(a) the manner in which, and purposes for which, the product has been marketed, its get-up, the use of any mark in relation to the product, and any instructions for, or warnings with respect to doing or refraining from doing anything with or in relation to the product;
 (b) what might reasonably be expected to be done with or in relation to the product; and
 (c) the time when the product was supplied by its producer to another."

**6–33** The subsection concludes by stating that the fact that products produced after an injury has occurred have a greater level of safety may not be used to infer that earlier products were defective. These factors will be discussed in turn. It should be noted that while, for the purposes of exposition, it is necessary to discuss them in isolation, in real life they will tend to interact with each other and overlap with such issues as the defences considered below and the question of causation.

*(a) Marketing, warnings and instructions*

It is probably the case that these factors only come into play **6–34** when it is not feasible to make the product safe through better design. It was said in the American case of *Schell v. AMF Inc.*[23] that "as a matter of policy, it is questionable whether a manufacturer which produces a machine without minimal available safeguards is entitled to escape liability by warning of dangerous condition which could reasonably have been avoided by a better design."

The importance of warnings is not a novelty: it has been **6–35** pointed out in negligence cases such as *Clarke v. Army and Navy Co-operative Society Limited.*[24] Mrs Clarke had purchased a bottle of disinfectant at the defendant's shop. There was no warning on the bottle, despite the fact that the defendant's shop manager had been informed by customers of incidents causing injury. When the plaintiff opened the bottle some of the contents flew out injuring her eyes. She sued, *inter alia*, alleging negligence in failing to issue a warning about this danger. The defendants were held to be in breach of their duty to the plaintiff in failing to attach a warning to the bottle. Collins M.R. said that there was:

"a duty, if there is some dangerous quality in the goods sold, of which he knows, but of which the purchaser cannot be expected to be aware, of taking reasonable precautions in the way of warning the purchaser that special care will be requisite."[25]

Where the danger is a matter of common knowledge a warning **6–36** will not be necessary,[26] but where warnings should be given they must be adequate, precise and appropriately placed. In this context the distinction between instructions and warnings is

---

[23] 567 f 2d 1259 (3d Cir 1977).
[24] [1903] 1 K.B. 155.
[25] The same point was made in *Vacwell Engineering Co. Ltd v. B.D.H. Chemicals* Ltd [1971] 1 Q.B. 88 where liability in negligence was found on the breach of a duty adequately to warn of the explosive properties of boron tribromide on contact with water. The importance of accurate instructions was demonstrated in relation to the merchantability and fitness for purpose of products in *Wormell v. R.H.M. Agriculture (East) Ltd* [1987] 1 W.L.R. 1091 where the problem was the ineffectiveness of herbicide, not personal injury.
[26] See *Yachetti v. John Duff & Son Ltd* [1943] 1 D.L.R. 194 where the Ontario High Court found that there was no need to warn of the danger of trichinosis from uncooked pork.

sometimes relevant. The function of a warning is to inform the user of the dangers of a product: directions or instructions for use are intended to indicate how the best results may be obtained when using the product. When dangers from failing to follow directions for use are not obvious such directions by themselves may not be sufficient to absolve the manufacturer from liability.

6–37   A good example of a warning which was not adequate comes from the Californian case of *Boyl v. California Chemical Co.*[27] The plaintiff used a liquid weedkiller frequently sold to ordinary consumers for garden use. The warnings given on the label by the defendant included the avoidance of breathing the spray mist, of contact with eyes, skin or clothing, and the necessity of washing after use. It also warned that livestock and poultry would be poisoned if allowed to feed on treated areas, which indicated that the defendant manufacturers knew of the weedkiller's propensity to contaminate the earth. The label also warned that the container should be washed after use and carefully disposed of. After using the weedkiller on her driveway the plaintiff rinsed the container, disposing of the rinsing water on some grass in her garden. Five days later she sunbathed in this area and absorbed some of the weedkiller into her skin causing serious injury. It was held that the defendants were negligent in failing to give an adequate warning of the danger of contact with contaminated earth.

6–38   That the location of the warning can be important is illustrated by *McLauglin v. Mine Safety Appliances*[28] where the warning was on the cardboard container in which the defective appliance was boxed, rather than on the appliance itself.

6–39   In addition to warnings, the way in which the product is promoted is relevant. A good example is to be found in *Watson v. Buckley, Osborne, Garret & Co. Ltd*[29] where the fact that a hair dye had been advertised as needing no preliminary tests contributed to a finding that the distributor had been negligent.

*(b)  Reasonable expectations about use*

6–40   This criterion raises the difficult question of how far abnormal use, or use not intended by the manufacturer, should be taken into consideration in determining whether a product is defective. Cases such as *Yachetii v. John Duff & Son Ltd*[30] where the

---

[27]   221 F.Supp. 669 (1963).
[28]   181 Ne 2d 430 (1960).
[29]   [1940] 1 All ER 74.
[30]   [1943] 1 D.L.R. 194.

purchaser had not carried out an obvious process will be relevant here. There the Ontario High Court found that there was no need to warn of the necessity to cook pork to avoid the danger of trichinosis. The American case of *Reid v. Spadone Machine Co*[31] may also be helpful. There it was held to be foreseeable that, if a dangerous machine for cutting up plastic could be used by two persons, it would be so used, because used in that way the job could be done faster. As designed, the machine, though not intended for use by two persons, was dangerous when so used. It was shown that it would have been fairly easy to have designed the machine so that one person could not have set the machine in motion while the other was in a position of danger and so the manufacturer was liable.

### (c) Time of supply

This factor requires a court to take into account standards applicable when the product was put into circulation, not those developed since the product was supplied. Another American case, *Bruce v. Martin Marietta Corp.*,[32] illustrates this point. This action arose out of the crash in 1970 of a plane, which had been manufactured by the defendants in 1952. When the plane crashed, seats in the passenger cabin broke loose from their floor attachments and were thrown forward against a bulkhead, blocking the exit. A fire broke out and it was alleged that the escape of passengers was impeded by the seats. Evidence was produced by the plaintiffs to show that seats could now be produced which would withstand a crash. The defendants showed that when the plane was built by them it met or exceeded all relevant design requirements, safety requirements, and other criteria prescribed by the regulatory body.

**6–41**

It was held that the plaintiffs had not shown that the ordinary consumer would expect a plane made in 1952 to have the safety features of one made in 1970. "A consumer would not expect a Model T to have the safety features which are incorporated in automobiles made today. The same expectation applies to airplanes."

**6–42**

### Other Factors

As section 3 makes clear, the factors listed are not the only ones which may be taken into account in determining whether a product is defective. What other factors might a court consider? It is well known that at a higher cost the consumer can buy a safer

**6–43**

---

[31]  404 A 2d 1094 (1979).
[32]  544 F. 2d. 442 (10th. Cir. 1976).

version of some products such as cars. It seems likely that in some cases the fact that various levels of safety are available to the consumer at varying prices will be a factor to be taken into account by the courts.

**6–44**     American courts have discussed whether it is appropriate to embark on a risk benefit analysis. In *Raney v. Honeywell Inc.*[33] the court observed that the determination of whether a design risk is "unreasonable" involves "a balancing of the probability and seriousness of harm against the costs of taking precautions . . . Factors to be considered include the availability of alternative designs, the cost and feasibility of adopting alternative designs, and the frequency or infrequency of injury resulting from the design." It may be that the United Kingdom courts will be prepared to take into account such factors. There may also be some situations, such as serious diseases, where the risk of side effects will be considered a reasonable price to pay for the possibility of cure.

DEFENCES

**6–45**     Section 4 sets out a number of defences open to the producer. The burden of proof is on the producer to establish the defence.

**6–46**     The manufacturer has a defence if he can show "that the defect is attributable to compliance with any requirement imposed by or under any enactment or with any Community obligation".[34] An example of a situation where this defence might apply is where safety regulations have been made in relation to a specific product under Part 2 of the Consumer Protection Act. The producer also has a defence if he can show that he did not supply the product to another. This could apply when stocks of a product are stolen from a manufacturer and reach the market through illicit channels.

**6–47**     Not unreasonably, section 4(1)(d) provides that it is a defence to show that there was no defect in the product at the time that the product was supplied. For this purpose it is important to note that the Act, in section 4(2) states what is the "relevant time" for this purpose. The basic idea is that a supplier should only be liable for defects present when he put it into circulation. In the case of manufacturers, ownbranders and importers this is the time at which they supplied the product to another. In the case of other persons it is the time when the product was last supplied by one of the producers just referred to.

---

[33]   540 F 2d 932 (8th Cir 1976).
[34]   Sched. 1 of the Interpretation Act 1978 applies to all legislation the definition contained in Sched. 1 of the European Communities Act 1972.

This defence will absolve a manufacturer from liability if he can show that some defect has arisen through damage caused to the product after it left his hands. This may take the form of deterioration through ordinary wear or tear; or the product may have become defective through unskilled servicing or maintenance.[35]   **6–48**

The final defence in section 4(1)(c) is intended to protect those involved in non-commercial activities such as those who provide home-made goods for a charity sale. They will have a defence where they can show that the only supply of the product to another by the person proceeded against was otherwise than in the course of a business,[36] and that that person is not a producer, own-brander or importer as defined in section 2(2) or, if he is, that he is not acting in that capacity with a view to profit.   **6–49**

### The State of the Art Defence

The most controversial defence is that which is popularly known as the state of the art defence, or sometimes the development risk defence. The directive permits such a defence but also provides that Member States may choose not to include such a defence in their national legislation. The United Kingdom has chosen to include the defence although its inclusion was not recommended by the Law Commissions or the Pearson Committee in their reports. Its inclusion is a major weakness of our products liability law. As a result, the difference between the new regime of strict liability and negligence based liability is much reduced.   **6–50**

The case for such a defence is superficially attractive. It seems unreasonable to hold someone liable for something that they could not have avoided in the state of knowledge when it was produced. However, this misses the main point of product liability regimes, which is to place liability on those who profit by production of a product, and who are best able to arrange to meet that liability. The argument also fails to meet the fact that retailers are strictly liable without such a defence. Such arguments did not persuade the Government, who were convinced by the arguments of industry to the effect that, particularly in the case of pharmaceuticals and aircraft, the prospect of strict liability without the state of the art defence would inhibit innovation. As a result the defence is set out in section 4(1)(e):   **6–51**

---

[35] For an example from a negligence case see *Evans v. Triplex Safety Glass Co. Ltd* [1936] 1 All E.R. 283.

[36] This is likely to be interpreted in the same way as similar phrases used in other consumer protection legislation. See, for example, the discussion of "in the course of trade or business" found in the Trade Descriptions Act 1968 at para. 11-09.

"that the state of scientific and technical knowledge at the relevant time was not such that a producer of products of the same description as the product in question might be expected to have discovered the defect if it had existed in his products while they were under his control."

**6–52** The European Commission sued the United Kingdom in the European Court of Justice, alleging that this formulation did not properly Article 7(e) which provides that a manufacturer shall not be liable if he proves:

"that the state of scientific and technical knowledge at the time when he put the product into circulation was not such as to enable the existence of the defect to be discovered."

**6–53** The Commission argued that the directive sets out an objective test where the Act, with its reference to the possibility of another producer discovering the defect, suggests a subjective test. It is even possible that this formulation of the defence would allow the courts to give the defence the meaning that it has been given in some American states. As was observed in one case "'state of the art' . . . is sometimes confused with 'standards of the industry'".[37] The European Court rejected the challenge by the Commission. They agreed that the test was an objective one and observed that "Article 7(e) is not specifically directed at the practices and safety standards in use in the industrial sector in which the producer is operating, but, unreservedly, at the state of scientific and technical knowledge, including the most advanced level of such knowledge, at the time when the product in question was put into circulation."[38] They went on to add that in order to have a defence:

"the producer of a defective product must prove that the objective state of scientific and technical knowledge, including the most advanced level of such knowledge, at the time when the product in question was put into circulation was not such as to enable the existence of the defect to be discovered. Further, in order for the relevant scientific knowledge to be successfully pleaded against the producer, that knowledge must have been accessible at the time when the product in question was put into circulation. On this last point .. the Directive raises difficulties of interpretation which, in the even of litigation, the national courts will have to resolve".[39]

---

[37] The Supreme Court of the state of Washington, *Cantu v. John Deere Co.*, 603 P 2d 839.

[38] [1997] All E.R. (EC) 481; [1997] 3 C.M.L.R. 923 at para. 26.

[39] [1997] 3 C.M.L.R. 923 at para. 29.

They concluded that there was no evidence that United Kingdom courts would fail to interpret section 4(1)(e) of the Act in this way. The *Richardson* case on p. 103 appears to support this view.

This is in line with what true state of the art is. To paraphrase **6–54** a leading American textbook,[40] it means that the design of the product took account of all scientific and technological knowledge available at the time of its production, including information from other industries and disciplines, or in research laboratories, so long as it is in published form and accessible to research workers through technical libraries, or similar sources. It does not, as some American courts have thought, provide a defence if it is shown that the product complied with the customary practice of the industry — a test that will almost invariably be much easier to satisfy. Fears about the state of the art defence also need to be seen in perspective. As was pointed out in the parliamentary debates, the true undiscoverable development risk is likely to be very rare. It is only to the category of design defects that it is likely to have any relevance. Where the defect is a manufacturing defect it is unlikely to have any relevance; and can have no application where the product is defective through a failure to warn.

## Components

Many products contain component parts made by various manu- **6–55** facturers. An excellent example is the motorcar where the manufacturer of the finished product may actually fabricate only the bodywork, the seats and the interior trim, but purchase many other parts such as brakes, gear boxes, tyres and electrical accessories from independent suppliers. As was pointed out above, a component manufacturer is liable as a producer for any defects in products of his which are incorporated in a finished product. In certain circumstances the component manufacturer will have a defence under section 4(1)(f). This is the case where the component supplier can show that the defect in the finished product which resulted from the article supplied by him was wholly attributable to the design of the finished product or to compliance with instructions given by the producer of the finished product.

*Verge v. Ford Motor Co.*[41] provides an example. Ford had built **6–56** the cab and chassis of a truck and supplied it to a manufacturer of garbage trucks who adapted it for such use. The plaintiff was injured when pinned between the truck and a garbage can. The

---

[40] Frumer and Friedman, *Products Liability*, para. 6.05.
[41] 581 F 2d 384 (3rd Cir 1978).

truck was not fitted with a device warning that the truck was reversing, and he alleged that Ford were liable for failing to install the device in the product supplied to the manufacturer. It was held that Ford were not liable. Any liability for failure to install a warning device in the cab was that of the manufacturer of the finished product, since the evidence was that it would not be feasible to install the safety device in question on all trucks of that type. Furthermore, there was no evidence that it would be feasible for Ford to determine which trucks were to be converted for refuse collection use.

**6–57**      This defence will be particularly important to manufacturers of components which are widely used in industry without the component manufacturer having any control over their use, such as nuts and bolts. Provided the component manufacturer has produced articles without a flaw and has correctly described his product, he will have no further responsibility for problems resulting from the use to which an assembler puts his product.

### Contributory negligence

**6–58**      As we have seen already, section 2(1) states that various persons are liable "where any damage is caused wholly or partly by a defect in a product". Thus where the damage is caused partly by the defect and partly by some third party the producer is liable to the victim, though he will be able by virtue of section 2(5) to obtain a contribution from the third party.

**6–59**      When the damage is caused partly by a defect in the product and partly by the fault of the victim, the normal rules of apportionment for contributory negligence apply. These are to be found in the Law Reform (Contributory Negligence) Act 1945.

**6–60**      The new product liability regime introduced by the Consumer Protection Act does not require proof that the loss suffered by the victim was foreseeable. This does not rule out consideration of causation. It is not enough to show that the product was defective and that the plaintiff was injured by it. It must be shown that there was a casual connection between these two facts. The Act states in section 21(1) that the damage must be "caused wholly or partly by a defect in a product". If the defendant can show some break in the chain of causation he will be able to avoid liability. Questions of causation will undoubtedly overlap with issues of improper use and contributory negligence.

### DAMAGE

**6–61**      For the purposes of liability for defective products damage is defined in section 5 to mean death or personal injury or any loss of or damage to any property including land. Although the Act does not state the basis on which damages are to be calculated, it is reasonable to assume that it will be on the normal delictual principles. Damages for personal injury will include damages for pain and suffering. Article 9 of the directive states that such damages are to be awarded if, as is the case in Scotland, they are awardable under domestic law. Where the victim has died as the result of his injuries, section 6(1)(c) preserves the rights of dependants and relatives to bring actions under the Damages (Scotland) Act 1976. Section 6(3) of the Act aligns the Congenital Disabilities (Civil Liability) Act 1976 with the new product liability regime.

Liability for damage to property is limited in various ways. **6–62** Damages are not available for any loss of, or damage to, the defective product itself. Compensation for other property is available only where the property is, to quote section 5(3), "of a description of property ordinarily intended for private use, occupation or consumption", and "intended by the person suffering the loss or damage mainly for his own private use, occupation or consumption's". Where compensation for property loss is sought section 5(4) provides that there is to be no award unless the amount awarded exceeds £275.

For the purpose of deciding who has the right to sue for loss to **6–63** property, and when such loss occurred, section 5(5) provides that it "shall be regarded as having occurred at the earliest time at which a person with an interest in the property had knowledge of the material facts about the loss or damage." Section 5(6) goes on to state that material facts:

"are such facts about the loss or damage as would lead a reasonable person with an interest in the property to consider the loss or damage sufficiently serious to justify his instituting proceedings for damages against a defendant who did not dispute liability and was able to satisfy a judgment."

The directive permits Member States to limit a producer's liabil- **6–64** ity for damage resulting from death or personal injury and caused by identical items with the same defect to be limited to an amount which is not less then 70 million ECUs (approximately £40 million). The United Kingdom has chosen not to take advantage of this facility.

### TIME LIMITS

The Prescription and Limitation (Scotland) Act 1973 is amended **6–65** by Schedule 1 of the Act and provides that product liability actions are extinguished 10 years after the product was supplied by its manufacturer, importer or the person who put his own name on it. No action shall be brought three years after the later of the date on which the cause of action accrued and the date of knowledge of the injured person.

## EXCLUSION OF LIABILITY

**6–66**  It will not be possible to contract out of liability under Part I of the Consumer Protection Act. Section 7 makes this clear stating that liability "to a person who has suffered damage caused wholly or partly by a defect in a product, or to a dependent or relative of such a person, shall not be limited or excluded by any contract term, by any notice or by any other provision."

## CIVIL LIABILITY UNDER THE CONSUMER PROTECTION ACT 1987 PART 2

**6–67**  The criminal law is used, as is discussed below, to try to ensure that only safe goods reach the market place. In addition to incurring criminal liability breach of the safety regulations can lead to civil liability. Section 41 of the Consumer Protection Act 1987 is one of those rare provisions in legislation imposing criminal penalties which explicitly states that this is the case. It provides that breach of safety regulations gives a right of action for breach of statutory duty to anyone affected. It is to be noted that while this applies to breach of the safety regulations it does not apply to breach of the general safety requirement. In practice little use seems to be made of this provision and there are no reported cases on it from any part of the United Kingdom.

## THE ROLE OF THE CRIMINAL LAW

**6–68**  The civil law controls on product standards discussed above apply *ex post facto*. Where the failure of a product to meet the required legal standard may cause personal injury or death it is important to attempt to prevent such a product being put into circulation at all. The Consumer Protection Act 1961[42] was the legislative response to the need identified by the Molony Report[43] for legislation governing dangerous products. Its central

---

[42]  The Consumer Protection Act 1961 was repealed by the Consumer Safety Act 1978, s. 10(1), Sched. 3, on October 1, 1987: Consumer Safety Act 1978 (Commencement No. 3) Order 1987 (S.I. 1987 No. 1681).

[43]  *Final Report of the Committee on Consumer Protection*, Cmnd. 1781 (1962)

feature was the creation of a power to make regulations specifying safety criteria for products. The Consumer Safety Act 1978 followed a review of product safety controls in a government consultative document[44] which revealed inadequacies in the earlier legislation. Among these were: criticisms of slowness in establishing and revising safety standards; the lengthy consultations involved when hazards came to light; and the absence of powers to deal promptly with new products which proved to be hazardous but which were not subject to existing regulations.

The 1978 Act met these criticisms by introducing three new techniques. Where the Secretary of State considered that a product or a component part of a product was not safe he was empowered to issue a "prohibition order" prohibiting the supply of goods which were considered to be unsafe, or permitting their supply only on such conditions as were specified in the notice.[45] Finally, a "notice to warn" could be served on any person, requiring that person to publish, at his own expense, a warning about unsafe goods which he had supplied. Further improvements to the legislation were made by the Consumer Safety (Amendment) Act 1986 which implemented many of the proposals in the 1984 White Paper.[46] This was concerned mainly with improving the enforcement of the legislation.

**6–69**

All this legislation was repealed by the Consumer Protection Act 1987,[47] which is primarily a consolidating measure, although it does include some new provisions, most notably the creation of a general safety requirement.[48] While there were other pieces of safety legislation, the law was reasonably clearly set out. That can no longer be said with the enactment of the General Product Safety Regulations 1994.[49] In order to try to make sense of the present law it will be necessary to discuss Part II of the 1987 Act and then the new regulations. This is because both are relevant and complement each other. As we shall see, the new regulations refer to the enforcement techniques of Part II.

**6–70**

## SAFETY REGULATIONS

The Consumer Protection Act 1987, like earlier safety legislation, gives the Secretary of State for Trade and Industry extensive powers to make regulations relating to the safety of

**6–71**

---

[44] Cmnd. 6398 (1976).
[45] See the Consumer Safety Act 1978, s. 3, Sched. 1 (repealed).
[46] Cmnd. 9302 (1984).
[47] Consumer Protection Act 1987, s. 48, Sched. 5. The repeals came into force on October 1, 1987: Consumer Protection Act 1987 (Commencement No. 1) Order 1987, (S.I. 1987 No. 1680), art. 3(k), Sched. 1, Pt 1.
[48] As to the general safety requirement, see para. 6.84 below.
[49] S.I. 1994 No. 2328

goods.[50] Regulations may be made to ensure that goods are safe; that unsafe goods are not made available generally, or to persons in whose hands they would be unsafe; and that appropriate information is provided. Section 11 (2) goes on to specify a wide range of matters with which the regulations may deal such as their composition, testing and inspection.[51] Before making such regulations the Secretary of State has a duty to consult organisations which appear to him to be representative of interests substantially affected by his proposal and any other persons he considers appropriate.[52]

**6–72**   The power to make safety regulations is exercisable by statutory instruments subject to annulment by resolution of either House of Parliament.[53] Under previous legislation regulations were subject to affirmative resolution of both Houses of Parliament.

**6–73**   Breach of safety regulations is not itself a criminal offence. It is an offence to supply (as widely defined in section 46[54]) where the regulations prohibit such supply. Offences are punishable on summary conviction by imprisonment for a term not exceeding six months or by a fine not exceeding level 5 on the standard scale or by both.[55]

**Prohibition notices and notices to warn**

**6–74**   The prohibition notices introduced by the Consumer Safety Act 1978 are re-enacted in the Consumer Protection Act 1987, as are notices to warn,[56] and the 1987 Act sets out in detail the procedure to be used when it is proposed to issue such notices.[57] In *R v. Liverpool City Council, ex parte Baby Products*[58] it was held that the Council were acting outside their powers in issuing a press release alleging that a product was dangerous. The statutory procedure under the safety legislation was the appropriate

[50]  See the Consumer Protection Act 1987, s. 11. For the goods to which s. 11 does not apply, see s. 11 (7).
[51]  A large number of regulations have been made covering such goods as toys, see the Toys (Safety) (Amendment) Regulations 1993 (S.I. 1993 No. 1547); cosmetics, see the Cosmetic Products (Safety)(Amendment) Regulations 1992 (S.I. 1992 No. 1525); and see the Low Voltage Electrical Equipment (Safety) Regulations 1989 (S.I. 1989 No. 728).
[52]  See s. 11(5). This function has been discussed in *R. v. Secretary of State for Health, ex p. United States Tobacco International Inc.* [1992] 1 Q.B. 353; [1992] 1 All E.R. 212.
[53]  s. 11(6).
[54]  See *Drummond-Rees v. Dorset County Council*, Dec. 2, 1996, English Divisional Court, unreported, on *Lexis*.
[55]  See generally s. 12. Level 5 is £5000: Increase of Criminal Penalties, Etc. (Scotland) Order 1984 (S.I. 1984 No. 526), art. 4.
[56]  See s. 13.
[57]  See s.13(2), Sched. 2.
[58]  November 23, 1999, English Divisional Court, unreported.

way to prevent the sale of goods suspected to be dangerous. The court conceded that this was cumbersome and slow and the Lord Chief Justice commented:

"I can imagine circumstances in which an emergency procedure to supplement the section 13 procedure would be desirable. The remedy for a defective statutory procedure is not, however, to ignore or circumvent it but to amend it".

**Suspension notices**

The Consumer Safety (Amendment) Act 1986 gave enforce- **6–75** ment authorities, in practice trading standards officers, an important new power to deal with dangerous goods when it introduced the suspension notice. This is re-enacted in the Consumer Protection Act 1987. A trading standards officer may serve a suspension notice prohibiting the supply of specified goods if he has reasonable cause to believe that any safety provision has been, or may be, contravened.[59] A suspension notice may not extend beyond six months and a further notice may only be served in respect of the same goods if proceedings have first been instituted for breach of a safety provision or for the forfeiture of the goods.[60] The owner of suspended goods may appeal against the suspension notice.[61]

In *R. v. Birmingham City Council, ex parte Ferrero Ltd*[62] the **6–76** English Court of Appeal held that the proper method of challenging a suspension notice was by means of the appeal procedure set out in section 15 of the Act, not by judicial review. Taylor L.J. (as he then was) said:

"The real issue was whether the goods contravened a safety provision and the section 15 appeal was geared exactly to deciding that issue. If the goods did contravene the safety provision and were dangerous to children then, surely, procedural impropriety or unfairness in the decision-making process should not persuade a court to quash the order. The determining factors are the paramount need to safeguard consumers and the emergency nature of the section 14 powers."

Where the power to suspend a supply has been exercised, an **6–77** enforcement authority is liable to pay compensation to any

---

[59] See s. 14(1), (5). A suspension notice may also require that the authority be informed of the whereabouts throughout the suspension period of suspended goods: s. 14(3). As to the contents of a suspension notice, see s. 14(2).
[60] See s. 14(1), (4). As to forfeiture of goods, see s. 17.
[61] See s. 15(1),(2), (4)
[62] (1990) 9 Tr. L.R. 148.

person having an interest in the goods, in respect of any loss or damage caused by reason of the exercise of the power, if there has been no contravention in relation to the goods of any safety provision and the exercise of the power is not attributable to any neglect or default by that person.[63]

**The defence of due diligence**

**6–78**	There is a due diligence defence in the Consumer Protection Act 1987,[64] but reliance on information supplied by someone else will not establish this defence unless it can be shown that it was reasonable in all the circumstances to have relied on the information having regard in particular to; (1) the steps which were taken, and which might reasonably have been taken, to verify the information; and (2) whether he had any reason to disbelieve the information.[65]

**6–79**	It has not been easy to take advantage of this defence. In *Riley v. Webb*,[66] a case under the 1961 Act, the defendants, who were wholesalers, showed that they had a condition on their order forms that orders were placed in the understanding that the goods met any relevant statutory requirements. They also argued that they were a small company and had dealt with the supplier of the unsafe goods for many years. Random sampling, they claimed, would have been unreasonable. The English Divisional Court held that the defendants could have taken a simple step to avoid breaching the Act. They could either have asked for specific assurances about the goods; or they could have imposed contract terms under which their suppliers would have had to ensure that the regulations had been complied with. By using only the general term in their order form they had not exercised due diligence.

**6–80**	In *Rotherham Metropolitan Borough Council v. Rayson (U.K.) Ltd*[67] a request to overseas suppliers to report any failures to meet United Kingdom standards had been sent to them, and the defendants had tested one packet out of an annual purchase of several thousand. The Divisional Court did not regard this as meeting the due diligence standard. In *P. & M. Supplies (Essex) Ltd v. Devon County Council*[68] the appellants had been con-

---

[63]	s. 14(7). Any dispute as to the right to or the amount of any compensation is to be determined by a single arbiter appointed, failing agreement between the parties, by the sheriff: s. 14(8).

[64]	*i.e.* s. 39. The offences in the Consumer Protection Act 1987, Pt 2, to which the defence relates are offences under ss. 10, 12(1)–(3), offences against safety regulations, and s. 14(6) offences in respect of suspension notices: s. 39(5).

[65]	s. 39(4).

[66]	(1987) 151 J.P. 372.

[67]	[1988] BTLC 292.

[68]	(1992) 11 Tr. L.R. 52.

victed of an offence against the Toys (Safety) Regulations 1974[69] relating to a soft toy. Evidence showed that 0.49 per cent of stock was tested randomly, and some samples were sent to the public analyst. Dismissing the appeal, the English Divisional Court said that it was for the company to produce evidence, preferably independent statistical evidence, to show the soundness of their sampling methods.

It is generally believed that a high proportion of dangerous goods are imported. For this reason the provision giving powers to the Commissioners of Customs and Excise to disclose information to those who enforce safety legislation, which was introduced by the Consumer Safety (Amendment) Act 1986, is re-enacted in the Consumer Protection Act 1987.[70] A customs officer may also, for the purpose of facilitating the enforcement of the safety provisions, seize any imported goods and detain them for not more than two working days.[71] **6–81**

Where there has been a contravention of the safety provisions the procurator fiscal may apply to a sheriff for an order for the forfeiture of any unsafe goods. The owner, or anyone having an interest in the goods, must be given notice of the application and may appear at the hearing to oppose the making of such an order.[72] **6–82**

### THE GENERAL SAFETY REQUIREMENT

The major innovation of Part 2 of the Consumer Protection Act 1987[73] is the enactment of a general safety requirement. Prior to its introduction, problems could arise where goods which were not the subject of safety regulations were found to be unsafe. If traders did not voluntarily remove them from the market, there were no powers to do so. It is to fill this gap that the general safety requirement was introduced. **6–83**

With the enactment of the General Product Safety Regulations 1994[74] the general safety requirement has a much restricted ambit. This is because the new regulations also contain a general safety requirement and provide that where it applies the requirement of the 1987 Act does not apply. **6–84**

It is a criminal offence to supply, offer or agree to supply, expose or possess for supply any consumer goods which fail to **6–85**

[69] S.I. 1974 No. 1367.
[70] See s. 37.
[71] See s. 31.
[72] See s. 17.
[73] The Consumer Protection Act 1987, Pt 2 (ss. 10–19), came into force on October 1, 1987: Consumer Protection Act 1987 (Commencement No. 1) Order 1987 (S.I. 1987 No. 1680), art. 3.
[74] S.I. 1994 No. 2328.

comply with the general safety requirements.[75] "Consumer goods" means any goods which are ordinarily intended for private use or consumption except (1) growing crops or things attached to land; (2) water, food, feeding stuff or fertilisers; (3) gas[76]; (4) aircraft (other than hang-gliders) or motor vehicles; (5) controlled drugs or licensed medicinal products; or (6) tobacco.[77] Goods fail to comply with the general safety requirement if they are not reasonably safe having regard to all the circumstances, including:

"(a) the manner in which, and purposes for which, the goods are being or would be marketed, the get-up of the goods, the use of any mark in relation to the goods and any instructions or warnings which are given or would be given with respect to the keeping, use or consumption of the goods;
(b) any standards of safety published by any person either for goods of a description which applies to the goods in question or for matters relating to goods of that description; and
(c) the existence of any means by which it would have been reasonable (taking into account the cost, likelihood and extent of any improvement) for the goods to have been made safer".[78]

**6–86** However, goods are not regarded as failing to comply with the general safety requirement in respect of anything which is shown to be attributable to compliance with a requirement imposed by any enactment or with any Community obligation.[79] Nor will goods be regarded as failing to comply with this requirement because they go no further than meeting any safety regulations made under the 1987 Act or any safety standards provided by that or any other enactment.[80]

### Defences in respect of the general safety requirement

**6–87** It is a defence to a charge that the general safety requirement has been breached for the supplier to show: (1) that he reasonably believed that the goods would not be used or consumed in the

---

[75] s. 10(1).
[76] *i.e.* gas which is, is to be, or has been, supplied by a person authorised to supply it by or under the Gas Act 1986, ss. 6–8 (authorisation of supply of gas through pipes).
[77] s. 10(7). For the meaning of "controlled drug", "feeding stuff", "fertiliser", "food", "licensed medicinal product" and "tobacco", see s. 19(1).
[78] s. 10(2)(a)–(c).
[79] s. 10(3)(a).
[80] s. 10(3)(b).

United Kingdom,[81] (2) that, being a retail supplier, he neither knew nor had reasonable grounds for believing that they did not comply with the general safety requirement,[82] or (3) that the terms on which he supplied or offered to supply the goods indicated that the goods which were to be acquired by someone else were not new.[83]

## THE GENERAL PRODUCT SAFETY REGULATIONS 1994

These regulations, which implement the E.C.'s General Product Safety Directive, follow the deplorable recent tendency of implementing directives in areas where there is already important domestic primary legislation by means of regulations instead of legislating afresh in the area. New primary legislation would have produced a more coherent and clearer legislative regime than the confusion with which industry, consumers and enforcement agencies have been saddled. It makes a mockery of the rhetoric about lifting the "burdens on business" of which we have heard so much.   **6–88**

The central provision of the regulations is found in regulation which states that "No producer shall place a product on the market unless the product is a safe product". The heading in the regulations calls this "the general safety requirement". This is supported by the following two regulations. Regulation 8 imposes various obligations on producers to give information to consumers and obtain information about the performance of their products. Regulation 9 requires a distributor to "act with due care in order to help ensure compliance with the requirements of regulation 7". In all these situations failure to observe the requirements of the regulations is a criminal offence.   **6–89**

Before considering these provisions in more detail it will first be useful to discover what products are covered and who are producers and distributors, remembering that where the safety requirement of these regulations applies that in the 1987 Act does not.   **6–90**

As we have seen above, the Consumer Safety Act has a list of products to which it does not apply. The products covered by the   **6–91**

---

[81] s. 10(4)(a).
[82] s. 10(4)(b). For this purpose goods are supplied in the course of carrying on a retail business if (1) whether or not they are themselves acquired for a person's private use or consumption they are supplied in the course of carrying on a business of making a supply of consumer goods available to persons who generally acquire them for private use or consumption; and (2) the descriptions of goods the supply of which is made available in the course of that business do not, to a significant extent, include manufactured or imported goods which have not previously been supplied in the U.K.: s. 10(5)(a), (b).
[83] s. 10(4)(c).

regulations is different and wider. Regulations 2 and 3 define them. Regulation 2 states that a "product" is "any product intended for consumers or likely to be used by consumers, supplied whether for consideration or not in the course of a commercial activity and whether new, used or reconditioned".

**6–92**     A number of points should be noted about this definition. As the definition of "product" goes on to make clear, it does not apply to one used "exclusively in the context of a commercial activity even if it is used for or by a consumer". Unlike the Consumer Protection Act, the regulations apply to second-hand products though, as regulation 3 shows, not all second-hand products. Regulation 3 exempts such products if they are antiques. A further important exemption set out in regulation 3 is "products supplied for repair or reconditioning before use". This only applies where the supplier clearly informs the person to whom they are supplied that this is the case.

**6–93**     Another important category of products exempt from the regulations is those where there are specific provisions in rules of Community law governing all aspects of the safety of the product. This means that there will be no overlap between these regulations and other Community product safety rules. For example, various Community directives contain a wide range of specific provisions governing the safety of medicinal products, medicated feeding stuffs and medicinal feed additives. Products which are licensed in the United Kingdom in accordance with these Community rules will not be subject to the General Safety Regulations. But it is important to note that this exemption applies only where the Community law relates to all aspects of the safety of the product. Regulation 4 makes clear that it does not apply where the product is subject to some other Community law which does not make provision about its safety.

**Producers**

**6–94**     The regulations place the primary duty of ensuring that only safe products are marketed on "producers" a term which is defined in regulation 2. It covers manufacturers established in the Community which, for the purposes of these regulations, means not just the member states of the European Union but the European Economic Area; a very much larger group of countries. The term "producer" also includes those who pass themselves off as manufacturers, such as own-branders and those who recondition products. Where the manufacturer is not established in the European economic area the producer, his representative or, if there is none, the importer is liable. "Producer" also includes other professionals in the supply chain, in so far as their activities may affect the safety properties of a product. This might bring transport or storage companies within the ambit of the definition.

## Distributors

As we shall see, certain duties are placed upon distributors. They   **6–95**
are defined as "any professional in the supply chain whose
activity does not affect the safety properties of a product".

## Safety

The definition of safety in regulation 2 bears some resemblance   **6–96**
to that in Part I of the Consumer Safety Act 1987 and is a
pragmatic one. A safe product is one:

> "which, under normal or reasonably foreseeable conditions of
> use, including duration, does not present any risk or only the
> minimum risks compatible with the product's use, considered
> as acceptable and consistent with a high level of protection for
> the safety and health of persons".

In assessing whether this standard has been met a number   **6–97**
factors related to the product are to be taken into account. These
are:

(1)  Its characteristics, including its composition, packaging,
     and instructions for assembly and maintenance;
(2)  its effect on other products where it is reasonably foresee-
     able that it will be used with them;
(3)  its presentation, labelling, instructions for use and disposal
     and any other indication or information provided by the
     producer;
(4)  the categories of consumers at serious risk when using the
     product, in particular children.

However, the fact that higher levels of safety can be obtained, or   **6–98**
that there are other products presenting a lesser degree of risk
does not of itself mean that a product is unsafe. An example of
this in practice might be provided by cars. Some, usually the
more expensive, models of cars have anti-lock braking systems.
This provision probably means that cars which do not have such
systems will not be regarded as unsafe because they do not have
such a system.

In assessing whether a product is safe regulation 10 is impor-   **6–99**
tant. Regulation 10(1) states that there is a presumption that a
product which conforms to United Kingdom rules laying down
health and safety requirements is safe. So, a product which

conforms to the safety regulations made under Part 1 of the Consumer Protection Act 1987 would be presumed to be safe. If there are no such rules, regulation 10(2) sets out factors to be taken into account in deciding whether a product meets the general safety requirement in regulation 7. These are voluntary United Kingdom standards which give effect to a European standard, or a Community technical specification. If there are no standards of these types, standards drawn up in the United Kingdom, health and safety codes of good practice in the product sector, or the state of the art and technology may be relied upon. In addition, the safety which consumers may reasonably expect is relevant.

**Duties of Producers**

6–100    In addition to the primary duty not to market unsafe products producers are also under an obligation to provide consumers with relevant information so that they may assess the risks inherent in a product where these risks are not immediately apparent.[84] They must also adopt measures commensurate with the characteristics of their products to enable consumers to be informed of the risks which these products might present and to take appropriate action, including, if necessary, withdrawing the product from the market. Such measures might include marking the products, or product batches, so that they can be identified. This would be important, if a fault were found, in arranging a product recall. Other measures are sample testing, investigating complaints and keeping distributors informed about the results of monitoring.

6–101    These requirements are said to apply to a producer "within the limits of his activity". This is a peculiarly opaque expression which is copied from the directive. it would appear to mean something like "in so far as it is within his power".

**Duties of Distributors**

6–102    Distributors as defined in the regulations are required by regulation 9 to act with due care in order to help ensure compliance with the general safety duty. In particular, they must not supply products which they know, or should have presumed, on the basis of the information available to them, were dangerous. They must, within the limits of their activities, participate in monitoring the safety of products, pass on information about their safety, and co-operate in action to avoid those risks.

[84]    reg. 8(1).

The regulations are enforced by using the techniques set out in **6–103**
the Consumer Protection Act 1987. As appropriate, therefore,
prohibition notices and notices to warn, suspension notices and
forfeiture may be used. Enforcement is in the hands of the
weights and measures authorities,[85] *i.e.* the island and district
councils. Breach of the general safety requirement, the obligation of a distributor to act with due care to ensure compliance
with it, and marketing or supplying unsafe products are criminal
offences.[86] A due diligence defence of the type common in
consumer protection legislation is provided.[87]

---

[85] Except for medicine, where it is mainly the responsibility of the Scottish
Executive.
[86] regs 12 and 13.
[87] reg. 14.

## CHAPTER 7

# SERVICES

**7–01**    Services encompass a very wide range of activities. They are as diverse as laundry and dry cleaning, furniture removal, home improvements, educational services, car maintenance and servicing and professional services. Even this latter category, which one might have supposed would include a relatively narrow range of services, displays astonishing diversity. The Monopolies Commission, when it was asked to investigate the professions, received evidence from 161 professional bodies, although some of those bodies were concerned with the same, or a closely related, profession. The Commission found it impossible to define the distinguishing characteristics of professions or to establish a definitive list; a feat that has taxed others.[1]

**7–02**    The service sector of the economy expanded enormously during the twentieth century and the range of services offered to the public is extremely varied. It is sometimes said that in the United Kingdom we have become a service economy. This is based on the fact that, like other developed economies, more than half of output is generated by the service sector.

**7–03**    While the service sector has expanded in economic terms, legally it has been somewhat neglected. The preliminary problem encountered in the range of services is the difficulty in determining into which legal category some kinds of services fall. In the case of most professional services this problem does not arise, the service clearly being *locatio operis faciendi*. As Professor McBryde observes "[t]his contract is very common in practice but has been somewhat neglected by our textbook writers."[2] Many non-professional services will fall into the same category where the essence of the service is the bringing about of a result as, for example, where a repair is to be effected or a thing is to be cleaned. In other cases classification is much less easy and

---

[1]    *Report on the General Effect on the Public Interest of Certain Restrictive Practices so far as they prevail in relation to the Supply of Professional Services* (Monopolies Commission), Cmnd. 4463 (1970), pp. 1, 3.

[2]    McBryde, *The Law of Contract in Scotland* (1987), p. 94.

is not aided by a paucity of authority, both institutional and judicial. The situation in England until recently was not dissimilar.

In England and Wales this was ameliorated by the passing of the Supply of Goods and Services Act 1982, Part II of which puts into statutory form some of the main terms to be implied in contracts for services. As Part II of the Act does not apply to Scotland it would be a useful service to Scottish consumers if similar legislation were introduced in this jurisdiction.               **7–04**

For the moment it is necessary to try to puzzle out the proper legal classification of some service contracts. The best illustration of the conceptual problems that this raises is to be found in what is sometimes referred to as the contract for work and materials. As the Scottish Law Commission pointed out, this is a term of art from English law and it does not seem to be the case that such a contract has been clearly recognised in Scots law.[3] Nevertheless, there are certain contracts into which consumers may enter which involve both the supply of goods and the provision of services. Examples of such situations are contracts for the construction of a building or its repair, the repair of a car, the installation of a central heating system and the provision of a meal in a restaurant. The problems presented in this area seem never to have been faced squarely in any case, although on occasions they would seem to have been worthy of some discussion. Professor Bell observed[4] that the contract *locatio operis faciendi* implied that the employer should provide the materials, otherwise the contract is one of sale. This is borne out by cases involving ships.[5]               **7–05**

The Scottish Law Commission suggested two other possible classifications. The arrangement might be seen as comprising two contracts, one of sale and the other for the hiring of services; or, the correct approach may be to regard it as a contract for services alone. Support for the latter view is available by implication from cases where the problem has been identified as arising not from any defect in the nature of the materials used but from shortcomings in the rendering of the service.[6]               **7–06**

If the arrangement is regarded as a sale combined with the hiring of services, the remedy where the materials used turn out to be defective will be those already discussed in relation to sale. Of course, if the employer specifies the materials to be used the               **7–07**

---

[3]   *Sale and Supply of Goods*, Scottish Law Commission Consultative Memorandum No. 58, 1983.

[4]   *Bell, Commentaries*, I, 485.

[5]   *Nelson v. William Chalmers & Co. Ltd*, 1913 S.C. 441; 1913 1 S.L.T. 190; *Reid v. Macbeth and Gray* (1904) 6 E (H.L.) 25; 11 S.L.T. 783.

[6]   *McIntyre v. Gallacher* (1883) 11 R. 64; *Brett v. Williamson*, 1980 S.L.T. (Sh.Ct.) 56; *Macintosh v. Nelson*, 1984 S.L.T. (Sh.Ct.) 82.

contractor cannot be held to stipulate that the goods are fit for
their purpose, although he would still be liable if they proved not
to be of satisfactory quality as occurred in the English case of
*Young and Marten Ltd v. McManus Childs Ltd.*[7]

**7–08**      If the third possibility is the correct legal categorisation, the
consumer in the past may have had the somewhat lower degree
of protection afforded by the obligation of the supplier to take
reasonable care in selecting the materials to be used. However,
Part IA of the Supply of Goods and Services Act 1982[8] now
applies in so far as goods are transferred. Sections IIB–IIE imply
terms in this contract in relation to title, description and quality.[9]
This situation may also give rise to problems relating to the
transfer of property in the materials. There seems now, as was
the case when Professor Bell considered the problem, to be little
authority on this point. Bell's view was that "where ... it is
resolvable into a contract for performing a particular piece of
labour, of which the articles sent are merely the materials, the act
of delivery seems not to be complete till the work be performed".[10]

**7–09**      In *Simpson v. Duncanson Creditors*[11] the situation was somewhat different, Simpson having contracted with Duncanson for
the construction of a ship. Duncanson was to supply the materials for the hull, Simpson the mast and some other fitments, and
payment was to be made in three stages as work progressed.
Duncanson became bankrupt after the first payment had been
made, and his trustee sought to include the unfinished ship
among the assets available for the creditors. The Court of
Session stated that the decision depended on the specific facts of
the case and preferred Simpson's argument that the vessel
"became his, *specification*, the builder being considered merely
as a mandatory, who acquired not to himself but to his
constituent". As the work proceeded such an appropriation took
place as prevented the creditors from attaching the ship without
refunding the sums advanced.

**7–10**      Bearing in mind the problems just discussed about how services
are classified legally, it is necessary to consider in more detail how
consumers are protected by the civil law when acquiring services.
Broadly speaking, the approach is the same as when goods are
purchased. The law implies in contracts for services certain terms
which, in the absence of any express provision in the contract,
will determine the rights and duties of the parties. The discussion

[7]   [1969] 1 A.C. 454; [1968] 2 All E.R. 1169.
[8]   Inserted by s. 6 of the Sale and Supply of Goods Act 1994.
[9]   For a discussion of these terms see Chap. 4.
[10]  Bell, *Commentaries*, I, 194.
[11]  (1786) Mor. 14204.

of these implied terms will focus on the *locatio operis faciendi*, as this is the most common contract concerning the provision of services.

Before examining the various terms implied in this contract it is first necessary to note that it will often be important to establish exactly what it was that the consumer and the provider of the service agreed should be done. *Brown v. J. Nisbet & Co. Ltd*[12] is a good example of this issue. The defenders had acquired a van which was not in a very good state of repair. They took it to the pursuer who ran a motor repair business and various repairs were carried out. When some problems later developed with the van the pursuers refused to pay for the repairs, alleging that the work had not been carried out properly. They claimed that it had been agreed that a complete overhaul of the van would be carried out. The repairer stated that he had not agreed to this but merely to put the van into good running order. There was evidence that the defenders had first obtained a quotation for the cost of a complete overhaul from another garage and, finding this to be too expensive, had then approached the pursuer who had offered to do work at a much lower cost. Looking at the evidence the sheriff came to the conclusion that "[t]he defenders tried to get along with something much less expensive". He found that the garage's evidence of the nature of the job agreed upon was to be preferred and, having agreed only to carry out limited work on the van, they were not liable for breakdowns which were unrelated to the repair work which they had been asked to do.

*Walter Wright & Co. Ltd v. Cowdray*[13] is another example of the objective approach which the courts take to this problem of assessing what the parties had agreed should be done. Electric motors on an estate had been damaged by floodwater and the pursuers, who were electrical engineers, were asked to dry out and test them. The engineers carried out this work. The defender refused to pay part of the charge for the work on the ground that it involved expensive repairs to one of the motors which had not been instructed. The sheriff considered the evidence and concluded from it that, looked at objectively, there was no justification for assuming that these repairs had been authorised.[14]

**7–11**

**7–12**

---

[12] (1941) 57 Sh.Ct.Reps. 202.
[13] 1973 S.L.T. (Sh.Ct.) 56.
[14] See also *Dalblair Motors Ltd v. J. Forrest & Son (Ayr) Ltd* (1954) 70 Sh.Ct. Reps. 107.

## THE IMPLIED TERMS THAT THE CONTRACTOR
## WILL EXERCISE REASONABLE SKILL AND CARE

**7–13**    A central issue in the provision of a service is the standard of quality which the client is entitled to expect. In contracts for services this is summed up in one of those Latin maxims with which lawyers seek to dazzle the uninitiated, *spondet peritiam artis et imperitia culpae enumeratur*. In English this means that a person is responsible for exercising skill in his trade or profession, and lack of such skill will be regarded as a fault. The standard is that of the reasonable practitioner of the particular trade or profession and there are a number of examples in the law reports.

**7–14**    *McIntyre v. Callacher*[15] is a good example of the application of the principle. Mr Gallacher was a Glasgow plumber who had been employed to carry out plumbing work in a row of tenements. This included sealing off some pipes. One of the pipes was not properly sealed off and some time later leaked causing damage to property on lower floors for which the landlord, Mr McIntyre, was liable. Evidence proved that the proper and workmanlike method of sealing a pipe was to solder it. In this case Mr Gallacher, or one of his workmen, had only hammered the end of the lead pipe together and it eventually leaked. He was thus liable for failing to carry out the job with the requisite level of skill.

**7–15**    In *Brett v. Williamson*[16] the sheriff principal referred to the fact that in building contracts arranged on either a fixed-price basis or, as in that case, on a "time and lime" basis, the problems resulting from unsatisfactory workmanship are particularly difficult to resolve. In that case the pursuer had undertaken to lay terazzo tiles and having done so in a manner which the defender regarded as unsatisfactory was obliged to bring an action for payment. It was argued for the pursuer that since such tile-laying was a specialist job but had been entrusted by the defender to him (who did not claim to be a specialist) he could not complain that the work was not up to the standard of a specialist. This argument was inspired by *Dickson v. The Hygienic Institute*[17] where it was said that a contractor need attain only "the skill which he professes or announces". As the sheriff principal pointed out, that did not go far enough for the pursuer's purposes because on examining the *Dickson* case it will be seen that Lord Dundas held that the standard of care is that of the type of practitioner which the client believed he or she was dealing with.

[15]   (1883) 11 R. 64.
[16]   1980 S.L.T. (Sh.Ct.) 56.
[17]   1910 S.C. 352; 1910 1 S.L.T. 111.

Applying this approach to the case before him the Sheriff Principal stated:

> "In my view, when a tradesman undertakes to carry out a particular job in his trade, his obligation is to carry it out properly, unless he either makes known to his customer when contracting that the job requires more special skill than he commands, or can show that the customer was aware of that when contracting with him. I consider that a tradesman who accepts instructions professes to be able to carry them out, and it is he — not the customer — who will normally know whether he has or lacks, the special skill which the job requires."

This approach has much to commend it especially, as is fre-    **7–16** quently the case with small building jobs, where the client commissions the work directly from the tradesman and does not engage the services of an architect or surveyor.

*Brett v. Williamson* was applied to slightly different circum-    **7–17** stances by the same sheriff principal in *Mackintosh v. Nelson*[18] where the pursuer claimed damages for loss sustained when seriously defective building work was carried out at her house. The defender had been an art teacher for several years before going into business on his own account as an industrial cleaning contractor who also undertook window cleaning, car valeting, external paintwork and landscape gardening. The pursuer had admired a sun lounge which the defender had built at his own home and had inquired whether he could do similar work at her house. While the pursuer understood that the defender was in business as a window cleaning contractor, it was clear from the evidence that he held himself out as being capable both of drawing up the necessary plans and carrying out the building work in a workmanlike manner. He argued that in the circumstances he should only be held to the standards of an amateur builder. The sheriff principal referred to his decision in *Brett v. Williamson* and was:

> "prepared to hold that the same considerations apply where one who is not a tradesman contracts to do work for another. In other words, he must be held to have professed the requisite skill to do the job which he undertakes. Plainly, if he says that the job may be more than he can promise to do well or if the customer is shown to have known that, it would be open to the court to hold that his customer had taken the risk of unsatisfactory work on himself."

[18] 1984 S.L.T. (Sh.Ct.) 82.

**7–18**    A different aspect of the problem of the standard of the work arises where the issue is not the competence which the tradesman professes but the advice or warnings which he gave to his customer before carrying out the job. *Terret v. Murphy*[19] is a good example. The owner of a furniture shop engaged the pursuer to paint an extension to his shop. He was eager to have the work completed and when the painter reported that supplies of the primer that he wished to use would not be available for several days he persuaded the painter to carry on with the job. This was done despite warnings from the painter that the absence of primer could result in problems later on. Problems did, indeed, arise and the owner of the shop withheld payment. Finding in favour of the painter the sheriff, to whom an appeal had been taken, pointed out that if a householder merely asked for a job to be done then the contractor would be liable if he did not draw attention to a particular risk. He went on:

> "But if, in spite of a clear warning from the painter that the work should be executed in a particular manner, the householder instructs him to proceed in a different way or without some recommended precaution, I cannot see why he should be entitled later on to say that the warning was not loud enough or that it was not repeated often enough or that he did not appreciate the full measure of the risk."

**7–19**    The result to be expected from the service performed is also related to the agreement between the parties. *Brown v. J. Nisbet & Co. Ltd* was referred to above in relation to this issue. It is to be noted that it also had implications for the liability of the repairer and the kind of result that the customer was entitled to expect. Had it been proved that he had agreed to a complete overhaul of the van the repairer might well have been liable for a failure to display the requisite level of competence when the van broke down if these were faults which had existed when he had been asked to work on it. As he had only been asked to carry out specific tasks, which it was proved that he had carried out in a workmanlike manner, he was not liable.

**7–20**    The principle has also been applied to professional services. One of the best known explanations of reasonable skill and care in relation to professional services is that of Lord President Clyde in *Hunter v. Hanley*[20] where he said:

> "where the conduct of a doctor, or indeed of any professional man, is concerned the circumstances are not so precise and

clear cut as in the normal case. In the realm of diagnosis and treatment there is ample scope for genuine difference of opinion and one man clearly is not negligent merely because his conclusions differ from that of other professional men, nor because he has displayed less skill or knowledge than others would have shown. The true test for establishing negligence in diagnosis or treatment on the part of a doctor is whether he has been proved to be guilty of such failure as no doctor of ordinary skill would be guilty of if acting with ordinary care."

This has been interpreted to mean that if any other professional can be found to agree with the actions of the doctor or other professional sued there is no negligence.[21] A close reading of the case suggests that this is going too far and that McNair J. in *Bolam v. Friern Hospital Management Committee*[22] correctly paraphrased the test when he said of the standard required of a doctor that: "it is sufficient if he exercises the ordinary skill of an ordinary competent man exercising that particular art."    **7–21**

This view certainly seems to be consistent with other professional negligence cases. It is the test laid down in *Jameson v. Simon*,[23] which involved the supervision of a building contract by an architect. There are numerous cases involving solicitors to similar effect of which *Hart v. Frame & Company*[24] is an early example.    **7–22**

A professional person does not give an absolute undertaking to achieve a particular result: that would be inappropriate in most cases of professional services. A doctor, in the nature of things, cannot undertake to cure his patients, and a lawyer can give no guarantee to a client that he will win his case.    **7–23**

This latter point was emphasised in a medical negligence case, *Eyre v. Measday*.[25] Mr and Mrs Eyre decided that they did not wish to have any more children and consulted the defendant, a gynaecologist, to discuss the sterilisation of Mrs Eyre. The defendant explained the nature of the operation and emphasised that it was irreversible and must be regarded as a permanent procedure. He did not explain that there was a small risk of failure. The Eyres believed that the result of the operation would be to render Mrs Eyre incapable of having further children. However, after the operation Mrs Eyre did become pregnant    **7–24**

---

[21] See Norrie, "Common Practice and the Standard of Care in Medical Negligence", 1985 J.R. 145. For a different view see Howie, "The Standard of Care in Medical Negligence", 1983 J.R. 193.
[22] [1957] 2 All ER 118.
[23] (1899) 1 F. 1211.
[24] (1839) McL & Rob. 595.
[25] [1986]1 All E.R. 488

and had another child. She sued the gynaecologist alleging, amongst other things, that there was an implied term that she would be rendered sterile by the operation.

**7–25**     It was held that the defendant had undertaken to carry out a particular type of operation rather than to render Mrs Eyre absolutely sterile and that his statement that the operation was irreversible was not an express guarantee that the operation was bound to achieve its objective. As the judge put it:

> "I think there is no doubt that the plaintiff would have been entitled reasonably to assume that the defendant was warranting that the operation would be performed with reasonable care and skill. That, I think, would have been the inevitable inference to be drawn, from an objective standpoint, from the relevant discussion between the parties . . . . However, that inference on its own does not enable the plaintiff to succeed in the present case. She has to go further. She has to suggest . . . that the defendant, by necessary implication, committed himself to an unqualified guarantee as to the success of the particular operation proposed, in achieving its purpose of sterilising her, even though he were to exercise all due care and skill in performing it. The suggestion is that the guarantee went beyond due care and skill and extended an unqualified warranty that the plaintiff would be absolutely sterile.
>
> On the facts of the present case, I do not think that any intelligent lay bystander (let alone another medical man), on hearing the discussion which took place between the defendant and the other two parties, could have reasonably drawn the inference that the defendant was intending to give any warranty of this nature . . . . But, in my opinion, in the absence of any express warranty, the court should be slow to imply against a medical man an unqualified warranty as to the results of an intended operation, for the very simple reason that, objectively speaking, it is most unlikely that he would intend to give a warranty of this nature".[26]

**7–26**     A case involving professional services which does show that a standard higher than that of due skill and care can be expected in certain circumstances is *Greaves & Co. (Contractors) Ltd v. Bayhnam Meikle & Partners*.[27] The plaintiffs, who were building

---

[26]   It was held in this case that the plaintiff had been adequately informed of the possibility that the operation might not be successful. For a case where the plaintiff succeeded because an adequate warning of the possibility of failure was not given see *Thake v. Maurice* [1986] Q.B. 644.

[27]   [1975] 1 W.L.R. 1095.

contractors, had agreed to design and build a warehouse for a customer. They employed the defendants, who were structural engineers to design the warehouse and advised them that it was essential that it should be capable of permitting materials to be moved around on fork lift trucks. Shortly after the warehouse was handed over to the customer the floor began to crack as a result of vibration caused by the forklift trucks. The plaintiffs accepted that they were liable to their customer and brought this action to recover, by way of indemnity, from the structural engineers the cost of repairs to the building.

It was held that on the facts as proved in this case there was a **7–27** term to be implied into the contract that the engineers would design a building that would be fit for the purpose which the plaintiffs had stipulated.

### TIME FOR PERFORMANCE

A perennial source of complaint from consumers is failure of a **7–28** contractor to complete a job in good time, or sometimes to complete it at all. The National Consumer Council's report *Service Please*[28] found that this was a very frequent source of annoyance to consumers. Problems in this area tend to fall into two categories. There are those cases where the date for the commencement or completion of the work has been agreed between the parties and subsequently ignored by the contractor. The other is where no time has been agreed for the completion of the work but the consumer thinks that the contractor has taken an unreasonably long time to complete the work.

The contract may specify the time by which the service is to be **7–29** completed. This is subject to the proviso that the contractor will not be liable for failure to comply with a time limit if his failure to do so is the fault of the client. This point was made in *T. & R. Duncanson v. The Scottish County Investment Co. Ltd*[29] where a plasterer was unable to complete his agreed tasks because the client had failed to ensure that other tradesmen, completion of whose work was necessary to allow him to start, had kept to their schedules.

If there is no complication such as that in the case just **7–30** mentioned, the question is whether time is of the essence. There is no problem where the contract explicitly says that this is the case. It should not be necessary to use the particular formula that time is to be of the essence. Any words that clearly indicate that this is the case should suffice.

---

[28] Lantin and Woodroffe (NCC, London, 1981).
[29] 1915 S.C. 1106.

**7–31**    The problem is more difficult where the contract does not have such a provision. Time will be assumed to be of the essence in a commercial contract. It is probably not the case that consumer contracts will fall into this category. Certainly, the reported cases have all been contracts between commercial parties.

**7–32**    If there is no express term about time a consumer is entitled to expect that a job will be completed within a reasonable time as was conceded in argument in *Davidson v. Guardian Royal Exchange Assurance*[30]; a case involving delay in repairing a car. The point is also illustrated by the English case of *Charnock v. Liverpool Corporation.*[31] Mr Charnock's car had been damaged in an accident and he took it to the defendant's for repair. An estimate for the work required was agreed but the job was not completed for eight weeks. Mr Charnock sued the repairers for the cost of hiring a car for three weeks, the period by which, in his opinion, the time taken for the repair exceeded what was reasonable. It was held that there was an implied term that the repairers would carry out the repair with reasonable expedition and on the facts eight weeks was not a reasonable time. Evidence had shown that the job should have taken not longer than five weeks.

**7–33**    Where a time has been stipulated in the contract for completion of the service but time is not to be regarded as of the essence of the contract it is open to the customer to make it of the essence. A good example of this comes from the English Court of Appeal case of *Charles Rickards Ltd v. Oppenhaim.*[32] Mr Oppenhaim had placed an order in August 1947 with the defendants for the construction of a body on the chassis of his car. The job was to be completed within six months or, at the most, seven months. The job was not completed within seven months and the plaintiff kept pressing for delivery. Eventually, on June 28, 1948 he wrote to the bodybuilders saying: "I regret that I shall be unable . . . to accept delivery . . . after July 25". When the car was not finished by the end of July Mr Oppenhaim cancelled his order and when the car was delivered to him in October 1948 he refused to accept it. It was held that the original stipulation making time of the essence of the contract had been waived but he was entitled to give reasonable notice once again making time of the essence. In determining what is reasonable notice the Court of Appeal drew attention to a dictum of Lord Parker of Waddington in *Stickney v. Keeble*[33] where he said:

---

[30]   1979 S.C. 192.
[31]   [1968] 1 WL.R. 1498.
[32]   [1950] 1 K.B. 616.
[33]   [1915] A.C. 386.

"In considering whether the time so limited is a reasonable time the Court will consider all the circumstances of the case. No doubt what remains to be done at the date of the notice is of importance, but is by no means the only relevant fact. The fact that the purchaser has continually been pressing for completion, or has before given similar notices which he has waived, or that it is especially important to him to obtain early completion, are equally relevant facts."

Applying this approach to the facts of this case it was decided **7–34** that the notice of June 28,1948 was a reasonable notice making time of the essence and Mr Oppenhaim was not obliged to take delivery.

### COST

The cost for a service will often be agreed beforehand and in that **7–35** event it is the price agreed that must be paid even if it is not in accordance with the normal practice in the trade or profession.[34] On occasions a professional man is instructed to carry through some piece of work but no discussion of the fee or payment takes place. The general rule is "that tradesmen and professional men who provide services of the kind by which they earn their livings are presumed not to do so gratuitously and are entitled to reasonable remuneration."[35] *Robert Allan and Partners v. McKinstray*[36] is a good example. A firm of architects after a meeting with a client prepared preliminary drawings for a house which he proposed to build. Thereafter the client requested and was supplied with more detailed information to enable a builder to provide an estimate of the cost of construction. When the project was abandoned by the client he refused to pay the architect's fees arguing that the work had been in the nature of an estimate and, the project having been abandoned, no fee was payable. The Sheriff Principal held that there was no evidence to displace the general rule quoted above and that the architects were entitled *quantum meruit* to a fee for the project.

There is a distinction to be made between cases such as *Robert* **7–36** *Allan and Partners v. McKinstray* and cases where no more has been done than the submission of an estimate or tender. This was pointed out in *Sinclair v. Logan*[37] where a builder had drawn up

---

[34] *Wilkie v. Scottish Aviation Ltd*, 1956 S.C. 198.
[35] *Robert Allan and Partners v. McKinstray*, 1975 S.L.T. (Sh. Ct.) 63, at p. 64, echoing Gloag, *Contract* (2nd. ed.), p. 291. See also *Bell v. Ogilvie* (1863) 2 M. *336; Landless v. Wilson (1880)* 8 R. 289; *Sinclair v. Logan*, 1961 S.L.T. (Sh.Ct.) 10.
[36] 1975 S.L.T. (Sh.Ct.) 63.
[37] 1961 S.L.T. (Sh.Ct.) 10.

plans for alterations to licensed premises, negotiated with the police and obtained approval from the licensing court before it became clear that the client was not going to go ahead with the project. In finding that the builder was entitled to a fee for the preliminary work that he had done the sheriff pointed out that:

> "The position of the pursuer is clearly distinguishable from that of a tradesman or contractor who submits a tender or estimate. The tender or estimate is in general submitted without any intention to benefit the person or authority requiring work to be done but purely to benefit the tradesman or contractor. It is generally submitted, in competition with others, so that the employment of the particular person submitting it is not a precondition to its submission.[38]

**7–37**  From this it is clear that the common practice of asking for an estimate for a proposed piece of work does not imply that the tradesman is entitled to charge a fee for this work. This was also held in *Murray v. Fairlie Yacht Slip Ltd*[39] where the company, having been asked to prepare an estimate for the cost of repairs, attempted to charge for bringing a yacht ashore and storing it for three months.

**7–38**  To establish a right to a fee more needs to be done than this and, as the quotation from *Sinclair v. Logan* makes clear, one element which will be relevant will be whether the client has derived any benefit from the services rendered. This seems to have been decisive in *Landless v. Wilson*,[40] where an architect submitted detailed plans for the development of a site in Glasgow which, in the end, the client did not proceed with. There was evidence that the client showed the plans to prospective purchasers of the site, and this and the general presumption referred to above resulted in a finding that the architect was entitled to a fee.

**7–39**  Where there is a contract for services but the amount to be paid has not been stated how is that amount to be calculated? The tradesman or professional is entitled to payment *quantum meruit*. This can be calculated by referring to a customary rate if there is one. To establish this it must be shown that the custom is reasonable, certain and notorious.[41] Failing this the court will fix reasonable remuneration which will be ascertained from such evidence as has been adduced. Evidence which might be

---

[38]  1961 S.L.T. (Sh.Ct.) 10, at p.12.
[39]  1975 S.L.T. (Sh.Ct.) 62.
[40]  (1880) 8 R. 289
[41]  *The Strathlorne Steamship Co. Ltd v. Hugh Baird & Sons Ltd*, 1916 S.C. (H.L.)134.

adduced would include the level of charges of other tradesmen or professionals in the area or reference to scale charges of a profession.

### DUTY TO TAKE CARE OF GOODS DEPOSITED

Some services will involve the contractor in taking possession of the customer's goods in order, for example, to effect a repair. In this situation the *locatio operis faciendi* is normally presumed to include as an inherent ingredient an element of *locatio custodiae*. The standard of care which the trader must observe is to take such care as a prudent man would take of his own property in the circumstances.[42] It has sometimes been described as an obligation to take reasonable care.

The onus of proving that reasonable care has been taken is on the trader. In *Sinclair v. Juner*[43] the garage which had undertaken to repair the pursuer's car failed to discharge this onus when they failed to produce any evidence about the cause of the fire which destroyed the customer's car. In *Forbes v. Aberdeen Motors Ltd*[44] the defenders were held not to have displayed the requisite degree of care when they left the pursuer's Bentley car in an unsupervised hotel car park in the middle of Aberdeen with the keys in the ignition. It was stolen by an inebriated naval rating whose motoring skills resulted in it suffering serious damage in an accident. Likewise, a garage was held liable for damage caused to a car in its custody when left in the street outside the garage overnight[45]; and, in an example from an earlier age, someone who undertook for reward to break in a horse was liable when it was injured when it bolted on being startled by an explosion under the stables. It was relevant that the explosion was not unexpected as the defender knew that a railway company was constructing a tunnel underneath his premises.[46]

One might have thought that the liability of a company operating a car park to someone leaving their motor bicycle in it might have been the same as in these cases. *Drynan v. Scottish Ice Rink Co. Ltd*[47] casts doubt on this. In the sheriff court it was held that leaving the scooter in the park and purchasing a ticket created a relationship of licensor and licensee, not that of custody. The correctness of this view must be in doubt but, as has been

**7–40**

**7–41**

**7–42**

---

[42] *Sinclair v. Inner*, 1952 S.C. 35; *Verrico v. George Hughes & Son*, 1980 S.C. 179.
[43] 1952 S.C. 35.
[44] 1965 S.C. 193.
[45] See *Vericco v. George Hughes & Son*, 1980 S.C. 179.
[46] *Laing v. Darling* (1850) 12 D. 1279.
[47] 1971 S.L.T. (Sh.Ct.) 59.

observed, "what suffices to create a contract of custody remains to be decided in Scots law".[48]

**7–43**    It is not clear whether the standard of care in cases of custody for reward is the same as in cases of gratuitous deposit. In *Copland v. Brogan*,[49] a case of gratuitous deposit, the Court of Session spoke of the standard in the same terms as have been used in cases of custody for reward.

### WHERE THE SERVICE INVOLVES THE PROVISION OF MATERIALS

**7–44**    At the beginning of this chapter the uncertainty about the legal classification of contracts for services which involved the provision of materials was referred to. This is no longer a problem as far as title, description and quality are concerned as the same terms are implied whether the contract is considered to be sale as far as the provision of materials is concerned, or something else. This is the result of the insertion of Part IA in the Supply of Goods and Services Act 1982.

## LIABILITY IN DELICT FOR NEGLIGENCE

**7–45**    So far, the standard of care and skill required of those who offer services has been discussed solely in terms of contractual liability. It is important to stress that there is also the possibility of liability for the delict of negligence. Indeed, in some situations there may be no other avenue open to the customer or client. An example of this is the situation of patients who allege that the treatment that they have received under the National Health Service has not been up to the required standard and that they have been harmed as a result. It appears from judicial decisions that such patients have no contractual relationship with the health service and can sue only in delict.[50] Such patients could not avail themselves of the implied terms. Negligence may also be the appropriate type of legal action because, in other circumstances, someone who has not contracted with the provider of the service has suffered loss as a result of his activities.

**7–46**    Lawyers will usually have a contractual duty to their clients so delictual liability may not be so important. However, *Ross v. Caunters*,[51] an English case, demonstrates where it might be

---

[48]   McBryde, *The Law of Contract in Scotland* (1987), p.106.
[49]   1916 S.C. 277.
[50]   *Pfizer Corporation v. Ministry of Health* [1965] 1 All E.R. 450, at p.455, *per* Lord Reid.
[51]   [1980] Ch. 297.

important. Mrs Ross was an intended beneficiary under a will drawn up by Caunters & Co., solicitors. They failed to tell the testator (the person making the will) that if a beneficiary, or the spouse of a beneficiary, witnessed the will the gift to that beneficiary would be invalid. Mrs Ross's husband witnessed the signature of the will by the testator and as a result Mrs Ross could not receive the legacy given to her in the will. She sued the solicitors who had drawn up the will for the amount of the legacy that she had lost saying that they had been negligent in not telling the testator that her husband should not act as a witness and in not noticing that he had done so. The solicitors' argument was that they were liable only to their client (now past caring about his will, or at least not in a position to do anything about it), not to people like Mrs Ross. Mrs Ross won. The English Court of Appeal held that the solicitors owed a duty to Mrs Ross who was clearly identified and intended to benefit under the will. There was thus a sufficiently proximate relationship with her to give rise to a duty of care to her.[52]

It is not clear whether the Scottish courts would reach the same conclusion on similar facts. In *Weir v. J.M. Hodge and Son*[53] an Outer House judge declined to follow English authority, feeling bound by *Robertson v. Fleming*[54] where the House of Lords had held that in the absence of privity of contract a solicitor was not liable to make reparation to third parties injured by negligent acts or omissions in the course of acting for a client. As the Lord Ordinary observed, this decision is out of sympathy with modern developments in the law of negligence. In *Macdougall v. Clydesdale Bank Trustees*[55] Lord Cameron also felt obliged to follow the decision while appearing to hint that it might not survive a challenge in the Inner House. However, in *Tait v. Brown & McRae*[56] Sheriff Principal Risk approved of it in relation to disappointed beneficiaries. However, he did emphasise that there were other circumstances in which solicitors, like other professional persons, could be liable in delict to those who were not their clients.[57]

**7–47**

---

[52] See *White v. Jones* [1995] 2 A.C. 207; [1995] 1 All ER 691, *Walker v. Geo H Medlicott & Son* [1999] 1 All E.R. 685; [1999] 1 W.L.R. 727, *Carr-Glynn v. Frearsons* [1999] Ch. 326, [1998] 4 All E.R. 225, [1999] 2 W.L.R. 1046, and for a case where a professional non-solicitor will maker was held to have a similar duty of care see *Esterhuizen v. Allied Dunbar Assurance plc* [1998] 2 F.L.R. 668.

[53] 1990 S.L.T. 266.

[54] (1861) 4 Macq. 167.

[55] *Macdougall v. Clydesdale Bank Trustees*, 1994 S.L.T. 1178; 1993 S.C.L.R. 832.

[56] 1997 S.L.T. (Sh.Ct.) 63.

[57] See *Midland Bank plc v. Cameron, Thom, Peterkins & Duncan*, 1988 S.L.T. 611; 1988 S.C.L.R. 209.

**7–48** An advocate does not have a contractual relationship with the lay client and so any action will have to be in delict. An advocate is to a certain extent immune from action for breach of duty. There is no direct authority on this point in Scots law, but it appears to be accepted that the immunity is now narrowly confined to things done in the conduct of a case in court. This is the position in England following *Rondel v. Worsley*[58] and *Saif Ali v. Sydney Mitchell & Co.*[59] It may be that the immunity is even more narrowly confined so that an advocate is liable for negligence "except insofar as the administration of justice requires that he should not be".[60]

**7–49** Surveyors may also incur liability to those, such as prospective mortgagors, if they are in breach of their duty to take reasonable care. This was established in *Smith v. Eric S. Bush & Co.*[61] which was followed in *Robbie v. Graham & Sibbald.*[62]

## REMEDIES

**7–50** The general principles relating to remedies for breach of contract apply to breaches of contracts for services and their application will depend on the particular circumstances of the case. There is a principle that damages are not normally recoverable for injury to feelings occasioned by a breach of contract.[63] It is recognised that there are exceptions to this principle which may be summed up by saying that it does not apply when the purpose of the contract is to provide pleasure. Such contracts are particularly likely to be contracts for the provision of services. In *Diesen v. Samson*[64] a photographer failed to turn up to take photographs of the pursuer's wedding and damages were awarded for the disappointment that this caused. In England damages have been awarded on this basis where package holidays have failed to live up to the claims made in the brochure,[65] and the principle was also applied where a firm of solicitors failed to take

---

[58] [1969] 1 A.C. 191.
[59] [1980] A.C. 198.
[60] Submission of the Faculty of Advocates to the Royal Commission on Legal Services in Scotland, p.20, quoted in Carey Miller, "Rationalising the Advocate's Immunity", 1979 S.L.T. (News) 109.
[61] [1990] 1 A.C. 831.
[62] 1989 S.C.L.R. 578. The defenders escaped liability because they were protected by an exclusion clause to which, at the time, the Unfair Contract Terms Act 1977 had no application in Scotland.
[63] *Addis v. Gramophone Co. Ltd* [1909] A.C. 488.
[64] 1971 S.L.T. (Sh.Ct.) 49.
[65] *Jarvis v. Swan Tours Ltd* [1973] 1 Q.B. 233; *Jackson v. Horizon Holidays Ltd* [1975] 1 W.L.R. 1468.

appropriate legal action to prevent the plaintiff's husband har-
assing her in breach of an injunction.[66]

## CRIMINAL LAW

The criminal law has a role to play in protecting consumers of    **7–51**
services. The main provisions are to be found in the Trade
Descriptions Act 1968 and Part 3 of the Consumer Protection Act
1987 which deals with prices. They are discussed in Chapter 11.

## SELF REGULATION

In addition to the legal rules which have been discussed above it    **7–52**
is important to note that codes of conduct drawn up by members
of some trade associations may offer assistance to consumers.
The Association of British Travel Agents, the electricity companies, the motor trade and funeral directors are examples of
providers of services who subscribe to such codes. Their chief
benefit is that codes can attempt to cope with matters which it
would be difficult, if not impossible, to deal with statutorily. For
example, the code governing electrical repairers provides that
where a home visit is needed "the first visit should (wherever
possible) be made within three working days from receipt of the
request". The Scottish Motor Trade Association code states that
"[s]pare parts should be readily available from the manufacturer
from the time that a new model is offered for sale continuing
throughout its production and for a reasonable period thereafter".[67]

## CASE STUDY: PACKAGE HOLIDAYS

The package holiday is an important part of many consumers    **7–53**
lifestyle and accounts for a significant part of their spending.
From a consumer protection perspective it is particularly interesting because it provides an example of various techniques
being used to protect the consumer. The criminal and civil law
are brought into play as well as self-regulation.
  While it is not the only relevant source of law in this area it will    **7–54**
be convenient to structure this discussion around the Package

---

[66] See *Heywood v. Wellers* [1976] Q.B. 446; and Jackson, 26 I.C.L.Q. 502 for a
review of some of the cases in this area.
[67] Available on the website of the Society of Motor Manuafcturers and Traders,
http://www.smmt.co.uk

Travel, Package Holidays and Package Tours Regulations 1992.[68] These regulations were enacted to implement the E.C. Package Travel Directive.[69] The regulations came into effect on December 3, 1992. They use both the civil and criminal law to improve the protection afforded to consumers.

**7–55**    Before looking at the regulations in detail it is first necessary to look at the definition of a package. Regulation 2 defines it as the pre-arranged combination of at least two of the following elements when offered for sale at an inclusive price and when the service covers a period of at least 24 hours or includes overnight accommodation. The three elements are: transport; accommodation, and other tourist services not ancillary to transport or accommodation and accounting for a significant proportion of the package.

**7–56**    The regulations set out various civil obligations of the package organiser or retailers. Regulation 4 provides that tour organisers or retailers must not provide consumers with information that is misleading. If they do they are liable to compensate consumers for any loss which is suffered. Particulars in brochures constitute implied terms of the contract unless the brochure states that the information in it may change and the changes are clearly communicated before the contract is concluded.[70] It is an implied term of the contract that the other party to the contract will ensure that the contract contains at least the information specified in Schedule 2.[71] This is basic information about the price, the means of transport, destination, type of accommodation, meals, and the payment schedule. The contract terms must be set out in writing or such other form as is accessible to the consumer who must be given a written copy of them.

**7–57**    In addition, the regulations imply various terms into contracts. Where the consumer is prevented from proceeding with the package there is an implied term that he or she may transfer the booking to any person who satisfies all the package conditions.[72] Surcharges have been a source of considerable friction in package tours and controls are placed on them. Price revision clauses are void unless they provide for the possibility of upward and downward revision. They must also state precisely how the revised price is to be calculated and that revisions are to be made solely to allow for variations in transport costs, service charges and currency fluctuations. In any event, they cannot be made less than 30 days before departure and the tour operator must absorb

[68]  S.I. 1992 No. 3288.
[69]  Directive 90/314.
[70]  reg. 6.
[71]  reg. 9.
[72]  reg. 10.

the first two per cent of any increase.[73] Further terms are implied by regulations 13 and 14. These deal with compensation for cancellation of the holiday and failure to provide a significant proportion of the services contracted for.

In many ways the central feature of the civil law provisions of **7–58** the regulations is to be found in regulation 15. This imposes strict liability on the package organiser or retailer for the proper performance of the contract, whether they are to be performed by him or another supplier. Failure to do so renders him liable for any damage caused, unless the failure is attributable to the consumer or due to unusual and unforeseeable circumstances beyond the control of the other party. This liability cannot be excluded but it may be limited in accordance with international conventions; and, in the case of damage other than personal injury, may be limited, provided that the limitation is reasonable.

One of the greatest problems that can beset a holidaymaker is **7–59** the insolvency of the tour operator or the financial failure of the travel agent. For some years there have been various methods of ensuring that holidaymakers will not suffer financial loss in these events. The Civil Aviation Authority licenses travel organisers who must have an Air Traffic Organiser's Licence (ATOL) which requires them to provide a bond. This amounts to 15 per cent of licensable turnover, or 10 per cent if the licence holder is a member of the Association of British Travel Agents which has arrangements to cope with these problems. For more serious failures the Air Travel Trust which succeeded to the assets of the Reserve Fund set up under the Air Travel Reserve Fund Act 1975 provides protection.

One of the most important aspects of the regulations is con- **7–60** tained in regulation 16, which places an obligation on tour operators and travel agents to provide evidence of security for the refund of money paid by customers and for their repatriation in the event of insolvency. This obligation is sanctioned by criminal penalties. Regulations 17 to 20 provide a choice of methods through which this obligation can be met. These include taking out a bond, having an Air Travel Organiser's Licence, being a member of a scheme which operates a reserve fund, or having insurance or placing money in a trust fund.

The scope of regulation 16 which implements Article 7 of the **7–61** directive was demonstrated in a decision of the European Court of Justice.[74] There it was said that:

---

[73] reg. 11.
[74] *Verein fürKonsumenteninformation v. Österreichische Kreditversicherrungs AG*, Case C-364/96.

"Article 7 of Directive 90/314 was to be interpreted as covering, as security for the refund of money paid over, a situation in which the purchaser of a package holiday who had paid the travel organiser for the costs of his accommodation before travelling on his holiday was compelled, following the travel organiser's insolvency, to pay the hotelier for his accommodation again in order to be able to leave the hotel and return home."

**7–62**    The criminal law is also used to ensure compliance with other requirements of the regulations. Regulation 5 makes it an offence for a holiday organiser to make brochures available to potential customers which do not indicate the price and adequate information about specified matters in a "legible comprehensible and adequate manner". A retailer who makes such a brochure available knowing that it does not comply also commits an offence. Regulation 7 requires tour operators or travel agents to make available before the contract is concluded general information about visa requirements applying to British citizens, information about health formalities, and arrangements for security of money paid over and repatriation arrangements. Failure to comply is also a criminal offence as is failure to provide "in good time before the start of the journey" certain information about what to do in the event of some problem arising during the holiday.

**7–63**    The use of the criminal law is, of course, not new in the package holiday world. As we shall see in Chapter 11, the Trade Descriptions Act 1968 has had considerable effect in ensuring high standards of accuracy in brochures. The law on price indications contained in Part III of the Consumer Protection Act 1987 also applies to package holidays.

**7–64**    Not only has the law been used to protect holidaymakers, but also the industry itself has taken steps to improve matters. One of the more successful codes of practice has been that of the Association of British Travel Agents (ABTA). This covers many of the matters now required by law under the Package Holiday Regulations. Two particularly important features are the compensation arrangements in the event of a travel agent or tour operator facing financial difficulties, and the low cost arbitration provisions. These are discussed in Chapter 12.

## CHAPTER 8

# THE PUBLIC SECTOR

A number of important goods and services are supplied by    **8–01**
nationalised or recently privatised companies. In addition, the
state through local and central government provides services and
facilities for its citizens. Health, education and the courts are
examples. In the latter case there has been an increasing tendency to apply consumer principles to the provision of these
services. In this chapter we look at the implications for consumers of the provision of services by these providers.

In the case of the nationalised and the privatised industries    **8–02**
where the consumer complains of defective goods or services the
remedy will usually be no different from that pursued against
any other supplier. The legislation and common law rules discussed in earlier chapters will be relevant. To this there are some
exceptions. The Post Office has statutory immunity from liability
for actions or omissions "in relation to anything in the post"
which is conferred by section 29 of the Post Office Act 1969.
Section 23 of the British Telecommunications Act 1981 excludes
British Telecom's delictual liability for failure to provide a
service or apparatus and for errors in telephone directories.

## REGULATED INDUSTRIES

A major feature of the last 20 years has been the privatisation    **8–03**
policy pursued by the previous Conservative administration
under which many nationalised industries have been returned to
private ownership. The major examples have been British Gas,
British Telecom, British Airways, the English and Welsh water
companies, the electricity and bus industries, the railways and
the coal industry. As a result, few major industries are in state
ownership, the Post Office being the most notable example.

While, in theory, these state monopolies have been broken, in    **8–04**
practice, in many cases, the privatised companies have near
monopoly power. British Telecom does face increasing competition but is by far the dominant enterprise in telecommunications

in the United Kingdom. While there is increasing competition in the gas and electricity industries this has been slow to develop and the regional power companies tend to be the dominant suppliers in their areas. The privatisation legislation recognised that, in most cases, there might not be a high level of competition in the markets supplied by the new corporations.

**8–05** To provide a proxy for the protection afforded to the consumer by competition in the market place the solution adopted in the privatisation legislation has been the creation of independent regulators with extensive powers to control the industries concerned. One objective announced in the Citizen's Charter was to bring the powers of all the public utility regulators up to the level of the strongest. This was done in the Competition and Service (Utilities) Act 1992. They can all now set and monitor service standards, ensure that consumers are aware of them, require payments to be made where the standards are not met, improve complaints procedures, encourage competition, and resolve disputes. In January 2000 the Government introduced a Utilities Bill into the House of Commons. This was, so far as Scotland was concerned, to deal with the telecommunications, gas and electricity industries. After the second reading the Secretary of State for Trade and Industry announced that the provisions relating to telecommunications were being deleted. The objectives of the bill are to achieve a fair balance between the interests of consumers and shareholders through changes to the regulators' duties, give new powers to the regulators, and establish an independent consumer council for each utility regulator. The current situation is discussed in the following paragraphs.

### TELECOMMUNICATIONS

**8–06** The Telecommunications Act 1984 set up the Office of Telecommunications (OFTEL) headed by the Director General of Telecommunications. The Director General's primary responsibility is to keep under review and to promote the provision of telecommunications in the United Kingdom. This includes the duty to exercise his powers so far as possible to ensure so far as practicable that there are provided throughout the United Kingdom telecommunications services which satisfy all reasonable demands for them. The Director General and the Secretary of State are under a duty to promote the interests of consumers, purchasers and other users in respect of the prices charged for, and the quality and variety of, services.[1]

---

[1] On the problems of regulating prices and quality see Barnes, "Quality Regulation: the UK experience of regulating BT" (1992) 2 Cons. Pol. Rev. 21.

The Director General of Telecommunications and OFTEL **8–07** also have, under the Telecommunications Act 1984, a duty to consider representations from users of telecommunications apparatus and services. OFTEL has accordingly taken over the investigation of complaints in relation to telecommunications, formerly carried out by the Post Office Users' National Council (POUNC). OFTEL is also advised by six Advisory Committees on Telecommunications (ACTs). Of these, four are regional and include the Scottish Advisory Committee on Telecommunications (SACOT). It was established by the Telecommunications Act 1984 and companies operating telecommunications systems are also required by their licences to consider its representations. The Chairman and members of the committee are private citizens appointed by the Secretary of State for Trade and Industry, and are independent of OFTEL. The other two ACTs are DIEL, the ACT for disabled and elderly people, and CFB which deals with communications for business. OFTEL also liaises with local Telecommunications Advisory Committees (TACs) of which there are about 170. Complaints should be taken up with the service provider and, if this does not result in their resolution, the customer should seek the help of the local TACs.

OFTEL will deal with complaints brought to it directly. The **8–08** major provider of telecommunications services, British Telecom, has its own code of practice which includes provision for taking unresolved complaints to a low-cost arbitration scheme which is referred to in Chapter 12.

## ENERGY

As mentioned above, the regulation of the gas and electricity **8–09** industries is in the process of being changed significantly. Already the original regulators, the Office of Gas Supply (OFGAS) and the Office of Electricity Regulation (OFFER) have merged their offices and will be known as the Office of Gas and Electricity Supply (OFGEM). The separate consumer councils for the gas and electricity industries are also being amalgamated and the arrangements for this are already well advanced. These changes require legislation and the Utilities Bill currently before Parliament provides for this. As this is not yet law it is necessary to describe the existing arrangements.

## GAS

The Gas Act 1986 created the Office of Director General of Gas **8–10** Supply who heads the Office of Gas Supply (OFGAS). Section 4 of the Act places duties on the Director General similar to those of the Director of Telecommunications. One important addition is the duty to protect the public from the dangers of gas supply.

**8–11** The Gas Consumers' Council (GCC) was also set up under section 2 of the Act. Its function is to represent the interests of gas consumers. The GCC has offices in each of the 12 regions of British Gas and can deal not only with gas supply but also with all issues affecting gas users. It can deal, for example, with complaints about appliances sold by British Gas, or its servicing and repairs, which do not come within the jurisdiction of OFGAS. The GCC can also deal with complaints about private gas installers and repairers.

**8–12** The GCC takes up complaints on behalf of consumers who have tried and failed to solve their problem direct with British Gas or the private installer/repairer. In addition, it will give advice about how best to tackle any problem not yet raised with British Gas, etc.

**8–13** Consumers complaining about British Gas should first approach the GCC who will inform OFGAS of any complaint which falls within OFGAS's powers. If the GCC cannot settle the complaint to the customer's satisfaction, then the facts will be passed to OFGAS for further action. Complaints can also be made direct to OFGAS. The Director General deals only with complaints about British Gas supply up to the point where the supply leaves the meter. In 1998 OFGAS received 61,887 complaints and enquiries.[2] The main issues raised were account disputes, marketing, doorstep selling and transfer problems.

### ELECTRICITY

**8–14** The Electricity Act of 1989 established the post of Director General of Electricity Supply who heads the Office of Electricity Regulation (OFFER). The duties of the Director General include ensuring that all reasonable demands for electricity are met and protecting the interests of consumers in respect of prices, terms and quality of supply. The Act requires the Director General to appoint consumers' committees, for each of the areas of the public electricity suppliers. These committees have a duty to make representations to, and consult with, their supplier, keep matters affecting the interests of consumers in the area under review and advise the Director General. There is, in addition, a National Consumers' Consultative Committee consisting of the Director General and the chairmen of all the consumers' consultative committees to review matters affecting the interests of consumers.

[2] Annual Report of the Director General of Gas Supply for 1998.

OFFER, together with the consumers' committees, has wide **8–15** responsibilities for investigating consumers' complaints about the performance of electricity suppliers. In general OFFER and the consumers' committees have responsibilities in relation to the supply of electricity up to, and including, the meter in the customer's home or premises. Neither has any responsibilities in relation to problems arising from the sale and use of electrical appliances, or with electrical work inside the home.

Where a complaint has been taken up with the supplier and **8–16** cannot be resolved it can be taken up with a regional office of OFFER who will investigate. If they are unable to resolve the problem straight away it may be considered by the local consumers' committee. The committees have no powers to enforce a decision and if they cannot effect a settlement they may have to involve the Director General who does have such powers. A decision by him has the same effect as a judgement of the county court or sheriff court. There are two main areas where the Director General might exercise his enforcement powers. These arise in cases of proposed or actual disconnection when a public electricity supplier has contravened its duty to give a supply; or where a supplier fails to meet a reasonable request from a potential customer for a supply.

### WATER

The restructuring of local government effected by the Local **8–17** Government (Scotland) Act 1994 has had implications for water and sewerage services which were previously services provided by the regional authorities. In response to public opinion in Scotland these services have not been privatised. Instead, they are provided by three new water authorities. These authorities have a duty to promote conservation and effective use of water resources, ensure that there are adequate supplies, and have regard to the interests of customers especially those with special needs occasioned by a persistent medical condition or family circumstances.

It was the Government's view that it would not be appropriate **8–18** for a service which was still in the public sector to have a regulator based on the model of the privatised public utility regulators. To provide protection for customers section 67 of the Act sets up the Scottish Water and Sewerage Customers' Council to represent the interests of customers, potential customers and former customers. Members of the council, who must be independent of the service providers, are appointed by the Secretary of State.

Section 68 states that the council is to keep under review all **8–19** matters appearing to affect the interests of customers, and to consult and make representations to the water authorities on these issues. In addition, it is to investigate complaints from customers and make representations about them to the authorities.

**8–20**     The Council can also make representations to the Secretary of State about the standard of service of the authorities and the manner in which the authorities conduct relations with customers. To enable it to carry out this duty, section 69 of the Act requires the authorities to provide it with such information as it needs. As well as the main Council there are three committees. These represent the interests of customers in the geographical areas of the water and sewerage authorities.

## THE CITIZEN'S CHARTER

**8–21**     Another approach to improving service in the public sector was launched in 1991 through the Citizen's Charter initiative. In a glossy White Paper, *The Citizen's Charter*,[3] the Government announced a programme to improve the quality of public services. This applied to a wide range of central and local government services as well as the privatised utilities. It recognised that in many of these areas competition has a limited role to play in ensuring high quality services. It stated that there were four main themes in the programme: quality, choice, the setting of standards, and value for money. In promoting these themes a number of mechanisms were to be used. In some cases further privatisation was to be the preferred method, in others the possibility of contracting out services was to be explored along with other ways of using competition. An important mechanism was the setting of targets such as the targets for train punctuality. Other important mechanisms were the creation of inspectorates to ensure that standards were being met, more effective complaints systems, and better redress for citizens when things go wrong.

**8–22**     The creation of effective complaints systems was of central importance to the charter initiative. A complaints task force chaired by Lady Wilcox, chairman of the National Consumer Council, was set up to review the procedures in various public services and it published a guide; *Effective Complaints Systems: Principles and Checklist.* Merely setting up complaints mechanisms is not enough — they must actually result in changes to the procedures that have caused the problem in the first place. If not, there is a danger that complaints procedures will be seen as a substitute for proper service.[4]

---

[3]   Cm. 1599 (1991).
[4]   See Williams and Goriely, "Big Idea — any effect?", (1994) 144 N.L.J. 1164.

The original *Citizen's Charter* set out the basic principles of    **8–23**
the initiative but it also envisaged that there would be further
charters dealing with specific areas. By the time that the present
Government came to review the operation of the charter programme in 1997 there were about 200 national charters. This
figure includes 40 that were termed "national charters" by the
previous administration and the "Charter Standard Statements"
drawn up by executive agencies and non-departmental public
bodies.[5] In addition, there are thought to be about 10,000 local
charters. Charters cover a diverse range of services including
health, education, public utilities and the courts. Of particular
interest in Scotland are a *Parents' Charter in Scotland* and *The
Justice Charter*. The former deals mainly with what parents can
expect of the schools which their children attend; the latter with
the court and procurator fiscal system, prisons and related
aspects of social work services.

The present Government, under the title of *Service First*, has    **8–24**
relaunched the Charter initiative. The purpose is the same as the
original one but the operating principles have been developed.
There are now nine principles of public service delivery.[6] These
are that every public service should set standards of service; be
open and provide full information; consult and involve users and
those who work in them; encourage access and the promotion of
choice; treat all fairly; put things right when they go wrong; use
resources effectively; innovate and improve; and work with
other providers.

How effective the charter initiative has been is difficult to say.    **8–25**
However, the present Government has observed that "[t]here is
little doubt among those people who commented on the original
Charter programme that it made a major contribution to the
improvement in public services during the 1990s"[7] The same
document also recognised that the Charter programme had
shortcomings which the recent National Consumer Council
report on local charters has highlighted.[8] These included a failure to include measurable standards and an inability on the part
of organisations to demonstrate what changes they had made in
response to perceived weaknesses in their services. Nevertheless, as two commentators have observed:

"The Charter approach . . . does indeed offer a redefinition of
the relationship between citizens and the state. The changes

[5]  Service First: The New Charter Programme (1998).
[6]  *ibid*. para. 2.8.
[7]  *ibid*. para. 2.1.
[8]  Local Charters — A Survey of Public Services, National Consumer Council,
     April 1998.

proposed are more fundamental than is immediately apparent. The shift in organisational culture that will be required
throughout the public sector will take years to achieve."[9]

## LOCAL GOVERNMENT

**8–26**    Related to the Service First programme is the Best Value initiative. This was a manifesto commitment of the Government and it
seeks to improve local government performance in the delivery
of services to local communities throughout Scotland. It has also
been extended to police forces and fire brigades. It aims to
ensure that the cost and quality of these services are at a level
acceptable to local people. This is to be achieved by increasing
the role of local people in deciding the priorities for local
government services; improving the way authorities manage and
review their business; and building on the experience and expertise of staff. In Scotland, unlike England and Wales, "Best Value
has developed on a partnership basis . . . although backed by the
threat of the re-imposition of [Compulsory Competitive Tender-
ing] in case of failure".[10]

**8–27**    In July 1997, the Secretary of State and the Convention of
Scottish Local Authorities (COSLA) set up a joint Task Force
on Best Value, comprising The Scottish Office, COSLA and the
Accounts Commission, to develop and implement Best Value
across local government. In their final report the task force
concluded:

> "that all Scottish local authorities have shown a commitment
> to Best Value and have attempted to incorporate the essential
> principles of Best Value in the way they serve their commu-
> nities. They have achieved varying levels of understanding
> and success in doing so, and we doubt that any would claim the
> process to be complete."[11]

**8–28**    The task force concluded that it would be desirable to provide a
legislative basis for Best Value but that this should not be highly
prescriptive to allow for flexibility in developing the programme.
They also recommended that it should apply across the public
sector.

---

[9]   See Williams and Goriely, "Big Idea — any effect?", (1994) 144 N.L.J.
      1164.
[10]  Best Value in Local Government: Final Report, Best Value Task Force, para.
      2.5.
[11]  *ibid.* para. 1.10.

## CHAPTER 9

# BUYING ON CREDIT

## INTRODUCTION

There can be no doubt about the importance of credit in our **9–01** society. Even a casual walk down any high street or a glance at newspaper advertising indicates the prevalence of credit; and the statistics on consumer credit confirm its immense importance in the economy. The amount of consumer credit outstanding in the United Kingdom in February 2000 was £116.82 billion. In addition, at the same date the lending secured on dwelling houses was £500.08 billion.[1]

The provision of credit has a long and chequered history, **9–02** becoming especially important in this country following the industrial revolution. This made credit granting both possible and necessary. If it was to become feasible for a much-increased volume of goods to be acquired it would be necessary for much of this increased consumption to be financed by the extension of credit. To depend on consumption being paid for out of short term savings would not have worked. In the latter half of the nineteenth century with increasing production of mass-produced consumer goods such as sewing machines and pianos, the credit market developed. Reliance on personal security alone would have been commercially imprudent and would have restricted the development of credit selling. The result was the development of hire-purchase. The advantage of this was that it provided the lender with security in the event that the purchaser defaulted. From the consumers' point of view it enabled them, in the words of the credit card slogan, "to take the waiting out of wanting". The Crowther Report noted that hire-purchase "has been one of the chief contributory causes of the great rise in the material standard of living of the British people in the last generation".[2]

---

[1] Bank of England Monetary and Financial Statistics Division Statistical Press Release, "Lending to Individuals", March 2000.
[2] *Consumer Credit: Report of the Committee*, 1971, Vol. 1, para. 2.3.17; hereafter referred to as Crowther.

**9–03**     Hire-purchase could be provided by the seller or manufacturer, though retailers would often not have the resources to finance hire-purchase transactions. There soon grew up finance companies, often companies expanding their activities from commercial financing into the developing area of consumer finance. The consumer credit market developed markedly during the twentieth century, not only in terms of the volume of credit extended, but also in the sophistication and range of methods used. The so-called credit boom of the late 1980s gave considerable impetus to these trends. Before considering the legal background to consumer credit it is necessary to summarise the main methods of obtaining credit and then to consider why special attention is paid to the protection of the consumer obtaining credit.

## METHODS OF OBTAINING CREDIT

**9–04**     There is a wide variety of methods of obtaining credit. One way of categorising these methods is, using a classification adopted by the Crowther Report, to divide them into lender credit and vendor credit. Lender credit involves transactions whose legal form is that of a loan of money, whether or not the loan is associated with a particular purchase. Vendor credit relates to transactions that, legally, are not loans but contracts for the sale or hire of goods. As there are some methods of obtaining credit that do not easily fit into either category, a third category of hybrid transactions is added.

### LENDER CREDIT

**9–05**     There are many ways of obtaining loans. Banks offer loans by way of overdraft where the customer is permitted to overdraw on a current account and the rate of interest is liable to fluctuate during the lifetime of the overdraft. There may be no fixed rate at which the customer is to pay off the loan. More common are bank loans, often marketed as "personal loans". In this case the customer borrows a fixed sum at a specified rate of interest and agrees to pay it off by regular instalments. Since the expansion of the facilities which building societies may offer, they, too, provide personal loans. The building societies are best known for offering loans for the purchase of property which are secured by way of mortgage.

**9–06**     Other institutions, such as finance houses, also provide loans and they are also available from a number of other sources. Insurance companies may make loans against the cash-in value of a life assurance policy; pawnbrokers will do so in return for the

pledge of some item of property; and credit unions will do so for
their members.

## VENDOR CREDIT

The most common form of vendor credit is hire-purchase. This is     **9–07**
an arrangement which combines the hire of goods with an option
to purchase. Typically, the retailer sells the goods to a finance
company which enters into the hire-purchase agreement with the
consumer. The consumer agrees to make a series of weekly or
monthly payments which are, technically, rental payments, so
the consumer is not at this point the owner of the goods and may
not dispose of them without the consent of the finance company.
The agreement gives the consumer an option to purchase the
goods on making a small final payment, an option which, in
practice, is normally exercised. The arrangement need not
involve a finance company as the retailer may enter into the hire-
purchase agreement directly with the consumer.

A very similar transaction is conditional sale. This is an agree-     **9–08**
ment for the sale of goods under which the property remains in
the seller until payment of the price. The main difference
between this and hire-purchase is that in conditional sale the
consumer automatically becomes the owner on making the final
payment, whereas in hire-purchase the consumer is not obliged
to do so.

Hire-purchase and conditional sale both give the person     **9–09**
providing credit a security over the goods. A third type of
transaction, credit sale, is very similar to conditional sale. The
difference is that the property in the goods passes immediately to
the consumer, so the seller has no security.

Another form of vendor credit is the leasing or rental agree-     **9–10**
ment. These have been common for many years in the
commercial sphere but have become more common in consumer
transactions, especially those relating to cars. The legal form is
that of a simple hire agreement similar to that entered into when
a car is hired for a short time from a car rental firm. The same
legal form can be used to finance a transaction where the lease is
for a fixed period at a rent equivalent to the sale price of the
goods and the cost of credit. The consumer does not have title to
the goods and so cannot pass a good title to anyone else. The
provisions of Part III of the Hire-Purchase Act 1964, which
protect those who acquire cars subject to a hire-purchase agreement, do not apply. As a result, there have been instances
recently of innocent purchasers of cars sold by persons who had

been leasing them being without a practical remedy when the true owners reclaimed their property.[3]

HYBRID TRANSACTIONS

### Check Trading

**9–11**   The following description is taken from the Crowther Report.[4]

> "Check trading is an outgrowth from the spontaneous development of mutual clubs in the industrial centres of the North of England. A check is a document, issued by the check trader and purchased by the customer, which entitles him to buy goods, of a wide variety, at any of a long list of shops. The customer buys a check for, say £10 or £20 or £30, paying [5p] in the pound at the start, and undertaking to pay a further [5p] in the pound weekly for 20 weeks — that is, a total of [£1.05] of face value. When he uses the check to buy goods, he is charged the cash price, and the amount of his purchase is noted on the back of the check. The check trader then reimburses the retailer, but after deduction of a discount which may range from $12\frac{1}{2}$ per cent to 15 per cent. Moreover, settlements are usually made monthly, which means that the average period during which the retailer is out of his money is probably from six to seven weeks."

**9–12**   Check trading is largely confined to the north of England and Scotland and the dominant company is Provident Clothing and Supply. The exact legal nature of cheek trading has never been authoritatively decided.[5]

### Credit Cards

**9–13**   Over the last 30 years credit cards have become increasingly popular in this country. The card is issued by a company specialising in the issue of cards which arranges that the card can be used to purchase goods and services from various traders. The cardholder receives a monthly statement from the credit card company. In one type of card, sometimes referred to as a "t and e" card (travel and entertainment), of which the best known is American Express, the customer is expected to pay off the full

---

3   The defrauded purchaser would have a claim against the seller for breach of the implied term about title in s. 12 of the Sale of Goods Act 1979. Often, in these cases, the person sued does not have the means to meet a decree.
4   Crowther, para. 2.4.1.
5   There is an English County Court decision, *Premier Clothing Co. Ltd v. Hillcoat*, Feb. 13, 1969, unreported, in which it was held that it was moneylending. Referred to in Crowther at para. 4.1.64.

amount each month. Apart from the period between paying for the goods or service with the card and the date by which payment must be made to the credit card company, there is no credit element. The other type of card, such as Access or Visa, gives the customer a choice. The full amount may be paid up and no interest charge incurred; or, subject to the payment of a minimum amount, the customer may choose to pay off the account in succeeding months. For this facility there is a charge which varies between 1.5-2% per month. In addition, it is becoming more common for card companies to charge an annual fee. Traders submit their accounts to the credit card company which pays them the amount of the account minus a commission charge.

There has been very little litigation concerning credit cards in any part of the United Kingdom. In *Re Charge Card Services Ltd*[6] the English Court of Appeal held that payment by credit card discharged the consumer's liability for the price to the trader. The cardholder was liable to pay the credit card company, whether or not the company paid the trader. If, as occurred in this case, the credit card company had failed to pay traders they could not recover from the cardholder.     **9–14**

## Budget Accounts

Budget accounts have become common, especially in retail stores. They are a form of revolving credit where the consumer agrees to make a regular monthly payment, say £20, and may then purchase goods of up to a certain multiple of this figure, perhaps ten times or £200. As each payment is made new purchases are permitted provided that the balance outstanding on the account does not exceed £200. A charge which covers interest is made at a specified rate on the amount outstanding at the end of the month.     **9–15**

The precise legal nature of these accounts has never been clear. They are not hire-purchase agreements but were thought by some to be money lending transactions. The Crowther Report noted that in the trade they "are usually treated as giving rise to a series of credit sale agreements" and this view derives support from certain Scottish decisions.[7]     **9–16**

## LEGAL REGULATION OF CREDIT GRANTING

The law on consumer credit was re-shaped by the Consumer Credit Act 1974 which adopted many of the recommendations of     **9–17**

---

[6]   [1988] 3 W.L.R. 764; [1988] 3 All E.R. 702; (1988) 4 B.C.C. 524.
[7]   Crowther, para. 4.1.64.

the 1971 Crowther Report on Consumer Credit. The committee carried out the most comprehensive review of the topic ever undertaken in this country. The report found the state of the law to be gravely defective, one of their most serious criticisms being that legislation regulated transactions on the basis of their form rather than their substance. Hire-purchase, some forms of moneylending and pawnbrokers were subject to strict regulation, whereas loans made by high street banks and the large finance houses were virtually unregulated.

**9–18**    The Crowther Committee considered that tinkering with the law would not be appropriate and recommended a complete revision. They suggested that two new Acts should be drafted: a Lending and Security Act which would rationalise the treatment of security interests and set up a security register, and a Consumer Sale and Loan Act which would govern the treatment of all forms of consumer credit, the linchpin of which would be a Consumer Credit Commissioner. The Consumer Credit Act is essentially the proposed Consumer Sale and Loan Act, the Government having decided that the Lending and Security Act was unnecessary.

**9–19**    As we shall see there is detailed regulation of the credit industry to a degree which is greater than that which normally obtains for protecting the consumer. Why should this be? The Crowther Report[8] summarised the factors which prevent the ideal of a fair balance between consumers and credit granters being attained in all cases. An important constraint is consumers' lack of knowledge both of the forms of credit available and their legal rights. In some cases inertia prevents appropriate action being taken. Some consumers are either reckless or improvident in their use of credit; and in other cases, through no fault of their own, families find themselves requiring to borrow because their income is inadequate. As they added, "[t]here is little point in talking of thrift to one who needs money to keep warm or to buy the minimum of food and clothing necessary for subsistence." Such people are particularly vulnerable to harsh and oppressive terms. Inequality of bargaining power and the existence of a small minority of sellers who indulge in trading malpractice causing great hardship were also noted. It should be added that the committee did not delude themselves that all these problems could be solved by legislation.

## THE CONSUMER CREDIT ACT 1974

**9–20**    The Consumer Credit Act with its 193 sections and five Schedules has been described by a judge as "an Act of extraordinary

---

[8]    See Crowther, Chap. 6.1 for a discussion.

length and complexity".[9] And even at this the Act is only a framework on which much flesh has been put by numerous statutory instruments. Such was its complexity that it was not until 1985 that it came fully into force. In addition, it must be remembered that it is not comprehensive. Aspects of the ordinary law of contract, such as the law on formation and misrepresentation still apply, and the Act does not apply to all credit contracts, as we shall see below.

## DEFINITIONS

Before looking at the various techniques which the Act uses to protect credit consumers it is vital to consider the scope of the Act. The central concept is the "regulated agreement" as, with some exceptions, it is only such agreements that are controlled by the Act. Before the term "regulated agreement" can be understood it is essential to look at various definitions which the Act uses. It will also be convenient at this point to consider some other definitions which will crop up later.  **9–21**

The draftsman of the Act invented some new terminology to distinguish various types of credit. In a novel departure from the methods normally adopted by parliamentary draftsmen he also provided examples of the terminology in Schedule 2 of the Act.  **9–22**

### Fixed and Running Account Credit

Section 10(1)(a) says that:  **9–23**

"running-account credit is a facility under a personal credit agreement whereby the debtor is enabled to receive from time to time (whether in his own person, or by another person) from the creditor or a third party cash, goods and services (or any of them) to an amount or value such that, taking into account payments made by or to the credit of the debtor, the credit limit (if any) is not at any time exceeded".

Section 10(3) includes provisions designed to prevent circumvention of this definition. Even if the credit limit is above £25,000 (the upper limit for a personal credit agreement) an agreement is still within the definition if at any one time the maximum amount which can be drawn down is under £25,000; or, having regard to all the relevant circumstances it is probable that the limit will not be exceeded. This latter situation is the subject of one of the examples in a schedule to the Act.  **9–24**

---

[9] Goff L.J. (as he then was) in *Jenkins v. Lombard North Central plc* [1984] 1 W.L.R.

**9–25**     Suppose that an individual runs a small shop which usually carries a stock worth about £5,000. A wholesaler makes a stocking agreement with him under which he undertakes to provide on short term credit the stock needed from time to time without any specified limit. This appears to provide unlimited credit, but because the circumstances show that the shop owner is never likely to be indebted for more than £25,000 the agreement is a consumer credit agreement.

**9–26**     The most common examples of running account credit are an overdraft or a shop revolving credit account. Fixed-sum credit is any other facility under which credit can be obtained. An obvious example would be a personal loan from a bank or a building society for a specific amount.

### Debtor-Creditor-Supplier Agreements

**9–27**     A debtor-creditor-supplier agreement can arise in three ways.[10] It occurs where a restricted use credit agreement is made to finance a transaction between a debtor and a creditor. An example would be a hire-purchase or credit sale agreement where the supplier provides the finance. Where, as is probably more common, a third party provides restricted use finance this, too, is a debtor-creditor-supplier agreement if made under pre-existing arrangements, or in contemplation of future arrangements between the creditor and the supplier. The typical hire-purchase arrangement, where the finance is provided by a finance company, is a good example, but credit card and check trading transactions provide further examples. The third situation deals with the case where a third party provides unrestricted use credit under pre-existing arrangements with the supplier in the knowledge that the credit is to be used to finance a transaction between the debtor and the supplier. This brings within the ambit of debtor-creditor-supplier agreements situations where a supplier, such as a retailer, has agreed to refer customers to a finance company which will provide them with loans which, though technically not limited to the purchase of a specific product, all parties know will be so used.

### Debtor-Creditor Agreements

**9–28**     Restricted use credit agreements which would be debtor-creditor-supplier agreements but for the fact that there are no pre-existing arrangements between the creditor and the supplier are known as debtor-creditor agreements. Restricted use credit arrangements to refinance any existing indebtedness of the

[10]  s.12

debtor are in the same category. So are unrestricted use credit agreements which are not made by the creditor under pre-existing arrangements with a supplier.[11] Examples are bank overdrafts, moneylenders' advances and loans from pawnbrokers.

**Linked Transactions**

Certain transactions are said to be linked to a regulated agreement. This is important, particularly in relation to withdrawal from, and cancellation of, agreements, as well as the provisions about extortionate credit bargains. A linked transaction is dealt with in section 19 and does not include a transaction for the provision of a security. Subject to this, it covers transactions entered into in compliance with a term in the principal agreement such as the taking out of a policy of life insurance by the debtor under a loan agreement. In a debtor-creditor-supplier agreement the sale and loan contract are linked; and there is a link where the debtor entered into a transaction in order to induce the creditor to enter into the principal credit agreement.

**9–29**

**Total Charge for Credit and Annual Percentage Rate**

A central feature of the recommendations of the Crowther Committee was the necessity for consumers to have better information about credit deals. This, it was hoped, would allow consumers to make rational decisions about credit transactions. It was also expected to benefit them by stimulating competition between lenders who would be exposed to a market where there was greater transparency.

**9–30**

In achieving this aim section 20 of the Act is one of its most important provisions. It requires the Secretary of State to make regulations for working out the true cost of credit to the borrower. This is known as the "total charge for credit" and is to be contrasted with the credit advanced. This is a most important concept for a number of reasons. For example, in relation to computing some of the monetary limits the total charge for credit is not included, only the amount of credit advanced. As we shall see, it is also relevant to the formalities which must be complied with in drafting a credit agreement, the liability of a debtor after a debtor-creditor agreement has been cancelled and the control of extortionate credit bargains. However, its most important function is probably as the first step in arriving at the

**9–31**

---

[11] s.12

Annual Percentage Rate (APR), an important piece of information which must be given to consumers and prospective consumers of credit.

**9–32**    The detailed working out of the total charge for credit and the related APR are set out in the Consumer Credit (Total Charge for Credit) Regulations 1980, as amended.[12] These are necessarily somewhat complex.[13] This is because a credit transaction may not merely include interest. There may well be other charges such as arrangement fees, maintenance charges, or insurance premiums. In giving a true picture of the cost of credit some or all of these charges may have to be taken into account. The main provisions of the regulations are regulations 4 and 5. Regulation 4 provides that, in calculating the total charge for credit, the total interest charge and any other charges at any time payable under the transaction by or on behalf of the debtor must be taken into account. Regulation 5 then provides that certain charges are to be excluded. Examples are premiums for insurance not taken out as a condition of the loan, or life insurance premiums where the proceeds of the policy will be used to repay the loan.

**9–33**    Having worked out the total charge for credit it is then possible to calculate the APR. The regulations provide three methods which may be used for doing this and there are 15 volumes of Consumer Credit Tables to assist traders.

**9–34**    The function of the APR is to provide a means of comparison between the cost of various kinds of credit and different credit offers of the same type. It has been argued that consumers have little understanding of APRs and tend to place more reliance on the size and frequency of repayments.[14] However, research by the Office of Fair Trading suggests that understanding of APRs is increasing. It was found that 64 per cent of those surveyed would generally draw the right conclusion from using APRs, even though they might not fully appreciate precisely what they represented.[15]

**Regulated Credit Agreements**

**9–35**    The meaning of this phrase requires a lengthy trawl through various sections of the Act starting with section 189(1), the definition section, which tells us that:

[12] S.I. 1980 No. 51 as amended by S.I. 1985 No. 1192 and S.I. 1989 No. 596 and the Consumer Credit (Total Charge for Credit, Agreements and Advertisements) (Amendment) Regulations 1999 (SI 1999 No. 3177).
[13] For detailed explanations of the calculation of the total charge for credit and APRs see Goode, *Consumer Credit Law and Practice* (Butterworths), Division 1C paras 29.121–29.300.
[14] *Consumers and Credit*, NCC (1980), Chap. 4.
[15] *Consumer Credit Deregulation*, 0Fr, June 1994, para. 7.14.

"'regulated agreement' means a consumer credit agreement, or consumer hire agreement, other than an exempt agreement, and 'regulated' and 'unregulated' shall be construed accordingly".

This raises a number of questions such as "what is meant by 'credit'?"; "what are consumer credit and hire agreements?"; and "which agreements are exempt?" "Credit" is very widely defined to include "a cash loan, and any other form of financial accommodation"[16] and the same section goes on specifically to say that a purchaser on hire-purchase obtains credit.

**9–36**

## Consumer Credit Agreement

The definition of a consumer credit agreement is to be found in sections 8. Section 8(2) defines a consumer credit agreement as:

**9–37**

"a personal credit agreement by which the creditor provides the debtor with credit not exceeding £25,000".[17] [A personal credit agreement is] an agreement between an individual ('the debtor') and any other person ('the creditor') by which the creditor provides the debtor with credit of any amount."[18]

It is important to note that the £25,000 limit is calculated by reference to the amount of credit advanced; interest charged is not included. For example, in the case of goods purchased on hire-purchase it is not the hire-purchase price of the goods which is relevant but the amount of the balance financed. Take the example of an individual who buys a car, the cash price of which is £26,000. Suppose that a deposit of £3,000 is paid and the finance charges are £7,000. Although the total purchase price at £33,000 is above the upper limit of the Act, the agreement is within the protection of the Act because the balance financed is only £23,000, *i.e.* the cash price minus the deposit.

**9–38**

The net result of the definition is that the Act applies to the common forms of instalment credit such as hire-purchase, conditional and credit sale as well as budget accounts, credit cards, loans and overdrafts.

**9–39**

## Consumer Hire Agreements

A consumer hire agreement is defined in section 15 as one which is made by an individual (the "hirer") for the hiring of goods to

**9–40**

---

[16] s. 9(1).
[17] s. 8 was amended with effect from May 1, 1998 by the Consumer Credit (Increase of Monetary Limits) Order 1998 (S.I. 1998 No. 996), art. 2.
[18] s. 8(1)

the hirer and which is not a hire-purchase agreement, is capable
of lasting for more than three months, and does not require the
hirer to make payments exceeding £25,000.

### WHO IS PROTECTED?

**9–41**  The definition of "individual" in the Act means that both consumer credit and consumer hire agreements may involve debtors
who are not what might usually be thought of as private consumers. This is because "individual" in the Act includes a
partnership or other unincorporated body of persons (not consisting entirely of bodies corporate).[19] Defining who should be
protected by consumer protection legislation is always difficult at
the margin, and the solution adopted in the Act is to make a
distinction between corporations (*i.e.* mostly limited companies)
and others. The merit of this approach is that it is easy to operate.
The disadvantage is that it does not identify all those requiring
protection. It can be argued that there are many small businesses
which have adopted the corporate form where those in control
are just as much in need of protection as private individuals or
those who choose to do business through partnerships or as sole
traders.[20]

### EXEMPT AGREEMENTS

**9–42**  Having discovered what a consumer credit agreement is, we next
must note that some of these agreements will be exempt from the
Act where an order has been made by the Secretary of State.
This can only apply to agreements where the creditor is a local
authority, building society, or one of a number of other organisations listed in the section such as insurance companies, friendly
societies, and organisations of workers or employers. An order
has been made, the effect of which is to exempt many loans
secured on land.[21]

**9–43**       Other parts of the same order based on other powers in
section 16 create further exemptions:

(1)  Debtor-creditor-supplier agreements financing purchases
of land which do not gain exemption under the previous
exemptions will be exempt if the number of payments to be
made does not exceed four.[22]

---

[19]  s. 189(1).
[20]  The inclusion of business consumers is under review at present, see the OFT's *Consultation Document on the Treatment of Business Consumers Under the Consumer Credit Act 1974*, Sept. 1993.
[21]  Consumer Credit (Exempt Agreements) Order 1989, (S.I.1989 No. 869).
[22]  *ibid.* art. 3(1)(b).

(2) A debtor-creditor-supplier agreement for fixed sum credit which is not hire-purchase or conditional sale where the number of payments to be made by the debtor in respect of the credit does not exceed four and must be made within 12 months of the date of the agreement. A straightforward example of this would be trade credit on terms such as payment within 30 days of invoice.[23]

(3) A debtor-creditor-supplier agreement which is not for hire-purchase or conditional sale and provides running account credit where the whole of the credit is repayable in one instalment. Examples are American Express or Diners Club cards.[24]

(4) A low interest exemption for debtor-creditor agreements, low being defined as an annual percentage rate which does not exceed 1 per cent above the highest base rate of an English or Scottish clearing bank in the 28 days prior to the making of the agreement.[25]

## PARTIALLY REGULATED AGREEMENTS

### Small Agreements

Small agreements as defined by section 17 of the Act are only partially subject to the controls in the Act. A small agreement is a regulated consumer credit agreement for credit not exceeding £50 which is not a hire-purchase or conditional sale agreement; or a regulated consumer hire agreement which does not require the hirer to make payments exceeding £50.  **9–44**

### Non-commercial Agreements

Non-commercial agreements are also freed from many of the controls of the Act such as those on the formalities about agreements and connected lender liability. Such an agreement is a consumer credit or consumer hire agreement not made by the creditor or owner in the course of a business carried on by him.[26]  **9–45**

## CONTROLLING BUSINESS ACTIVITIES

Various parts of the Consumer Credit Act regulate the way in which those in the credit industry can carry on their businesses. There are controls on advertising, canvassing for business, the  **9–46**

---

[23] S.I. 1989 No. 869, art. 3(1)(a)(i). *Zoan v. Roumba* [2000] All E.R. 620, CA.
[24] *ibid.* art. 3(1)(a)(ii).
[25] *ibid.* art. 4.
[26] s. 189(1).

marketing of credit cards, and the operation of credit reference agencies. The most important of the controls on the credit industry takes the form of the licensing system.

## THE LICENSING SYSTEM

9–47    The creation of an effective and comprehensive licensing system was one of the central recommendations of the Crowther Report. It pointed out that protective measures focusing on individual transactions, important as they are, have limited efficacy.[27] One of the members of the Crowther Commission has explained in more detail the necessity for having a licensing system:

> "No consumer legislation, however sophisticated, is likely to have more than a marginal impact if it is not underpinned by effective enforcement machinery. The Hire-purchase Acts provided no mechanism whatever for systematic enforcement. The onus was placed on the individual consumer to take the initiative in invoking the Acts. In many cases he was not equipped to do so, through ignorance of his rights, timidity or inability to incur the legal costs that might be involved. The reputable trader or finance house would endeavour to comply with the law. The less scrupulous creditor, against whose activities the legislation was primarily aimed, could afford to cock a snook — provided he stood clear of the small number of criminal offences provided by the statutes — since at worst he would lose the occasional case, and this loss was far outweighed by the benefits to be derived from diligent and persistent flouting of the statutory requirements and the recovery from uninformed debtors of sums which they could not legally have been compelled to pay."[28]

9–48    The Consumer Credit Act set up a licensing system covering, not just moneylending and pawnbroking, as had been the case prior to the Act, but all activities relating to credit. The operation of the licensing system is the task of the Director General of Fair Trading.[29]

9–49    Section 21 of the Act provides that licences are required to carry on a consumer credit or consumer hire business; and section 147 extends the licensing provisions to "ancillary credit businesses". An "ancillary credit business" means the following:

(1)   credit brokerage;

---

[27]   Crowther, para. 6.3.3.
[28]   Goode, *The Consumer Credit Act* (1979), p. 103.
[29]   s. 1.

(2)   debt-adjusting;
(3)   debt-counselling;
(4)   debt-collection;
(5)   the operation of a credit reference agency.

Most of these are self-explanatory, but the term "credit broker-   **9–50**
age" requires more comment. In addition to businesses acting as
brokers in the ordinary sense of the term it covers many dealers
and services providers. It is for this reason that retailers, for
example, even though they themselves do not provide credit,
must have a licence, because they introduce customers to sources
of finance such as hire-purchase companies.

Local authorities and bodies corporate with statutory powers   **9–51**
to carry on business are not required to have licences.

Applications for licences are made to the Director General of   **9–52**
Fair Trading and, since 1991, licences last for five years. Prior to
that time the period was 15 years and there will be many
businesses with such licences. The Office of Fair Trading estimate that there are now about 150,000, and in 1998–99 they
issued, renewed or agreed to vary consumer credit licences for
37,000 traders, of which approximately 21,000 were new licences.[30] There are two types of licence: a "standard licence" which
can be issued to sole traders, partnerships and companies, and
"group licences" which are issued where the Director General
considers that it is in the public interest to do so, rather than
require those affected to apply individually. Group licences have
been issued to the Law Society of Scotland and Citizens' Advice
Scotland.

To obtain a licence an applicant must show that the name   **9–53**
which the business will use is not misleading or otherwise
improper; and that "he is a fit person to engage in activities
covered by the licence".[31] In deciding on fitness the Director
General must have regard to any circumstances appearing to
him to be relevant. In particular he will consider evidence
tending to show that the applicant has committed offences
involving fraud, dishonesty, or violence; broken the law relating
to credit; discriminated on the grounds of sex, colour, race or
ethnic origin; or engaged in business practices which are oppressive, deceitful, unfair or improper.[32] The record of an associate of
the applicant such as an employee or agent or director of a
company seeking the licence will also be relevant.

---

[30] *The Office of Fair Trading: Protecting the Consumer from Unfair Trading
Practices*, Report by the Comptroller and Auditor General, H.C. 57, Session
1999–00, London, The Stationery Office.
[31] s. 25(1).
[32] s. 25(2).

**9–54**   In obtaining information about the suitability of applicants the Director General depends on information from various sources, but that from trading standards departments is particularly important. If the Director General is "minded to refuse" an application he must inform the applicant who may make written representations and request an opportunity to make oral submissions.[33] Appeal against a refusal of a licence lies to the Secretary of State.[34]

**9–55**   In addition to the power to refuse a licence, the Director General may revoke or suspend one that has been issued.[35] The grounds on which this may be done are that the holder has engaged in conduct which would have prevented a licence being granted in the first place. The procedures for dealing with such cases are similar to those where it is intended to refuse a licence.[36]

**9–56**   In practice few licences are refused or revoked. In 1998–99, for example, the OFT refused only 15 of the 21,200 applications for a new licence, one of the 10,000 applications for a renewal, and revoked 18 existing licences. Significantly, almost 800 traders did not proceed with applications for licences after queries from the OFT.[37] The Comptroller and Auditor General was critical of the effectiveness of the methods used to check on the suitability of applicants and, in particular, noted that arrangements to obtain evidence from trading standards departments are not working well. This seems to be related to a sharp drop in the number of licences revoked since 1995–96 despite a rise in consumer complaints.[38]

SEEKING BUSINESS

**9–57**   In any context accurate information is of importance to a consumer in coming to a rational decision about the purchase of goods and services. Where a purchase is to be made on credit this is particularly important as consumers contemplating taking on credit commitments are especially vulnerable. There is much pressure through the media to acquire goods and services, and the availability of credit can beguile people into taking on commitments that they cannot afford. In addition, it is not easy

[33] s. 27.
[34] s. 41.
[35] s. 32.
[36] The operation of the system is described in the *Annual Report of the Director General of Fair Trading*, 1993, pp. 14 and 15.
[37] *The Office of Fair Trading: Protecting the Consumer from Unfair Trading Practices*, Report by the Comptroller and Auditor General, H.C. 57, Session 1999–00, London, The Stationery Office, para 3.12.
[38] *ibid.* para 3.21.

to make comparisons between various offers of credit in the absence of common methods of setting major terms such as the rate of interest.

For these reasons the Consumer Credit Act has placed considerable importance on pre-contractual information. There are controls on advertising, requirements to provide quotations to those considering credit arrangements, and restrictions on canvassing credit agreements and distributing credit cards. **9–58**

## Advertising Controls

Part 4 of the Act regulates advertising in two principal ways. Under section 46 it is an offence to publish an advertisement which is false or misleading in a material respect. Section 44 requires the Secretary of State to make regulations as to the form and content of advertisements. These controls are in addition to other more general controls on advertising such, for example, as the Control of Misleading Advertising Regulations 1988.[39] **9–59**

The controls in the Consumer Credit Act cover any advertisements indicating that the advertiser is willing to provide credit or hire facilities. There are certain exceptions in section 43 which relate to advertisers who do not carry on a consumer hire or credit business, or a business in the course of which credit secured on land is provided to individuals, and certain agreements subject to foreign law. Also exempt from the advertising controls are those advertisements which indicate that the credit must exceed £25,000 and that no security is required, or that the security is to consist of property other than land; and those directed only to bodies corporate. **9–60**

The regulations made under the powers in section 44 of the Act are now to be found in the Consumer Credit (Advertisement) Regulations 1989[40] which came into force on February 1, 1990. The principles underlying them are that advertisements should contain nothing misleading and should give a reasonable picture of the terms on which credit is to be granted, especially its cost. They also require information about any personal factors which will be taken into account in considering whether to offer credit, and the inclusion of so-called "wealth warnings" in advertisements relating to mortgages. All methods of advertising are covered though the amendments[41] which came into effect in February 2000, which have the effect of exempting certain credit advertisements from the requirement to contain one or both of **9–61**

---

[39] S.I. 1988 No. 915
[40] S.I. 1989 No. 1125.
[41] See the Consumer Credit (Content of Quotations) and Consumer Credit (Advertisements) (Amendment) Regulations 1999 (SI 1999 No. 2725).

the warning statements "Your home is at risk if you do not keep up repayments on a mortgage or other loan secured on it" and "The sterling equivalent of your liability under a foreign currency mortgage may be increased by exchange rate movements". This exemption applies to television and radio advertisements broadcast in the course of programming whose primary purpose is not advertising, and to advertisements on film. The same amendments have been made in relation to hire advertisements.

**9–62**   The approach of the regulations, which do not apply to credit or hire for business purposes, is to divide advertisements into three types: simple, intermediate and full. Simple advertisements can give no more than the name of the credit provider and an indication of the type of business carried on. Intermediate advertisements may consist only of the advertiser's name, address or telephone number and an invitation to obtain written quotations for credit terms. Full advertisements include much more information about the credit or hire facilities and, in particular, involve disclosure of details about the cost of credit, the frequency and amount of repayments and any deposit.

**9–63**   Failure to comply with the regulations is a criminal offence.[42] Any agreement entered into, following an advertisement which did not comply with the regulations, is not invalid.

**9–64**   There have been frequent criticisms of the complexity of these regulations and the Director General of Fair Trading has accepted that they require revision. In his review of the Act he has recommended that they should be replaced by much less complex regulations focusing on the central information of importance to consumers, such as the cost of credit.[43]

**Quotations**

**9–65**   In November 1996, the then Minister for Competition and Consumer Affairs announced that the Government had decided to proceed with some of the recommendations made in the Director General's report referred to above. As part of the deregulation initiative, the Consumer Credit (Quotations) Regulations 1989,[44] were repealed, without replacement, by the Consumer Credit (Quotations)(Revocation) Regulations 1997,[45] as of March 10 1997. There are, therefore, no current regulations in force. This means that traders who provide credit facilities are

[42]   s. 164 and Sched. 1.
[43]   See *Consumer Credit Deregulation: A review by the Director General of Fair Trading of the scope and operation of the Consumer Credit Act 1974*, June 1994, Chap. 5.
[44]   S.I. 1989 No. 1126.
[45]   S.I. 1997 No. 211.

no longer under a legal obligation to set out the terms in a specified form when their customers ask for a written quotation. While in most circumstances advertisements for credit or hire facilities must state that written quotations are available on request — and businesses are obliged to supply such quotations when they are asked to do so — the way the necessary information is presented is now solely a matter for individual traders, so long as it does not mislead their prospective clients.

## Canvassing

The Moneylenders Acts banned the peddling of loans from door   **9–66**
to door. Similar but more wide-ranging controls are included in the Consumer Credit Act. Canvassing debtor-creditor agreements (of which the most common type will be personal loans) off trade premises is a criminal offence. So is soliciting the entry of an individual into such an agreement during a visit carried out in response to a request made on a previous occasion, if the request was not in writing and signed by the person making it. "Canvassing" means making oral representations off trade premises. Premises are still trade premises if a business is carried on there by the creditor, a supplier, the canvasser or, even the consumer. It does not matter that the place is only a temporary place of business such as a stand at a trade show.[46]

The Director General has exercised a power to exempt from   **9–67**
these rules the solicitation of agreements permitting the debtor to overdraw on certain types of current account, provided that the debtor already keeps an account with the creditor.[47]

## Circulars to Minors

In line with the policy of protecting vulnerable consumers, the   **9–68**
Act makes it a criminal offence to send to a person under 18 years old, with a view to financial gain, any document inviting him or her to borrow money, obtain goods or services on credit, hire goods, or even apply for information about doing any of these things. It is a defence for the accused to show that he did not know and had no reasonable cause to suspect that the person to whom the document was sent was a minor. However, where the address to which the document is sent is a school, or other

[46] ss. 48 and 49.
[47] See determination of the Director General of June 1, 1977, printed in Goode, *Consumer Credit Encyclopaedia* (1979), Vol. 3.

educational establishment for minors, reasonable cause to suspect that the recipient is under 18 will be assumed.[48]

**Distribution of Credit Tokens**

9–69 Mass mailings of Access cards gave rise to widespread criticism some years ago with the result that this practice is now banned by section 51 of the Act.[49] The section applies to "credit tokens" which are defined as:

> "a card, check, voucher, coupon, stamp, form, booklet or other document or thing given to an individual by a person carrying on a consumer credit business, who undertakes:—
>
> (a) that on production of it (whether or not some other action is also required) he will supply cash, goods and services . . . on credit, or
>
> (b) that where, on the production of it to a third party (whether or not any other action is also required), the third party supplies cash, goods and services he will pay the third party for them (whether or not deducting any discount or commission), in return for payment to him by the individual."[50]

9–70 This definition covers two party cards operated by department stores as well as three party cards such as American Express, Access and Visa. It also includes checks and vouchers issued by check and voucher trading companies, and cash cards issued by banks and building societies for use at automatic teller machines.

9–71 Credit tokens, such as credit cards, may only be distributed in response to a written and signed request. There are exceptions in the case of renewals and where the agreement is a small debtor-creditor-supplier agreement.[51]

### CREDIT REFERENCE AGENCIES

9–72 Those who lend will wish to have as much assurance as possible that borrowers will pay back what they have been lent. In the past lenders may have tended to do this through personal knowledge of clients. With the scale of credit today that is not possible and attempts to interview all borrowers would be prohibitively

---

[48] s. 50.
[49] For the only case arising out of a breach of s. 51, see *Elliot v. Director General of Fair Trading* [1980] 1 W.L.R. 977.
[50] s. 14(1).
[51] See definition at paras 9–44

expensive. Many lenders have streamlined the process by using credit scoring techniques to determine whether credit should be granted. Credit scoring is a method of assessing applications for credit using statistical techniques and is widespread amongst stores and financial institutions throughout the United Kingdom. Specialist consultants design individual scorecards for lenders using information about previous credit accounts which have been analysed to show which personal details are associated with good payment records and which with bad. When an individual applies for credit from that company, information on the application form will be combined with information from other sources to obtain a credit score.[52] Usually the other information is obtained from credit reference agencies which are organisations specialising in storing information about people's credit history.

Given the importance of credit scoring and access to credit, the accuracy of the information held by credit reference agencies is vital. Their existence also raises other issues related to privacy. For this reason the Consumer Credit Act contains protections for consumers. Section 157 imposes a duty on a creditor, owner or negotiator to respond within seven working[53] days to a written request for the name and address of any credit reference agency from which information has been sought about the customer's financial standing. The application must be made within 28 days after the end of antecedent negotiations as defined in section 56.[54] **9–73**

This obligation is complemented by section 7 of the Data Protection Act 1998 which casts a duty on a credit reference agency to give consumers a copy of any file relating to them which they have, putting it into plain English if necessary. This duty only arises where the consumer has made a written request (accompanied by a fee of £3) and given sufficient details to enable the agency to identify the file. As well as providing the information an agency must also send consumers a statement of their right to have mistakes corrected. **9–74**

This statement refers to the right set out in section 159 to have wrong and prejudicial information removed from a file or amended. Where the agency complies it must give the consumer a notice stating that it has done so and send a copy of the amended entry. Where the agency and the consumer cannot reach agreement on the issue either side may apply to the Director General of Fair Trading who will resolve the matter. **9–75**

---

[52] For further detail on how credit scoring works see *Which?*, July 1989, p.316.
[53] See the Consumer Credit (Credit Reference Agency) Regulations 1977 (S.I.1977 No. 329), reg. 3.
[54] See para. 9-79.

**9–76**    Part III of the Data Protection Act 1984 is also relevant and gives individuals whose personal data is held by a data user or data bureau an action for damages if loss is occasioned to them through unauthorised destruction, disclosure or access. There is also a right to compensation where loss is caused as a result of the information being inaccurate.

## FORMATION AND CANCELLATION OF THE AGREEMENT

### MAKING AN AGREEMENT

### Antecedent Negotiations

**9–77**    In practice there will frequently be situations where an important role in a credit transaction will be played by a person who does not provide the credit or with whom the consumer has no legal relationship because the goods are transferred to the financier before being transferred to the consumer. A typical example would be a hire-purchase transaction where the consumer selects the goods in a shop which does not provide hire-purchase finance itself, but has arrangements with a financier. As we have seen, the consumer's contract is with the hire-purchase company and the shop drops out of the picture. However, what if, in the course of discussions in the shop, false or misleading statements were made to the consumer? Under common law the hire-purchase company would not have any responsibility for the activities of the shop. The consumer would have no contractual link with the shop and thus might not be able to obtain redress.

**9–78**    Section 56 seeks to deal with this situation. The central provision is section 56(2) which states that:

> "Negotiations with the debtor ... shall be deemed to be conducted by the negotiator in the capacity of agent of the creditor as well as in his actual capacity."

**9–79**    The "antecedent negotiations" which are covered by section 56, in addition to those carried out by the owner or hirer, are set out in section 56(1). The first are those:

> "conducted by a credit-broker in relation to goods sold or proposed to be sold by the credit-broker to the creditor before forming the subject-matter of a debtor-creditor-supplier agreement within section 12(a)".

**9–80**    Section 12(a) refers to restricted-use credit. The typical situation would be a hire-purchase transaction where the credit-broker is the shop which sells the goods to the hire-purchase company which then hire-purchases them to the consumer.

The second situation is where negotiations have been:  **9–81**

"conducted by the supplier in relation to a transaction financed or proposed to be financed by a debtor-creditor-supplier agreement within section 12(b) or (c)".

This covers negotiations such as those conducted by a supplier  **9–82**
before putting consumers into contact with a finance house which, under pre-existing arrangements, provides them with loans enabling them to purchase goods or services from the supplier.

The creditor will be liable under section 56(4) for contractual  **9–83**
statements and misrepresentations made by the negotiator during the antecedent negotiations. These begin when the negotiator and the consumer first enter into communication, and for this purpose an advertisement can constitute communication. It is important to note that section 56(3) prevents attempts to exclude liability under the section.

Section 56 does not apply to implied terms or to hire contracts,  **9–84**
as opposed to hire-purchase contracts.[55] It will sometimes overlap with section 75 which is discussed below. Indeed, the two Scottish decisions on section 75 should really have been decided under section 56.[56]

Creditors or owners can be liable for a very wide range of  **9–85**
representations. It must be noted that the liability is for antecedent negotiations "in relation to goods sold or proposed to be sold" in the case of section 56(1)(b) and "in relation to a transaction financed or proposed to be financed" in the case of (1)(c). However, in *Powell v. Lloyds Bowmaker Ltd*[57] a narrow and unrealistic view of section 56(1)(b) was taken. Mr Powell had traded his Vauxhall in part exchange against a Toyota which he wished to purchase. The vendors negotiated finance on the deal and agreed that they would settle an existing hire purchase commitment (with a finance company called AIB) on the vehicle being traded in. The vendors did not settle the commitment and Mr Powell raised an action for damages basing his claim on the

---

[55] See *Lloyds Bowmaker Leasing Ltd v. MacDonald* [1993] C.C.L.R. 65; [1999] G.C.C.R. 3443 (Sheriff Court) and the English Court of Appeal decision, *Woodchester (Equipment Leasing) Ltd v. British Association of Canned and Preserved Food Importers and Distributors Ltd* [1995] C.C.L.R. 51; [1999] G.C.C.R. 1923.

[56] See *United Dominions Trust v. Taylor*, 1980 S.L.T. (Sh.Ct.) 28 and *Forward Trust Ltd v. Hornsby and Windermere Aquatic Ltd* [1996] C.C.L.R. 18 discussed at paras 9-122 to 9-125. The same error occurred in the English case of *Porter v. General Guarantee Corp. Ltd* [1982] R.T.R. 384.

[57] [1999] G.C.C.R. 3523.

proposition that by virtue of section 56(1)(b) the vendors were the deemed agents of Lloyds Bowmaker, who were thus liable for their failure to pay off the earlier hire purchase commitment. The sheriff disagreed with a decision of an English County Court judge in *UDT v. Whitfield*[58] where, on very similar facts, the finance company was held liable. He accepted that "the legislation is intended to benefit consumers and that the Crowther Report laid some stress on the need to base the law on commercial reality as opposed to legal abstractions". While agreeing that it could have applied to a representation about the price of the car he did not consider that it applied to the promise to pay off the existing hire-purchase debt.

**9–86** The English Court of Appeal decided *Forthright Finance Ltd v. Ingate*,[59] shortly after the *Powell* case. Staughton L.J. examined the decisions of *UDT v. Whitfield* and *Powell v. Lloyds Bowmaker Ltd* and the legislative origins of section 56. He stated:

> "In my judgement what s. 56(1)(b) means is that there must be goods sold or proposed to be sold by the credit-broker to the creditor, which will form the subject matter of a debtor-creditor-supplier agreement. If that condition is fulfilled, one next inquires whether there were negotiations in relation to those goods. If there were, then all that was said by the credit-broker in those negotiations is deemed to have been said on behalf of the creditor. On the other hand, what is said in any other negotiations which do not relate to those goods, is not deemed to be said on behalf of the creditor. The question is then a simple one of fact, were the negotiations in this case all relating to the goods to be sold?"[60]

**9–87** On the facts he found that only one transaction was involved and that the *UDT* case was rightly decided. Henry L.J., in agreeing, indicated that section 56 should be construed widely, stating that:

> "a narrow construction of the words would not only be artificial but would fly in the face of the clear purpose of this Act to protect consumers. While I would favour a wide construction of the words on that ground alone, subs. (4) of s. 56 seems to be to put the matter beyond doubt in favouring a wide construction."

---

[58] [1987] C.C.L.R. 60.
[59] [1997] 4 All ER 99.
[60] *ibid.* p.105.

**Form and Content of Agreements**

In a further attempt to ensure that consumers know exactly what they are doing, the Act requires the Secretary of State to make regulations as to the form and content of regulated agreements.[61] These must have provisions to ensure that a debtor or hirer is made aware of:

(a) the rights and duties conferred or imposed on him by the agreement;

(b) the cost of credit;

(c) the protection and remedies available under the Act;

(d) any other matters which it is desirable that creditors should know.

**9–88**

The regulations may require that specified information be included in a particular way, be excluded, or be brought clearly to the attention of a debtor or hirer.

**9–89**

The Consumer Credit (Agreement) Regulations 1983[62] set out in great detail the form, content, legibility and signature of documents containing regulated consumer credit and hire agreements. Different types of agreement require different types of information to be given and the regulations set out the requirements for each type in schedules. These have in common the fact that the kind of information which must be given falls into five main categories:

**9–90**

(1) a heading on the first page of the document prominently stating the legal nature of the agreement;

(2) the name and address of each party;

(3) financial information, such as the subject matter of the agreement, the timing and amount of payments, and the cost of credit, including the APR;

(4) other information about the agreement, such as details of any security provided and charges payable on default;

(5) the protection and remedies available under the Act.

The regulations also require that there should be a signature box in an agreement and go into detail on exactly how this is to be set out. In the case of credit-token agreements the name, address and telephone number of the person to whom notice is to be given of loss or misuse must be included.

**9–91**

---

[61] s. 60.
[62] S.I. 1983 No. 1553.

**9–92**    Failure to comply with the agreement regulations can have serious consequences for the creditor or hirer. Before dealing with that issue it is better to consider first the related rules in the Act dealing with the signing of agreements, the provision of copies to the debtor, and rights to cancel or withdraw.

## Proper Execution of an Agreement

**9–93**    Execution of an agreement is the technical term for the signing of it by both parties. The Act has stringent requirements about proper execution of an agreement which go well beyond simply ensuring that both parties put their names to it. To be properly executed, as the Act calls it, the following requirements must be complied with:

(1)    The document must be in the prescribed form containing all the prescribed terms and conform to the agreement regulations;

(2)    It must contain all the terms of the agreement apart from the implied terms;

(3)    It must be legible;

(4)    The requirements of sections 62 and 63 about supplying copies (see below);

(5)    The cancellation provisions of section 64 or the special provisions of section 58 for a consideration period where there is a heritable security (see below).

(6)    It must be signed in the prescribed manner by the debtor and the creditor or owner.[63]"

**9–94**    The agreement regulations require the debtor or hirer to sign within the signature box in the agreement. Where the debtor or creditor is a partnership or unincorporated association the signature may be that of someone signing on its behalf.

## Copies of the Agreement

**9–95**    The debtor or hirer must get at least one copy of an agreement and sections 62 and 63 have detailed rules about this. If the debtor signs an agreement at the same time as the creditor, a copy of the executed agreement must be given to the debtor then and there. Where an unexecuted agreement is presented to the debtor and he or she signs it but the creditor does not sign at that time, the debtor must then and there be given a copy of the unexecuted agreement. In addition, within seven days of the

[63]    Requirements 1–3 and 6 are found in s. 61.

agreement being signed by the creditor a further copy must be sent. Where an agreement is sent to the debtor a copy must also accompany it. If the agreement has already been signed by the creditor and so becomes an executed agreement on the debtor signing it, no further copy need be sent. If, however, the creditor has not signed it at that stage a copy of the executed agreement must be sent within seven days of being signed by the creditor. Copies of credit token agreements need not be given within seven days of being made as long as they are given before, or at the same time as, the credit token is given to the debtor.[64]

## Special rules for cancellable agreements

In the case of cancellable agreements these rules are modified. A copy of a cancellable agreement must contain a notice in the form prescribed by the regulations,[65] drawing attention to the right to cancel and saying how and when it may be exercised as well as the name and address of a person to whom notice may be given. As we have seen, in some cases a second copy of an agreement must be sent. In the case of a cancellable agreement it must be sent by post.[66] Where a second copy of an agreement is not required a notice containing the information about cancellation must be sent by post.

**9–96**

## Consequences of Improper Execution

Where an agreement has not been properly executed it can, at best, only be enforced against a creditor or hirer by an order of the sheriff court.[67] In some circumstances it cannot be enforced at all. The importance of this is emphasised when it is realised that enforcing the agreement includes the retaking of goods or land.[68]

**9–97**

Where an agreement is improperly executed because requirement 1 (document to be in the prescribed form) is not complied with the agreement cannot be enforced even with a court order according to section 127(3). However, the severity of this provision is qualified and the sheriff has power to order enforcement of the agreement even though there has been a failure to comply

**9–98**

---

[64] See s. 63(4). Because of the practical difficulties in some cases of complying with the requirements about copies the Consumer Credit (Cancellation Notices and Copies of Documents) Regulations 1983 (S.I. 1983 No. 1557) derogate from the full rigour of the copies rules. They also prescribe the form and content of documents to be issued as executed copies.

[65] See s. 64(1)(a) and the Consumer Credit (Cancellation Notices and Copies of Documents) Regulations 1983 (S.I. 1983 No. 1557).

[66] s. 63(3).

[67] s. 65(1).

[68] s. 65(2). See *Dimond v. Lovell* [2000] 2 All E.R. 897, HL.

with the agreement regulations. This is the case if the signed document contains all the prescribed terms that should have been in the agreement and has been signed, albeit not necessarily in the manner set out in the regulations.

**9–99**     In the case of a cancellable agreement, if the requirements of sections 62 and 63 about the provision of copies have not been complied with no enforcement order is possible unless the creditor supplies a copy of the executed agreement before legal proceedings are commenced. Providing the debtor or hirer with a copy at this time, of course, gives them the right to cancel.[69] If the creditor or hirer has omitted to give notice of the right to cancel a cancellable agreement, as required by section 64, the omission is regarded as so serious that there can be no enforcement of the agreement in any circumstances.[70]

## WITHDRAWAL AND CANCELLATION

### Withdrawal

**9–100**     It is a general principle of contract law that an offer may be revoked prior to acceptance. There is such an opportunity in the context of a consumer credit agreement where the debtor signs the agreement before the creditor or owner signs it. At this point there is an offer by the prospective debtor which has yet to be accepted by the creditor. The consumer, therefore, has an opportunity to withdraw from the agreement.

**9–101**     The Consumer Credit Act clarifies how this may be done. Section 57 provides that no special form of wording is required; all that is required is that it "indicates the intention of the [consumer] to withdraw from a prospective regulated agreement".[71] The notice of withdrawal can be written or oral. The same section also sets out the list of persons to whom such a notice can be given. Notice can, of course, be given to the creditor or hirer, but, in addition, it can be given to others who are deemed to be agents of the creditor or hirer. A credit-broker or supplier who is the negotiator in antecedent negotiations is deemed to be such an agent. Surprisingly, perhaps, so is any person who, in the course of a business carried on by him, acts on behalf of the debtor or hirer in any negotiations for the agreement. This means that if, for example, a solicitor was carrying on negotiations on behalf of a client it would be sufficient for the client to give notice of withdrawal to his own solicitor.[72]

---

[69] s. 127(4)(a).
[70] s. 127(4)(b).
[71] s. 57(2).
[72] s. 175 provides that the deemed agent is under a contractual duty to the creditor or owner to transmit the notice to the him forthwith.

Withdrawal has the same effect as cancellation and is **9–102**
discussed below.[73]

**Cancellation**

In some circumstances someone who has entered into a con- **9–103**
sumer credit or hire agreement may cancel it. The period during
which an agreement may be cancelled is popularly known as the
"cooling off" period. The reasons for such protection in the
context of the Hire-Purchase Acts, which is where it was first
introduced, is succinctly set out by Professor Goode:

"It was aimed primarily at the doorstep salesman who, taking
advantage of the unsuspecting housewife, would there and
then sign her up ... to an onerous agreement for goods she
might not be able to afford, frequently inducing her entry into
the agreement by oral misrepresentations of various kinds,
secure in the knowledge that no-one else was present to
overhear him and that the organisation he represented would
rely on the agreement to disclaim any responsibility for his
statements."[74]

The present cancellation provisions apply to a much wider range **9–104**
of agreements than the Hire-Purchase Acts rules did. They are
set out in sections 67 to 73 of the Act.

A regulated consumer credit or hire agreement may be can- **9–105**
celled if two conditions are met. First, oral representations by an
individual acting as, or on behalf of, the negotiator must have
been made in the presence of the debtor or hirer during the
course of antecedent negotiations. In addition, the subsequent
agreement must not have been signed by the debtor or hirer at
trade premises of either the creditor or owner, or the negotiator,
or any party to a linked transaction (other than the debtor or
hirer or a relative of his). While it is often said that the cancellation provisions apply to doorstep sales it should be noted that
they can apply in other circumstances. If, for example, the
consumer discusses the proposed transaction at a shop or in the
offices of a finance company but takes the agreement away and
signs it at home it will be cancellable.

The "cooling-off" period begins when the debtor or hirer signs **9–106**
the unexecuted agreement. It ends five days after the second
statutory notice or copy is received by the debtor or hirer. To
exercise the right to cancel a notice must be served within the
cancellation period on one of a number of people. This notice,

[73] See paras 9-109 to 9-111.
[74] Goode, *The Consumer Credit Act* (1979), p.196.

unlike notice that one is withdrawing from a prospective agreement, must be in writing. However, it need not be in any particular form. It is sufficient if it "indicates the intention of the debtor or hirer to withdraw from the agreement".[75] If it is posted it is deemed to be served on the recipient at the time of posting, whether or not it ever arrives.[76]

**9–107** The notice can be given to any one of several people. These are the same people to whom an intention to withdraw from a prospective agreement may be sent,[77] as well as anyone specified in the statutory cancellation notice.[78]

**9–108** The effect of a notice of cancellation is to cancel the agreement and any linked transaction; and to withdraw any offer by the debtor or hirer, or a relative, to enter into a linked transaction.[79]

To this there are some exceptions. Where the agreement is a debtor-creditor-supplier agreement for restricted-use credit to finance the doing of work or the supply of goods to meet an emergency it cannot be cancelled. If the same sort of agreement is used to finance the supply of goods which have been incorporated in land or something else before service of the notice of cancellation it cannot be cancelled.[80]

**9–109** Section 71 makes clear that where an agreement other than a debtor-creditor-supplier agreement for restricted-use credit is cancelled it still remains alive for the purposes of repayment of credit and the payment of interest. This provision would be important where the credit under a personal loan had been advanced before the end of the cooling-off period. It would be inequitable if the consumer could simply keep the loan. While the section prevents this, its other provisions are likely to discourage lenders from advancing loans early as there are considerable disadvantages from their point of view.

**9–110** Some linked transactions also survive the cancellation of an agreement. These are insurance contracts, guarantees, and deposit and current accounts.[81]

**Consequences of cancellation**

**9–111** The debtor or hirer can recover any sum paid under the agreement or linked transaction except for the first £5 of any fee or

---

[75] s. 69(1).
[76] s. 69(7).
[77] See para. 9.101.
[78] s. 69(1).
[79] See para. 9.101.
[80] s. 70(2).
[81] Consumer Credit (Linked Transactions)(Exemptions) Regulations 1983 (S.I. 1983 No. 1560). Insurance contracts might be cancellable under the Insurance Companies Act 1982.

commission charged by a credit-broker. Any sum payable by the debtor or hirer or his relative under the agreement ceases to be payable. For any sum repayable the consumer has a lien on any goods in his possession under the cancelled agreement.[82]

Should the consumer have acquired goods under a restricted **9–112** use debtor-creditor-supplier agreement which is subsequently cancelled, they must be restored to the person from whom they were obtained. All that is required of consumers is that they should, if they receive a written request, hand them over at their own premises. While the goods are in their possession they must take reasonable care of them. This obligation does not apply to perishable or consumable goods which are consumed prior to cancellation. In this case the consumer will receive a windfall.[83]

Should goods have been given in part-exchange, the debtor or **9–113** hirer is entitled to their return in substantially the same condition as when they were given. This must be done within 10 days of cancellation by the consumer, otherwise the debtor or hirer is entitled to a sum equal to the part-exchange allowance.[84]

**Certain conveyancing transactions**

Because of the conveyancing difficulties that would arise, the **9–114** cancellation provisions do not apply to agreements secured on heritable property. Instead there is a "consideration period" during which the consumer can reflect on the wisdom of the proposed transaction and, if he or she has second thoughts, withdraw from it. The way that this works is that the creditor or hirer must, at least seven days before sending an agreement for signature, send a copy. With this copy must be sent a notice in the prescribed form indicating the consumer's right to withdraw and saying how and when the right may be exercised. During the period for consideration the creditor must not approach the consumer in any way except in response to a specific request from the consumer.[85]

This consideration period does not apply in two situations.[86] **9–115** The first is where the agreement is a restricted-use credit agreement to finance the purchase of the heritable property which is the subject of the security. The other is where the agreement is for a bridging loan in connection with the purchase of the land subject to the security, or other land. The reason for this is that in both these situations speed may be of the essence if the deal is not to fall through.

---

[82]  s. 70.
[83]  s.72.
[84]  s.73.
[85]  ss. 58 and 61(2).
[86]  s. 58(2).

## DURING THE AGREEMENT

**Implied Terms**

**9–116**  In a credit transaction there will be terms relating to the credit and others relating to the goods or services supplied. We will first look at the latter. This leads to discussion of terms relating to the quality of the goods or services, the title of the supplier and the date of delivery. In all credit transactions there will be implied terms relating to such matters. The source of these terms will depend on the type of contract concerned. In many credit transactions the goods will be supplied under a contract of sale and the implied terms will be those to be found in sections 12 to 14 of the Sale of Goods Act 1979. This is so in the case of conditional sale, credit sale and the supply of goods paid for by means of a credit card. In the case of hire-purchase the implied terms are almost exactly the same but they are to be found in sections 8 to 11 of the supply of Goods (Implied Terms) Act 1973 as redrafted by the Consumer Credit Act 1974. The exact wording is to be found in Schedule 4, paragraph 35. As these terms are so similar to those in the Sale of Goods Act reference should be made to the discussion in Chapter 5. The ability of a trader to exclude these terms is restricted and this is discussed in Chapter 10.

**9–117**  As a result of the insertion in the Supply of Goods and Services Act 1982 of a Part IA applying to Scotland[87] there are there are now statutory implied terms for hire. These are set out in sections 11H–11K. They are very similar to those in contracts of sale and other contracts for the supply of goods.[88]

**9–118**  While the use of implied terms in credit transactions is nothing new, there is a novel provision relating to the liability of those involved in such transactions. In certain circumstances, the consumer has a claim not only against the supplier of the goods or service but also the provider of the credit. Section 75 of the Act provides that:

> "(1) If the debtor under a debtor-creditor-supplier agreement falling within section 12(b) or (c) has, in relation to a transaction financed by the agreement, any claim against the supplier in respect of a misrepresentation or breach of contract, he shall have a like claim against the creditor, who, with the supplier, shall accordingly be jointly and severally liable to the debtor."

---

[87]  By the Sale and Supply of Goods Act 1994, s. 6 and Sched. 1.
[88]  For discussion see Chap. 4.

This is what is commonly known as "connected lender liability" **9–119**
and it has considerable advantages for consumers where it
applies. For the section to apply four conditions must be met:

(1) the cash price of the goods or service being supplied must
exceed £100 but not be more than £30,000 (including
VAT);

(2) there must be a debtor-creditor-supplier agreement regulated by the Act, *i.e.* an agreement where credit of not more
than £25,000 is advanced to an individual and which is not
exempt under the Act;

(3) the provider of the credit is in the business of giving credit
and the credit agreement is made in the course of that
business; and

(4) the credit is advanced under pre-existing arrangements, or
in contemplation of future arrangements, between the provider of credit and the supplier.

One of the most common situations where connected lender **9–120**
liability applies is a credit card transaction such as Access or
Visa. It would also apply where a consumer wished to buy a car
from a motor dealer and the dealer arranged finance with a
finance company with whom he had pre-existing arrangements.
It would not apply where the consumer wished to buy the car and
went to his bank and arranged a personal loan, even where the
bank was aware that the loan was specifically for the purchase of
the car. In this case the credit is not advanced under pre-existing
arrangements between the supplier and the bank and there is not
a debtor-creditor-supplier agreement. It should also be noted
that debit cards provided with current accounts are not within
this protection, nor are payment cards like Diner's Club or
American Express where credit must be paid off at the end of
each month.

Section 75 has no relevance to hire-purchase, conditional sale **9–121**
or credit sale agreements, despite the comments of the judge in
*Porter v. General Guarantee Corporation*[89] in relation to a hire-
purchase agreement. This is because of the way in which such
agreements are structured. The dealer sells the goods to the
finance company which then supplies them to the consumer. Any
claim for breach of the supply contract must be against the
finance company which is both creditor and supplier as far as the
consumer is concerned.

---

[89] [1982] R.T.R. 384.

**9–122**     There has been practically no litigation on this section. An OFT
report says that there have been no reported or unreported cases
in the English High Court.[90] The only reported case seems to be
the sheriff court decision in *United Dominions Trust Ltd v.
Taylor*.[91] In that case Mr Taylor had purchased a second hand car
from a dealer in Glasgow. The purchase was financed through a
loan from the defenders which had been arranged by the dealer
who had arrangements for this purpose. This was, therefore, the
kind of transaction to which section 75 could apply. The car
proved to be so unsatisfactory that after several months Mr Taylor
sought to rescind the contract of sale. He also stopped making
payments to the finance company and, when sued, invoked section
75. He argued that because the dealer had made misrepresentations to him about the condition of the car he had an action for
rescission against the dealer. By virtue of section 75 he said that he
had a like claim against the finance company, *i.e.* a claim to rescind
the loan contract. This the sheriff principal accepted.

**9–123**     The case has been the subject of considerable academic criticism and is generally thought to have been wrongly decided.[92]
The Sheriff Principal relied on the policy of the Act and the
wording of the section to justify his decision. Both, it is submitted, are weak arguments. The policy argument that credit and
supply contracts that are linked stand or fall together is simply
not consistently applied throughout the Act. The policy of the
section is to make the creditor vicariously liable for the actions of
the supplier. Where the debtor has a claim against the supplier,
say for breach of the implied term about satisfactory quality, he
or she may assert it against either the supplier or the creditor.
The argument on the language of the section would seem to
point that way too. The use of the word "claim" suggests a
monetary claim rather than a right of rescission.

**9–124**     Ironically, in this case, had Mr Taylor been better advised and
a better case presented to the sheriff-principal, the same result
could have been achieved by a legally correct route. It is not clear
why Mr Taylor did not invoke section 56.

**9–125**     While, in Mr Taylor's situation, section 56 would have allowed
him to escape from the credit transaction, it will not work in
some other cases. However, someone in the predicament in

---

[90]   See *Connected Lender Liability: a review by the Director General of Fair
Trading of section 75 of the Consumer Credit Act 1974*, OFT, March 1994,
p. 11.
[91]   1980 S.L.T. (Sh.Ct.) 28. Followed in *Forward Trust v. Hornby*, 1995 S.C.L.R.
574.
[92]   For a comment by a Scottish commentator see Davidson, "The Missing
Linked Transaction" (1980) 96 L.Q.R. 343. Other criticisms are to be found in
1981 J.B.L. 179, and Guest and Lloyd, *Encyclopaedia of Consumer Credit*,
p. 2074/3.

which Mr Taylor found himself may well not wish to continue with the loan. If it is accepted that *United Dominions Trust Ltd v. Taylor* is wrongly decided is there another solution? It is suggested that there is. A court might accept that the credit contract was void for frustration, though there must be some doubt about this.[93] Alternatively, the debtor might invoke the early repayment provisions of the Act. They provide only a partial solution because the rebate takes into account the setting up charges involved in credit transactions and the debtor will still be out of pocket. The part of the loan which the debtor cannot recover through the early repayment provisions could be regarded as loss flowing directly from the supplier's breach of contract. This could be included in a claim against the supplier or against the creditor as part of a section 75 claim.

While creditors are liable under section 75 it should be noted **9–126** that they are entitled to be indemnified by suppliers for any liability incurred. They can, and this is the policy of the section, protect themselves by ensuring that dealers with whom they enter into arrangements are reputable.

In relation to section 75 liability there are some grey areas, **9–127** mostly in relation to credit card transactions. Credit card companies take the view that it does not apply where the card was first taken out prior to July 1977, the date when the section came into force. However, they voluntarily accept section 75 liability in such cases but limit it to the amount of the transaction charged to the cardholder's account. They also argue, but with much less plausibility, that transactions by authorised users are not covered by section 75 and that in some situations payments for travel and package holidays are not covered.[94]

Some credit granters take the view that section 75 liability is **9–128** unfair to them, and during the review of it recently conducted by the Director General of Fair Trading lobbied hard to persuade him to restrict it.[95] In a 1994 report he observed that "connected lender liability is, and remains, an important consumer protection measure that has proved its worth over the years. It is an integral part of the safeguards for consumers built into the Act".[96] However, in a second report issued in 1995, he recommended that in credit card transactions liability should be limited to the amount charged to the card in respect of the purchase in question.[97]

---

[93] See 1981 J.B.L. 179.
[94] For arguments against the views of the credit card companies see the OFT's report, *Connected Lender Liability*, pp. 28–31, supra.
[95] *ibid.*
[96] *ibid.* p. 33.
[97] *Connected Lender Liability: A Second Report by the DCFR on section 75 of the Fair Trading Act 1975*, OFT, May 1995.

## INFORMATION REMEDIES

**9–129**     As part of the policy of ensuring that consumers have appropriate information, the Act provides in sections 77 and 78 that they have the right to obtain information from the creditor about such matters as the amount already paid and the amount owing. To supplement the early repayment provisions in sections 94 and 95, section 97 obliges the creditor to inform consumers of the amount required to settle their accounts. Those hiring goods have similar rights under section 79. Those who have agreed to act as sureties are entitled, on payment of a fee, to similar information.[98]

## NOTICE ABOUT CERTAIN ACTIONS

**9–130**     Agreements will often allow creditors to demand early repayment, recover possession of goods or land, or treat any right under the agreement as terminated. Such action cannot be taken without giving the consumer at least seven days notice in an approved form.[99] Debtors must be given at least seven days notice of variations of agreements before they can become effective.[1]

## APPROPRIATIONS OF PAYMENTS

**9–131**     A debtor who has more than one agreement with a creditor may not be able to make a payment which discharges the total sum due under the agreements. Section 81 provides that each agreement should be credited with that proportion of the payment which each sum due bears to the whole sum due under the various agreements. For example, suppose that there are two agreements under which £100 and £50 are due and the debtor can only afford to pay a total of £90. £60 will be appropriated to the agreement under which £100 was due and £30 to that under which £50 was due.

## LIABILITY OF CREDIT CARD HOLDERS

**9–132**     Unless the card has been used with the consent of the cardholder, the maximum liability of the cardholder is £50. However, if someone has acquired the card with the consent of the cardholder there is no limit on liability. Once the cardholder has

---

[98]   See ss. 107–109.
[99]   s. 76 and the Consumer Credit (Enforcement, Default and Termination Notices) Regulations 1983 (S.I. 1983 No. 1561) as amended by S.I. 1984 No. 1109.
[1]   s. 82 and the Consumer Credit (Notice of Variation of Agreements) Regulations 1977 (S.I. 1978 No. 328) as amended by S.I. 1979 Nos. 661 and 667.

given notice of loss or misuse there is no further liability. Notice
is effective when received. If given orally the credit token agreement can stipulate that it is not effective unless confirmed in
writing within seven days.[2]

## TERMINATION AND DEFAULT

In this section we are, with the possible exception of the early    **9–133**
settlement rules, dealing with cases where consumers have run
into financial difficulties. In such a situation they are particularly
vulnerable and the policy of the law is to provide a measure of
protection against the worst excesses of some elements of the
credit industry. As a practical point, it may be said in passing that
consumers encountering difficulties are well advised to seek help
sooner rather than later. Generally speaking, creditors are willing to be accommodating where, as is usually the case, the
difficulties stem from some unexpected cause such as domestic
problems, unemployment or illness.

### TERMINATION

At this point termination is being considered in the sense of the    **9–134**
statutory right of the debtor or hirer voluntarily to bring the
agreement to an end. Later, we shall be discussing the circumstances surrounding termination by the creditor or hirer.

As a response to financial difficulties, termination, using the    **9–135**
rights given in sections 99 to 101 of the Act will rarely be in the
consumer's interests. However, the facility is available.

Regulated hire-purchase and conditional sale agreements may    **9–136**
be terminated by the debtor at any time before the final payment
falls due by giving notice to anyone who is entitled to receive
payments under the agreement. To this right there are two
exceptions, both relating to conditional sale agreements. Such an
agreement relating to land, title to which has passed to the buyer,
or one relating to goods where the property has vested in the
debtor who has transferred the goods to someone else, cannot be
terminated.

Termination only operates for the future. Section 99(2) makes    **9–137**
clear that liability which has accrued prior to termination is not
affected. On termination the debtor must pay the difference
between what has been paid and half the total price of the goods.
In making this calculation any installation charge is deducted
first and the whole of that charge added as it is clearly reasonable
that such a charge should be payable. It is possible that the

---

[2]  s. 84(5)

amount due could be less if it can be shown that the creditor's loss is less.

**9–138** In the case of a consumer hire agreement there is also a right to terminate, but the earliest time at which this can occur is 18 months after the making of the agreement. Notice of not less than the shorter of the shortest payment interval or three months must be given. Because early termination can cause hardship to the owner there are three circumstances in which the right is not available. These are: where the total payments, ignoring sums payable on breach, exceed £1,000 in any year; where the goods are let out for the hirer's business and were selected by him and acquired by the owner at his request from a third party; and, finally, where the hirer requires the goods to re-let them in the course of business.

**EARLY SETTLEMENT**

**9–139** At any time during a regulated consumer credit agreement the debtor may give notice to the creditor of an intention to complete payments early.[3] This is only economic if there is a rebate on the total charge for credit and regulations prescribe how this is to be calculated.[4]

**DEFAULT**

**9–140** Where the debtor is in default of the obligations under a regulated consumer credit or hire agreement the Act provides various protections. We have already seen that before a creditor can take action against a debtor a default notice must be served specifying the breach and what action needs to be taken to remedy it. If it is not capable of remedy the amount of compensation required and the date by which this must be paid has to be stated. *Eshun v. Moorgate Mercantile Co. Ltd*[5] is an example of the result of failure to comply with the similar provisions of the Hire-Purchase Act 1965. The defendant finance company was ordered to pay compensation to the debtor for the loss caused by terminating his agreement.

**9–141** A remedy which is open at common law to creditors in the case of hire-purchase and conditional sale is repossession of the goods. Under these agreements the consumer does not acquire title to the goods initially and it is usual for agreements to provide that there shall be this right in case of default. This can operate very harshly where the consumer has paid a substantial

---

[3] s. 94.
[4] See the Consumer Credit (Rebate on Early Settlement) Regulations 1983 (S.I. 1983 No. 1562) as amended by S.I. 1989 No. 596.
[5] [1971] 1 W.L.R. 722; [1971] 2 All E.R. 402.

proportion of the price, and in the past some creditors abused their rights. As a result, "snatch back" provisions were enacted in the Hire-Purchase Act 1938. Similar provisions are now found in sections 90 and 91 of the Consumer Credit Act.

Under these provisions, if the debtor has paid one third or **9–142** more of the total price of the goods, and the property in the goods remains in the creditor, the goods are known as "protected goods". This means that the creditor is not entitled to recover possession from the debtor except on an order of the sheriff court. Where an installation charge is part of the total price the amount relevant for deciding whether the goods are protected is calculated by adding the installation charge to one third of the remainder of the total price. It is not possible for a creditor to circumvent this protection by making a fresh agreement which includes goods additional to those which were protected under an earlier agreement, or by modifying an agreement.[6]

This protection also applies where the debtor has died. In this **9–143** case the person in possession of the goods benefits initially from the protection and, after confirmation has been granted, the executor.[7]

The "protected goods" provision only applies where the goods **9–144** have been recovered "from the debtor". This includes anyone to whom the debtor has entrusted the goods, such as a garage in which a car has been left for repair, or someone to whom the goods have been lent. However, if the goods have been abandoned the restrictions on repossession do not apply. This is illustrated by *Bentinck Ltd v. Cromwell Engineering*[8] where the debtor had obtained a car on hire-purchase. After the car had become protected goods he defaulted on the repayments and the car was seriously damaged in an accident. Following the accident the debtor took the car to a garage and then disappeared and could not be traced. The hire-purchase company did manage to trace the car, which by then had been at the garage for some months, and repossessed it. In this action against the defendants, who had agreed to act as sureties, it was held that there was such clear evidence of an intention to renounce all rights to the goods that the equivalent of section 90 did not apply.

Protected goods may be repossessed without a court order if **9–145** the debtor consents. The cases show that the courts will wish to be satisfied that the consent is a genuine and informed consent. In *Chartered Trust v. Pitcher*[9] the debtor, having lost his job,

---

[6] s. 90(3) and (4).
[7] s. 90(6).
[8] [1971] 1 Q.B. 324.
[9] [1987] R.T.R. 72.

telephoned the hire-purchase company to say that he could not keep up the payments on his car and was advised to write to them asking them to repossess the car. The letter that he wrote clearly showed that he did not want to do this and that he was hoping that some other solution might be possible. Without telling him that the car was protected goods, and that on an application to repossess the court might reschedule the payments, the car was repossessed. It was held that this was in breach of what is now section 90.[10]

9–146    Where the debtor does not choose to hand over the goods it is arguable that in Scotland it is always necessary to obtain a court order to recover them. This is certainly the case where the goods are on someone's premises whether or not they are "protected goods". Section 92(1) of the Consumer Credit Act 1974 provides that:

> "Except under an order of the court, the creditor or owner shall not be entitled to enter any premises to take possession of goods subject to a regulated hire-purchase agreement, regulated conditional sale agreement or regulated consumer hire agreement."

9–147    Section 173 provides that this provision cannot be overridden by anything in the agreement between the debtor and the creditor.[11]

9–148    This leaves the question of the creditor's right to repossess goods which are not on "premises". In practice this means repossessing goods found in the street or a public road and will apply mainly to cars, motorcycles, caravans and the like. Before there can be any question of repossession the debtor must be in breach of an agreement which has a term allowing the creditor in those circumstances to repossess the goods (which invariably agreements do have). The creditor must also have served a default notice (as required by section 87) which has expired.

9–149    The reason that it is suggested that it is never possible to repossess goods under Scots law is that the policy of the law is against such a self help remedy as the nineteenth century institutional writer, Professor Bell, explained:

> "Possession attempted to be acquired by force may be resisted by force; but possession, being once obtained in this way, must be reclaimed by the true creditor judicially; the party who has

---

[10]   The facts of this case are less likely to recur now as the statutory default notice must give more detailed information about a debtor's rights than was the case at the time of this case or the harsh and unrealistic decision in *Mercantile Credit Co. Ltd. v. Cross* [1965] 2 Q.B. 205.

[11]   If the goods are on someone else's premises, *e.g.* a garage, it would appear that the consent needed is that of the owner of those premises.

ceased to possess being bound to trust to the protection of the law for restitution, and not to the strength of his own arm."[12]

If this is the case where possession has been obtained by force how much more powerful where possession has initially been obtained perfectly legally under a hire-purchase or conditional sale agreement. Professor Walker expresses similar views in his book, *Remedies*,[13] though he would allow more latitude to those recovering property.[14] Nevertheless he points out that the repossession must be carried out without committing trespass, assault or any other wrong. This will often be quite difficult to achieve if, for example, the hirer is in the vicinity. In short, Professor Gow's observation[15] that "it seems that the owner who resorts to self help acts at his peril" has still much to commend it. The parliamentary draftsman also thinks so to judge by the statement in the notice required by paragraph 7 of Schedule 2 of the Consumer Credit (Enforcement, Default and Termination Notices) Regulations 1983. After pointing out that protected goods can only be recovered by the creditor against the wishes of the debtor by means of a court order it adds "[i]n Scotland he may need to get a court order at any time".

9–150

### JUDICIAL CONTROL

As part of the policy of trying to provide adequate protection for those involved in credit transactions, the Consumer Credit Act 1974 gives wide powers to the sheriff court in relation to credit agreements. Such powers do, of course, suffer from the inherent disadvantage of private law remedies that consumers must take some action. It is well known that consumers rarely invoke these protections.

9–151

Before considering the various ways in which the courts can regulate agreements it is worth noting the rules about jurisdiction. We have already seen that actions relating to consumer credit agreements must be brought in the sheriff court. This is an advantage for consumers in that expenses in that court are lower than in the Court of Session. In addition, the jurisdiction rules assist the consumer in that actions relating to the enforcement of such agreements, and most other actions relating to them, must be brought in the sheriff court of the place where the debtor is domiciled or carries on business.[16] However, if the purpose of the

9–152

---

[12] *Dictionary and Digest of the Law of Scotland* (7th ed.), p.826.
[13] p.39
[14] Walker, *Remedies*, pp. 263-264.
[15] *The Law of Hire Purchase* (2nd ed., 1968).
[16] s. 141(3A)(a) and (b) which were added by the Civil jurisdiction and Judgements Act 1982, Sched. 12, Pt 2, para. 4.

action is to determine proprietary or possessory rights or security rights over moveable property, the action may be brought in the sheriff court of the place where the property is located.[17]

## ENFORCEMENT ORDERS

**9–153**    We have already seen that in certain circumstances an agreement can only be enforced by means of a court order. Indeed, in the case of a cancellable agreement, if the rules about supplying copies have not been complied with there is no possibility of enforcing, even by means of a court order. This is also the case where the agreement has not been properly executed. However, enforcement is still possible if all the prescribed terms have been set out in a document even if the statutory formalities have not been complied with.

**9–154**    Where an application has to be made to the sheriff it must be dismissed only if the sheriff considers that it is just to do so taking into account two sets of circumstances. First, account must be taken of the prejudice caused to any person by the contravention, and the degree of culpability for it. In addition, the powers which the court has under sections 135 and 136 must also be taken into account. These give wide powers to vary agreements; and the implication of referring to them in this context is that, by using them, it may be possible to remove any disadvantageous aspects of an agreement by their use.

## TIME ORDERS

**9–155**    Section 129 of the Act gives wide powers to the sheriff to make time orders. These are orders which permit the sheriff to adjust the rate and time of payments of instalments by debtors, hirers or sureties. In addition, they can be used to specify the time within which a breach of an agreement, other than non-payment of money, should be rectified.

**9–156**    A time order may be made in a variety of circumstances. It is possible where there has been an application for an enforcement order or in any other action to enforce a regulated agreement or a security, or to recover possession of goods or heritable property to which an agreement relates. Debtors or hirers can apply for a time order where default notices have been served on them.

**9–157**    In deciding on the making of a time order the sheriff must consider whether it is just to do so taking into account whether the sum suggested is reasonable, having regard to the means of the debtor, hirer or surety. Section 130 deals with the situation

---

[17]    s. 141(3A)(c).

where the debtor has made an offer to pay instalments which has been accepted by the creditor. In such a case a time order may be made without hearing evidence of means. In the case of hire-purchase and conditional sale agreements only, time orders dealing with instalments may deal with sums not yet due.[18] Sheriff Fitzsimmons has recently held that wide as these powers are they do not extend to varying the rate of interest.[19] In England, the Court of Appeal has held in *Southern and District Finance plc v. Barnes*[20] that this is possible under section 136 and approved of the decision of a county court judge who used this power.

### FINANCIAL RELIEF FOR HIRERS

Those who hire goods do not have the benefit of the protected goods rule which applies only to hire-purchase and conditional sale agreements. Prior to the Consumer Credit Act they could find themselves in a particularly difficult and unfair position when they ran into financial difficulties.[21] They might have had use of the goods for only a short time yet, on failure to keep up payments, might become liable to pay substantial sums. Section 132 now provides a solution in this situation. It applies where an owner has recovered possession of goods otherwise than by court action. The hirer may ask the sheriff to order that the whole or part of any sum paid should be repaid, and that the obligation to pay any sums owed should cease.

**9–158**

The only reported case on section 132 appears to be *Automotive Financial Services Ltd v. Henderson.*[22] The defenders had leased a car, the purchase price of which was £8,144, from the pursuers. After the agreement had run for six months they got into financial difficulties, stopped making the rental payments, and the pursuers repossessed the car. By this time the defenders had made payments of £2,150 under the lease. The car was sold by the pursuers for £6,000 and they then sued for £3,840 as an amount due under the terms of the agreement. The defenders asked the Sheriff Principal to exercise his discretion under section 132 but he refused to do so saying:

**9–159**

"To suggest that somehow the payments made should entitle the defenders to relief seems to me an unlikely proposition

---

[18] s. 130(2).
[19] See *Murie McDougall Ltd v. Sinclair*, 1994 SLT (Sh. Ct.) 74; 1994 S.C.L.R. 805.
[20] [1996] 1 F.C.R. 679.
[21] For an example see *Galbraith v. Mitchenhall Estates Ltd* [1965] 2 Q.B. 473.
[22] 1992 S.L.T. (Sh. Ct.) 63.

unless the defenders can set out a good reason why the pursuers should be satisfied in the commercial sense with what they have received. The defenders have not attempted to do so. Looking at the matter another way they have not even started to suggest that the payment sought is by way of a penalty."

**9–160**    The Sheriff Principal upheld the decision on appeal saying that this was an exercise of discretion based on a proper assessment of relevant materials. He did not think that it was appropriate to use either of the formulae which the defenders had put forward to justify invoking the section's protection. These were to base the operation of section 132 on the interest and administration costs incurred by the lessors during the period during which the defenders had the car; or the monetary value of the depreciation of the car during the same period.

**9–161**    On the facts this seems a suitable case for the exercise of section 132. For a car, the purchase price of which was £8,144, the pursuers were found to be entitled to recover just short of £12,000 from the defenders within six months of entering into the agreement. Even allowing for the fact that the pursuers will have incurred various costs this seems excessive. The problem may have been that the sheriff did not feel able to exercise his discretion on the basis of the financial information put before him by the defenders. The moral of this case may be that more sophisticated accounting information should be produced to support an application.

### SPECIAL POWERS RELATING TO HIRE-PURCHASE AND CONDITIONAL SALE AGREEMENTS

**9–162**    In cases of hire-purchase or conditional sale agreements section 133 contains special provisions involving *return orders* and *transfer orders*. Such orders may be made where an application for an enforcement order or time order has been made, or where the creditor has brought an action to recover possession of goods. These powers can be exercised together with the power to make a time order or vary an agreement. The *return order* is self explanatory, being an order for the return of goods to the creditor.

**9–163**    A *transfer order* can only apply where the agreement relates to more than one item of goods. In such a situation an order can be made transferring to the debtor the creditor's title to some of the goods and the return to the creditor of the remainder. Such an order can only be made where the debtor has already paid an amount at least equal to the part of the total price which relates to the goods transferred and one third of the unpaid balance of the total price. The goods transferred shall be "such of the goods to which the agreement relates as the court thinks just".[23]

## EXTORTIONATE CREDIT BARGAINS

One of the most far-reaching powers given to the courts is the power in sections 137–140 to reopen a credit bargain which it finds to be extortionate so as to do justice between the parties. This power has its origins in the provisions of the Moneylenders Acts but goes much further. Unlike most of the other provisions of the Consumer Credit Act, it applies not only to regulated credit agreements but also to all credit agreements with individuals. This means that a loan of £250,000 to an individual could be challenged on this ground. It does not apply to hire agreements where section 132 may be seen as the nearest parallel. **9–164**

It is one of the weaknesses of this part of the Act that section 139(1) provides that a sheriff can reopen a credit bargain on the grounds of extortion only on the application of the debtor or a surety. It was held in *United Dominions Trust v. McDowell*[24] that the sheriff cannot do so of his own volition.[25] **9–165**

Section 138(1) provides that a credit bargain will be extortionate if either it: **9–166**

"(a) requires the debtor ... to make payments ... which are grossly exorbitant, or

(b) otherwise grossly contravenes ordinary principles of fair dealing."

In making a judgement on these matters sheriffs are to have regard to evidence adduced on prevailing interest rates, the age, experience, business capacity and health of the debtor. They must also take account of the financial pressure that he or she was under at the time the bargain was entered into, as well as any other relevant considerations. From the creditor's point of view the sheriff must consider the degree of risk taken, having regard to any security provided, the relationship to the debtor, and whether or not a colourable cash price was quoted for any goods or services. This latter point is included to prevent a transaction being dressed up to seem as if the rate of interest is lower than, in truth, it is by inflating the alleged purchase price. **9–167**

An important point to note is that dealing with the burden of proof. Section 171(7) provides that where a debtor or surety **9–168**

---

[23] s. 133(3).
[24] 1984 S.L.T. (Sh. Ct.) 10.
[25] The Consumer White Paper pointed out at para. 5.21 that this is under review at the moment.

alleges that a bargain is extortionate it is for the creditor to prove the contrary. This can be important, particularly if the matter is finely balanced. It is, of course, necessary for the debtor to produce some sort of evidence to give substance to the allegation, rather in the way that, in a criminal trial where a defence such as provocation is alleged, the accused must produce some evidence to show that there is an issue to discuss.

**9–169** It is important to note that the test applies to the credit bargain, not just a credit agreement. If one or more other transactions are to be taken into account in computing the total charge for credit the test applies to the credit agreement and those other related transactions. These might include various fees such as arrangement fees.

**9–170** If a sheriff finds that a credit bargain is extortionate there are wide powers "for the purpose of relieving the debtor or a surety from payment of any sum in excess of that fairly due and reasonable".[26] The whole, or any part, of any obligation imposed by the credit bargain may be set aside and the creditor may be made to repay the whole, or any part, of a sum paid under the credit bargain or any related agreement by the debtor or a surety. In addition, the sheriff has power to alter the terms of the credit agreement or any security instrument and direct the return to a surety of any property provided as security.

**9–171** These are potentially draconian powers and it is, perhaps, not surprising to find that little use has been made of them. In its 1991 report, *Unjust Credit Transactions*,[27] the Office of Fair trading could find only 23 court cases in which they had been used or mentioned, in only four of which was the debtor successful. There seems to have been no Scottish case in which a debtor has raised the issue, although there is passing reference to it in two reported cases.[28]

**9–172** One reason for the small number of cases may be the absence of guidance in those that have been reported; and the evidence that they contain that the courts will not easily be persuaded that a bargain is extortionate. There has been some division of opinion on whether the courts should look for guidance to the Moneylenders Act. In one of the few English High Court deci-

---

[26] s. 139(2).

[27] *Unjust Credit Transactions: A report by the Director General of Fair Trading on the provisions of sections 137–140 of the Consumer Credit Act 1974*, OFT, Sept. 1991.

[28] In *Bank of Scotland v. Davis*, 1982 S.L.T. 20 there is a reference to the potential relevance of the power; and in *United Dominions Trust v. McDowell*, 1984 S.L.T. (Sh.Ct.) 10 the sheriff seems to have decided that the bargain was extortionate. His decision was overruled on appeal on other grounds and the sheriff principal expressed doubt about the correctness of the view that the bargain was extortionate.

sions, *Ketley v. Scott*,[29] it was said that "sections 137–140 are a completely new set of provisions and it is idle to seek guidance from the old Moneylenders Acts of 1900 and 1927 to try to interpret them". However, in a later Court of Appeal decision[30] Russell L.J. notes with apparent approval the view in *Halsbury's Statutes* that "it seems that the word extortionate is to be equated with the words 'harsh and unconscionable'", which appear in the Moneylenders Act. Neither of these cases is binding on a Scottish court, but it is submitted that *Ketley v. Scott* demonstrates the correct approach. If Parliament had intended to use the previous test it would have used the earlier language. In providing new language it must be assumed to have intended to alter the test.

What factors seem to have been important in the successful cases? In *Barcabe v. Edwards*[31] an English county court substituted a flat rate of 40 per cent which would have given an APR of 92 per cent under the original terms of a loan. The debtors had borrowed £400 for the purchase of a car at a flat rate of almost 100 per cent, an APR of 319 per cent. The fact that they had little business capacity, that there was no unusual risk for the lender, and that one of the debtors could not read were taken into account, as was evidence that similar lenders were charging flat rates of 20 per cent. **9–173**

In *Devogate v. Jarvis*[32] the debtors had borrowed £10,000, on security, to pay off existing debts at an APR of 39 per cent. An APR of 30 per cent was substituted, despite the fact that the original rate was not unusual for the type of loan, the court taking into account the fact that there was security justifying a lower rate. Also relevant was the inequality of bargaining power flowing from the desperate financial circumstances of the debtors. The relatively low risk and the fact that the loan was secured were also important in the judge reducing the flat rate of interest from 42 per cent to 21 per cent in *Prestonwell Ltd v. Capon.*[33] The fact that the debtors were under financial pressure, had little business acumen and did not have access to proper legal advice were also relevant. An interesting aspect of this decision is that the judge did not limit comparisons of interest rates to the consolidation loans sector of the market in which it had been obtained. **9–174**

Another successful case is *Shahabinia v. Gyachi*[34] where loans with flat rates of interest of 78 per cent, 104 per cent and 156 per cent were considered extortionate and reduced to a flat rate of 30 per cent. **9–175**

[29] [1981] I.C.R. 243.
[30] *Shahabinia v. Gyachi* (1989) Lexis.
[31] [1983] C.C.L.R. 11.
[32] 1987, county court, unreported.
[33] 1988, county court, unreported.
[34] *ibid.*

**9–176**     *Falco Finance Ltd v. Michael Gough*[35] is one of the few cases
where the agreement was found to be extortionate under section
138(1)(b), on the ground that it grossly contravened ordinary
principles of fair dealing rather than involving grossly exorbitant
payments. This involved a dual rate mortgage under which the
"normal" interest payments of 13.99 per cent (flat rate) were
initially discounted to 8.99 per cent, providing every monthly
payment was made on time. This concession was lost perma-
nently for the life of the mortgage if any payment was missed or
was in any way deficient. The court viewed this as unacceptable
as there was no attempt to calculate, in any genuine way, the loss
to the company by late payment, or conversely any gain received
by prompt payment; the conditions to retain the concession were
so harsh that it was almost impossible to comply with them for
the whole period; and there was no possibility of reclaiming the
concession.

**9–177**     Some guidance can be obtained from unsuccessful cases. The
OFT report notes that the highest rate of interest not held to be
extortionate has been 48 per cent. One of these was *Ketley v.
Scott*,[36] where the debtor had business experience and the risk
was relatively high. The judge also observed that even if he had
found the extortion test had been satisfied he would not have
given relief on the ground that this would not have been just
between the parties. The reason for this was that the debtor had
been deceitful in not disclosing the full extent of his financial
commitments and had falsified the value of the house on the
security of which the loan was given.

**9–178**     While it is not easy from case reports to assess the fairness of
decisions it is difficult to dispel the impression that in some cases
the courts have been less than realistic and unwilling to make full
use of the width of the definition of extortionate. A good
example is *Wills v. Wood*.[37] An elderly lady with little business
experience and no capital, except her cottage, borrowed £3,000
secured on the cottage at 12 per cent. The county court judge
found the bargain extortionate on the second limb of the definition, observing that the debtor was in severe financial difficulties
with no source of income or capital from which to meet her
liabilities. He added that had "she received independent advice I
am satisfied she would have been strongly advised against borrowing". The Court of Appeal upheld the creditor's appeal
stating that the debtor was of full age and capacity and no
"unworldly recluse". It was suggested that she could have sold
her cottage to meet her debts. The Master of the Rolls noted that

---

[35]  (1999) 17 Tr. L.R. 526, Macclesfield County Court.
[36]  [1981] I.C.R. 243.
[37]  (1984) 128 S.J. 222.

the word was *extortionate*, not *unwise*, and that the situation came nowhere near one in which the court could reopen the bargain.

*Coldunell Ltd v. Gallon*[38] is another case the result of which might occasion some surprise. The borrowers were a man of 86 and his wife of 91 who borrowed money on the security of their home which was their only capital asset. The creditor knew that the money was needed to help their son, who promptly ran off with it, and that they had not had independent legal advice. In the English Court of Appeal Oliver L.J. said that a creditor could discharge the burden of proof "by showing that the bargain was on its face a proper and not extortionate commercial bargain and that [the creditor] acted in the way that an ordinary commercial lender would be expected to act". In finding that this bargain was not extortionate he added that there was no obligation on the creditor to ensure that the couple had obtained independent legal advice or that the security was executed in the presence of a solicitor. **9–179**

In the circumstances it is not surprising that the Office of Fair Trading believes that the extortionate credit provisions have not dealt adequately with the problem of socially harmful lending which the Crowther Report identified.[39] This it believes is because the drafting of the Act is unnecessarily restrictive, or has been interpreted in that way, with undue emphasis on the cost of credit. New forms of lending have emerged into which no sensible person with independent advice would enter but which creditors have induced them to do by exploitation or deception. Another reason is consumer ignorance of the law and a reluctance to resort to the courts because it might jeopardise future access to credit. This is in addition to the various practical, cultural and financial factors which tend to inhibit going to court. **9–180**

The Office of Fair Trading recommends sweeping reforms deal with harmful lending. While noting that the E.C. Directive on Unfair Contract Terms might alleviate the problem, it considers that the problem is sufficiently serious to warrant specific legislation. The Office proposes that the concept of "unjust credit transaction" should replace that of "extortionate credit bargain". A finding that the transaction involved excessive payments, not grossly exorbitant payments, should be a factor in determining whether the transaction was unjust. A new test of deception, oppression, impropriety or unfairness, using the criteria used to assess the fitness to hold a consumer credit licence, would replace the "ordinary principles of fair dealing" test. One **9–181**

[38] [1986] 1 All E.R. 429, C.A.
[39] *Unjust Credit Transactions*, para. 4.18.

of the most important proposals is that, in addition to the right of
a debtor to invoke this protection, sheriffs should have power of
their own motion to reopen agreements, and the Director General, and other enforcement authorities, should be given power
to apply to the courts for a declarator that a credit transaction is
unjust. With a view to linking with the licensing regime, it is also
proposed that the courts should be required to notify the Director General of all cases where an unjust credit transaction has
been reopened.[40]

**9–182**    These proposals, as the OFT report recognises, are not a
complete answer to the problem of socially harmful lending.
They need to be complemented by enforcement action against
illegal moneylending and those who regularly act oppressively
against consumers. Better advice and information would also
alleviate the problem for consumers. The development of other
forms of lending would also be beneficial. Credit unions have not
had the success in Scotland (or the United Kingdom as a whole)
that they have had, for example, in Ireland or North America.
Even the advent of all these measures would still not solve the
problems of those most at risk and there is no escape from the
conclusion that wider questions of social policy are involved in
this issue.

---

[40]  See *Unjust Credit Transactions*, Chap. 5.

CHAPTER **10**

# UNFAIR CONTRACT TERMS

## INTRODUCTION

This chapter is concerned with the problem of the fairness of **10–01**
terms found in contracts. It will deal mainly, but not exclusively,
with exclusion clauses. Such clauses are often unfair to consumers but other terms of a contract can also be unfair and, as we
shall see, to some extent these too can be controlled.

The problem of exclusion clauses or exemption clauses, as **10–02**
they are also called, is one that has a long history. It is common
to find one party to a contract limiting or excluding entirely the
legal liability that would otherwise attach. Everyday examples
are to be found in any package holiday brochure, car hire
contract or a furniture remover's contract. The following are
some examples:

(1) All cars parked at the owner's risk.

(2) All photographic materials are accepted on the basis that
    their value does not exceed the cost of the material itself.
    Responsibility is limited to the replacement of films. No
    liability will be accepted, consequential or otherwise, how-
    ever caused.[1]

(3) In the case of loss or damage the liability of the company is
    limited to the value of the garment.

(4) All claims must be notified to the company within seven
    days.

(5) Our liability to you in contract law or in tort or delict or
    otherwise howsoever arising in relation to this contract is
    limited to £1,000,000 for any one incident or related series

---

[1] This is taken from *Woodman v. Photo Trade Processing Ltd*, June 20, 1981,
Exeter County Court, unreported.

of incidents and £2,000,000 for any series of incidents related or unrelated in any period of 12 months.

**10–03**  Such clauses are frequently found in standard form contracts. These are contracts drawn up by one party setting out the terms on which it will do business. Such contracts are not necessarily objectionable. Indeed, they can be seen as the legal or administrative counterpart of mass production and marketing. Using such forms cuts out the necessity for detailed negotiation in every transaction and saves time and money. Standard forms and their exclusion clauses work best where both parties know and understand their significance and can take appropriate action to protect themselves against any potential hardship resulting from the other side limiting its liability.

**10–04**  These are conditions which generally do not exist in the typical consumer transaction. How many of us even realise that when we travel by rail, for example, that we are travelling on the rail companies' Conditions of Carriage which contain exclusion clauses? Even where we do know that there are exclusion clauses in the small print of, say, a car hire contract, how often do we stop to read them. If we did read them would we understand them and would it make any difference? Lord Denning answered that question in his usual forthright way. "The big concern said, 'Take it or leave it.' The little man had no option but to take it."[2]

**10–05**  The underlying approach of the law has been informed by the doctrine of freedom of contract. This fails to take account of the power imbalances in consumer situations, a fact which has been recognised both by the common law and by legislation. How the law has intervened to control the use of exclusion clauses is discussed below under three main headings. First, we consider the role of the common law; then the intervention of the legislature, mainly through the Unfair Contract Terms Act 1977; and finally, the regulations implementing the Unfair Contract Terms Directive are discussed.

## COMMON LAW CONTROLS

**10–06**  In controlling exclusion clauses the common law applies two techniques. The first is to consider whether the clause is part of the contract, *i.e.* has it been incorporated into the contract? If so, the second question is: does it cover the situation that has arisen? These techniques are in addition to the various doctrines referred to below under which contracts may be struck down

---

[2]  *George Mitchell (Chesterhall) Ltd v. Finney Lock Seeds Ltd* [1982] 3 W.L.R. 1036, at p. 1043.

because of some other element of unfairness. The protection of those under the age of 18 whose contracts may be reopened if "prejudicial" is also relevant as is the law on extortionate credit bargains.[3]

## INCORPORATION

The parties may have agreed that the exclusion clause is to be **10–07** part of the contract. The easiest way to demonstrate this is to show that a document including that clause has been signed. There can then be no argument, in the absence of fraud or misrepresentation, that the consumer is bound by the agreement. Support for this proposition can be found in *Henderson v. Stevenson* where, in a Scottish appeal to the House of Lords, the Lord Chancellor observed that where a document had been signed "there might, indeed, be a question what was the construction of the contract, or how far the contract was valid. But there could be no question whatever that the contract, such as it was, was assented to and entered into by the person who received the ticket".[4]

A case where this principle did not apply because the effect of **10–08** the clause had been misrepresented to the consumer is *Curtis v. Chemical Cleaning and Dyeing Co.*[5] Staff at a dry cleaners incorrectly assured a customer that a clause exempted the cleaners only for limited kinds of damage when it covered any kind of damage. Fraudulent conduct by the party seeking to rely on the clause would have the same effect. It should be remembered that the concept of fraud in Scots law in relation to the annulment of obligations is wide and, as Professor Smith pointed out, can cover not only what Bell in his *Principles* called "a machination or contrivance to deceive", but also conduct inconsistent with bona fides.[6]

Quite commonly there is no signed document and the trader **10–09** relies on an unsigned document such as a railway ticket, a receipt for dry-cleaning or a notice on the premises. The notice or ticket may itself contain the exclusion clause or it may refer, as for example, railway tickets do, to another document. What is the effect of such documents or notices? It must first be shown that the exclusion clause is contained in a contractual document, as

---

[3] See Chap. 9.
[4] (1875) 2 R. (H.L.) 71, at p. 74. The English case of *L'Estrange v. Graucob* [1934] 2 K.B. 394, provides an example of the harsh consequences of this rule in operation. It has been argued that the case could have been decided differently.
[5] [1951] 1 All ER 631.
[6] See Smith, *Short Commentary on the Law of Scotland* (1962), p. 833.

*Taylor v. The Corporation of the City of Glasgow*[7] demonstrates. Mrs Taylor had gone to public baths run by the corporation. On entering she paid for the facility that she wished to use and was given a ticket. On the front were the words "For conditions see other side" and on the reverse were words excluding the corporation's liability for injury caused to users of the baths. As a result of the negligence of the corporation Mrs Taylor sustained serious injuries in a fall. The corporation sought to rely on the exclusion clause on the ticket. The Inner House held that the clause did not protect the corporation because it was not a contractual document. It was merely "a domestic check on the defenders' running of their establishment, the register and the ticket having taken the place of the old-fashioned turnstile. It also performed the function of a receipt . . . this voucher aspect of this 'ticket' was the significant aspect". The court refused to attach the same significance to this kind of ticket as courts have traditionally done to tickets relating to contracts of carriage or deposit.

10–10    To be effective the exclusion clause must be brought to the attention of the other party before the contract is made. This is the rationale of *Olley v. Marlborough Court*[8] where a couple booked and paid for a room on arriving at the reception desk of an hotel. In their room was a notice exempting the hotel from liability for loss of personal belongings. Some of their belongings were stolen from the room and the hotel sought to rely on the exemption clause. It was held by the English Court of Appeal that the guests' contract had been concluded when they booked the room and the notice which they saw subsequently was not part of that contract. This approach was also one reason for the decision in *McCutcheon v. MacBrayne*,[9] a Scottish appeal to the House of Lords.

10–11    Where the document containing the exclusion clause can be said to be contractual in nature it is still necessary to show that the party relying on the clause has done, to quote Lord Dunedin in *Hood v. The Anchor Line (Henderson Brothers) Ltd*, "what was reasonably sufficient to bring to [the other party's] notice the existence of the condition."[10] It was stated in the same case that what is reasonable notice depends on the facts.

10–12    As indicated above, it appears that the courts will be more easily satisfied that reasonable notice has been given where contracts of carriage or deposit are concerned. The high point

[7]   1952 S.C. 440.
[8]   [1949] 1 K.B. 532.
[9]   1964 S.C. (H.L.) 28.
[10]  1918 S.C. (H.L.) 143, at p. 149.

was probably reached in the English case of *Thompson v. London Midland & Scottish Railway Co.*,[11] where it was held that an illiterate lady whose niece had bought a ticket for her had been given reasonable notice of a clause by a reference on the ticket to the fact that it was issued subject to the conditions set out in the company's timetable. The conditions could be found on page 552 of that timetable which could be purchased for 6d. The Inner House came to a similar decision in *Gray v. London and North Eastern Railway Co.*[12] Mr Gray had bought his own ticket and admitted that he knew that there was writing on it, though he had not read it.

The courts have not found notice to be sufficient where a **10–13** ticket for a ferry crossing contained an exclusion clause on the back but there was no reference to this on the face of the ticket.[13] The same result occurred where the face of the ticket did refer to conditions on the back but the reference was in the smallest known type and presented in such a way as easily to be overlooked.[14]

In other situations the courts have been less inclined to incor- **10–14** porate exclusion clauses. In *Grayston Plant Ltd v. Plean Precast Ltd* it was said in the Inner House that it is wrong to apply "the principles of the 'ticket' cases, which are based on matters of practicability and reasonableness peculiar to 'ticket' contracts ... to a very different kind of case".[15] The court went on to refer with approval to the dictum of Denning L.J. in *Spurling v. Bradshaw*[16] that "the more unreasonable the clause is, the greater the notice which must be given of it". In *Thornton v. Shoe Lane Parking Ltd*[17] Lord Denning had suggested that there were some clauses that were so oppressive that they would only be effective if placed in a box in red print with a hand pointing to them.

In theory it seems that an exclusion clause might be incorpo- **10–15** rated even though no notice was given on the occasion when a problem arose if it was merely one of a number of occasions when the parties had contracted. This is referred to as incorporation by means of a course of dealing and might arise where a

[11] [1930] 1 K.B. 141.
[12] 1930 S.C. 989.
[13] *Henderson v. Stevenson* (1875) 2 R. (H.L.) 17.
[14] *Williamson v. The North of Scotland and Orkney and Shetland Navigation Co.*, 1916 S.C. 554.
[15] 1976 S.C. 206.
[16] [1965] 1 W.L.R. 461
[17] [1971] 2 Q.B. 163. See also *Interphoto Picture Library Ltd v. Stiletto Visual Programmes Ltd* [1988] 1 All E.R. 348, C.A.

consumer has frequently contracted with the same trader and their contracts have normally contained an exclusion clause. This argument was put forward in *McCutcheon v. MacBrayne*,[18] where the pursuer's car had been lost when MacBrayne's ferry sank. The pursuer was a frequent customer of MacBraynes both for transporting vehicles and livestock. It was their usual, though not invariable practice, to require the customer to sign a risk note which contained an exclusion clause. They did not do so on the relevant occasion but argued that the pursuer, through a course of dealing with them, knew that goods were shipped on standard terms containing such a clause. This argument failed in the House of Lords. It was accepted that there could be incorporation in this way, but the course of dealing must be both consistent and lengthy. In this case the evidence showed that the pattern of dealings was not consistent, a risk note having to be signed on some occasions but not on others. While there are examples of incorporation by means of a course of dealing in the law reports none concerns a consumer contract.

## CONSTRUCTION

**10–16**     If it is established that the clause is part of the contract the next step is to consider whether it protects the party relying on it in the circumstances. With the passage of the Unfair Contract Terms Act 1977 the courts will probably not resort to some of the mental gymnastics that were necessary in the past to do justice. However, it is still true that the courts will construe exclusion clauses strictly and against a party seeking to rely on them. The principle, often known by the Latin tag, the *contra proferentem* rule, can be traced back to Stair[19] and has frequently been employed by the courts. In *McKay v. Scottish Airways Ltd* it was said in the Outer House in a judgment approved by the Inner House that:

> "It is well settled that clauses exempting a carrier from liability fall to be construed strictly and *contra proferentem* . . . . Only clear and unambiguous language will suffice to exclude a common law liability, and as the language used in conditions

---

[18]   1964 S.C. (H.L.) 28

[19]   "*Verba sunt interpretanda contra proferentem* (words must be construed unfavourably to those who drafted them) where the parties are skilful, or are known to have trusted skilful persons in forming of the writs; and therefore the same should be as much extended in favour of the other party, as their sense can bear." *Institutes* (More's edition) IV. 42. 21.

expressed on a ticket is language framed and devised by the carriers themselves, it will . . . fall to be construed in the sense most unfavourable to the carrier who sells the ticket and most favourable to the passenger who buys it."[20]

An example of the principle in operation in a consumer context  **10–17**
is *Graham v. The Shore Porters Society*.[21] Mr Graham arranged to have his belongings moved from Glasgow to Aberdeen by the defenders. While in their custody they were destroyed by fire. The carriers argued that they were protected by the following clause in the contract:

> "The contractors shall not be responsible for loss and damage to furniture and effects caused by or incidental to fire or aircraft, but will endeavour to effect insurance on behalf of the customer on receipt of instructions".

Applying the *contra proferentem* rule, the Court of Session held  **10–18**
that this clause did not protect the carriers. They were liable to their customer under the contract to take reasonable care of his goods and also had a statutory duty to him. The court considered that the clause only excluded liability for statutory duty and that the carriers still owed their contractual duty of care to the customer.

The courts look with particular disfavour on clauses seeking to  **10–19**
exempt one party from the consequences of negligence on the ground that it is inherently unlikely that this is what the parties intended. It has, however, always been accepted in Scotland, which did not flirt with the doctrine of fundamental breach as the English courts did, that a properly worded clause could exclude any kind of liability. With the passing of the Unfair Contract Terms Act 1977 the House of Lords has made clear that it will approach construction of clauses in a less hostile manner. In particular, it has been stated that clauses limiting liability will be treated less unfavourably than those entirely excluding it.[22] The cases in which this point has been made are commercial cases and may not be relevant to consumer situations.[23]

---

[20]  1948 S.C. 254, at p. 256.
[21]  1979 S.L.T. 119.
[22]  *Ailsa Craig Fishing Ltd v. Malvern Fishing Co. Ltd*, 1982 S.L.T. 377.
[23]  See *Mars Pension Trustees v. County Properties and Developments Ltd*, 1999 S.C.L.R. 117 (I.H.) where Lord Prosser considered the proper approach to construing contracts where there was an attempt to exclude liability which would otherwise attach. This was in the context of a case to which the legislative controls did not apply.

## A WIDER PRINCIPLE?

**10–20**   It is arguable that Scots common law had the capacity to control terms in contracts, including exclusion clauses, on more general grounds.[24] In *McKay v. Scottish Airways Ltd*[25] Lord Cooper observed that the:

> "remarkable feature of these conditions is their amazing width, and the effort which has evidently been made to create a leonine bargain under which the aeroplane passenger takes all the risks and the company accepts no obligation, not even to carry the passenger or his baggage nor even to admit him to the aeroplane."

**10–21**   He went on to note that it had not been "argued that the conditions were contrary to public policy nor that they were so extreme as to deprive the contract of all meaning and effect as a contract of carriage". He reserved his opinion on these matters but was clearly inviting lawyers to develop a wider principle for attacking exclusion clauses. This has not been done and there is now less need or scope for such an approach with the enactment of the Unfair Contract Terms Act 1977 and the Unfair Terms in Consumer Contracts Regulations 1999.[26]

## STATUTORY INTERVENTION

**10–22**   In the absence of some wider principle, such as Lord Cooper appeared to be advocating, the common law controls on exclusion clauses were bound to have limited power to protect consumers even in the hands of the most sympathetic judges. With care, it was possible to ensure that exclusion clauses were incorporated in contracts, and careful drafting could ensure that they were appropriate to exclude or limit the liability of the trader. As Lord Reid recognised, "[t]his is a complex problem which intimately affects millions of people and it appears to me that its solution should be left to Parliament."[27] Legislative action has been taken in a number of forms; the most important of which are the Unfair Contract Terms Act 1977 and the Unfair Terms in Consumer Contracts Regulations 1999.

---

[24]   See McBryde, "Extortionate Contracts", 1976 J.L.S.S. 322 where a number of cases are referred to.

[25]   1948 S.C. 254, at p. 263.

[26]   S.I. 1999 No. 203, which replaced the original regulations of the same name. See S.I. 1994 No. 3159.

[27]   *Suisse Alantique Societe d'Armement Maritime SA v. N-V Rotterdamsche Kolen Centrale* [1967] A.C. 361, at p. 406.

## THE UNFAIR CONTRACT TERMS ACT 1977

The Unfair Contract Terms Act 1977 followed the second report **10–23**
on exemption clauses by the Law Commissions[28] and was introduced as a private member's bill. The title of the Act is confusing
in that it both understates and overstates its scope. The title of
the original bill, the Avoidance of Liability Bill, more accurately
describes its purpose. The Act does not deal with all terms in
contracts which might be considered unfair. It may be the case
that the price is thought to be too high or the contract gives wide
latitude to the supplier in relation to delivery. Neither of these
terms would be within the scope of the Act. On the other hand,
the title is too narrow in that it applies not only to contract terms
but also with notices attempting to restrict or exclude liability for
negligence.

It is important to note that before one need consider the **10–24**
relevance of the Act it must be established that the clause is
validly incorporated into the contract. This point is expressly
made in section 24(2), so the common law on incorporation is
still relevant. Similarly, even if the clause is validly incorporated
it must be demonstrated that it covers the breach that has
occurred.

Part 2 of the Act applies exclusively to Scotland, and Part 3, **10–25**
which applies to the whole of the United Kingdom, is also
relevant. The Act applies to more than just consumer transactions, but it is only with these that this chapter is concerned.

### Scope

The approach of the Act is to set out those types of contract to **10–26**
which it applies. This covers a wide range of contracts and
certainly includes many contracts which would be regarded as
consumer contracts, such as contracts for the supply of goods
and services.[29] Contracts relating to the liability of an occupier of
land to persons entering or using it are covered. This is important
as it will cover situations such as attendance at cinemas, theatres,
zoos and sporting events. Since April 1, 1991 the controls of the
Act apply to non-contractual notices.[30] A notable exception to
the scope of the Act is insurance contracts. The insurance
industry argued that it would be very difficult to distinguish
between a genuine attempt to define the insured risk and an
exclusion of liability.

---

[28] See *Exemption Clauses: Second Report* (1975) Scot. Law Com., No. 39.
[29] See s. 15.
[30] As a result of The Law Reform (Miscellaneous Provisions)(Scotland) Act
1990, s. 68.

**10–27**    The Act does not define an exclusion clause. There are various references to terms which "exclude or restrict" liability and section 25(3) amplifies what this means. It makes clear that it includes making the liability or its enforcement subject to any restrictive or onerous conditions. Clauses requiring claims to be notified within a short time limit would be covered by this. Clauses which exclude or restrict any right or remedy or hamper someone in pursuing a remedy are also caught. An example would be a clause limiting a consumer to a remedy in damages where he or she would otherwise be entitled to rescind the contract. A third way in which the phrase is amplified is by stating that it covers clauses excluding or restricting any rule of evidence or procedure.

**10–28**    Section 23(5) is important in that it states that references to excluding or restricting liability for breach of an obligation or duty "shall include a reference to excluding or restricting the obligation or duty itself". This is an anti-avoidance provision designed to stop attempts to get round the controls on exclusion clauses by saying that one party has no legal obligation in the first place. For example, it is clear that section 20 of the Act covers attempts to exclude or restrict the obligation to provide goods of satisfactory quality. What section 25(3) makes clear is that this cannot be subverted by clauses stating that the subject matter of the sale is an article not guaranteed to meet those standards.[31] In *Ferguson v. Littlewoods Pools Ltd*[32] the "honour clause" seeking to make the arrangement between a pools company and its clients one that gave rise to no legal obligations was considered. In *obiter dicta* it was considered that such a clause might be subject to the Act. This, presumably, would be by applying s 23(5). In *Halloway v. Cuozzo*[33] the English Court of Appeal in a very similar situation appear to have assumed that the provisions of the Act did not affect the existence of a contract and, even if they did, the honour clause would be found to be reasonable.

**10–29**    The Act is aimed at exclusion of liability by businesses. "Business" is defined in section 25(1) as including "a profession and the activities of any government department or local or public authority".

**Consumer Contracts**

**10–30**    The term "consumer contract" is used in several sections of Part 2 of the Act and, by and large, the controls on consumer

---

[31]   See Peel, "Making More Use of the Unfair Contract Terms Act 1977: Stewart Gill Ltd v. Horatio Myer & Co Ltd" (1993) 56 M.L.R. 98.

[32]   1997 S.L.T. 309 (O.H.).

[33]   (1999) unreported Lexis.

contracts are more stringent than on contracts between businesses. It is therefore advantageous for the person faced with an
exclusion clause to be able to show that they come within the
definition. It is helpful to consumers that the party claiming that
the contract is not a consumer contract bears the burden of
proving that proposition. It is defined in section 25(1) as follows:

"a contract (not being a contract of sale by auction or competitive tender) in which

(a)  one party to the contract deals, and the other party to the
contract ('the consumer') does not deal or hold himself
out as dealing, in the course of a business, and
(b)  [where the contract involves the transfer of the ownership or possession of goods] the goods are of a type
ordinarily supplied for private use or consumption".

This definition shows that consumers can have exclusion clauses      **10–31**
imposed on them when buying at auctions. The status of consumer is lost, not only if the dealing is in the course of a business,
but also if it occurs while holding oneself out as so dealing. This
points out the pitfalls for those private individuals who, for
example, gain access to wholesale stores that make it clear that
they deal only with trade customers.

There may be some difficulty in deciding whether goods are      **10–32**
"ordinarily supplied for private use or consumption". There are
some articles which are mainly purchased by businesses but
which are not infrequently acquired by private individuals.
Examples might be provided by equipment hiring businesses
where a wide range of apparatus is available for hire. Some of the
more sophisticated items will probably normally be hired to
business users, but it is quite possible that someone might hire
them for their own private purposes.

It appears that businesses can in some circumstances come      **10–33**
within the definition of consumer. Suppose that a firm of solicitors buys a carpet for its office. This is an article which is
"ordinarily supplied for private use or consumption", but is it to
be regarded as purchased "in the course of a business"? The view
of the English courts has been that it is not.[34]

---

[34]  See *Peter Symmons & Co. v. Cook* (1981) 131 N.L.J. 758. The approach of the
English Court of Appeal in *Stevenson v. Rogers* [1999] Q.B. 1028, a decision
on the meaning of in the course of a business in s. 14 of the Sale of Goods Act
1979 suggests that a narrower view should be taken of the meaning of
*consumer* in the 1977 Act. his case is under appeal to the House of Lords.

**Clauses controlled by the Act**

10–34   The Act controls attempts to exclude or restrict liability by means of contracts or notices in four main situations. These are in relation to breach of duty; in consumer and standard form contracts; indemnities and guarantees; and terms implied in contracts for the supply of goods.

*Breach of Duty*

10–35   The Law Commissions in their second report on exemption clauses concluded that "clauses or notices exempting from liability for negligence are in many cases a serious social evil"; it is hardly surprising that section 16 of the Act should control their use. Section 16 covers more than just liability for negligence. It speaks of breach of duty which covers a number of different situations, as the definition of breach of duty in section 25 of the Act makes clear. The first of these is breach of any obligation to take reasonable care or exercise reasonable skill which arises from the express or implied terms of a contract. Thus, exclusion clauses in a wide range of trades and professions are covered. These would include contracts by professional people such as accountants, solicitors or architects, as well as non-professional services provided by garages or dry cleaners. All these service providers have an obligation to perform their services with reasonable skill and care.

10–36   The definition also applies to any common law duty to take reasonable care or exercise reasonable skill. This covers situations where the delictual duty of care arises as developed in the line of cases originating with *Donoghue v. Stevenson*. Finally, it also includes the common law duty to take reasonable care under section 2(1) of the Occupiers Liability (Scotland) Act 1960. In a consumer context this might be relevant where attempts to exclude liability are made at playgrounds, funfairs and other places of amusement or recreation.

10–37   Where a clause or notice attempts to exclude liability for death or personal injury arising from breach of any of these duties it is void and of no effect. This is a most important and wide-ranging provision. Cases such as that of *Taylor v. The Corporation of the City of Glasgow* would now never reach the courts as, no matter what the ticket said or whether it could be regarded as a contractual document, anything which purported to exempt from liability for personal injury or death could have no effect.

10–38   Where an exclusion clause seeks to exclude liability for other loss or damage arising from breach of duty it can be relied on, but only to the extent that it is "fair and reasonable" to do so.[35] What is fair and reasonable is discussed later. This provision redresses the balance between consumers and those who provide them with such services as drycleaning, car-parking or furniture removing.

The controls in section 16 are not intended to affect the **10–39** defence of *volenti non fit injuria.* This is a defence to a delict action which applies where it can be shown that a person willingly accepted the risk of injury. It could be argued that although an exclusion clause could not protect a defender from liability it could prevent liability arising in the first place if it were interpreted as a warning of a risk. Section 16(3) prevents this result by providing that where a contract term is void by virtue of section 16 of the Act the fact that a person agreed to, or was aware of, that term "*shall not of itself* be sufficient evidence that he knowingly and voluntarily assumed any risk". [Emphasis added.]

*Consumer and Standard Form Contracts*

Section 17 of the Act controls attempts in consumer and stand- **10–40** ard form contracts to exclude contractual liability. It overlaps with other sections of the Act and it must be remembered that it may be more advantageous to use one of those other provisions. For example, as we shall see below, in some circumstances it is not possible to exclude liability imposed by the implied terms found in the Sale of Goods Act 1979. This is clearly more useful than relying on this provision which applies only a reasonableness test.

The section deals with both consumer and standard form **10–41** contracts. As we are concerned only with consumers all references will be to consumer contracts, the meaning of which has been discussed at paragraph 10–30, above. The reasonableness test is applied to three situations. It applies where a trader tries to limit liability when in breach of contract; claims to be entitled to perform the contract in a way substantially different from that which was reasonably expected of him; or claims that he is entitled to render no performance at all.

In practice, section 17 is likely to apply most frequently to **10–42** contracts for services. *McKay v. Scottish Airways Ltd*[36] contains the sort of clause which would be subject to the first and third of the situations which the section deals with. The second part could apply to the sort of clause often found in package holiday

[35] s. 16(1)(b).
[36] 1948 S.C. 259.

contracts which permits the tour operator to alter the itinerary or
the dates of the holiday.[37]

*Indemnities*

**10–43**   Indemnity clauses are clauses that require one party to a contract
to take responsibility for the legal liability of someone else. Such
clauses are not unusual in the contracts of cross channel ferry
firms. While, strictly speaking, not exclusion clauses they have a
similar effect and are made subject to a reasonableness test by
section 18.

*Guarantees*

**10–44**   Guarantees are often given by manufacturers of products and
can be a very useful addition to the rights which a consumer has
under the Sale of Goods Act 1979 against the retailer. There
have been examples of such guarantees conferring additional
advantages on consumers but excluding the manufacturer's common law liability under *Donoghue v. Stevenson*.[38] Section 19 of
the Act renders void attempts to do this. The section applies only
to goods "of a type ordinarily supplied for private use or consumption", the meaning of which has been discussed above.

*Terms Implied in Contracts for the Supply of Goods*

**10–45**   In Chapter 5 we saw that certain terms relating to title, description and the quality of goods are implied in contracts of sale by
sections 12 to 15 of the Sale of Goods Act 1979. Similar terms are
implied in contracts of hire-purchase by the Supply of Goods
(Implied Terms) Act 1973. Section 20 renders void clauses
purporting to exclude or restrict these terms in consumer contracts.[39]

**10–46**   There are several other contracts under which goods may be
transferred. Until the amendment of the Supply of Goods and
Services Act 1982 by the Sale and Supply of Goods Act 1994, the
implied terms in such contracts were found, not in statute, but
the common law. The 1994 Act, which came into force on
January 3, 1995, added a Part IA to the 1982 Act setting out
implied terms which are very similar to those implied in contracts
of sale.[40] In consumer contracts transferring the property in goods

[37] For an example in a case which arose before the Act see *Anglo-Continental
Holidays Ltd v. Typaldos Lines (London) Ltd* [1967] 2 Lloyd's Rep. 61.
[38] 1932 S.C. (H.L.) 31.
[39] These provisions first appeared in the Supply of Goods (Implied Terms) Act
1973.
[40] The terms are discussed in Chap. 5.

clauses purporting to exclude or restrict such terms are void. Contracts affected will include those for work and materials and barter. This is achieved by an amended version of section 21 of the Unfair Contract Terms Act 1977.

Contracts of hire, which are not contracts for the "transfer of **10–47** property in goods", are treated slightly differently. Exclusion clauses in these contracts are controlled by section 21 of the Unfair Contract Terms Act. Attempts in consumer contracts to exclude the implied terms about correspondence with description or sample, quality, or fitness for purpose are void. However, exclusion of the terms about the right to transfer possession and the enjoyment of quiet possession are subject to the test of fairness and reasonableness.

**The Reasonableness Test**

In some circumstances an exclusion clause is only effective if **10–48** "fair and reasonable". To assist in determining what this means there is guidance in the Act. Before looking at those guidelines there are two points that need to be kept in mind. The first concerns the onus of proof. Section 25(4) states that this falls on the party asserting that the clause is reasonable. The other point concerns the time at which any test of reasonableness should be applied. The Act draws a distinction between contractual terms and non-contractual notices. In the case of contractual terms section 24(1) states that the test must be satisfied having regard "to the circumstances which were, or ought reasonably to have been, known to or in the contemplation of the parties when the contract was made."

In the case of non-contractual notices section 24(2A) states **10–49** that one must have "regard to all the circumstances obtaining when the liability arose or (but for the provision) would have arisen."

The English case of *Bellamy v. Newbold*[41] turned on the **10–50** question of when the test should be applied. Following the discovery of defects in a house the sellers paid compensation to the purchaser who had signed a form acknowledging that this payment was in full and final settlement of all present and future claims. Some time later there was a dispute about the boundaries of the property and the sellers sought to apply this statement to that claim. It was held that the statement did not apply to the boundary dispute as this had not been in the contemplation of the parties at the time that it had been drawn up.

The Act provides not one but three sets of guidelines. The **10–51** most elaborate guidance is given in relation to clauses relating to

---

[41] 1986, Court of Appeal, unreported.

the supply of goods controlled by sections 20 and 21 of the Act. As far as consumers are concerned the only situation where these sections apply a reasonableness test is where, in a contract of hire, a clause excludes the implied term about the right to transfer possession or the enjoyment of quiet possession of the goods. In this case section 24(2) directs that regard shall be had to the guidelines in Schedule 2 of the Act. These guidelines are as follows:

"(a) the strength of the bargaining positions of the parties relative to each other, taking into account (among other things) alternative means by which the customer's requirements could have been met;
(b) whether the customer received an inducement to agree to the term, or in accepting it had an opportunity of entering into a similar contract with other persons, but without having to accept a similar term;
(c) whether the customer knew or ought reasonably to have known of the existence and extent of the term (having regard, among other things, to any custom of the trade and any previous course of dealing between the parties);
(d) where the term excludes or restricts any relevant liability if some condition is not complied with, whether it was reasonable at the time of the contract to expect that compliance with that condition would be practicable;
(e) whether the goods were manufactured, processed or adapted to the special order of the customer."

**10–52** If the clause or notice seeks to restrict liability to a sum of money two further guidelines are included in section 24(3). These are:

"(a) the resources which the party seeking to rely on that term could expect to be available to him for the purpose of meeting the liability should it arise;
(b) how far it was open to that party to cover himself by insurance."

**10–53** In the other cases where the Act applies a reasonableness test to consumer contracts, such as section 16 dealing with breach of duty leading to loss other than death or physical injury and the consumer contracts covered by section 17, the only guidelines are the two just referred to. These can only operate where liability is limited to a specified sum. However, one reason for setting out the Schedule 2 guidelines in full, despite their limited application, was that they encapsulate the factors which judges would take into account even if they had not been set out.

Indeed, in the English Court of Appeal it has been observed that "the considerations there set out are normally regarded as being of general application to the question of reasonableness".[42]

Relatively few cases have come before the courts on the issue **10-54** of reasonableness and most of the specifically consumer cases are decisions of the English county courts. Some guidance on the approach of the appellate courts is set out by Lord Bridge in *George Mitchell (Chesterhall) Ltd v. Finney Lock Seeds Ltd.*[43] The case was decided under the earlier Supply of Goods (Implied Terms) Act 1973, but Lord Bridge expressly said that his comments were relevant to the Unfair Contract Terms Act:

> "It would not be accurate to describe such a decision as an exercise of discretion. But a decision under [the Supply of Goods (Implied Terms) Act or the Unfair Contract Terms Act] will have this in common with the exercise of a discretion, that . . . the court must entertain a whole range of considerations, put them in the scales on one side or the other and decide at the end of the day on which side the balance comes down. There will sometimes be room for a legitimate difference of judicial opinion as to what the answer should be, where it will be impossible to say that one view is demonstrably wrong and the other demonstrably right. It must follow, in my view, that, when asked to review such a decision on appeal, the appellate court should treat the original decision with the utmost respect and refrain from interference with it unless satisfied that it proceeded on some erroneous principle or was plainly and obviously wrong."

One can see an example of this approach in the speech of Lord **10-55** Griffiths in the only consumer cases on this point to reach the House of Lords, *Smith v. Eric S. Bush & Co.; Harris v. Wyre District Council.*[44] While emphasising that it is impossible to draw up an exhaustive list of factors to be taken into account and that he was dealing with dwelling houses of relatively modest value, he was able to isolate certain matters which should always be considered. These were the relative bargaining strengths of the parties; the practicality of obtaining advice from another source taking into account time and cost; the difficulty of the task undertaken by the service provider; and the financial consequences of the decision on reasonableness. In these cases where the valuation of a house was concerned the factors all pointed in the direction of finding it unreasonable for a surveyor to exclude

---

[42] *Stewart Gill v Horatio Myer & Co* [1992] 1 Q.B. 600, at p 608.
[43] [1983] 2 A.C. 803.
[44] [1990] A.C. 831; [1989] 2 All E.R. 514.

liability. The disclaimer was imposed on the client who had no
effective power to object; given the value of the house it was
unreasonable for the buyers to seek an alternative valuation; the
task was straightforward; and the consequences of being made
liable could be covered by insurance.[45] In *Melrose v. Davidson &
Robertson*[46] it was stated that for the reasons given by Lord
Griffiths in those cases it could not be disputed that the disclaimer was not fair and reasonable.[47]

**10–56**   In *Woodman v. Photo Trade Processing Ltd*[48] the relevance of
choice was an important issue. The plaintiff had taken photographs of a friend's wedding to the defendants for processing.
They failed to return the photographs and when sued relied on a
clause in their contract limiting liability to the replacement cost
of the film. It was held that this clause was unreasonable because
it excluded liability for negligence as well as accident. The
evidence showed that there was no alternative to the defendant's
terms as all other processors used the same terms. It was also
relevant that the defendant's could have insured against the
liability. In *Moores v. Yakeley Associates Ltd*,[49] on the other
hand, in a case where an architect's limitation of liability clause
was found to be reasonable the facts that the consumer had been
advised by a solicitor, the clause was clearly brought to the
client's attention and the market for architects' services was
highly competitive were considered to be relevant.

**10–57**   In *Waldron-Kelly v. British Railways Board*[50] a clause in
British Rail's conditions of carriage relating compensation to the
weight of the goods, not to their value, was held to be unreasonable. The plaintiff's suitcase had been lost by British Rail. On
their basis of calculating compensation £27 would have been
payable, whereas the value of the contents was £320.

**10–58**   Although far removed from the consumer sphere, *Stag Line v.
Tyne Ship Repair Group; The Zinnia*,[51] a shipping case, has some
pointers to the attitudes of the courts in relation to reasonableness. Staughton J. observed:

> "I would have been tempted to hold that all the conditions are
> unfair and unreasonable for two reasons: first they are in such
> small print that one can barely read them; secondly the

[45] [1989] 2 All E.R. 514, pp. 531–532.
[46] 1993 S.C.L.R. 365.
[47] The Scottish cases are reviewed in Stewart, "15 Years of Fair Contracts in
Scotland", 1993 S.L.T. (News) 15.
[48] 1981, Exeter County Court, unreported.
[49] 1998 Lexis English High Court.
[50] [1981] 3 C.L.33.
[51] [1982] 2 Lloyd's Reps. 211.

drafting is so convoluted and prolix that one almost needs an
LL.B. to understand them."

These remarks were obiter but it is interesting that they should **10–59**
have been made in the context of a commercial contract where
the parties were of equal bargaining strength and had suitably
qualified persons to scrutinise their contracts. It seems almost
certain that a consumer contract of which the same criticisms
could be made would be considered to be unreasonable.

## THE UNFAIR TERMS IN CONSUMER CONTRACTS REGULATIONS 1999[52]

These regulations implement the E.C. Directive on Unfair **10–60**
Contract Terms[53] of April 5, 1993 and replace the 1994 regulations of the same name which came into effect on January 1,
1995.[54]

The directive is based on Article 100a of the Treaty of Rome **10–61**
which is primarily concerned with the establishment of the single
market. The recitals in the directive point out that the many
disparities in contract terms in the Member States create a
distortion of the market and may deter consumers in entering
into cross-border transactions.

The criticisms of the method of implementation of the Gen- **10–62**
eral Safety Directive apply with even greater force to this
directive. As it adds to the law relating to unfair terms the
obvious course would have been to implement it by means of
primary legislation recasting this whole area of law.[55] Instead, the
regulations are superimposed on the existing Unfair Contract
Terms Act 1977. In the case of the General Safety Directive such
a course could be justified on the ground that the primary
legislation and the regulations implementing the directive were
complementary. No such answer is available in the case of the
Unfair Terms Directive. The 1977 Act and the regulations overlap. Anyone seeking to ascertain whether a term is valid must
check it against both the Act and the regulations. It is quite
possible that a term would survive scrutiny under the 1977 Act
but be found to be unfair under the regulations.

The central provision of the regulations is regulation 8(1) **10–63**
which provides that "[a]n unfair term in a contract concluded
with a consumer by a seller or supplier shall not binding on the

---

[52] S.I. 1999 No. 2083.
[53] Directive 93/13 ([1993] O.J. L95/29).
[54] Those regulations, S.I. 1994 No. 3159, came into force on July 1, 1995, six
months after the date set out in the directive for implementing it.
[55] The White Paper announced that the government was considering a consolidation of the 1977 Act and the regulations and had commissioned research
on its feasibility.

consumer". This short sentence introduces a potentially revolutionary rule into our contract law. While this provision looks very similar to the controls introduced by the 1977 Act, and does indeed overlap with them to some extent, there are also important differences.

**10–64**     An obvious difference is that the regulations apply to unfair terms in contracts. The 1977 Act, as we noted at para. 10–23, is misleadingly named, for it applies, in the main, only to clauses excluding and limiting liability. There are many other situations where a term can be unfair but, because it is not such a clause, it is not subject to the controls of the Act. The regulations apply much more widely. For example, they can apply to terms about delivery dates; terms which give the supplier the right to increase the contractual charges unilaterally; or to terminate the contract without adequate notice. Bankers' contracts with their customers often permit the bank to close an account or withdraw a bank card with little notice. None of these would be regarded as exemptions or exclusions of liability and would not be subject to the Act. They can be challenged under the regulations.

**10–65**     An important similarity between the existing common law and the new regulations is that both apply the *contra proferentem* rule. Regulation 7 enjoins traders to "ensure that any written term of a contract is expressed in plain, intelligible language" and goes on to say that "if there is doubt about the meaning of a written term, the interpretation most favourable to the consumer shall prevail". This rule does not apply to proceedings brought by the Office of Fair Trading and others for an interdict which are discussed below. The point of this is to prevent traders, in effect, taking advantage of the *contra proferentem* rule in proceedings for an interdict. Were they to do so and succeed in opposing the award of an interdict banning use of a term they would be at liberty to use a term which was to some degree obscure.

**10–66**     An important difference is in the scope of the regulations. Regulation 4(1) states that they apply "in relation to unfair terms in contracts concluded between a seller or supplier and a consumer". The definition of "consumer" in regulation 3 is narrower than that in the 1977 Act. For the purposes of the Act businesses can, in certain circumstances, be regarded as consumers as occurred in *R. & B. Customs Brokers Co. Ltd v. United Dominions Trust.*[56] This is not the case under the regulations as "consumer" is defined as "any natural person who ... is acting for purposes which are outside his trade, business or profession".

[56]  [1988] 1 All E.R. 847.

"Seller" and "supplier" are also defined differently in the   **10–67**
regulations.[57] In both cases they mean "any natural or legal
person who ... is acting for purposes related to his trade,
business or profession, whether publicly or privately owned".
"Related to" is much wider than the equivalent phrase in the
1977 Act which is "in the course of a business". In *R. & B.
Customs Brokers Co. Ltd*[58] it was held that to come within that
test: "the transaction should be an integral part of the business
concerned, or one which he or she carries out with sufficient
regularity or a one off adventure in the nature of a trade."

"Related to" will bring under the control of the regulations   **10–68**
transactions such as the isolated sale of a capital item by a
business which does not deal in that sort of item.[59]

*Unfair Contract Terms*

There is a significant difference between the definition of seller   **10–69**
or supplier in the 1999 Regulations and that in the original set.
The original regulations referred to sellers of goods and services.
This assumed that the directive did not apply to contracts relating to heritage. It is not clear from the directive whether such
contracts are covered by it, but the DTI's guidance notes took
the view that they were not and this was reflected in the 1994
Regulations.[60] The new regulations indicate a change to a neutral
stance as the definitions of seller and supplier make no reference
to the supply of goods or services. The definition follows that in
the directive precisely. Whether contracts relating to heritage
are covered is debatable using the evidence of the English
language version of the recitals. In some of the other Community
languages it is clearer that they are included.[61]

Schedule 1 of the original regulations excluded certain types   **10–70**
of contract. It is no surprise to find that this schedule is not
reproduced in the new regulations as it would not have occurred
to anyone that most of the excluded types of contract would have
been subject to the regulations anyway. They included contracts
relating to employment, the incorporation or businesses, contracts relating to succession rights, and contracts relating to

---

[57] See reg. 3.
[58] [1988] 1 All E.R. 847.
[59] *cf. Davies v. Sumner* [1984] 1 W.L.R. 1301.
[60] See DTI, *Implementation of the E.C. Directive on Unfair Terms in Consumer
Contracts: A Consultation Document*, Oct. 1993. Footnote 1 to the commentary to draft reg. B(I) cites four recitals which plainly refer to suppliers of
goods.
[61] The OFT take the view that heritage is covered and have persuaded traders
to delete or amend unfair terms in such contracts. S. and C. Bright, "Unfair
Terms in Land Contracts: Copy Out or Cop Out?" (1995) 111 L.Q.R. 655.

rights under family law. The only reason that they appeared in the original regulations seems to have been because they are referred to in one of the recitals to the directive. It is understood that their appearance there was an oversight and as they do not appear in the body of the directive they have been excised from the new regulations.

**10–71**    Two other types of terms to which the regulations do not apply appeared in Schedule 1 to the old regulations, and they have been preserved in the new regulations. These are terms which reflect mandatory statutory or regulatory provisions including Community legislation which has direct effect; and the provisions or principles of international conventions to which the Member States or the Community are party. The latter would exempt from the controls of the regulations clauses in transport contracts which comply with the Warsaw Convention. These exclusions, which are drafted in terms much closer to the wording of the directive, are now to be found in regulation 4(2).

**10–72**    It is important to emphasise that insurance contracts are subject to the regulations. They are one of the most important exclusions from the 1977 Act but did not escape the controls in the directive. However, the exclusion of the so-called "core provisions" of a contract (discussed below) from consideration for unfairness means that insurance contracts do get some protection from control under the regulations.

**10–73**    It is not all contract terms to which the regulations apply. Regulation 5(1) makes clear that it is only those "where the term has not been individually negotiated". According to regulation 5(2) a term shall "always be regarded as not having been individually negotiated where it has been drafted in advance and the consumer has therefore not been able to influence the substance of the term". The fact that some terms or parts of terms have been individually negotiated will not prevent the regulations applying "if an overall assessment of [the contract] shows that it is a pre-formulated standard contract". Regulation 5(4) is important here in that it puts the burden of showing that a term was individually negotiated on the supplier or seller. This definition sounds rather like a way of saying in statutory terms what the Law Commissions in their *Second Report on Exemption Clauses*[62] thought it best to leave unsaid in the 1977 Act. It is useful in making clear that a contract does not cease to be a standard form contract because some parts of it have been negotiated. For example, in a contract for double glazing the vast majority of the terms will be standard form terms on which there will be no negotiation. The customer will probably not even read them and, would be an unusual customer if he or she fully

---

[62] Law Com. No. 69; Scot. Law Com. No. 39, para. 157.

understood them. However, there will be some terms which will be discussed. The price will be one and the delivery dates another.

Article 9 prevents the controls in the regulations being circum- **10–74** vented by attempts to say that the contract is governed by the law of a state outside the Community.[63] They apply in such a case if the contract has a close connection with the territory of a Member State."

The key aspect of the regulations is the meaning of unfairness **10–75** which is the criterion by which terms are to judged. Superficially, there are similarities with the Unfair Contract Terms Act 1977. The degree to which this is helpful is limited for the concept of unfairness in the regulations is somewhat different. The core of the definition of unfairness is to be found in regulation 5(1) which says that:

> "A contractual term . . . shall be regarded as unfair if, contrary to the requirement of good faith, it causes a significant imbalance in the parties' rights and obligations arising under the contract, to the detriment of the consumer".

How will this be applied? Regulation 6(1) goes on to say that the **10–76** time for applying the test is the time of the conclusion of the contract. It also states that "the nature of the goods or services for which the contract was concluded", the circumstances attending its conclusion, and all other terms of the contract or of another contract on which it is dependent must be taken into account.

From this list of things which may be taken into account in **10–77** deciding on the fairness of the terms of a contract there are two exceptions. Regulation 6(2) says that:

> "In so far as it is in plain, intelligible language, the assessment of fairness of a term shall not relate—
>
> (a) to the definition of the main subject matter of the contract, or
> (b) to the adequacy of the price or remuneration, as against the goods or services supplied in exchange."

---

[63] The "Community" means the European Economic Community and the other states of the European Economic Area; and "member state" means a State which is a contracting party to the EEA Agreement signed at Oporto on May 2, 1992 and adjusted by the protocol signed at Brussels on March 17, 1993. Liechtenstein, however, is not included until the EEA Agreement comes into force in relation to it. See reg. 2(1).

**10–78**  This excludes two kinds of clause from the fairness test. The definition of the subject matter exception is designed to exclude clauses describing what the deal is about. From the recitals to the directive it can be discovered that insurance contracts are in mind here, though they are not the only possible examples. Insurance contracts were excluded from the Unfair Contract Terms Act 1977 on the ground that it would be very difficult to distinguish between exclusion clauses and those clauses which defined the insured risk. The directive and the regulations do not go as far as this. Their approach is to say that terms defining or circumscribing the risk are not on their own to be subject to the fairness test. However, contracts of insurance are still subject to the regulations. In addition, the price of the goods or service are not subject to the fairness test. This will be seen as a major gap in the regulations, as one of the most significant features of a transaction is the price.

**10–79**  In *Director General of Fair Trading v. First National Bank plc*[64] it was argued by the Bank that a clause setting out the consequences of default in a regulated consumer credit agreement was a "core provision". The Court of Appeal agreed with counsel for the Director General that it did not "define the main subject matter of the contract". It was a term which dealt with the situation where there was a breach of contract. Neither could it be said to concern the adequacy of the remuneration "as it relates only to a case where the borrower is in default and then merely providing for the continuation of the contractual rate after judgment". They thus agreed with this part of the judgment of Evans-Lombe J., who had stated that:

> "I do not think that the average borrower seeking a home improvement loan from the Bank would consider default provisions as one of the important terms of the agreement which he would have under consideration in deciding whether or not to accept an offer of advance. He would be considering the cost to him of the loan which would be the interest calculable under clause 3 on the basis that he repaid the advance by paying the instalments required on the due date."[65]

**10–80**  However, it must be stressed that both these exceptions are subject to qualification. Both apply only "in so far as the term is in plain, intelligible language". It is not clear what standard this is imposing. Does it mean language that is intelligible to a lawyer

[64] [2000] All E.R. 759 C.A.
[65] *Director General of Fair Trading v. First National Bank plc* [2000] 1 All E.R. 240.

— which is a standard that many standard clauses barely meet at present. Or does it mean language that the average person finds intelligible. From the recitals it would appear that it is the latter. The relevant recital after referring to the need for plain language states that the consumer should be given the opportunity to examine all the terms. This envisages the ordinary person reading the contract and therefore the kind of language used must be such that he or she will find plain and intelligible. This is certainly the approach of the OFT who have stated[66] that they take the view "that the standard of 'plainness' and 'intelligibility' of contract terms must normally be within the understanding of ordinary consumers *without legal advice*". A good many standard form contracts do not survive scrutiny on that ground. Insurance contracts are a prime example, but there are many more.

The other qualification to the exclusion of these two factors **10–81** from the fairness test is that while they are not subject to it on their own, they can still be relevant to the fairness of other terms. This is not at all clear from the regulations but is clearly set out in the recitals to the directive. So, for example, if it can be shown that a service at the high price charged is usually accompanied by the supplier taking full legal responsibility for its provision then a clause exempting from that liability might be regarded as unfair. On the other hand, if the price were considerably lower the exemption clause might be regarded as fair.

With these considerations disposed of we are left with the **10–82** central features of unfairness of a term. These are that it is one that "contrary to the requirement of good faith ... causes a significant imbalance in the parties' rights and obligations arising under the contract, to the detriment of the consumer".

The last of these criteria, detriment to the consumer, is prob- **10–83** ably the easiest to explain. It would seem simply to be making the point that only the consumer can take advantage of the regulations.[67]

The requirement of "significant imbalance" would seem to **10–84** mean no more than the application of a *de minimis* rule eliminating minor imbalances in the rights and obligations of the parties. As Willet has argued,[68] it can hardly mean that the imbalance is particularly extreme. This would run counter to the idea of the having an *Indicative and Illustrative List of Terms Which May be Regarded as Unfair* in Schedule 3.

---

[66] *Unfair Contract Terms: A Bulletin issued by the Office of Fair Trading*, Issue 2, September 1996, para 2.13.
[67] See "Unfair Contract Terms Directive", in Brownsword, Howells and Wilhelmsson, *Welfarism in Contract Law* (1994).
[68] "Directive on Unfair Terms in Consumer Contracts" (1994) 2 Cons. L.J. 114.

**10–85**     This brings us to the concept of good faith. The central aspect of unfairness is that the term is "contrary to the requirement of good faith". There has been much comment about the novelty of this is in English and Scots law. Whatever may be the case in English law the fact is that it does have antecedents in Scots law. Professor T.B. Smith asserted in his *Short Commentary* that it was an underlying feature of the Scots law of obligations. He pointed to the various doctrines such as facility, force and fear, undue influence and control of minors' contracts on what is now the ground of prejudice, and argued that these were but specific examples of the wider principle of good faith. Professor Gow in *The Mercantile and Industrial Law of Scotland* notes that "Sale is a bargain bonae fidei"[69] and goes on to point out that:

> "Our doctrine of bona fides is of considerable importance *in re mercatoria* [in commercial matters] and its vigorous restatement, especially in an era of instalment credit and buyers, whose pockets appear large enough to impel them into an activity now become essential to the national economy but are not large enough to enable them lightly to embark upon litigations, is urgently required."[70]

**10–86**     Professor Smith also went on to argue that "the principles of bona fides which are latent in the Scottish law of contract could with advantage be resuscitated to deal with problems of the twentieth century".[71]

**10–87**     Both writers acknowledged that the principle had fallen into disuse. The implementation of the E.C. Directive is an opportunity to begin its revival. Surprisingly, the new regulations give less assistance than the original set in interpreting the concept of good faith. The original regulation 4(3) had directed that in determining whether a term satisfied the good faith requirement regard should be had to the criteria set out in Schedule 2. These criteria contained more than a passing similarity to the criteria in Schedule 2 of the 1977 Act. They included such matters as the parties' bargaining strength, whether the consumer received an inducement to agree to the term, whether the goods or services were supplied to a special order and the extent to which the supplier had dealt fairly and equitably with the consumer. Their inclusion was clearly intended to placate the fears of English lawyers, in particular, about the use of the unfamiliar concept of good faith so familiar to civil lawyers. In one of the few reported case in which the fairness of a term has been raised in litigation

---

[69] (1964), p.161.
[70] *ibid.* pp.178–179.
[71] *Short Commentary*, p. 46.

between private parties, *Falco Finance Ltd v. Gough*[72] the judge placed considerable emphasis on these criteria.

The absence of these guidelines from the new regulations does **10–88** not mean that they are no longer relevant. Here we have one of the disadvantages of slavish adherence to the copy-out technique in implementing E.C. directives. Those less familiar with the regulations and their European background will find the application of the fairness test more difficult. In practice there should be no difference in application between the two sets of regulations. This is because the recitals clearly state that the factors formerly set out in Schedule 2 to the regulations are to be taken into account in determining fairness. As the regulations implement an E.C. directive it is legitimate, as *Litster v. Forth Dry Dock & Engineering Co.*[73] demonstrates, to refer to the recitals to assist in interpreting the regulations.

While the Schedule 2 guidelines have disappeared from the **10–89** regulations the somewhat delphic "indicative and non-exhaustive list of terms which may be regarded as unfair", to quote regulation 5(5), remains and is now to found in Schedule 2 to the new regulations. Neither the regulations, nor the directive nor its recitals give any further guidance on the status of this "grey list" as it has come to be known. There is no indication that terms appearing in it should be presumed to be unfair. However, given the nature of many of the terms this is the conclusion to which one must come.

This grey list has many similarities to the sort of terms, which **10–90** are controlled by the 1977 Act. Included are terms which exclude liability for death or personal injury or the implied terms in contracts for the supply of goods and services; those which give the seller or supplier the right to end or extend the contract at his discretion; or in other ways to alter the terms of the contract. As one might expect, terms imposing harsh obligations to pay compensation in the event of breach as well as barriers to the use of the courts to decide disputes are also in the list. A common characteristic of the list is that the terms included are very much to the advantage of the trader.

It was argued in the first edition of this book that the concept **10–91** of good faith covered both what is sometimes referred to as procedural good faith and substantive good faith. This was the view of the English Court of Appeal in the only case relating to the regulations to be heard in one of the higher courts in the United Kingdom. In *The Director General of Fair Trading v.*

---

[72] [1999] Tr. L 526; see also *Gosling v. Burrard-Lucas,* [1999] 1 C.L. 197, Tunbridge Wells County Court, November 4, 1998; and *Kindlance Ltd v. Murphy* 1997 Lexis, a judgment of a master in the NI Chancery Division.
[73] [1990] 1 A.C. 546.

*First National Bank plc*[74] they pointed out that "'good faith' has a special meaning in the regulations, having its conceptual roots in civil law systems". They went on to quote with approval commentators who have referred to the fact that it involves both procedural and substantive good faith. That is, it covers unfairness in the way in which the bargain is arrived at, sometimes referred to as unfair surprise, as well as unfairness because the bargain is very much weighted in favour of the seller or supplier.

**10–92** In this case the Director General was challenging the fairness of a term in a loan agreement subject to the Consumer Credit Act 1974. The term provided that if the borrower defaulted on a repayment the bank could demand repayment of the outstanding balance on the customer's account and interest at the rate set out in the loan agreement. It went on to add that where court action was necessary, interest would be payable at this rate on the judgment. The significance of this is that interest on the judgment would not otherwise have been payable. In practice what happens in cases of default is that after a court action has commenced borrowers agree to pay off the debt by instalments and the action is settled without a proper court hearing taking place. Despite making the agreed repayments to pay off the debt the borrower finds that further sums are owed to the bank by way of interest at the contractual rate on the judgment. The Director General's argument was that this rendered the term in the agreement unfair because when a borrower took out a loan it was not made clear that this could be one of its effects. It also meant that, in practice, borrowers did not have an opportunity to avail themselves of the opportunity to apply for time orders under the Consumer Credit Act 1974 which could have provided that interest should not be payable. At first instance[75] Evans-Lombe J. had considered this term to be fair. The Court of Appeal disagreed and found that it "does create unfair surprise". They stated that:

> "The test of unfairness is not to be judged by personal concepts of inherent fairness apart from the requirements of the Directive and Regulations, and we are far from convinced that a borrower would think it fair that when he is taken to court and an order for payment by instalments has been tailored to meet what he could afford and he complied with that order, he should then be told that he has to pay further sums by way of interest. The borrower's attention is not specifically drawn to

---

[74] See note 64 above.
[75] *Director General of Fair Trading v. First National Bank plc* [2000] 1 All E.R. 240.

the point by the Bank at or before the conclusion of the contract nor at any later time prior to the making of the order nor in the order itself and the evidence shows that it comes as a disagreeable surprise to the borrower to find that due compliance with the order for payment by instalments, so far from eliminating the debt to the Bank, may leave because the bargain is very much weighted in favour of the seller or supplier."

In a number of cases the directive has added nothing to the protection Scottish consumers already have under the 1977 Act. In other ways it has extended considerably that protection. How far it does this will depend on the interpretation of the regulations by the judiciary. The experience of the application of the reasonableness test in the 1977 Act augurs well for this. It is generally agreed that this has redressed the balance in favour of consumers. This assumes that consumers are able to obtain access to the courts. The regulations take account of the danger that this may not occur in the procedures for enforcing the new rules to which we now turn.    **10–93**

### Enforcement

It is a trite observation that consumer protection laws are of very little value if they cannot be enforced. As we will see in Chapter 12 this is a major problem in Scotland, as in many other jurisdictions. Giving individual rights to consumers is of limited value especially where those against whom they must be asserted are much more powerful. Article 7 of the directive requires Member States to "ensure that in the interests of consumers and of competitors, adequate and effective means exist to prevent the continued use of unfair terms." It goes on to add that the means referred to:    **10–94**

"shall include provisions whereby persons or organisations, having a legitimate interest under national law in protecting consumers, may take action according to the national law concerned before the courts or before competent administrative bodies for a decision as to whether contractual terms drawn up for general use are unfair, so that they can apply appropriate and effective means to prevent the continued use of such terms."

Originally, this was implemented by giving the Office of Fair Trading powers, modelled on those in the Control of Misleading    **10–95**

Advertisements Regulations 1988,[76] to seek an interdict in the
Court of Session. The current regulations require the Director
General of Fair Trading[77] to consider complaints about unfair
terms and to apply for an interdict "against any person appearing
to the Director ... to be using, or recommending use of, an
unfair term drawn up for general use in contracts concluded with
consumer.[78] The Director General has also been given new
powers[79] to assist investigations of allegedly unfair terms. A
major innovation of the 1999 Regulations is the extension of the
power to enforce to various other "qualifying bodies" set out in
Schedule 1. This followed the launching of litigation in England
by the Consumers' Association asserting that the 1994 Regulations had not properly implemented the enforcement provisions
of the directive. Two groups of organisations now have enforcement powers. The first group of "qualifying bodies" to which
enforcement powers have been extended ten statutory bodies:
the Data Protection Registrar, the Directors General of Electricity Supply and for Gas for both Great Britain and Northern
Ireland, as well as the Directors General of Telecommunications
and of Water Services and the Rail Regulator. Also included in
this part are the weights and measures authorities in Great
Britain as well as the Department of Economic Development in
Northern Ireland which is the weights and measures authority
there.[80] This means that trading standards departments now have
enforcement powers under the regulations. In addition, the
Consumers' Association also is a qualifying body.[81] These organisations may only seek an interdict after they have given the
Director General notice of their intention to do so. This is part of
a process of ensuring the co-ordination of action and the avoidance of duplication of effort.[82]

**10–96**     The court to which an application for an injunction or interdict
may be made is the Court of Session or the Sheriff Court, and in
the rest of the United Kingdom the High Court or the County
Court. Conferring jurisdiction on the Sheriff Court and the
County court is an innovation which follows the model of Part III

---

[76] S.I. 1988 No. 915.
[77] reg. 10.
[78] reg. 12(1).
[79] reg 13.
[80] It is expected that the Financial Services Authority will be added to the list
    when the Financial Services and Markets Bill, currently before Parliament, is
    enacted.
[81] The reason for the distinction is that the power to require information from
    those allegedly using unfair terms is not extended to qualifying bodies falling
    into the second category of which the Consumers' Association is the only
    example at present.
[82] See *Unfair Contract Terms: a case report bulletin issued by the Office of Fair
    Trading*, Issue no. 8, Dec. 1999, pp. 4 and 5.

of the Fair Trading Act 1973 which permits the Director General to take action against traders who persistently act unfairly towards consumers. This facility will be particularly useful for trading standards departments who are likely to take action against local traders; and will also be appropriate where other bodies entitled to seek interdicts sue local businesses.

None of the new qualifying bodies has exercised its powers but **10–97** it is to be expected that their approach will be similar to that of the OFT which has sought to persuade traders to remove or amend terms. The Director General has put considerable resources into the creation of an unfair terms unit within his office, and its operation over the past five years must be one of the greatest successes of the office. By the end of March 1999 it had received 3753 complaints. 26 per cent of these were not proceeded with either because they were duplicate or defective complaints or could be dealt with more appropriately under other legislation. 29 per cent resulted in no further action because they were not about contract terms, involved terms not subject to the regulations or the unfairness test, were closed for some other reason or were not considered to be unfair. It was possible to deal with 15 per cent by advice or warning. In 10 per cent or 383 cases an informal undertaking to stop using the term was given by a business, and in eight cases businesses were required to give formal undertakings. The remaining 20 per cent of cases have still to be dealt with.[83] Two spectacular examples of the benefits of the regulations are contained in a recent report which shows that the agreement of a mortgage company to remove unfair penalties in their loan agreements has saved consumers £65.2 million and amendments to mobile telephone contracts is estimated to save consumers between £60 million and £80 million.[84]

## OTHER STATUTORY CONTROLS

The Unfair Contract Terms Act 1977 and the Unfair Terms in **10–98** Consumer Contracts Regulations 1999 are, undoubtedly, the most important controls on exclusion clauses. Brief mention should be made of some other statutory controls. Section 29 of the Public Passenger Vehicles Act 1981 invalidates a provision in a contract for the conveyance of passengers in a public service vehicle which purports to restrict the liability of a person in respect of death or personal injury. The Warsaw Convention on

---

[83] The Office of Fair Trading's *Unfair Contract Terms Bulletin No.7.*
[84] *The Office of Fair Trading: Protecting the Consumer from Unfair Trading Practices,* Report by the Comptroller and Auditor General, H.C. 57 Session 1999–00, p. 53.

carriage by air which is given effect to by the Carriage by Air Act 1961 controls their use in contracts of air travel. The Defective Premises Act 1972, section 6(3), renders void any attempt to contract out of the provisions of the Act. The Trading Stamps Act 1964 prevents the implied terms relating to the title of the promoter of the trading stamp scheme and the quality of the goods being excluded. There are many examples in the Consumer Credit Act 1974 of provisions designed to protect debtors and hirers out of which it is not possible to contract as a result of section 173 of that Act. Similarly, section 7 of the Consumer Protection Act 1987 provides that it is not possible to contract out of the strict delictual duty imposed on producers of defective products.

## CHAPTER 11

# CONTROL OF TRADING PRACTICES

This chapter deals with the control of unfair trading practices. **11–01** There has been a traditional reluctance by government in this country to intervene in this area. Nevertheless, there are several areas where the law does impose specific controls on certain types of trade practices and a number of these are discussed below. In addition, it should be noted that the material on exclusion clauses might well have been included here instead of in a separate chapter. Similarly, while the Trade Descriptions Act 1968 is discussed in this chapter there is other material in Chapter 3 which deals with controlling trade practices. Attention is also drawn to Chapter 9 where the control of trade practices relating to credit are discussed. The credit licensing system provides a good example of one technique which may be used to regulate trade practices.

A number of methods are used to control unfair or deceptive **11–02** trade practices. The criminal law is sometimes used to ban or control a practice; statute may intervene to alter the civil law, as it does in relation to exclusion clauses; or a combination of criminal and civil law controls may be used. More recently, administrative methods have been introduced, notably through the Fair Trading Act 1973. In addition to the use of legal techniques it has become increasingly common to resort to self regulation of industry through codes of practice. This chapter begins by looking at the most important example of the use of the criminal law to control trading practices — the Trade Descriptions Act 1968 and the related Property Misdescriptions Act 1991. A varied collection of practices which are statutorily controlled by criminal and civil methods is then discussed after which the important work of the Office of Fair Trading is considered. There follows a look at the role of self regulation.

Before looking at how the law intervenes it is worth consider- **11–03** ing why such intervention is necessary at all. There are some who argue that intervention by the state to control unfair or deceptive trading practices is unnecessary. They assert that competition will usually ensure that those who promote unfair methods of trading will not flourish and that consumers who have been injured by unfair practices can resort to traditional legal remedies.[1] It is true that there are common law crimes that might be seen as having some role to play; and that the common law doctrines of fraud, facility and circumvention, undue influence, and force and fear might have relevance. In practice, such private law remedies are of limited use. The cost of invoking them, if their availability is known, is often prohibitively expensive. In any event, in the more serious cases of malpractice the trader may be difficult to find by the time that the consumer realises that he or she has been the victim of a swindle. This argues for measures which will deter and for institutions with the muscle to police the market.

## STATUTORY CONTROL

### TRADE DESCRIPTIONS

**Introduction**

**11–04**   The Trade Descriptions Act 1968 has an important role in the protection of purchasers of goods and services through the criminal law. The Act aims to protect consumers against false or misleading claims about goods and services. Legislation of this kind is not new; the earliest example is the Merchandise Marks Act 1862, which was replaced by the more effective Merchandise Marks Act 1887. While the consumer derived some benefit from the Merchandise Marks Acts 1887 to 1953,[2] these Acts were not designed primarily to protect consumer interests.

**11–05**   It was part of the remit of the Molony Committee[3] to review this legislation, and it made four main recommendations in this regard. It recommended that the definition of a "trade description" should be widened considerably to include characteristics of goods which were of significant interest to consumers. Powers to define the meaning of terms used in trade and to require that the consumer be provided with essential information about goods were advocated. The committee also laid stress on the

[1]   See, for example, Posner, *The Federal Trade Commission* (1969–70) 37 University of Chicago L.R. 47.
[2]   The Merchandise Marks Acts 1887–1953 comprised the Merchandise Marks Act 1887, 1891, 1911, 1926 and 1953, the Merchandise Marks (Prosecutions) Act 1894, and the Patents, etc. (International Conventions) Act 1938.
[3]   *Final Report of the Committee on Consumer Protection* (the Molony Report) Cmnd. 1781 (1962).

need to ensure that new legislation should cover any trade description likely to be taken as relating to goods, whether in advertisements or elsewhere. Its final main recommendation, and one of immense importance, was that there should be specific provisions about enforcement which should be the duty of local weights and measures authorities.

The Trade Descriptions Act 1968 incorporated most of the **11–06** proposals of the Molony Committee and, indeed, went further. The most significant excursions beyond the Molony Committee's recommendations were in relation to services and prices which are discussed below.

The Trade Descriptions Act 1968 protects the purchaser of **11–07** goods by creating criminal offences relating to the making of false trade descriptions and the importation of goods bearing false indications of origin or bearing infringing trade marks. The Act also enables regulations to be made defining terms used in connection with goods[4] and the display of information in advertisements.

The two principal criminal offences in relation to goods are set **11–08** out in section 1. Any person who, in the course of a trade or business (1) applies a false trade description[5] to any goods, or (2) supplies or offers to supply any goods to which a false trade description is applied, is guilty of an offence. As was pointed out by the Lord justice-Clerk (Grant) in an early decision on this part of the Act, "the offences created by section 1 are offences of strict liability subject only to the statutory defences provided".[6]

It is to be noted that the trade description must be applied "in **11–09** the course of a trade or business" a phrase which is not defined in the Trade Descriptions Act 1968. In *Roberts v. Leonard*[7] it was held that professional people were included in the Act. The trade or business need not be retail, nor need the offender's business be primarily concerned with transactions of the kind which give rise to the prosecution.[8]

This was made clear in the *Havering London Borough v.* **11–10** *Stevenson*,[9] where a car-hire firm which regularly sold off cars from its fleet of cars when it wished to replace them was held to be doing so in the course of its trade or business as a car-hire firm. This decision was distinguished in the House of Lords in *Davies v. Sumner*[10] on its facts but, as Lord Keith of Kinkel, who

---

[4] See the Trade Descriptions Act 1968, s. 7.
[5] *ibid.* s. 1(1)(a), (b).
[6] *Macnab v. Alexanders of Greenock Ltd,* 1971 S.L.T. 121.
[7] (1995) *The Times,* May 10, DC.
[8] Sales in members clubs are not regarded as being in the course of a business see *John v. Matthews* [1970] 2 Q.B. 443; [1970] 2 All E.R. 643.
[9] [1970] 1 W.L.R. 1375.
[10] [1984] 1 W.L.R. 1301; [1984] 3 All E.R. 831, H.L.

delivered a speech with which his brethren concurred, observed, its correctness was not challenged by counsel for the accused. *Davies v. Sumner* decided that goods are not dealt with "in the course of a trade or business" unless there is a degree of regularity in such dealing as part of the normal practice of the business. Thus, the trading-in of a used car by the accused who was a self-employed courier who used his car almost exclusively for his business was held not to be done in the course of a business. Sporadic sales of pieces of equipment, which were no longer required by a business, would, likewise, not be considered to fall within the purview of the Act.

**11–11**     In *Elder v. Crowe*[11] the High Court of Justiciary dealt with a case raising the question whether there was a course of trade. Trading standards officers found 300 bottles of counterfeit perfume, many of them in cellophane wrappers, in a house occupied by the appellant and he was charged with offering to supply goods to which a false trade description had been applied. He argued that the goods were not offered for supply in the course of a trade or business as what was involved was merely a "one-off" transaction. He was convicted and appealed to the High Court. There the dictum of Lord Keith in *Davies v. Sumner*,[12] that a one-off adventure in the nature of trade, carried through with a view to profit, can itself constitute a trade, was approved. As there was evidence entitling the sheriff to conclude that this was such a case the appeal was refused.

**11–12**     For the purposes of the Act, statements published in newspapers, books, periodicals, in films or sound or television broadcasts are not deemed to be made in the course of a business unless they form part of an advertisement.[13]

**11–13**     Offences, as the vast majority of the reported cases demonstrate, normally arise from descriptions applied to goods for sale, but they may also arise from a purchase. This occurred in *Fletcher v. Budgen*,[14] where a car dealer informed a private customer that his car was irreparably damaged and fit only for scrap. Nevertheless, the seller, who was paid £2 for the car by the dealer, later saw it advertised at £135. It transpired that repairs costing £56 been carried out to put it in a saleable condition. The dealer was convicted of applying a false trade description. The English Divisional Court held that the Trade Descriptions Act

---

[11]   1996 S.C.C.R. 38.
[12]   [1984] 1 W.L.R. 1301 at 1305.
[13]   Trade Descriptions Act 1968, s. 39(2) (amended by the Cable and Broadcasting Act 1984, s. 57, Sched. 5, para. 19) and the Broadcasting Act 1990 s. 203(1) and Sched. 20, para. 11.
[14]   [1974] 1 W.L.R. 1056; [1974] 2 All E.R. 1243, D.C.

1968 applied to buyers in the course of a business as well as those selling in the course of a business.

"Any person" includes bodies corporate or unincorporated by **11–14** virtue of the Interpretation Act 1978.[15] Limited companies are thus subject to the Act, as are partnerships, which, in any event, had been held in *Douglas v. Phoenix Motors Ltd*[16] in relation to a Scottish partnership to be bodies corporate, being legal persons distinct from the partners of whom they are composed, under the Partnership Act 1890.[17]

A person applies a trade description to goods if he (1) affixes **11–15** or annexes it to or in any manner marks it on or incorporates it with (a) the goods themselves, or (b) anything in, on or with which the goods are supplied; or (2) places the goods in, on or with anything which the trade description has been affixed or annexed to, marked on or incorporated with, or places any such thing with the goods; or (3) uses the trade description in any manner likely to be taken as referring to the goods.[18]

It is to be noted that, contrary to the recommendation of the **11–16** Molony Committee,[19] trade descriptions may be applied orally as well as in written form.[20] However, where an oral misdescription is alleged, a prosecution must be brought within six months of the commission of the offence[21]" and not 12 months which is the normal time limit for summary proceedings.[22]

"Goods" includes ships and aircraft, things attached to land **11–17** and growing crops.[23] It was widely accepted, despite the reference to things attached to land, that houses were not within the scope of the Trade Descriptions Act 1968.[24] This omission has now been repaired by the Property Misdescriptions Act 1991 which is discussed below.

The Trade Descriptions Act 1968 prohibits "false" descrip- **11–18** tions. Ironically, this is itself somewhat misleading when one considers the manner in which it is amplified. The Act, of course, prohibits those trade descriptions which are blatantly deceptive, but it also encompasses that which, though not false, is misleading; that is to say, likely to be taken for such an indication of any

[15] Interpretation Act 1978, s. 5, Sched. 1.
[16] 1970 S.L.T. (Sh. Ct.) 57.
[17] s. 4(2).
[18] Trade Descriptions Act 1968, s. 4(1)(a)–(c).
[19] *Final Report of the Committee on Consumer Protection* (the Molony Report), Cmnd. 1781 (1962).
[20] Trade Descriptions Act 1968, s. 4(2).
[21] *ibid.* s. 19(4), and the Criminal Procedure (Scotland) Act 1975, s. 331(1).
[22] *ibid.* s. 19(3).
[23] *ibid* s. 39(1). "Ship" includes any boat and any other description of vessel used in navigation.
[24] *Review of the Trade Descriptions Act 1968*, Cmnd. 6628 (1976), p. 27.

of the matters specified as trade descriptions.[25] To secure a conviction it is not sufficient that a trade description be false in the above sense; it must be false to a material degree.[26]

**11–19**    In determining whether a description is false the relevance of disclaimers has been a controversial issue.[27] The Trade Descriptions Act 1968 is silent on their effect, but in a number of cases their use has been accepted, albeit within very strict limits. There is no Scottish case in which this issue has arisen, although it seems significant that one of the findings in fact made by the sheriff in *Beattie v. Tudhope*[28] was that there was no disclaimer. One may speculate and hope that the Scottish courts would take as vigorous an approach to this problem as have English courts. The leading decision is *Norman v. Bennett*[29] where, in one of the many "clocking" cases, that is cases involving car odometers which have been turned back, the Lord Chief Justice laid down the following principle:

> "where a false trade description is attached to goods, its effect can be neutralised by an express disclaimer or contradiction of the message contained in the trade description. To be effective any such disclaimer must be as bold, precise and compelling as the trade description itself and must be as effectively brought to the notice of any person to whom the goods may be supplied. In other words, the disclaimer must equal the trade description in the extent to which it is likely to get home to anyone interested in receiving the goods."[30]

**11–20**    Even where the disclaimer meets this test the courts will look at its wording to see if that may create a false impression on the mind of the reader. *Corfield v. Starr*[31] is a good example. There the disclaimer read "[w]ith deep regret due to the Customers' Protection Act we can no longer verify that the mileage shown on this vehicle is correct". The English Divisional Court regarded this reference to a fictitious statute, with its implication that

---

[25]   Trade Descriptions Act 1968, s. 3(2). Anything which, though not a trade description, is likely to be taken for an indication of any of those matters and, as such an indication, would be false to material degree is deemed to be a false trade description: s. 3(3). A false indication that any goods comply with a standard specified or recognised by any person or implied by the approval of any person is deemed to be a false trade description if there is no such person or no specified standard, recognised or implied: s. 2(4).

[26]   *ibid.* s. 3(1).

[27]   Bragg, "More Mileage in Disclaimers" (1982) 2 L.S. 172.

[28]   1984 S.L.T. 423; 1984 S.C.C.R. 198.

[29]   [1974] 1 W.L.R. 1229; [1974] 3 All E.R. 351, D.C.

[30]   *ibid.* at p. 1232; *ibid.* at p. 354.

[31]   [1981] R.T.R. 380, D.C.

the mileage was correct but could not be so stated, as rendering the disclaimer ineffective.

Some confusion has been introduced into this area by mis-understanding of *Kent County Council v. Price.*[32] A market trader had copies of various items of clothing bearing well-known brand names such as *Adidas, Levi's* and *Reebok* which he was selling at very low prices. Beside these items was a notice with the words "Brand Copy". On appeal the English Divisional Court refused to overturn the decision of the magistrates to acquit the defendant on the ground that the notice was an effective disclaimer. This has sometimes been seen as a counter-feiters' charter but looked at more carefully the decision is explicable as an example of the reluctance of an appeal court to alter the findings of fact of a trial court. The comments about disclaimers were obiter and a number of issues were not explored in detail.[33]

**11–21**

In the light of the strict attitude of the courts it is suggested that the review of the Act was right in recommending that the matter be left to be regulated by case law rather than amending the Act. Among those bodies favouring incorporation of the principles presently found in the case law into the Act was the Law Society of Scotland.[34]

**11–22**

The term "trade description" is defined comprehensively in the Trade Descriptions Act 1968. It is an indication, direct or indirect, and by whatever means given, of any of the following matters with respect to any goods or parts of goods; that is to say:

**11–23**

(1)  quantity,[35] size or gauge;

(2)  method of manufacture, production, processing or recon-ditioning;

(3)  composition;

(4)  fitness for purpose, strength, performance, behaviour or accuracy;

(5)  any physical characteristics not included in heads (1) to (4);

---

[32]  (1993) unreported ref. CO/2796/92, DC.

[33]  Simmonds, "A Counterfeiter's Charter", *Trading Standards Review*, August 1993, p.22 and Smith "A Licence to Sell Counterfeit Goods?", Sol Jo 20 August 1993, p. 822; and see the comments on the case in  *Trading and Consumer Law* (Butterworths) 3-267.

[34]  *Review of the Trade Descriptions Act 1968*, Cmnd. 6628 (1976), p. 51.

[35]  "Quantity" includes length, width, height, area, volume, capacity, weight and number: Trade Descriptions Act 1968, s.2(3).

(6)  testing by any person and results thereof[36];

(7)  approval by any person or conformity with a type approved by any person;

(8)  place or date of manufacture, production, processing or reconditioning;

(9)  person by whom manufactured, produced, processed or reconditioned;

(10) other history, including previous ownership or use.[37]

**11-24**  The cases under the Merchandise Marks Acts 1887 to 1953 provide examples of what might be regarded as a misdescription in relation to composition. For example, it has been held to be a false description to describe artificial silk stockings as "silk".[38] In addition, it has been held that "composition" is wide enough to cover the different articles which are comprised in a package of goods, as where a gas cooker was described as being supplied with a hand-held battery torch for ignition.[39]

**Fitness for purpose**

**11-25**  Fitness for purpose, strength, performance, behaviour or accuracy have frequently been relevant to the description of second-hand cars. For example, auctioneers have been convicted under this provision, having applied the description "good condition" to a car which was not roadworthy.[40] In England the courts have been prepared to hold that expressions such as "beautiful car" and "immaculate condition" could be false descriptions within this provision in appropriate circumstances

---

[36]  It should be noted that the provisions under heads (6) and (7) may be seen as being buttressed by the provision which includes in the definition of "false trade description" statements that goods comply with specified standards or are approved by specified standards or are approved by specified persons even if such standards or persons are fictitious: see the Trade Descriptions Act 1968, s. 34.

[37]  Trade Descriptions Act 1968, s. 2(1). Approval marks applied to motor vehicles in respect of any international agreement to which the U.K. is a party are deemed to be a trade description: see the Road Traffic Act 1972, s. 63. See the Motor Vehicle (Designation of Approval Marks) Regulations 1979 (S.I. 1979 No. 1088).

[38]  *Allard v. Selfridge & Co. Ltd* [1925] 1 K.B. 129.

[39]  *British Gas Corporation v. Lubbock* [1974] 1 WL.R. 37; [1974] 1 All E.R. 188.

[40]  *Aitchison v. Reith and Anderson (Dingwall and Tain) Ltd*, 1974 J.C. 12; 1974 S.L.T.

when applied to a car which to external examination seemed in good condition but internally was not.[41]

Somewhat controversially, in *Formula One Autocentres Ltd v. Birmingham City Council*[42] it was held that the term "Formula One Master Service" was a trade description within this paragraph. This arose from a check on the quality of the servicing offered by a garage. Trading standards officers arranged to have a car serviced by the appellants having first noted that there were various faults that the service ought to have rectified. When the car was returned without several of these faults having been attended to as the servicing schedule promised, a prosecution was brought under section 1 of the Act rather than section 14 which relates to services. It was held that there were false trade descriptions, first of "performance" and second, of "accuracy". It was also held that a false trade description had been applied to goods, namely the Rover car.[43]

**11–26**

Whilst the vast majority of the cases on fitness for purpose, etc., have involved cars, *Sherratt v. Gerald's the American jewellers Ltd*[44] demonstrates that it can be applied to other products. In that case the misdescription was to describe as a "diver's watch"; a timepiece which, on immersion in a bowl of water, filled with water.

**11–27**

### Details of manufacture, etc.

Statements which mislead about origin are caught by the provision in respect of place or date of manufacture, etc., and there are a number of examples from the Merchandise Marks Acts case law.[45] The provision in respect of the person by whom goods are manufactured, etc., has recently become important in the campaign to combat commercial counterfeiting. It can be the appropriate provision to invoke in cases of video piracy or the counterfeiting of computer equipment.[46]

**11–28**

---

[41] *Kensington and Chelsea Royal London Borough Council v. Riley* [1972] R.T.R. 122, D.C.; *Robertson v. Dicicco* [1972] R.T.R. 431, D.C.; *R v. Ford Motor Co Ltd* [1973] 3 All E.R. 489;[1974] 1 W.L.R. 1220, CA.

[42] *The Times*, December 29, 1998, DC (transcript ref: CO/3641/98).

[43] The necessity to resort to s. 1 in this way to overcome the need to prove *mens rea* under s. 14 will disappear when the promise in the White Paper to amend s. 14 is implemented.

[44] (1970) 114 S.J. 147, D.C.

[45] *Holmes v. Pipers Ltd* [1914] 1 K.B. 57, D.C.; *Sandeman v. Cold* [1924] 1 K.B. 107, D.C.

[46] Rowell, "Commercial counterfeiting — Analysis of Trading Standards Statistics" (1984) 92 *Monthly Review* 202. A trade mark could contribute to a misleading trade description see *Re Swiss Miss Trademark* [1998] R.P.C. 889, CA.

**Other history**

**11–29** Undoubtedly the most frequently invoked category of mis-description is the provision in respect of other history, including previous ownership or use. The vast majority of cases under the rubric have been those involving the altering of car odometers. Since *Macnab v. Alexanders of Greenock Ltd*[47] there has been no doubt that this is appropriate. In that case Lord Justice-Clerk Grant stated that: "[t]he distance which a car has travelled seems to me to be just as much a part of its history as the places where it has been and the persons who have owned it. The mileometer figure is, if accurate, a silent historical record of previous use."[48]

**11–30** Trade Descriptions, where they relate to animals, include sex, breed or cross, fertility and soundness, and in relation to semen, include the identity and characteristics of the animal from which it was taken and measure of dilution.[49] The Trade Descriptions Act 1968 excludes from the ambit of the term "trade description" various marks and descriptions applied in pursuance of the Consumer Protection Act 1987 and a number of statutes relating to agriculture and horticulture.[50] Where food and drug legislation has already prohibited the application of a description, such a description is deemed not to be a trade description within the meaning of the Act.[51] A similar provision applies to descriptions prohibited by the Medicines Act 1968.[52]

**Conclusion**

**11–31** As the above analysis demonstrates, the scope of the term "trade description" is very wide. It has been argued by consumer organisations that to make it even more extensive the Trade Descriptions Act 1968 should adopt the practice adopted in some other countries and enact a general prohibition on the use

---

[47] 1971 S.L.T. 121.
[48] *ibid.* at p. 124. See also *Tarleton Engineering Co. Ltd v. Nattrass* [1973] 1 W.L.R. 1261; [1973] 3 All E.R. 699, D.C.
[49] Trade Descriptions Act 1968, s. 2(2).
[50] Trade Descriptions Act 1968, s. 2(4) (amended by the Agriculture Act 1970, ss. 6(4), 87(3),113(3), Sched. 5, Pt. 5; the European Communities Act 1972, s. 4, Sched. 3, Pt. 3, Sched. 4, para. 4(2); the Consumer Safety Act 1978, s. 7(8); and the Consumer Protection Act 1987, s. 48(1), Sched. 4, para. 2(1)(a)).
[51] *ibid.* s. 2(5)(a)(amended by the Consumer Safety Act 1978, s. 7(8); the Food Act 1984, s. 134(a), Sched. 10, para. 11; and the Consumer Protection Act 1987, Sched. 4, para. 2(1)(b)). See also *H. P. Bulmer Ltd and Showerings Ltd v. Bollinger S A and Champagne Lanson Pere et Fils* [1978] R.P.C. 79; [1977] 2 C.M.L.R. 625, C.A.
[52] *ibid.* s. 2(5)(b) (added by the Medicines Act 1968, Sched. 5, para.16).

of misleading descriptions.[53] The review committee rejected this view on the basis that the precision of the present method was desirable in a criminal statute and helpful to enforcement authorities and traders alike. It also pointed out that few suggestions for additions to the list of trade descriptions[54] have been made. Nevertheless it did recommend some extensions to the present list. Indications of the identity of a supplier or distributor and the standing, commercial importance or capabilities of a manufacturer, producer or supplier of goods were recommended as "[w]e very much doubt whether the provisions of section 2(1)(i) go anything like far enough to provide the protection which we think desirable."[55] Another proposal was that false and misleading indications of the contents of books, films and recordings, including their authorship should be brought within the scope of the Act.[56] To resolve a possible doubt about the scope of the Act relating to testing[57] it was recommended that, unless the contrary is expressed, an indication that goods have been tested should mean that they have either passed the test or would do so if tested.[58] Like the other recommendations in the review of the Act these useful proposals have not been acted upon.

*Trade Descriptions in Advertisements*

Advertisements present special problems, some of which are dealt with in the Trade Descriptions Act 1968.[59] Advertisements are, by nature, general statements about categories of goods and, therefore, trade descriptions contained in advertisements are to be taken as referring to all goods of the class, whether in existence at the time the advertisement was published or not.[60] In determining whether goods fall into a class, regard must be had, in addition to the form and content of the advertisement, to all matters which would affect a customer's judgement on this matter including the time, place, manner and frequency of the advertisement.[61]     **11–32**

A false statement is made when it is communicated to someone, so that in the case of a written advertisement it is made     **11–33**

---

[53] *Review of the Trade Descriptions Act 1968,* Cmnd. 6628 (1976), p. 39.
[54] *i.e.* under the Trade Descriptions Act 1968, s. 2(1).
[55] *Review of the Trade Descriptions Act 1968*, Cmnd. 6628 (1976), p. 127.
[56] *ibid.* p. 128.
[57] *i.e.* the scope of the Trade Descriptions Act 1968, ss. 2(1)(f), 3(3).
[58] *Review of the Trade Descriptions Act 1968*, Cmnd. 6628 (1976), p. 129.
[59] *i.e.* where in an advertisement a trade description is used in relation to any class of goods: Trade Descriptions Act 1968, s. 5(1). Section 5 applies to the Hallmarking Act 1973.
[60] See the Trade Descriptions Act 1968, s. 5(2)
[61] *ibid.* s. 5(3)

when the advertisement is read by each reader.[62] Thus, there are as many offences as there are readers of an advertisement. In Scotland the problem of multiple prosecutions which this may give rise to appears to be dealt with appropriately by means of administrative procedures adopted by the prosecuting authorities.[63]

**11–34**   The Trade Descriptions Act 1968 enables orders to be made requiring advertisements about goods to contain or refer to information, whether or not a trade description.[64]

*Trade Descriptions and Services*

**11–35**   Despite the fact that the Molony Report[65] did not so recommend, the Trade Descriptions Act 1968 applies to the provision of services, accommodation and facilities. It is an offence for any person in the course of any trade or business to make a statement which he knows to be false, or recklessly to make a statement which is false, about any of five matters relating to the provision of services, accommodation or facilities.[66] These are (a) their provision or nature; (b) the time, manner in which or persons by whom they are provided; (c) their location; or (d) that they have been examined, approved or evaluated by any person.[67]

**11–36**   The terms "services", "accommodation" or "facilities" are not defined, or fully defined, in the Act.[68] There has been some doubt whether professional services are regulated by the Act but in *R. v. Breeze* the argument that they were not was rejected.[69] In the only reported Scottish case[70] to deal with the meaning of the term "facilities" it was held, adopting the same approach as the English decisions, that to provide a facility was to provide someone with the wherewithal to do something for himself. Thus the provision of a guarantee with a television set was a facility. A

[62]  *Wings Ltd v. Ellis* [1985] A.C. 272.
[63]  *Review of the Trade Descriptions Act 1968*, Cmnd. 6628 (1976), p. 84.
[64]  See the Trade Descriptions Act 1968, s. 9 and the Trade Descriptions (Sealskin Goods) (Information) Order 1980 (S.I. 1980 No. 1150).
[65]  *Final Report of the committee on Consumer Protection* (the Molony Report), Cmnd. 1781 (1962).
[66]  Trade Descriptions Act 1968, s. 14(1)(a),(b). "Services" does not include anything done under a contract of service: s. 14(4). In relation to any services consisting of or including the application of any treatment or process or the carrying out of any repair, the matters specified in s. 14(1) are to be taken to include the effect of the treatment, process or repair; s. 14(3). The Secretary of State of Trade and Industry may make orders defining terms for the purpose of s. 14.
[67]  *ibid.* s. 14(1)(i)–(v).
[68]  As to "services", see the 1968 Act, s. 14(3),(4).
[69]  [1973] 1 W.L.R. 994; [1973] 2 All E.R. 1141, CA.
[70]  *Smith v. Dixons Ltd*, 1986 S.C.C.R. 1.

closing down sale has been held not to be a facility within the meaning of the Act.[71]

*Meaning of "false"*

"False" means false to a material degree.[72] Anything (whether or   **11–37**
not a statement as to any specified matters[73]) likely to be taken
for such a statement as to any of those matters as would be false
is deemed to be a false statement as to that matter.[74] A statement
made regardless of whether it is true or false is deemed to be
made recklessly, whether or not the person making it had reasons for believing that it might be false.[75]

It has been commonplace to draw attention to the differing   **11–38**
bases of liability under sections 1 and 14 of the Act.[76] Section 14
is often said to be markedly different in requiring proof of *mens
rea*. In the light of the House of Lords discussion of section 14 in
*Wings Ltd v. Ellis*[77] it is necessary to revise this assessment. As
Lord Scarman put it, "the basic issue between the parties is
whether . . . section 14(1)(a) creates an offence of strict, or more
accurately, semi-strict, liability or is one requiring the existence
of full *"mens rea"*.[78] Lord Scarman found that it fell into the
category of "semi-strict" liability in so far as it "can be committed unknowingly, *i.e.* without knowledge of the act of
statement."[79] This he justified on the ground that it advanced the
social purpose of the legislation which was, in a simple and
straightforward way, to protect consumers. He also pointed out
that the Act is "not a truly criminal statute. Its purpose is not the
enforcement of the criminal law but the maintenance of trading
standards. Trading standards, not criminal behaviour, are its
concern".[80] In these circumstances he deduced that the intention
of the legislature was not to include *mens rea* as an ingredient of
the offence.

An offence is committed if a statement known to be false is   **11–39**
made on the defender's behalf in the course of a business. It is
irrelevant that the defender did not know that the statement had

---

[71] *Westminster City Council v. Ray Alan (Manshops) Ltd* [1982] 1 WL.R. 383,
   D.C.
[72] Trade Descriptions Act 1968, s. 14(4).
[73] *i.e.* the matters specified in the 1968 Act, s. 14(1): see para. 11-32.
[74] *ibid.* s. 14(2)(a).
[75] *ibid.* s. 14(2)(b).
[76] In para 3.19 of the White Paper the Government indicated that, subject to
   consultation, they intended to remove the distinction.
[77] [1985] A.C. 272.
[78] *ibid.* at p. 290.
[79] *ibid.* at p. 295.
[80] *ibid.* at p. 293.

been made. This was the case in *Wings Ltd v. Ellis,* where a holiday firm was convicted when one of its brochures, containing a false statement was read, some months after first being issued, by a customer who obtained it from a travel agent.[81] As *Wings Ltd v. Ellis* shows, statements are made not only on first publication of a document, but on all later occasions when members of the public read them.

**11–40**    In the only other decision on section 14 of the Act by the House of Lords, the difficult problem of distinguishing between statements of fact, which if false are contrary to section 14, and statements as to future conduct, which are not, was discussed.[82] The bald assertion of this dichotomy conceals some of the problems. The existence of an intention can be a fact like anything else and thus within the prohibition. In a number of cases the difficulty has been that it could not be shown that the accused had at the time he made the assertion no intention to do what he promised.[83] However, *British Airways Board v. Taylor*[84] demonstrates that assertions about future conduct can be within the Act. In that case a passenger who had a return ticket from London to Bermuda received from BOAC a written confirmation that he had a booking on a specific flight. When he arrived at the airport he was informed that the flight was full and he was not permitted to travel on that flight. It was shown that BOAC, in common with other airlines, adopted a policy which could lead to this situation. In these circumstances its assertion that the passenger was assured of a seat on the flight was, to its knowledge when made, false. This principle was applied in *Herron v. Lunn Poly (Scotland) Ltd.*[85]

## Miscellaneous Provisions in respect of Trade Descriptions, etc.

*Marking orders*

**11–41**    The Secretary of State for Trade and Industry is empowered by the Trade Descriptions Act 1968 to make orders requiring that goods be marked with or accompanied by certain information.[86] Failure to comply is a criminal offence.[87]

---

[81]   [1985] A.C. 272, at p. 293.
[82]   *British Airways Board v. Taylor* [1976] 1 W.L.R. 13; [1976] 1 All E.R. 65, H.L.
[83]   *Beckett v. Cohen* [1972] 1 W.L.R. 1593; [1973] 1 All E.R. 120, D.C.
[84]   [1985] A.C. 272.
[85]   1972 S.L.T. (Sh.Ct.) 2.
[86]   Trade Descriptions Act 1968, s. 8.
[87]   *ibid.* s. 8(2).

*Imported goods*

The Trade Descriptions Act 1968 makes it a criminal offence to **11–42** import into the United Kingdom goods bearing false indication of their place of origin.[88]

*False representation as to royal approval, etc.*

In addition to the prohibitions relating to false trade descriptions **11–43** already discussed in relation to the supply of goods and services the Trade Descriptions Act 1968 bans false representations as to royal approval or award. It is an offence in the course of a trade or business to give a false indication that goods or services are of a kind supplied to or approved by any member of the royal family.[89] It is also an offence to make unauthorised use of any device or emblem signifying the Queen's Award to Industry.[90]

*False representations as to supply of goods or services*

The Trade Descriptions Act 1968 creates an offence of falsely **11–44** claiming that goods or services supplied by a person are of a kind supplied to any person.[91] This is a strict liability offence, but is subject to the general defences set out in the Act.

**Defences**

Like other consumer protection measures sanctioning behaviour **11–45** by means of strict criminal liability, the severity of the Trade Descriptions Act 1968 offences is mitigated by the defence of due diligence.[92] There is also a defence of innocent publication of advertisements.[93] Although strictly speaking the provision regarding offences due to the fault of another person is not a defence, it is convenient to deal with it here.[94] There has been some doubt as to whether the defences apply in respect of the offence of making false or misleading statements as to services,[95] but this has been dispelled by the decision of the of Lords in *Wings Ltd v. Ellis.*[96]

---

[88] Trade Descriptions Act 1968, s. 16.
[89] *ibid.* s. 12(1).
[90] *ibid.* s. 12 (2).
[91] *ibid.* s. 13.
[92] *ibid.* s. 24.
[93] *ibid.* s. 25.
[94] *ibid.* s. 23.
[95] *ibid.* s. 14.
[96] [1985] A.C. 272.

**11–46**      In *R. v. Southwood*[97] it was held that the defences could not be used where the charge was one of applying a false description to goods. In that case a motor trader had "clocked" a car. The invoice given to the purchaser contained a disclaimer on which the defendant relied as demonstrating that he came within the reasonable precautions defence. The English Court of Criminal Appeal found such a course of action illogical and refused to countenance this as a defence.

*Defence of due diligence*

**11–47**   To establish the defence of due diligence the accused must establish two things: (1) that the commission of the offence was due to his[98] mistake, or reliance on information supplied to him or to the act or default of another person, an accident or some other cause beyond his control[99]; and (2) that he took all reasonable precautions and exercised all due diligence to avoid the commission of the offence by himself or by anyone under his control. Where the accused is relying on the act or default of, or on information supplied by, another person he must give, at least seven days before the date of the hearing, written notice to the prosecution giving such information as he has identifying the other person.[1]

**11–48**      These defences apply to all the offences created by the Trade Descriptions Act 1968. However, in addition there is a separate defence in respect of the offence of supplying or offering to supply goods to which a false trade description has been applied,[2] which provides that it is a defence to prove that the accused did not know, and could not with reasonable diligence have ascertained, that the goods did not conform to the description or that the description had been applied to the goods.[3]

**11–49**      The defence of due diligence has given rise to frequent litigation. The part of the defence involving ascription of fault to "another person" has revealed a weakness in the Trade Descriptions Act 1968 where large corporate traders[4] are concerned. It has been held that a branch manager of a large retailing chain was "another person", it not being possible to identify him as the

[97]  [1987] 1 W.L.R. 1361.
[98]  *Birkenhead and District Co-operative Society Ltd v. Roberts* [1970] 1 W.L.R. 1497; [1970] 3 All E.R. 391, D.C.
[99]  Trade Descriptions Act 1968, s. 24(1).
[1]  *ibid.* s. 24(2).
[2]  *ibid.*
[3]  *ibid.* s. 24(3).
[4]  As to offences by corporations, see the Trade Descriptions Act 1968, s. 20.

*alter ego* of the company.[5] Only very senior members of the company could be so regarded. The extent to which reliance on this defence may undermine the purpose of the Act should not be over-emphasised. In another case it was pointed out that the defence was not available unless all reasonable inquiries had been made to try to establish the actual person responsible for the offence and that it was not sufficient simply to produce a list of all the staff who might have been responsible.[6]

It should also be noted that shifting the blame to another **11–50** person is only one ingredient of the defence, the other being that the accused took all reasonable precautions and exercised all due diligence. The courts have not been easily satisfied on this score. The case law would seem to support the proposition that to avail himself of this part of the defence the accused must show that he had set up a system designed to prevent errors and also that that system was adequately operated. The two Scottish cases which discuss the reasonableness of precautions and due diligence certainly set high standards. In one of these cases the defence was not available, but the High Court of Justiciary would not have held it to have been satisfied.[7]

The circumstances were that a car sold by the accused com- **11–51** pany had been serviced by it some months before and the company was not considered to have taken all reasonable precautions to avoid a misdescription of the car's mileage because it was proved that it had taken no steps to check its own records. In the other case the failure of the accused's managing director to check that his instructions had been carried out showed want of due diligence.[8] It was also stated by the High Court that where auctioneers applied descriptions concerning the condition of cars which they offered for sale it was not sufficient, to meet the reasonableness requirement of the defence, merely to carry out a cursory external examination. The Lord Justice-Clerk (Wheatley) observed that the accused "were under no obligation to give any description of the condition of the car, but, if they elected to do so they should have taken some reasonable steps to see that their description was warranted."[9]

A similarly strict line was taken by the High Court in *Ford v.* **11–52** *Guild*,[10] in which a motor dealer appealed against a conviction

---

[5] *Tesco Supermarkets Ltd v. Nattrass* [1972] A.C. 153; [1971] 2 All E.R. 127, H.L.
[6] *McGuire v. Sittingbourne Co-operative Society Ltd* [1976] Crim.L.R. 268, D.C.
[7] *Macnab v. Alexanders of Greenock Ltd,* 1971 S.L.T. 121.
[8] *Aitchison v. Reith and Anderson (Dingwall and Tain) Ltd,* 1974 J.C. 12; 1974 S.L.T. 282.
[9] *ibid.* at pp. 17–18; *ibid.* at p. 287.
[10] 1990 J.C. 55; 1990 S.L.T. (Sh. Ct.) 502; 1989 S.C.C.R. 572.

for supplying a car to which a false trade description had been applied. The dealer had bought the car from D, a private individual, who told him that the mileage reading was correct. It was slightly above average for the age of the car but appeared to be consistent with its condition. D gave his name and address and the name and address of B, the previous owner, but could not produce any service documents. The address of B proved to be false and he could not be traced. The appeal was dismissed. Although the dealer had no reason to disbelieve D's information he had made no attempt to confirm that B existed and the sheriff had been entitled to find that he had not established under section 24(3) that he could not have ascertained the truth.

*Offence due to the fault of another person*

**11–53**    Sometimes referred to as the "by-pass" provision, section 23 of the Trade Descriptions Act 1968 enables a prosecution to be brought against a person whose act or default has caused another person to commit an offence, even if that other person has not been prosecuted. It is a provision that has been borrowed from the food and drugs legislation, where it has a long history. The version used in the 1968 Act is not clearly drafted and, read literally, it is difficult to make sense of it. It could be argued that the first person would not have committed an offence if he could bring himself within the due diligence defence of section 24 by proving that the offence was due to the act or default of another and that he had exercised due diligence. In *Coupe v. Guyett*[11] Widgery L.C.J. suggested that sections 23 and 24 could be fitted together. Where the first person referred to in section 23 has a defence on the merits and without reliance on section 24, it is not possible to operate section 23 so as to render guilty the person whose act or default gave rise to the matter in complaint. He argued that section 23 comes into play only where the first person escaped prosecution by taking advantage of the due diligence defence of section 24.

**11–54**    Unlike the other sections of the Act creating criminal offences, section 23 is not prefaced by the words "in the course of a business". It has been held in England that a private individual not acting in the course of a business can be prosecuted under it.[12]

---

[11]  [1973] 1 W.L.R. 669; [1973] 2 All E.R. 1058, D.C.
[12]  *Olgeirsson v. Kitching* [1986] 1 All E.R. 746; [1986] 1 WL.R. 304; D.C. See also Ervine, "Private Sellers and the Trade Descriptions Act", 1986 S.L.T. (News) 217.

**Enforcement and Penalties**

Enforcement of the Trade Descriptions Act 1968 is the duty of **11–55**
the district councils as the local weights and measures authorities.[13] Prosecutions are carried out by the procurator fiscal, who
decides whether a prosecution should be brought. There has
been some disquiet in Scotland that the level of prosecutions is
significantly lower than in England and Wales.[14]

In order to carry out their duties under the Act, trading **11–56**
standards officers are given various powers. They may make test
purchases,[15] enter premises at all reasonable hours to ascertain if
the Act is being observed and, if they have reasonable cause to
suspect that an offence has been committed, may require production of books and documents and seize goods.[16] On obtaining
a warrant from a sheriff or justice of the peace admission to
premises, by force if necessary, is permissible.[17] Where goods are
seized in exercise of these powers, the enforcement authority
may in certain circumstances be liable to pay compensation to a
trader.[18] Obstruction of an enforcement officer in the exercise of
his duty is a criminal offence.[19]

The penalties for most offences under the Trade Descriptions **11–57**
Act 1968 are, on summary conviction, a maximum fine not
exceeding the prescribed sum[20] and, on indictment, a fine or a
term of imprisonment not exceeding two years, or both.[21] The
offence of obstructing an enforcement officer in the exercise of
his duty[22] carries a fine not exceeding level 3 on the standard
scale.[23]

---

[13] Weights and Measures Act 1985, s. 69(3).
[14] Purdom and Walker, *The Enforcement of the Trade Descriptions Act in Scotland,* Scottish Consumer Council (1980).
[15] See the Trade Descriptions Act 1968, s. 27. As to notice of test and intended prosecution, see s. 30(1).
[16] *ibid.* s. 28 (amended by the Consumer Credit Act 1974, s. 192(3)(a), Sched. 4, para. 28, and the Consumer Protection Act 1987, s. 48(1), Sched. 4, para. 2(2)).
[17] See the Trade Descriptions Act 1968, s. 28(3).
[18] *ibid.* s. 33.
[19] *ibid.* s. 29.
[20] *ibid.* s. 18(a). The prescribed sum is now £5,000: the Criminal Procedure (Scotland) Act 1975, s. 289B (added by the Criminal Law Act 1977, s. 63(1), Sched. 2, para. 5, substituted by the Criminal Justice Act 1982, s. 55(2), amended by the Criminal justice Act 1991, s. 17(2).
[21] Trade Descriptions Act 1968, s. 18(b).
[22] Consumer Protection Act 1987, s. 29(1),
[23] *ibid.* s. 29(1), and the Criminal Procedure (Scotland) Act 1975, ss. 289F(8), 289G(2)(added by the Criminal Justice Act 1982, s. 54).

## MISLEADING PRICES

**11–58** The control of misleading indication of prices has proved to be a difficult and controversial matter. On the one hand it is important not to impede the working of the competitive process by unnecessary restrictions but, on the other hand, it is difficult by simple methods to catch those determined to exploit the loopholes in legislation. Section 11 of the Trade Descriptions Act 1968 sought to regulate price advertising, but it proved necessary to buttress it with the Price Marking (Bargain Offers) Order 1979.[24] This proved unpopular both with traders and trading standards officers, and Part III of the Consumer Protection Act 1987 introduces a different approach to the regulation of price advertising.

**11–59** Instead of attempting to prohibit specific practices, as the earlier legislation did, the Consumer Protection Act 1987 creates a wide general offence of giving to consumers a misleading indication as to the price of any goods, services, accommodation or facilities.[25] This applies whether the indication was misleading when it was originally given or later becomes so.[26] An indication of the price or the method of determining a price is misleading if what is conveyed, or what consumers might reasonably be expected to infer from the indication or any omission from it, includes any of a number of factors.[27] These are indications:

(1) that the price is less than, or the method is not what, in fact it is;

(2) that the applicability of the price or method does not depend on facts or circumstances on which its applicability does in fact depend;

(3) that the price or method covers matters in respect of which an additional charge is made;

(4) that a trader has no genuine belief that a price increase or reduction or alteration of a method is imminent; and

(5) that facts or circumstances by reference to which a consumer might reasonably be expected to judge the validity of a comparison are not accurate.[28]

---

[24] Price Marking (Bargain Offers) Order 1979, (S.I. 1979 No. 364) (amended by S.I. 1979 No. 633 and S.I. 1979 No. 1124).
[25] See the Consumer Protection Act 1987, s. 20(1).
[26] *ibid.* s. 20(1), (2).
[27] *ibid.* s. 21(1), (2).
[28] *ibid.* s. 21(1)(a)–(e), (2)(a)–(e), (3).

It is made clear that references to services do not include **11–60**
references to services provided to an employer under a contract
of employment[29] and that references to services or facilities do
not include references to services or facilities provided by
authorised persons or appointed representatives in carrying on
an investment business.[30] However, it is emphasised that the
provision of credit[31] or banking or insurance services, the purchase or sale of foreign currency,[32] the supply of electricity and
the provision of off-street car parks and caravan sites[33] are
included.[34] This somewhat curious provision is explained by the
fact that all these services have been the subject of frequent
complaints on account of the quality of price advertising. Reference to accommodation or facilities does not include
accommodation or facilities being made available by means of
the creation or disposal of an interest in land, except where it is
the creation or disposal of the *dominium utile* of land comprising
a new dwelling or a leasehold in such a dwelling where at least 21
years remains unexpired.[35]

For the most part the defences available are similar to those **11–61**
applicable to offences under the Trade Descriptions Act 1968.
The due diligence defence set out in the Consumer Protection
Act 1987 applies.[36] It is a defence for a person (1) to show that a
price indication complied with regulations made under Part III[37]
of the Act[38]; (2) that he was a bona fide publisher of an

---

[29] Consumer Protection Act 1987, s. 22(2). By virtue of s. 22(5), "contract of employment" and "employer" have the same meaning as in the Employment Protection (Consolidation) Act 1978 (see s. 153(1)).
[30] *ibid.* s. 22(3). By virtue of s. 22(5), "appointed representative", "authorised person" and "investment have the same meaning as in the Financial Services Act 1986 (see ss. 1(2), 44, 207(1)).
[31] "Credit" has the same meaning as in the Consumer Credit Act 1974. See Consumer Protection Act 1987, s. 22(5).
[32] In relation to a service consisting in the purchase or sale of foreign currency references in Consumer Credit Act 1974, Pt 3, to the method by which the price of the service is determined include references to the rate of exchange: s. 22(4).
[33] "Caravan" has the same meaning as in the Caravan Sites and Control of Development Act 1960 (see s. 29(1)): Consumer Protection Act 1987, s. 22(5).
[34] Consumer Protection Act 1987, s. 22(1)(a)–(e).
[35] *ibid.* s. 23.
[36] *ibid.* ss. 24(5), 39. In respect of offences under Pt. 3 (ss. 20–26), s. 39 only applies to the offence of giving a misleading price indication under s. 20(1).
[37] *ibid.* s. 26.
[38] *ibid.* s. 24(1). This defence is only available in respect of offences under s. 20(1),(2).

advertisement[39]; or (3) that he was the author of a recommended
price and did not offer goods, services, accommodation or facilities himself but reasonably assumed that the recommended price
was, for the most part, being followed.[40]

**11–62**    A defence which gave rise to a good deal of controversy
during the parliamentary progress of the Consumer Protection
Bill is that in respect of the code of practice. The Secretary of
State, after consulting the Director General of Fair Trading and
such other persons as may be appropriate, may by order approve
a code of practice giving practical guidance about price indications.[41] Failure to comply with this code does not by itself give
rise to any criminal or civil liability, but it will have evidential
value[42] in that contravention of the code may be relied on for the
purpose of establishing that an offence had been committed or of
negativing a defence, while compliance with the code may be
relied on to show that no offence has been committed or that
there is a defence.[43]

### Enforcement

**11–63**    The enforcement of the provisions in respect of misleading price
indications is the duty of district councils as the weights and
measures authorities.[44] The penalties for the offence of giving a
misleading price indication are, on conviction on indictment, a
fine, and on summary conviction, a fine not exceeding the
statutory maximum.[45]

### PROPERTY MISDESCRIPTIONS

**11–64**    Although house purchase is most people's most expensive purchase it was generally agreed that houses for sale did not come
within the ambit of the Trade Descriptions Act 1968.[46] Although

---

[39]  Consumer Protection Act 1987, s. 24(3). This defence is only available in
respect of offences under s. 20(1), (2). "Advertisement" includes a catalogue,
a circular and a price list: s.24(6). In proceedings for an offence under s. 20(1),
(2), in respect of an indication published in a book, newspaper, magazine, film
or radio or television broadcast or in a programme included in a cable
programme service, it is a defence to show that the indication was not
contained in an advertisement: s. 24(2),(6).

[40]  *ibid.* s. 24(4). This defence is only available in respect of an offence under
s. 20(1).

[41]  *ibid.* s. 25(1), (3), (4).

[42]  *i.e.* in proceedings for an offence under the 1987 Act, s. 20(1), (2).

[43]  1987 Act, s. 25(2).

[44]  *ibid.* s. 27.

[45]  *ibid.* s. 20(4). As to the time limit for bringing prosecutions, see s. 20(5). "The
statutory maximum" means the prescribed sum as defined in the Criminal
Procedure (Scotland) Act 1975, s. 289B.

[46]  See *Review of the Trade Descriptions Act 1968: A Report by the Director
General of Fair Trading,* Cmnd. 6628 (1976), para. 70.

it was recommended that this omission should be rectified as long ago as 1976,[47] this did not happen until the Property Misdescriptions Act 1991 was passed.[48] It makes it a criminal offence to make false or misleading statements about various matters in the course of an estate agency or property development business. The prescribed matters are set out in the Property Misdescriptions (Specified Matters) Order 1992[49] which came into force on April 4, 1993. They include location or address, aspect, view, outlook and environment, availability and proximity of services and facilities, accommodation and measurements, physical characteristics, surveys, history, and the identity of the builder. In addition, various matters relating to the tenure and incidents of ownership as well as rates and charges are included.

Like the offences in section 1 of the Trade Descriptions Act **11–65** 1968 the offence created by this Act is one of strict liability. The Act also has a due diligence defence in section 2 in the interpretation of which the cases on the similar defence in the 1968 Act will be relevant. The false statement must be made in the course of an estate agency or property development business, "otherwise than in providing conveyancing services". A statement is made in the course of an estate agency business if (but only if) the making of the statement is a thing done as mentioned in subsection (1) of section 1 of the Estate Agents Act 1979. This means anything done for the purposes of introducing a client to a third party who wishes to dispose of or acquire an interest in land.[50] Given the fact that solicitors offer estate agency services in Scotland, it may be difficult to decide when they are offering estate agency services and when they stray over the line into conveyancing service.

Enforcement is in the hands of the district councils as weights **11–66** and measures authorities.[51] The penalty for a breach of the Act is, on summary conviction, a fine not exceeding the statutory maximum which is currently £5,000[52]; and, on indictment, to an unlimited fine.

### DOORSTEP SELLING

Complaints about high pressure selling methods employed by **11–67** some sales representatives when they visit consumers in their

---

[47] Cmnd. 6628 (1976).
[48] See Styles, "The Property Misdescriptions Act 1991" (1992) 37 J.L.S.S. 486.
[49] S.I. 1992 No. 2834.
[50] There is a similar provision in relation to the making of statements in the course of a property development business.
[51] Property Misdescriptions Act 1991, s. 3 and Schedule.
[52] See n. 45.

homes are not uncommon. They are particularly prevalent in relation to the sale of double glazing and encyclopaedias, but have arisen in other sectors as well.[53] The E.C. Doorstep Selling Directive[54] which was implemented in this country by the Consumer Protection (Cancellation of Contracts Concluded away from Business Premises) Regulations 1987[55] provides a civil remedy.

**11–68**    Although often referred to as a control on doorstep selling, the regulations apply more widely. Regulation 3 provides that they apply where a trader makes a contract relating to goods or services[56] during an unsolicited visit to the home of a consumer,[57] or to another person's home; and also to a person's workplace. They can also apply to a visit which was requested if it results in a contract to supply goods or services other than those concerning which the consumer requested the visit. For the regulations to apply in those circumstances the consumer must not have known, or could not reasonably have known, when the visit was requested, that the supply of those goods or services formed part of the trader's business activities. Finally, the regulations also apply to contracts concluded during an excursion organised by a trader away from trade premises.

**11–69**    The 1998 amendment to the regulations seeks to close loopholes in the regulations by amplifying the meaning of "unsolicited visit" in a new regulation 3(3). A visit by a trader is considered to be unsolicited if it follows an earlier unsolicited visit during which he, or someone acting in his name or on his behalf, indicated that he, or the trader in whose name or on whose behalf he was acting, was prepared to make a subsequent visit to the consumer. The definition is also amended to make it

---

[53]    Life assurance is notorious and since the Insurance Companies Act 1982 there has been a right to cancel certain policies of insurance. See para. 11-88.

[54]    Directive 85/577, of December 20, 1985, to Protect the Consumer in Respect of Contracts Negotiated away from Business Premises [1985] O.J. L372, p. 31.

[55]    S.I. 1987 No. 2117 as amended by The Consumer Protection (Cancellation of Contracts Concluded away from Business Premises) (Amendment) Regulations 1988 (S.I. 1988 No. 958) as of July 1, 1988; and The Consumer Protection (Cancellation of Contracts Concluded away from Business Premises) (Amendment) Regulations 1998 (S.I. 1998 No. 3050) as of December 31, 1998.

[56]    The Court of Justice of the European Community has ruled, in *Bayerische Hypotheken-und Wechselbank AG v. Dietzinger*, Case C–45/96; [1998] All E.R. (E.C.) 332, that the directive does not apply to a contract of guarantee concluded by a natural person who was not acting in the course of his trade or profession where repayment of a debt contracted by another person who was acting in the course of his trade or profession was being guaranteed.

[57]    "Consumer" means a person, other than a body corporate, who, in making a contract is acting for purposes which can be regarded as outside his business. See reg. 2(1).

clear that it covers a visit following an unsolicited telephone call where the person who visits the consumer is not the same as the person who made the telephone call, but the person who made the telephone call was acting in his name or on his behalf.

Not all contracts are subject to the regulations. As we have seen in Chapter 9, the Consumer Credit Act has provisions for a cooling off period for "cancellable agreements". Where these apply they should be followed, even if the contract would also fall under these regulations.[58] Contracts for the provision of credit of less than £35, other than hire-purchase and conditional sale contracts, are exempt, as are other contracts under which the consumer will not make payments of more than £35. There is an important exception also for the supply of food, drink or other goods intended for current consumption by use in the household and supplied by regular roundsmen. Obvious examples would be milk or bread deliveries. Catalogue traders who leave their catalogues with their customers and expect to have a continuous relation with them are exempt from the regulations if their catalogues and contracts contain a prominent notice that the consumer may return the goods within seven days of their receipt.[59]     **11–70**

Also excluded from the regulations are contracts for the sale of land, heritable securities and bridging finance in connection with the purchase of land. Contracts for the construction or extension of a building are exempt. However, the regulations explicitly state that they do apply to a contract to supply goods and incorporate them in a building; and a contract for the repair of a building.[60] Contracts for fitted kitchens or double glazing are, therefore, clearly within the regulations. Investment agreements under the Financial Services and Markets Act 2000 and contracts of insurance governed by the Insurance Companies Act 1982 are also exempt.     **11–71**

Where the regulations apply, consumers have a cooling off period of seven days from the making of the contract. During this period they may cancel the contract by giving written notice of cancellation. This need be in no particular form as long as it indicates the intention of the consumer to cancel the contract. The fact that there is a cooling off period must be brought to the attention of consumers by an easily legible notice which must be given at least as much prominence as any other information in the document. It must contain the information set out in the schedule to the regulations and a cancellation form in the form set out there. The notice must be given to the consumer at the     **11–72**

---

[58] reg. 4(2).
[59] reg. 3(2)(c).
[60] reg. 3(2)(a).

Consumer Law in Scotland

time of making the contract or, where consumers offer to enter into a contract in their homes, when they make that offer. Failure to comply with this requirement means that the contract is not enforceable and that the trader commits a criminal offence.[61]

**11–73**     Where consumers exercise their rights to cancel, any money that they have paid becomes repayable and there is a lien for its repayment over any goods supplied under the contract which may be in the possession of a consumer. Subject to this lien, consumers who are in possession of goods are under a duty to take reasonable care of them pending their return to the supplier. Although under no obligation to deliver the goods to the supplier other than at their own homes, consumers may choose to return them to the person on whom a cancellation notice could have been served. These duties to take reasonable care of the goods and to return them are statutory duties and are actionable as such.[62] There are detailed provisions in the regulations dealing with the return of goods given in part-exchange[63] and the repayment of credit.[64]

## DISTANCE SELLING

**11–74**     Distance selling by which is meant a sales method where the buyer and supplier do not come face to face up to and including the moment at which the contact is concluded is becoming increasingly important. Mail order selling is an important and long-standing example and telephone sales and tele-shopping are other examples. E-commerce is an increasingly important growth area. Few aspects of distance selling are subject to statutory regulation in the United Kingdom beyond those controls which apply generally to the supply of goods and services. This will change with the implementation of the Distance Selling Directive[65] which should have occurred by June 4, 2000.

**11–75**     This directive covers contracts concluded between a consumer and a professional using the various forms of distance selling. Distance selling of financial services is not included because the Commission intends to deal with this in a separate measure. The directive requires certain information to be given by distance sellers such as their identity, the principal characteristics of the product or service, its price, delivery costs, payment methods and conditions of delivery. Most importantly, there is a cooling off period of at least seven days starting from the day on which

---

[61]   regs 4 and 4A.
[62]   reg. 7(8).
[63]   reg. 8
[64]   reg. 6.
[65]   97/7/EC O.J. L144 4, June 1997, p.19.

the consumer receives the product during which he or she may withdraw from the contract. The DTI have been consulting on the implementation of the directive. At the end of June 2000 their website stated that regulations would come into force later this year.

## TRADING STAMPS

Trading stamps are a much less popular method of promoting the sale of goods and services than was the case a few years ago. Their use is regulated by the Trading Stamps Act 1964, which makes it a criminal offence for trading stamp schemes to be promoted by entities other than companies registered under the Companies Act 1985 or an industrial and provident society.[66] Companies promoting such schemes must issue stamps which are to be used in connection with the sale or hiring of goods[67] only if they bear on their face in clear and legible characters a value expressed in or by reference to current coin of the realm.[68] Every stamp book and catalogue must contain a prominent statement of the name of the promoter and the address of the promoter's registered office.[69] Failure to provide these pieces of information is a criminal offence as is the publication of advertisements which seek to indicate the value of stamps by comparing their worth with what the holder of them may pay for goods or services to obtain them, or in terms which are deceptive or misleading.[70] Shops participating in trading stamp schemes are required to post notices stating the cash value of stamps and the basis on which customers are entitled to obtain stamps.[71] Where the promoter of a trading stamp scheme has issued a catalogue it

**11–76**

---

[66] See the Trading Stamps Act 1964, s. 1(1), (3), (4) (amended by the Companies Consolidation (Consequential Provisions) Act 1985, s. 30, Sched. 2). For the meaning of "trading stamp", see the Trading Stamps Act 1964, s. 10(1) (substituted by the Consumer Credit Act 1974, s. 192, Sched. 4, para. 26(3)), and for the meaning of "trading stamp scheme", see the Trading Stamps Act 1964, s. 10(1).

[67] Barter is not included. For the meaning of "goods", see the Trading Stamps Act, s. 10(1).

[68] Trading Stamps Act 1964, s. 2(1)(substituted by the Consumer Credit Act 1974, Sched. 4, para. 24). The stamps must also bear on their face in clear and legible characters the name of the company or its business name or the name of the industrial and provident society: Trading Stamps Act 1964, s. 2(2). For the meaning of "stamps", see s. 10(1).

[69] *ibid.* s. 5(1). For the meaning of "stamp book", see s. 10(1).

[70] Trading Stamps Act 1964, s. 6(1). For this purpose an advertisement issued by way of display or exhibition in a public place is to be treated as issued on every day on which it is so displayed or exhibited: s. 6(3).

[71] *ibid.* s. 7(1)(a), (2). For the meaning of "cash value" and "shop", see s. 10(1).

must be kept where it can be conveniently consulted by customer.[72]

**11–77**    The holder of trading stamps having a value of more than 25p
is entitled to redeem them for cash by presenting them at the
registered office of the promoter of the scheme or in some other
way afforded by the promoter.[73] Where stamps are exchanged
for goods the Trading Stamps Act 1964 implies stipulations that
the promoter has a right to give the goods in exchange, that they
are free from encumbrances and are of satisfactory quality.[74]
Restriction or exclusion of these stipulations is prohibited by the
Trading Stamps Act 1964.[75]

## PYRAMID SCHEMES

**11–78**    Various get rich quick schemes appear from time to time which
depend on participants obtaining benefits by recruiting others.
These money circulation or "snowball" schemes (which are not
to be confused with genuine multi-level marketing operations)
are often little more than consumer frauds. As a judge explained
in a recent case:

> "The number of persons who are sufficiently gullible to be
> persuaded to join may be very large but it is obviously finite.
> So is the amount of money which can be raised by a scheme of
> this kind. The scheme is bound to come to an end sooner or
> later. When it does, most of its members will have lost their
> money. This is not merely likely, it is a mathematical cer-
> tainty."[76]

**11–79**    In the past some of these schemes have been closed down
because they were illegal lotteries.[77] In a further attempt to
control them the pyramid selling provisions in Part XI of the Fair
Trading Act have been amended by the Trading Schemes Act
1996.[78]

---

[72]  Trading Stamps Act 1964, s. 7(1)(b), (5).
[73]  See generally the Trading Stamps Act 1964, s. 3 (amended by the Decimal
      Currency Act 1969, s. 10(3), Sched. 2, para. 77, and the Consumer Credit Act
      1974, s. 192, Sched. 4, para. 25). For the meaning of "to redeem", see the
      Trading Stamps Act 1964, s. 10(1).
[74]  *ibid.* s. 4 (substituted by the Supply of Goods (Implied Terms) Act 1973,
      s. 16(1)) and amended with effect from Jan. 3,1995 by the Sale and Supply of
      Goods Act 1994).
[75]  Trading Stamps Act 1964, s. 4(1).
[76]  Millet L.J. in *Re Senator Hanseatische Verwaltungsgesellschaft Gmbh* [1996]
      4 All E.R. 933 at 942.
[77]  The case referred to in the previous footnote involving the Titan scheme is an
      example.
[78]  See also the Trading Schemes Regulations 1997 (S.I. 1997 No. 30) and The
      Trading Schemes (Exclusions) Regulations 1997 (S.I. 1997 No. 31).

## UNSOLICITED GOODS AND SERVICES

In the late 1960s the practice of inertia selling developed. It **11–80**
consists of sending out goods which have not been ordered,
either by themselves or with other goods that have been ordered,
in the hope that the recipient will in fact pay for them. Demands
for payment of increasing hostility then follow, often alarming
the recipient, who will frequently be unaware of his legal rights.
On general contractual principles no obligation could be created
in this way, but whether the recipient had any duty to keep the
goods safely or any right to appropriate them to his own use was
obscure. To combat this problem the Unsolicited Goods and
Services Act 1971 was enacted.

The Unsolicited Goods and Services Act 1971 attacks the **11–81**
problem in two ways. First it clarifies the civil law by providing
that unsolicited[79] goods become the property of the recipient,
provided that he has no reasonable cause to believe that they
were sent with a view to being acquired for the purpose of a trade
or business, if the sender[80] fails to repossess them within six
months of the day on which the recipient received them.[81] The
recipient can become the owner before the expiration of the six
month period by giving notice of not less than 30 days to the
sender that he has received the unsolicited goods and stating
when and where they may be uplifted.[82]

The criminal law is also invoked to control this abuse by **11–82**
making it a criminal offence, without reasonable cause, to
demand or assert a right to payment for unsolicited goods.[83] The
penalty for this offence is doubled if the sender threatens legal
proceedings, causes the recipient's name to be placed on a list of
defaulters or debtors, or threatens to do so, or has any other
collection procedure invoked.[84] Regulations make detailed provision for the form and content of invoices accompanying
unsolicited material if they are to avoid being regarded as
demands for payment.[85]

---

[79] "Unsolicited" means, in relation to goods sent to any person, that they are
sent without any prior request made by him or on his behalf: Unsolicited
Goods and Services Act 1971, s. 6(1).

[80] "Sender", in relation to any goods, includes any person on whose behalf or
with whose consent the goods are sent, and any other person claiming through
or under the sender or any such person: *ibid.* s. 1(4).

[81] *ibid. s.* 1(1), (2)(a).

[82] *ibid.* s. 1(2)(b), (3).

[83] *ibid.* s. 2(1), and the Criminal Procedure (Scotland) Act 1975, ss. 289f(S),
289(2) (added by the Criminal justice Act 1982, s. 54).

[84] *ibid.* s. 2(2), and the Criminal Procedure (Scotland) Act 1975, ss. 289f(8),
289(2).

[85] See the Unsolicited Goods and Services (Invoices, etc.) Regulations 1975,
(S.I. 1975 No. 732).

**11–83**     The only reported case in respect of demands of payment is *Readers' Digest Association Limited v. Pirie*[86] which suggests a basic weakness in the Act. The *Readers' Digest*, as the result of errors by junior employees, had demanded payment for unsolicited goods. Its conviction was quashed by the High Court of Justiciary on the ground that there was no evidence to show that anyone (who could be regarded as acting as the company) did not have reasonable cause to believe that there was a right to payment.

**11–84**     It is a criminal offence to send anyone a book, magazine or leaflet (or advertising material for such a publication) which is known to be unsolicited and which describes or illustrates human sexual techniques.[87] It has been held that even to send an advertisement for such a publication even though it did not itself illustrate human sexual techniques is a crime.[88]

### RESTRICTIONS ON STATEMENTS

**11–85**     The now moribund procedure under Part II of the Fair Trading Act 1973 produced three sets of regulations governing trading practices.[89] The Consumer Transactions (Restrictions on Statements) Order 1976 makes it a criminal offence to display, at any place where consumer transactions[90] are effected, notices which would be void under the obligations implied by law in consumer transactions[91] or the similar terms implied under the Trading Stamps Act 1964.[92] It is also forbidden to make such statements in advertisements, on goods or containers in which goods are supplied or in documents given to a consumer or someone likely to enter into a consumer transaction.[93] Where statements about

---

[86]   1973 J.C. 42; 1973 S.L.T. 170.

[87]   See the Unsolicited Goods and Services Act 1971, s. 4, and the Criminal Procedure (Scotland) Act 1975, ss. 289B, 289E (added by the Criminal Justice Act 1982, s. 54).

[88]   *Director of Public Prosecutions v. Beate Uhse (U.K.) Ltd* [1974] Q.B. 158; [1974] 1 All E.R. 753, D.C.

[89]   *i.e.* the Consumer Transactions (Restrictions on Statements) Order 1976 (S.I. 1976 No. 1813); the Mail Order Transactions (Information) Order 1976 (S.I. 1976 No. 1812); the Business Advertisements (Disclosure) Order 1977 (S.I. 1977 No.1978).

[90]   For the meaning of "consumer transaction", see the Consumer Transactions (Restrictions on Statements) Order 1971, *supra*, art. 2(1)(substituted by S.I. 1978 No. 127).

[91]   *i.e.* under the Unfair Contract Terms Act 1977, s. 20, which entrenches the terms implied by the Sale of Goods Act 1979. Consumer Transactions (Restrictions on Statements) Order 1976, *supra*, art. 3(a)(i) (substituted by S.I. 1978 No. 127).

[92]   *i.e.* Consumer Transactions (Restrictions on Statements) Order 1976, *supra*, s.4(1)(c) and art. 3(a)(ii).

[93]   *ibid.* art. 3(b)–(d). For the meaning of "advertisement", "consumer" and "container", see art. 2(1).

a consumer's rights are made, whether on the goods or their packaging or in a document, a clear and conspicuous statement must be added explaining that the purchaser's statutory rights are not affected.[94] This applies both to manufacturers' guarantees and notices and statements made by retailers.[95]

## MOCK AUCTIONS

The Mock Auctions Act 1961 seeks to control spurious auctions. **11–86** The objection to such auctions is that "they may be described as a sale conducted by a person . . . whose ultimate aim is to sell goods to the gullible purchasers at highly inflated prices".[96] The auctioneer often begins by giving away or selling at very low prices some inexpensive goods. Somewhat higher priced goods will then be offered and the highest bidder, possibly an unidentified accomplice of the auctioneer, receives an unexpected rebate of the purchase price. Then, with an atmosphere of excitement created, other articles are put up for sale. These will probably not have been available for inspection and may be of inferior quality.

The Mock Auctions Act 1961 seeks to regulate the above **11–87** practices by making it a criminal offence to promote, conduct or assist at a mock auction.[97] A mock auction is one where goods are sold by way of competitive bidding and the highest bidder pays an amount less than his highest bid or part of the price is repaid or credited to him.[98] Alternatively if, during the course of an auction, articles are given away or offered as gifts or the right to bid for any lot is restricted to those who have bought or agreed to buy other articles, the Act is breached.[99] Judging by some of the reported cases this piece of legislation is an extreme example of seeking to protect the gullible from their own folly.[1]

## INSURANCE

Following disquiet about the practices of some insurance sales- **11–88** men there is a "cooling off" period in respect of ordinary

[94] S.I. 1976 No. 1815, art. 4.

[95] *ibid.* art. 5.

[96] Organisation for Economic Co-Operation and Development Annual Report on Consumer Policy (Paris, 1974), p. 11.

[97] s. 1(1).

[98] s. 1(3)(a). A sale of goods is not taken to be a mock auction if it is proved that the reduction in price, or the repayment or credit, as the case may be, was on account of a defect or of damage discovered or sustained after the bid was made: s. 1(4). For the meaning of "sale of goods by way of competitive bidding" and "competitive bidding", see s. 3(1).

[99] s. 1(3)(b), (c).

[1] *Aitchison v. Cooper*, 1982 S.L.T. (Sh. Ct.) 41 where the auctioneer invited bids of £50 for "what was on his mind".

long-term insurance business. "Long term business" includes life assurance, contracts to pay annuities on human life and insurance on death which is to remain in effect for not less than five years.[2] The insurance company may not enter into such contracts unless it sends a statutory notice in the prescribed form either before or at the time the contract is entered into.[3] The principal point of this notice is that it must inform the client that he or she has a statutory right to cancel the insurance policy.[4] This can be done by serving a cancellation notice on the insurer or his agent within 10 days of receiving the statutory notice or before the end of the earliest day on which he knows both that the contract has been entered into and that the first or only premium has been paid, whichever is the later.[5]

## TIMESHARE

**11–89**    Timeshare is a right to use accommodation at a holiday development or resort for a specified number of weeks each year over a specified period of time or in perpetuity. To acquire this right an "owner" pays a lump sum to a "developer". In addition, there are usually annual service charges and there may also be optional annual fees for participation in a scheme to exchange timeshares with others. A report[6] by the Director General of Fair Trading acknowledged that most timeshare owners were satisfied with their purchases. It also noted that there was also a great deal of evidence to suggest that all too often timeshare was not sold in a healthy market where well-informed consumers dealt with responsible traders. The Government responded to proposals in the report for increased protection by bringing forward the Timeshare Act 1992. That act was extensively amended with effect from April 29, 1997[7] to implement the E.C. Timeshare Directive.[8]

**11–90**    One of the common complaints of disenchanted timeshare owners is that they were subjected to high pressure selling techniques and did not realise what they were accepting. To combat this section 2 of the Act provides a cooling-off period of 14 days. Failure to provide a customer with notice of this right and a blank notice of cancellation form is a criminal offence. The Act also covers "timeshare credit agreements" which are those

---

[2]    See the Insurance Companies Act 1982, s. 1(1), Sched. 1.
[3]    *ibid.* s. 75.
[4]    See the Insurance Companies Regulations 1981 (S.I. 1981 No. 1654), regs 70, 71, Scheds. 10–12.
[5]    See the Insurance Companies Act 1982, ss. 76, 77.
[6]    *Timeshare,* Office of Fair Trading, 1990.
[7]    Timeshare Regulations 1997 (S.I. 1997 No. 1081).
[8]    O.J. L. 280 29.10.94, p.83.

financed by credit but which do not come within the cooling off provisions of the Consumer Credit Act 1974. Here the same notice of cancellation rights must be given.

The approach of the Act is firstly to try to ensure that con- **11–91** sumers make a properly informed decision to buy a timeshare, and then to give a period for reflection during which they can cancel the arrangement. To further the first objective section 1A requires a time share operator to provide anyone who requests it with information about the accommodation. Failure to do so is a criminal offence. If the consumer purchases a timeshare this information is deemed to be a term of the contract. One of the common complaints of disenchanted timeshare owners is that they were subjected to high pressure selling techniques and did not realise what they were accepting. To combat this section 5 of the Act provides that a cooling-off period must be provided during which the consumer can choose to cancel the contract. Timeshare operators must give consumers who have entered into a time share agreement a notice informing them or this right and the "cooling-off" period must be at least 14 days from the date of the contract.[9] Not only may consumers withdraw from the contract during the cooling-off period, the operator cannot enforce the agreement during that period. That means, for example, that the seller may not ask for or accept any money from the consumer during it.[10] The 14 day cooling-off period will be extended to three months and ten days if the operator fails to include certain information which must be given under section 1A about the timeshare.

### ESTATE AGENCY

Estate agency has been the subject of much criticism over many **11–92** years because of the sharp practices of a minority of those involved in it.[11] The Estate Agents Act 1979 controls certain aspects of the work of estate agents. The Act does not control entry into the profession: instead, it creates a system of negativing licensing. The Director General of Fair Trading is given powers to ban a person from acting as an estate agent if he finds that they are unfit to do so. The grounds which may render a person unfit are set out in section 3 of the Act. They include convictions for fraud, dishonesty or violence; convictions for breach of the Estate Agents Act; failure to comply with other obligations under that Act; and discrimination.

---

[9] Timeshare Act 1992, s. 2.
[10] *ibid.* s. 5B.
[11] See *Estate Agency: A report by the Director General of Fair Trading,* OFT, March 1990.

**11–93**     In addition, sections 12 to 21 of the Act impose duties on estate agents. They must give certain information about their charges and when these are payable. There is a duty to declare any conflict of interest or personal interest in the transaction. Where deposits are taken from a purchaser, there are duties relating to keeping the money in a clients' account. Failure to observe the duty to provide the client with information about charges results in the contract being unenforceable without the approval of the sheriff.[12]

**11–94**     The only reported case on this provision is *Solicitors Estate Agency (Glasgow) Ltd v. MacIver*[13] where a client refused to pay his estate agent's fees because an advertising discount obtained by the agent had not been disclosed. This breached both section 18(2)(a) and (d) as a failure to give details of any payment which is not part of the agent's remuneration but forms part of the payment to him, and a failure to give details of the method of calculating the advertising charges. The sheriff, before whom the client had argued only that there was a breach of section 18(2)(d), did not think it fair to refuse to enforce the payment but ordered the payment of approximately three quarters of the fee. On appeal the sheriff principal stated that the deliberate policy of concealing the advertising discount would have justified refusing to enforce the contract but that the sheriff's decision was not such an erroneous exercise of his discretion as to merit being altered. However, as he found that two provisions of the section had been breached he considered that the degree of culpability was so high that it would not be just to enforce the contract at all.

**11–95**     Enforcement of the Act is under the overall supervision of the Director General of Fair Trading, but district councils also have enforcement powers.

## THE ROLE OF THE OFFICE OF FAIR TRADING

**11–96**     The origins and structure of the Office of Fair Trading have been discussed earlier.[14] Here we focus on two weapons to fight unfair trade practices with which the OFT has been armed by the Fair Trading Act. It should also be remembered that the OFT has formidable powers under the licensing provisions of the Consumer Credit Act 1974. The creation of the OFT and the provision of these powers recognise the necessity to combat unfair trade practices using more modern, purpose built tools

[12]  Estate Agents Act 1979, s. 18(6).
[13]  1990 S.C.L.R. 595.
[14]  See Chap. 1.

than those available from the armoury of traditional legal techniques.

**PART II OF THE FAIR TRADING ACT 1973**

Part II of the Fair Trading Act 1973 provided a procedure under **11–97** which unfair trade practices could be banned using the mechanism of the criminal law. It applied where the Director General of Fair Trading found that there was a "consumer trade practice" which adversely affected the interests of consumers with respect to their economic interests or their interests with respect to health, safety or other matters. He could send to an independent committee, known as the Consumer Protection Advisory Committee, a dossier setting out the evidence of harm and his proposals for the banning of the practice in the form of a statutory instrument. If the committee agreed with the Director General's proposals, or agreed to them with modifications, they would be forwarded to the Secretary of State who, if he thought fit, could make the necessary order. The thinking behind this procedure was that it would provide a speedier method of proscribing unfair practices than is possible using primary legislation. A number of references were made to the committee and several of these resulted in orders.

For example, the Consumer Transactions (Restriction on **11–98** Statements) Order 1976[15] makes it a criminal offence to mislead consumers about their statutory rights when acquiring goods.[16] The Part II procedure is referred to briefly here because it is in abeyance. While Part II of the Act has not been repealed the members of the committee were not reappointed on the expiry of their terms of office.[17] Sir Gordon Borrie, who had experience of it both as a member of the Consumer Protection Advisory Committee and as Director General of the Office of Fair Trading, notes that it "has not been a success story ... [rather] an example of a bold idea smothered by an excess of nervous caution. The difficulty seems to have been that its provisions were too narrowly drawn and the three-stage procedure was too cumbersome.[18] It seems likely that Part II may be revived. The consumer White Paper stated that amendments to the Fair

---

[15]  S.I. 1976 No. 1813.
[16]  See also the Mail Order Transactions (Information) Order 1976 (S.I. 1976 No.1812), and the Business Advertisements (Disclosure) Order 1977 (S.I. 1977 No. 1918).
[17]  See Department of Trade and Industry Press Notice, Sept. 24, 1982, printed in the *Annual Report of the Director General of Fair Trading 1982* (1983–84 H.C. 20), p.45.
[18]  Borrie, *The Development of Consumer Law and Policy— Bold Spirits and Timorous Souls* (1984), pp.126–127.

Trading Act 1973 will include a power for the Secretary of State to make orders by secondary legislation to specify that certain unfair practices (for instance those associated with so-called "one day sales") should become criminal offences"[19] This follows a pilot project conducted by the OFT.[20]

<h3 align="center">PART III OF THE FAIR TRADING ACT 1973</h3>

**11–99**     More effective have been the powers under Part III of the Fair Trading Act to discipline traders who have persisted in a course of conduct which is detrimental to the interests of consumers. It recognises that neither the criminal law nor the invocation of the civil law by individual consumers are sufficient deterrents to the unfair conduct of some traders. Relatively small fines lead some traders to ignore criminal sanctions and treat the occasions when they are convicted as minor inconveniences. Some are prone to refuse to honour their civil obligations to consumers knowing that the chances of an action being raised against them are remote.

**11–100**     Part III allows the Director General to exercise various powers. Before this can be done it must be shown that the statutory criteria have been satisfied. Section 34 of the Act provides that action may be taken where a person who has been carrying on a business has, in the course of that business, persisted in a course of conduct which is detrimental to the interests of consumers whether those interests are economic or health, safety or other interests. In addition, the conduct must be unfair to consumers. The section goes on to say that unfairness in this context can arise in one of two ways. First, breaches of the criminal law can be taken into account whether or not they have resulted in prosecution. It is not uncommon for breaches of the Trades Descriptions Act 1968 to be relied on to show unfairness. Other statutes which might be relevant are the Food Safety Act 1990, the Consumer Protection Act 1987 which creates the offence of giving a misleading price indication, or the Consumer Credit Act 1974. However, it should be noted that any criminal offence may support an allegation of unfairness. It does not need to be one specifically designed to protect consumers.

**11–101**     In addition to breaches of the criminal law, unfairness may be demonstrated by persistent breaches of the civil law regardless of whether or not legal proceedings have been brought in a court. There can be many examples of such conduct. The selling of goods which are not fit for their purpose or not of satisfactory

---

[19]   White Paper, para. 7.6.
[20]   *Consumer Affairs: The Way Forward*, OFT, 1998, para. 3.10.

quality as required by the Sale of Goods Act 1979, or the failure of the provider of a service to provide the service to a reasonable and workmanlike standard have resulted in action being taken. Others would be failure to honour the terms of a guarantee given when goods were purchased; inducing customers to enter into contracts for the purchase of goods by making false statements about their description and availability; and failure to provide redress for consumers when their rights have been infringed.

In deciding whether to take action section 34 permits the **11–102** Director General to take account of complaints received by him from consumers or others and any other information which he has collected or which has been provided to him. In practice, the main source of information leading to the use of these powers is Trading Standards Departments. The Office of Fair Trading and local Trading Standards Departments work together closely and how they operate has been set out in detail in Office of Fair Trading guides.[21]

It is important to note that there must be a course of conduct **11–103** which has been persisted in. A single act, no matter how serious, will not be enough. When a series of convictions, decrees and complaints against a trader amounts to persistent conduct will vary from case to case. All relevant factors must be taken into account such as the trader's attitude to his or her conduct, the nature and scale of the business, the period over which the breaches took place, the degree of repetition and the seriousness of the breaches and whether the trader has followed or allowed a policy or practice which has had the effect of causing the breaches of the law. The OFT's most recent guidance states that "Between six and ten complaints, backed by clear and precise evidence, will generally be enough".[22] It does however qualify this by pointing out that no exact figure can be given because every case differs.

Even where there appears to be sufficient evidence to seek an **11–104** assurance from the trader the OFT and the trading standards department may decide that a warning from a senior OFT official may be sufficient. Having been convinced by the information provided by a trading standards department that the Part III powers should be used, the Director General is obliged under section 34 to use his "best endeavours" to obtain a satisfactory written assurance from the trader that the conduct will cease and he will not carry on any similar course of conduct in the future.

---

[21] *Assurances by Traders: guidance on the operation of Part III of the Act*, OFT, 1985 and *Part III Assurances: a new approach*, OFT, 1993.

[22] See *Part III Assurances*, at n. 12.

When assurances are sought from a body corporate, an assurance may also be sought from a director, manager, secretary or other similar officer or from a person who has a controlling interest in it.[23] This is done by sending a recorded deliver letter to the trader and, if there is no response, following this up with one reminder a month later.

**11–105**      Many cases will be disposed of by means of a written assurance. Should the trader not be willing to provide a suitable assurance or, having given one, it is broken, the Director General may take court proceedings leading to an undertaking or an order. The appropriate court is the Restrictive Practices Court. However, in certain circumstances the action can be raised in the sheriff court (or, in England, the county court). This may occur where the case does not involve a company with a paid up share capital of more than £10,000 and a question of law or fact of such general application as to justify reserving it for the Restrictive Practices Court is not in issue. *Director General of Fair Trading v. Boswell*[24] is the only example of the OFT having to raise an action under Part III in Scotland, and arose from the failure of the trader concerned to provide an assurance.

**11–106**      Should an assurance given to a court or a court order be broken the trader would then be subject to proceedings for contempt of court. This has not happened in Scotland but has occurred on several occasions in England. In 1982 a double-glazing supplier who was in breach of an order gave an undertaking to comply. Within months he was in breach of this undertaking and, following an application by the Director General, was imprisoned for 14 days for contempt of court with a warning that any continuation of this conduct would lead to lengthy imprisonment.[25] During 1985 a London company retailing electronic consumer goods was fined £1,950 (and ordered to pay costs) for failing to observe undertakings given to the court in 1978; and a Bournemouth television retailer and repairer was fined £1,000 (and ordered to pay costs) for failing to comply with a court order.[26] Since then contempt proceedings have occurred in a number of cases in three of which suspended prison sentences have been imposed. In the others fines were imposed, in one case amounting to £50,000. In 1999 a second-hand car dealer who had first signed assurances in 1984 but had a subsequent

---

[23]  Fair Trading Act 1973, s. 38.
[24]  1979 S.L.T. (Sh. Ct.) 9.
[25]  *Annual Report of the Director General of Fair Trading 1983* (1983–84 H.C. 495), p.21.
[26]  *Annual Report of the Director General of Fair Trading 1985* (1985-86 H.C. 403), p.19.

history of serious consumer complaints was imprisoned for $15\frac{1}{2}$ months for contempt of court in failing to comply with a court order.[27]

Up to the end of 1998, the latest time for which statistics are **11–107** available, approximately 840 assurances, undertakings or court orders had been made including twelve orders in contempt of court cases.[28] The vast majority are assurances given to the Director General without resort to court action. Approximately one quarter of these have involved businesses in the car and motoring sector while there have been significant numbers in the electrical, home improvements and mail order sectors.[29]

When an assurance has been given the OFT may wish to **11–108** publicise the fact. It has been held in England that this is permissible so long as it is ancillary to the purpose of Part III. It was pointed out that Part III is not a punitive procedure and that should not be the purpose of publicity.[30] Publicity is often important if monitoring of the conduct of a trader is to be effective. The present practice of the OFT is to issue press releases in some cases and in others to insert paid advertisements in the appropriate media.

In its first decade Part III appeared to work well. A former **11–109** Director General of Fair Trading said that he has "no doubt about the effectiveness of Part III . . . it is a valuable power which has demonstrated its worth over the years."[31] More recently it appears to have worked less well. The current Director General noted that "[d]espite its laudable objective, the present law is inadequate and does not deal with those who continuously deceive consumers or take advantage of ignorance, inexperience, or trust".[32] Nevertheless, it is recognised that it could be made more effective and proposals for achieving this were set

---

[27] Referred to in *The Office of Fair Trading: Protecting the Consumer from Unfair Trading Practices*, Report by the Comptroller and Auditor General, figure 36 at p 58, H.C. 57 Session 1999–00, London, the Stationery Office.

[28] These figures were calculated using the figure given in the figure in the DTI's 1994 consultation paper, *Reform of Part III of the Fair Trading Act 1973* and adding the figures given in the annual reports of the Director General of Fair Trading for 1995–98.

[29] *Annual Report of the Director General of Fair Trading 1991* (1991–92 H.C. 38), p. 29.

[30] *R. v. Director General of Fair Trading, ex p. F. H. Taylor & Co. Ltd* [1981] I.C.R. 292, D.C.

[31] Sir Gordon Borrie, *Regulating Business — Law and Consumer Protection Agencies,* a paper delivered at the Consumer Law Conference held at Trinity College Dublin, March 23 and 24, 1984.

[32] *Consumer Affairs: the way forward*, para. 4.10, OFT 1998. See to similar effect the Better Regulation Task Force report, *Consumer Affairs*, Central Office of Information, 1998.

out in the OFT's *Trading Malpractices*[33] which is discussed at the end of this chapter.

## SELF REGULATION

**11–110**    In Chapter 1 reference has already been made to the role of the Office of Fair Trading in encouraging sectors of trade and industry to develop codes of conduct. In addition, some other codes have been developed outwith this scheme by other sectors; a good example being the British Code of Advertising Practice. A major function of such codes is to raise standards in trade and industry and bring benefits to consumers, which might not easily be secured by legislation. It is difficult to know how successful such codes have been in this respect. Research carried out for the OFT has suggested that codes do result in a reduction in undesirable trading practices such as the use of exclusion clauses.[34] However the achievements of these codes has been limited, as the OFT itself recognised in its report *Raising Standards of Consumer Care: progressing beyond codes of practice*.[35]

**11–111**    While it is arguable that they may have some success it is widely recognised that they do have limitations as well as advantages.[36] Codes are more flexible than statutes in that they can be altered more easily; those who know the problems of the sector intimately can design them; and they shift the cost of regulation from the state to the private sector. It is also argued that members of a trade association are more likely to comply with rules in a code whose drafting they have been able to influence. On the other hand they can only affect those who adhere to them through membership of the relevant trade association and it may well be that the sort of trader who most requires to improve the standards of his or her business is not likely to be a member of a trade association. Even amongst members of a trade association it may be difficult to attain high levels of compliance; and it is not always the case that trade associations devote much effort to ensuring compliance with their codes. Enforcement also depends on a willingness to discipline members from time to time and to publicise this. There is also the potentially anti-competitive effect of codes in that where they are most

---

[33]    *Trading Malpractices: A report by the Director General of Fair Trading following consideration of proposals for a general duty to trade fairly*, OFT, July 1990.

[34]    Pickering and Cousins, *The Economic Implications of Codes of Practice*, UMIST, 1980.

[35]    OFT, 1998.

[36]    For a discussion of the advantages and disadvantages as well as self regulation in a consumer context see *Models of Self-regulation: an overview of models in business and the professions*, National Consumer Council, 1999.

widespread in their coverage they may inhibit consumer choice.

Despite the limited achievements of the codes sponsored by the OFT there has recently been increased debate about the use of codes to improve standards in the interests of consumers. The National Consumer Council's paper *Models of Self-Regulation*[37] has already been referred to. The Better Regulation Task Force is studying the issue and has issued an interim report.[38] In the consumer White Paper the Government indicated that it saw codes of practice approved by the OFT as an important method of raising the standards of service that consumers can expect from business. It proposes, subject to further consultation, to confer powers on the OFT to give a seal of approval to codes that implement certain core principles.[39] One must wonder how beneficial these codes will be when two of these core principles, truthful advertisements and fair contracts, are already legal obligations. However, the other principles relating to helpful information, informed staff, complaints handling and publicity about the codes may confer benefits on consumer. Much will depend on the sectors chosen for the development of codes. As the White Paper points out, e-commerce is one area where there could be considerable benefits for consumers and for businesses. Consumers wish to be sure that electronic payments will be secure and that they will be able to get speedy redress should there be any problems with their transactions. E-commerce will not develop as business would wish if this objective is not attained so there should be considerable willingness for business to create effective self-regulation.

**11–112**

## REFORM: A DUTY TO TRADE FAIRLY?

Whatever the merits or demerits of codes of practice there is no doubt that they have limitations as methods of improving trading standards. So do our statutory methods of dealing with unfair practices as the Director General of Fair Trading observed in his introduction to *Trading Malpractices*:

**11–113**

> "The traditional approach to the framing of consumer protection legislation suffers from a number of drawbacks. Consumers' rights may be ignored if it is only individual consumers who can enforce them. With the focus on redressing or punishing past misbehaviour, there is much less attention on putting things right for the future. Enforcement

[37] See previous note.
[38] *Self-Regulation: Interim Report*, October 1999.
[39] White Paper, Chap. 4.

authorities can face intractable problems in trying to apply
detailed legislation to the known facts relating to a particular
transaction or practice. The criminal law — with its high
burden of proof — can be both blunt and unwieldy as a
regulatory instrument. There is not normally the flexibility to
take into account business behaviour which takes advantage
of the ignorance, inexperience or trust of some consumers or
otherwise exploits particular types of vulnerability. Many
malpractices fall just outside existing law — or traders can be
just one step ahead."[40]

**11–114**   To deal with this problem the OFT produced new proposals in
1990 for dealing with unfair trading practices in this report. This
was the culmination of a long process begun when the idea of a
statutory duty to trade fairly was floated in the OFT's discussion
paper on *Home Improvements* in 1982. More detailed proposals
were set out in a discussion paper entitled *A General Duty to
Trade Fairly* issued in August 1986. This advocated the creation
of a broad statutory duty to trade fairly which would reinforce
the existing civil and criminal law. The statutory duty would be
supported by codes of practice, which would set out the practices, which would be regarded as acceptable or unacceptable.
Further consultation resulted in more limited proposals which
rejected as too ambitious the earlier attempt to combine raising
trading standards with improvements in redress procedures. It is
essentially these proposals in the 1990 report which the OFT has
again recommended to ministers. In the consumer White Paper[41]
the Government has indicated that it intends to legislate in this
area "when parliamentary time allows" to quote their implementation plan.

**11–115**      Their first limb of the OFT's proposals aims to streamline the
present Part III which is recognised as being "convoluted and
susceptible to delay". The requirement that a trader has persisted in a course of conduct should be deleted as this can result
in lengthy delays while a series of complaints is investigated
during which the evidence may become stale. It is also recommended that the duty on the Director General to use his best
endeavours to obtain an undertaking should be abolished as this
provides some traders with an opportunity to drag out the
procedure. The procedure can also be criticised as essentially
negative and failing to provide a method of changing trading
practices. This is tackled by recommending that a caution, as the
new technique would be called, could be served on traders
requiring them to modify their trading practices.

---

[40]   para. 1.4.
[41]   7.07–7.10.

In addition, the report suggests that local trading standards **11–116** departments should be given the power to serve cautions as most problems tend to occur at local level. The OFT would continue to have the same powers but would use them only where some point of general importance was at issue or the problem arose at regional or national level. It would also be possible for the enforcement authorities in an urgent case to by-pass the assurance stage and go straight to court to obtain undertakings or an order. As a safeguard against abuse of the power a trader could challenge the legal validity or terms of the caution in the sheriff court.

Allied to these proposals is an important redefinition of the **11–117** concept of fairness. Borrowing from foreign models it is proposed that, as well as behaviour which involves breaches of existing legal requirements, the definition of "unfair" should be extended by adding two general provisions. The first would relate to "deceptive or misleading" business practices, supported by a non-exhaustive list of illustrative acts or practices. The second, "unconscionable" practices, is intended to deal with malpractices which would generally be regarded as indefensible or objectionable by virtue of their oppressive or exploitative nature. To assist in identifying what was unconscionable the legislation would include a set of factors to be taken into account in individual cases.

The previous Government had included a commitment to **11–118** "improve our powers to deal with rogue traders" in its 1992 election manifesto and on its re-election a revised version of the OFT's proposals was set out in a consultation paper.[42] Most of the proposals for improving the operation of Part III were retained except that trading standards departments were not to have the power to issue "warnings", as it is proposed to call what were previously referred to as "cautions".

The extension of the grounds on which Part III powers may be **11–119** exercised was also scaled back. The concept of unconscionable conduct was dropped as being too wide and too subjective readily to be enforced. The idea of statutory, illustrative lists of unacceptable practices that are deceptive or misleading was also dropped. The reason given was that there would have been considerable enforcement complications and might have been litigation as to whether particular conduct was or was not precisely covered in the list.[43]

It is not quite clear whether the present government's pro- **11–120** posals are the same as the original OFT proposals. It is clear that

---

[42] *Reform of Part III of the Fair Trading Act 1973: A Consultation Paper*, DTI, Dec. 1994.
[43] *ibid.* Appendix B, pp. 6 and 7.

they do intend to arm trading standards officers with the new powers. What is not clear is whether they intend to delete the reference to unconscionable conduct as part of the definition of unfairness. There are arguments to be made in favour of this view. This concept has given a good deal of difficulty in some other jurisdictions. The new standard of "deceptive, misleading, or oppressive practices" proposed in the earlier consultation may well be as effective. However, it is to be hoped that the present Government's proposals will not omit the addition of an illustrative list to this general statement. It was made clear in the *Trading Malpractices* report that such a list would be prefaced by a statement that it was without prejudice to the general statement.

**11–121**     In addition to these proposals, the DTI's consultation paper on implementation of the Injunctions Directive[44] contains far-reaching proposals to extend the powers of various bodies to protect consumers. The purpose of the directive is to permit consumer protection bodies to apply to the courts or administrative authorities in their own and other Member States for orders to stop traders breaching consumer law. This will be possible where the collective interests of consumers under certain E.C. directives are threatened. It will not be a means of seeking redress for individual grievances. The directives concerned are those on misleading advertising and the advertising of medicines, doorstep selling and distance selling, consumer credit, timeshare, package holidays, unfair terms and T.V. broadcasting. For example, if misleading advertising was being directed at United Kingdom consumers by mail from Holland Consumers' Association or a trading standards department could seek an injunction in the Dutch courts to stop it.

**11–122**     The consultation paper envisages that the directive will be implemented in a similar way to the Unfair Terms Directive. Various named bodies will be authorised to take action under the various directives with a lead body co-ordinating action. In the case of several of the directives this will be the OFT. Relevant regulators will be amongst the named bodies as will trading standards departments. It is likely that the Consumers' Association will be included as it is already in the case of the Unfair Terms Directive.

**11–123**     While it is true that there is not at present a duty to trade fairly, the combined effect of a number of pieces of legislation comes close to that point and the enactment of the OFT's proposals and the implementation of the Injunctions Directive would emphasise that. This chapter has discussed a number of practices which

---

[44] *Injunctions Directive: Implementation of Directive 98/27/EC on Injunctions for the Protection of Consumers' Interests*, DTI, February 2000.

are forbidden. The Consumer Credit Act 1974, in addition to restricting certain practices, comes close, through the licensing provisions, to imposing a duty to trade fairly on the credit industry. Section 10 of the Consumer Protection Act 1987 imposes a general duty to supply safe goods. The Unfair Contract Terms Act 1977 prevents the use of certain terms in contracts and applies a standard of fairness and reasonableness to others. This has been taken further in the regulations implementing the Unfair Contract Terms Directive. Clearly we are inching closer to having a general duty to trade fairly.

## CHAPTER 12

# CONSUMER REDRESS AND ENFORCEMENT[1]

## INTRODUCTION

**12–01**  As the earlier chapters have shown, there is now an impressive body of law protecting the consumer as well as various organisations, notably local authority trading standards and environmental health departments, who enforce it and provide advice to consumers. However, in many cases it is up to individual consumers to take action to assert their rights.

**12–02**  It is a commonplace of debate on consumer protection that settling disputes between consumers and traders is a major problem. Much discussion has centred on this issue. The Scottish Consumer Council, like its parent body the National Consumer Council, has devoted considerable resources to it. The Office of Fair Trading has also been in the van of efforts to deal with the issue in a number of ways. In 1991 it devoted a major conference to the topic of redress, the results of which are set out in *Consumer Redress Mechanisms*[2] and in its recent strategy document[3] it confirmed its continuing commitment to improving access to redress. As one would expect, the consumer White Paper devotes a chapter to redress and stresses the importance of an integrated system of information and redress.[4] The problem is not confined to Scotland or the United Kingdom, as the Florence Access to Justice Project amply demonstrated.[5] At European level it has featured prominently in all the consumer protection initiatives of the European Union and was given further impetus with the publication of a Green Paper,

---

[1]  Some of the material in this chapter, especially that on small claims and ADR, first appeared in Mackay and Moody, *ADR in Scotland* (1995). I am grateful to the editors for permission to use it here.

[2]  *Consumer Redress Mechanisms: A report by the Director General of Fair Trading into systems for resolving consumer complaints*, OFT, London, 1991.

[3]  *Consumer Affairs: the way forward*, para. 5.11.

[4]  *Modern Markets: confident consumers*, Chap. 6.

[5]  See Cappelletti and Weisner, *Access to justice*, Vol. 11, Book I, Pt 4.

*Access of Consumers to justice and the Settlement of Consumer Disputes in the Single Market.*[6]

To set the scene for what follows it will be useful to indicate **12–03** the scale of consumer complaints about goods and services. The best source of information on this is derived from the statistics of consumer complaints published by the OFT and the annual consumer dissatisfaction surveys that it has published. These surveys show a consistently high level of complaints. Around 40 per cent of the adult population of the United Kingdom felt that they had some cause for complaint and 76 per cent took some action. Those complaining about goods were much more likely to succeed, 74 per cent being successful as against 34 per cent of those complaining about services. Within categories success was much more likely if the complaint related to a low value item such as food, drink or clothing rather than higher value products such as household appliances or cars.

Although the surveys show that approximately three out of **12–04** four consumers took some action about their complaint, few went beyond a complaint to the supplier. Fewer than one in a thousand of all consumers, or under one quarter of a per cent of those with complaints, resorted to any kind of redress mechanism.[7] A complaint to the supplier of the goods or service is the appropriate first step and in many cases this will resolve the problem with, or without, the assistance of some other agency. Should it not be possible to reach a settlement what courses are open to the consumer? This is what we investigate below.

## COURT PROCEEDINGS

The traditional answer is to point to the courts. In Scotland the **12–05** appropriate court for most consumer disputes is the sheriff court. There are three main procedures, which may have to be used to resolve a dispute. The ordinary cause will be the appropriate one where the value of the claim is over £1,500. This is a relatively complex procedure which, in practice, requires professional assistance. If the claim is for between £751 and £1,500 the summary cause procedure may be used. This was introduced in 1975 in an attempt to provide a simpler and quicker procedure. While it is

---

[6] Commission of the European Communities, COM (93) 576 final, Brussels, Nov. 1993. In the recent Commission *Consumer Policy Action Plan 1999–2001* (1999/C 206/01) the Commission notes that "Access to justice for consumers in pursuing their complaints is still imperfect" and promises to take steps to improve enforcement mechanisms.

[7] See *Consumer Redress Mechanisms: A report by the Director General of Fair Trading into systems for resolving consumer complaints*, OFT, 1991; see Chap. 3.

certainly simpler than the ordinary cause procedure it has lengthy
and complicated rules and does little to provide realistic access to
justice for consumers. To try to achieve this a small claim procedure was introduced into the sheriff court in 1988.

**12–06**     The legislative basis for the small claims procedure is to be
found in section 35 of the Sheriff Court (Scotland) Act 1971 as
amended by section 18 of the Law Reform (Miscellaneous
Provisions) (Scotland) Act 1985. The definition of a small claim
is to be found in the Small Claims (Scotland) Order 1988.[8] It is
wide enough to cover most consumer claims (though it also
covers many other types of case) where the amount claimed does
not exceed £750. The detailed rules of the procedure are set out
in the Act of Sederunt (Small Claims Rules) 1988.[9]

**12–07**     The Scottish Executive has announced that the financial limits
of the Sheriff Court procedures will shortly be altered. The small
claims limit will be raised to £1,500 and the Summary Cause limit
to £5,000. At the same time personal injury claims will no longer
competent as small claims.

**12–08**     A small claim is begun by filling in a form, known as a summons,
setting out the names and addresses of the person making the
claim and the person sued, as well as a brief account of what is
being claimed. This form, together with the appropriate fee, is
lodged with the sheriff clerk who, where the pursuer is an individual,[10] will arrange for it to be served on the defender. Where the
defender intends to dispute the claim this is done by completing
and returning the appropriate part of the summons.

**12–09**     In a disputed case the next stage is called the preliminary
hearing and is intended to focus the issues prior to the full
hearing at which a decision will be reached. The rules provide
that the case may be resolved by the sheriff at the preliminary
hearing if sufficient facts are admitted. In practice, as the
research[11] into the procedure shows, few cases are resolved in
this way.

**12–10**     Where the case is not resolved at the preliminary hearing a full
hearing is held. Like the preliminary hearing this is held in public
"in such manner as the sheriff considers best suited to the
clarification of the issue before him: and shall so far as practica-

---

[8]   S.I. 1988 No. 1999.
[9]   S.I. 1988 No. 1976. The rules are currently under review following and the
      Sheriff Court Rules Council issued a *Consultation on Proposed New Rules for
      Summary Cause and Small Claim in the Sheriff Court*, Scottish Courts
      Administration, 1998. It is expected that a revised set of rules will be
      introduced in 2000.
[10]  This privilege applies to anyone who is not a partnership or company so could
      be availed of by a one-man business.
[11]  *Small Claims in the Sheriff Court in Scotland: An assessment of the use and
      operation of the procedure,* Central Research Unit Papers, Scottish Office,
      1991.

ble, be conducted in an informal manner."[12] To make it more realistic to expect the parties to present their own cases the legislation dispenses with the rules relating to the admissibility or corroboration of evidence.[13] For those who do not wish to present their own cases advocates or solicitors are not the only alternatives as lay representatives are permitted. In practice, relatives, CABx staff and trading standards officers have acted in this capacity.

A major barrier to going to court is expense, or the fear of it, in a system where the losing party will normally have to meet the expenses of the winner. Small claims procedure resolves this problem by providing that in disputed cases involving less than £200 no expenses of any kind are recoverable by the successful party; and that above this figure an award of expenses is limited to £75. When the new financial limits are introduced these figures will also change. **12–11**

The Scottish small claims procedure has the potential to be a genuinely radical approach to resolving consumer (and other) disputes. The research into its first year of operation showed some positive features. It deals speedily with cases in a way that bears favourable comparison with its English equivalent and trade arbitration schemes; and, as was to be expected, advisers were unanimous in acknowledging the fairness of sheriffs. Court staff were also found to be very helpful to litigants, and the explanatory literature was well received. **12–12**

As has been pointed out more than once,[14] much depends on the approach of the sheriff whose role is central to the operation of the process. Here the limitations of the procedure in practice have been exposed. The research into its operation revealed a variety of approaches in different courts. Variation, while it cannot be entirely eliminated, is inimical to the development of confidence in the system by consumers and, perhaps more importantly, those who frequently provide them with advice. Too often, preliminary hearings are held in an atmosphere which does not encourage individuals to represent themselves. Commonly, they take place before a sheriff in traditional court dress in a normal court room where a number of solicitors are waiting to deal with other business. Full hearings tend to be held in less busy surroundings but, again, traditional court rooms are normally used instead of other rooms such as jury rooms. However, there are examples of good practice, such as the "consumer **12–13**

---

[12] r. 19.
[13] See the Sheriff Courts (Scotland) Act 1975, s. 35; and the Civil Evidence (Scotland) Act 1988, ss. 1 and 2.
[14] See for example, *Consumer Redress Mechanisms*, OFT, 1991, p. 47; and Ervine, "The New Small Claims Procedure", 1989 S.L.T. 65.

court", as it is commonly termed, in Glasgow which deals with cases involving unrepresented parties.

**12–14**     Insufficient attention seems to have been given to the particular needs of persons bringing small claims on their own. Simple things such as good signposting within court buildings is essential for people who will, in all probability, be making their first and possibly only visit to a court. There is, as the Director General of Fair Trading has pointed out, scope for improved timetabling of cases to prevent litigants spending long periods waiting for their cases to begin; and for experiments with evening or weekend hearings.[15] This is one of a number of issues which is under review by the Lord Advocate at the moment.

## LEGAL AID

**12–15**     In theory the availability of legal aid should have overcome the problems of lack of access to the courts. There are two forms of assistance in civil matters. Under the Legal Aid (Scotland) Act 1986 it is possible to get advice and assistance from a solicitor on any matter of Scots law and to assert rights in any way short of going to court. In addition, there is a legal aid scheme which funds litigation in the civil courts. In both cases these services are means tested and their availability has diminished dramatically in the past few years as a result of the Government's policy of reducing public expenditure. It is estimated that the proportion of the population eligible for legal aid in Britain fell from 79 per cent in 1979 to 47 per cent in 1990. Further restrictions on eligibility applied in 1993 will have reduced this proportion still further.[16]

## THE SPECULATIVE ACTION

**12–16**     On public policy grounds it is illegal for solicitors to pursue a case on the basis that they will be remunerated by a share of any sum recovered. This is often referred to as the contingent fee system and is widely used in the United States. However, the speculative action has a long and honourable history in the Scottish legal system. This is the name given to the practice of solicitors taking on a case on the understanding that they will receive no fee for their services unless they are successful. The Law Reform (Miscellaneous Provisions) (Scotland) Act 1990 provides a variation of this action. Where a lawyer takes a case on a speculative basis they can now do so under an agreement with the client that they will receive, if successful, up to twice the normal party and party level of expenses. In the event of failure the solicitor is not entitled to a fee but may recover

---

[15]   *Consumer Redress Mechanisms*, OFT, 1991, p. 50, n. 8.
[16]   For further detail on the provision of legal aid and advice see White and Willock, *The Scottish Legal System* (2nd ed., 1999), pp. 288–296.

outlays from the client who is also liable for the other side's legal expenses. An experienced practitioner has suggested that these new provisions are not likely to prove attractive to lawyers as expenses on a party-and-party basis do not normally properly remunerate them.[17]

## ALTERNATIVE DISPUTE RESOLUTION

Given the difficulties experienced by consumers in using the courts to resolve disputes, it is not surprising that other avenues have been explored. These are now often known collectively as Alternative Dispute Resolution (or ADR). There is no definitive or agreed definition of ADR but one that might be used is that it is any means of providing a resolution of a dispute between two or more parties which does not involve traditional court procedures.[18] In this sense the small claims procedure referred to above is a form of ADR. In addition, there have been a number of interesting developments which are discussed below involving conciliation, mediation, arbitration and ombudsmen schemes.

**12–17**

### MEDIATION

The most common situation in which mediation or conciliation of consumer disputes takes place is in the context of complaints procedures under codes of conduct drawn up by trade associations in consultation with the Office of Fair Trading. Under the Fair Trading Act 1973 the Director General of Fair Trading has a duty to "encourage relevant trade associations to prepare, and to disseminate to their members, codes of practice for guidance in safeguarding and promoting the interests of consumers".[19] There are currently 49 codes in operation covering such diverse sectors as credit, footwear, photography, package holidays and funerals.[20] With one exception the codes have been drawn up by groups who are organised on a United Kingdom basis. The one exception is the Scottish Motor Trade Association which is one of the organisations which drew up the Code of Practice for the Motor Industry.

**12–18**

The codes have model complaint-handling schemes which encourage consumers to deal with complaints initially by contacting the trader. The second stage is conciliation by the trade

**12–19**

---

[17] See Semple, "Fees in Speculative Actions" (1994) 39 J.L.S.S. 57.
[18] Ervine, *Settling Consumer Disputes: A review of alternative dispute resolution*, National Consumer Council, 1993, pp. 2-3. See also by the same author *ADR in Consumer Disputes* in the book cited at p. 300, n. 1.
[19] Fair Trading Act 1973, s. 123(4).
[20] For a list of the codes and the redress facilities that they offer see *Butterworths Trading and Consumer Law* 1 [5065].

association concerned, and many complaints do not proceed beyond this stage.[21] As the National Consumer Council's report, *Out of Court*, points out, little is known about how conciliation operates in practice. That study found that consumers tended to perceive conciliation as biased towards the trader. Partly for this reason, the Association of British Travel Agents (ABTA), whose complaint-handling scheme is the best known of the trade schemes, has abandoned the conciliation stage. The financial services complaint handling schemes referred to in more detail at paragraphs 12–26 and 12–27 also include conciliation in their procedures.

**12–20**  Information is available about the operation of the Scottish Motor Trade Association's complaints procedure and is set out in Table 1.

**12–21**  The SMTA in a note accompanying the entry on complaints in its 1994 *Annual Reports & Accounts* points out that informal conciliation of disputes can be highly successful and accounts for almost all the cases in the column "Complaints resolved formally but outwith the Committee". Formal consideration by the Complaints Committee is the stage between informal conciliation and a possible reference to arbitration.

**12–22**  An interesting new development is an experimental consumer mediation project in Edinburgh. Consumer Advice Scotland launched a pilot mediation project in February 1995 which was not limited to consumer cases. Mediation is undertaken by qualified mediators nominated by the Centre for Dispute Resolution (CEDR) and is free to both parties.[22]

**Table 1**

|                                                    | 1992 | 1993 | 1994 |
|----------------------------------------------------|------|------|------|
| Complaints received                                | 681  | 465  | 28   |
| Referred elsewhere                                 | 63   | 34   | 28   |
| Complaints resolved formally but out-with Committee | 465  | 321  | 284  |
| Pending                                            | 19   | 8    | —    |
| Considered by committee                            | 134  | 102  | 105  |
| Resolved in favour of complainant                  | 54   | 42   | 27   |
| Resolved in favour of SMTA member                  | 80   | 60   | 78   |
| Referred to arbitration                            | —    | 5    | 4    |

*Source:* SMTA Annual Report and Accounts

---

[21]  See *Consumer Redress Mechanisms*, OFT, 1991, p. 31.
[22]  On the provision of Mediation in the civil sphere in Scotland see *Alternative Dispute Resolution in Scotland*, Mays and Clark, Central Research Unit, The Scottish Office, 1996

## ARBITRATION

Arbitration as a method of private dispute resolution has a long    **12–23**
history and is widely used in commercial disputes. Its advantages
are that disputes can be decided by an adjudicator who is an
expert in the subject matter of the dispute and that they are held
in private. Speed and cheapness are not necessarily characteristics of arbitration.[23] In Scotland, common law provides the
framework, though there is now statutory intervention.[24] For
reasons of cost arbitration, until relatively recently, has not been
a realistic option for consumers.

Most consumer arbitrations take place as a result of arbitra-    **12–24**
tion schemes contained in codes of practice drawn up by trade
associations in consultation with the Office of Fair Trading
referred to above. Arbitration under codes is only one part of the
process of complaint handling. The codes make clear that complaint should be taken up with the trader concerned and that
Citizens' Advice Bureau or Trading Standards Departments
may be able to offer assistance in resolving a dispute. Most codes
provide for conciliation prior to arbitration. If conciliation by the
trade association does not achieve a settlement most of the codes
provide arbitration as an alternative to raising an action in the
sheriff court.

Originally, the Consumer Arbitration Agreements Act 1988    **12–25**
sought to ensure that arbitration was a genuine alternative to the
courts in cases involving consumers and that they were not
forced to submit to arbitration. That Act has now been repealed
and replaced by provisions in the Arbitration Act 1996 sections
89 to 91. These extend the Unfair Terms in Consumer Contracts
Regulations 1999 to arbitration agreements. Section 91 provides
that for the purposes of the regulations such agreements are
deemed to be unfair where the amount claimed is up to
£5,000.[25]

To use one of the OFT approved arbitration schemes the    **12–26**
consumer must pay a registration fee which is usually of the
order of £40, though it is refunded where the consumer is
successful. The arbiter under most schemes is appointed by the
Chartered Institute of Arbitrators, though the scheme operated
by the Scottish Motor Trade Association is different in that it has

---

[23] Indeed, some types of arbitration may be more expensive than using the
courts as the parties have to meet not only the costs of their lawyers but also
the costs of the arbitrator and the venue.

[24] See the Articles of Regulation 1695, of the Parliament of Scotland, the
Arbitration (Scotland) Act 1894, and the Administration of Justice (Scotland) Act 1972, s. 3.

[25] The Unfair Arbitration Agreements (Specified Amount) Order 1999 (S.I.
1999 No. 2167).

its own panel of independent arbiters. To reduce costs, arbitrations are almost invariably on a documents only basis. Each side
provides the arbiter with its written submissions and relevant
documents. Normally, the parties have no direct contact with the
arbiter except in the case of the Glass and Glazing Federation's
scheme where site visits are quite common.

**12–27** In addition to the schemes approved by the Office of Fair
Trading there are a number of other low cost schemes. Virgin
Trains and British Telecom both have such schemes as has the
Royal Institution of Chartered Surveyors. In the financial sector
the Security and Futures Authority provides another example of
the use of arbitration. This stems from the requirement in the
Financial Services Act 1986, which reshaped regulation in this
area, that the Securities and Investments Board (renamed the
Financial Services Authority in 1997) and the self-regulatory
bodies must have effective complaint handling procedures. All
these schemes have in common that the client should take up a
complaint in the first instance with the company concerned. It is
only if this proves ineffective and conciliation does not resolve
the problem that arbitration may be resorted to. Where arbitration is offered its outcome is binding on both parties. The arbiter
is appointed by the chairman of the SFA's own Arbitration
Service from a panel of arbiters who may appoint experts to
assist them. The dispute may be resolved on a documents only
basis or there may be a hearing. Unless the arbiter agrees, there
is no legal representation at a hearing. To use the arbitration
service there is a fee of £10 and only where a case is considered
to be frivolous or vexatious will costs be awarded up to a
maximum of £500.

**12–28** Not a great deal is known about the operation of these various
arbitration schemes. Only with the publication of the National
Consumer Council's study, *Out of Court*,[26] has empirical evidence about any of them become widely available. This study
looked at the three most heavily used schemes, those of the
Association of British Travel Agents (ABTA), the Glass and
Glazing Federation (GGF) and British Telecom (BT). Unfortu-
nately, the schemes do not keep statistics on a regional basis so it
has not proved possible to produce figures relating to Scotland.

**12–29** In the course of the study the researchers learnt that many of
the schemes operating under codes of practice are hardly ever
used. At the date of the study the funeral scheme had never been
used and the photography scheme only once. The main reason

[26] *Out of Court: A consumer view of three low-cost trade arbitration schemes*,
National Consumer Council, London, 1991.

for this is probably consumer ignorance of their existence which is related to under-resourcing of the schemes.[27]

The number of arbitrations under the ABTA scheme rose **12–30** from 87 in 1977 to 1,312 in 1993. In these cases consumers in the last three years have been successful in over 80 per cent of cases.[28] In the case of the GGF scheme the number of arbitrations rose from 12 in 1982 to 47 in 1989 with consumers being successful, at least to some extent, in about 75 per cent of cases on average.[29] The BT scheme dealt with 83 arbitrations in 1987 and this rose to 125 in 1989.[30]

Of the three schemes studied in detail claims in the BT scheme **12–31** were lowest on average at £222.28, whereas ABTA claims averaged £648.64, and GGF claims £1,691.82. The main criticisms of the ABTA scheme were that it took too long and that awards were low. The GGF scheme was also criticised for slowness and for difficulty in enforcing awards in some cases. The BT scheme was criticised for the fact that the arbiters had to rely on technical evidence from BT itself.

The one purely Scottish arbitration scheme is that run by the **12–32** Scottish Motor Trade Association. From Table 1 the number of cases referred to arbitration can be seen. As no research has been carried out into its operation no further comment can be made about it.

### MED-ARB

This is an abbreviation for mediation and arbitration where the **12–33** same person acts successively as mediator and then, if a mediated solution is not found, as arbiter. An example of this is to be found in the financial services sector in the complaints procedure of the Investment Management Regulatory Organisation (IMRO). This procedure involves an ombudsman scheme but, in practice, it appears to operate in two clear stages. The ombudsman attempts conciliation and if that does not effect a resolution of the dispute the ombudsman can refer it to an arbitrator who is one of a panel of experienced commercial lawyers. The other ombudsmen schemes discussed below, could also be seen as falling within this category but are probably best regarded as being in a category of their own.

---

[27] See *Consumer Redress Mechanisms*, OFT, 1991, pp. 31 and 32.
[28] The figures for cases are taken from *Out of Court*, Appendix 1, Table 2.1. for the years to 1989 and supplemented by information from ABTA for the years 1991, 1992 and 1993. The amounts awarded in arbitration during the NCC study were 46 per cent of those claimed.
[29] *ibid.* Table 2.5.
[30] *ibid.* Table 2.6.

## OMBUDSMEN

**12–34**  One of the most interesting additions to the range of redress mechanisms available to consumers in the United Kingdom over the past decade has been the ombudsman. The concept has been borrowed from public sector which in its turn had adapted an institution that originated in Scandinavia. A Parliamentary Commissioner for Administration, more commonly referred to as "the Ombudsman", was first appointed in 1967 to investigate allegations by individuals of maladministration by central Government. This was followed by the creation of a Health Services Ombudsman in 1973 and local government ombudsmen, or Commissioners for Local Administration, to give them their official title, in 1974.

**12–35**  In response to increasing number of consumer complaints, first the insurance industry and then the banks created ombudsmen. The Building Societies now have one as well to meet the requirement of the Building Societies Act 1986 that societies have adequate dispute resolution procedures. The most recent financial sector ombudsman is that of the Personal Investment Authority (PIA) who was appointed in June 1994 following the recognition of the PIA as the self regulatory organisation for retail investment. Also, in the private sector there is an ombudsman for corporate estate agents and, most recently, since 1994, a Funeral Ombudsman. These ombudsmen are creatures of private schemes. The Pensions Ombudsman was created by the Social Security Act 1990 and differs from the other ombudsmen in that investigations can be carried out into maladministration in both the private and the public sectors. All these ombudsmen have jurisdiction throughout the United Kingdom. The one specifically Scottish ombudsman is the Legal Services Ombudsman created by the Law Reform (Miscellaneous Provisions) (Scotland) Act 1990 to carry on, with slightly extended jurisdiction, the functions of the Lay Observer.

**12–36**  The financial services ombudsmen schemes[31] in the private sector vary in detail, but the function of the various office holders is to investigate complaints from customers and to resolve them by conciliation, if possible, and ultimately by issuing a decision. In the private sector the schemes have fairly similar structures. Overall responsibility lies with a board of directors composed of industry representatives while a council, which has a majority of

---

[31]  See Rawlings and Willett, *Ombudsmen Schemes in the Financial Sector* (1994) 17 J.C.P. 307 and Morris and Little, *The Ombudsmen and Consumer Protection* in P. Cartright (ed), Consumer Protection in Financial Services, (Kluwer, London, 1999).

independent members, appoints the ombudsman and oversees the operation of the scheme.

One thing that can be said about these ombudsman schemes is that they have become popular. In 1985 the Insurance Ombudsman had 872 cases passed to him whereas in 1998 that figure had risen to 19,304, by which time a deputy ombudsman and many more ancillary staff had been appointed. The trend is similar in the cases of the other financial services ombudsman schemes. In 1986, 217 cases were referred to the Banking Ombudsman, whereas the figure for 1998/99 was 12,713. In the case of the Building Societies Ombudsman scheme the ombudsman received 306 within his terms of reference in 1986/87. By 1996/97 this had risen to 11,624.[32]     **12–37**

As the schemes in the financial sector have been running for some time the National Consumer Council decided to evaluate their effectiveness in providing simple, accessible, cheap, quick, efficient, fair and independent procedures from the viewpoint of the consumer. Their study[33] looked in detail at two of the schemes in the private sector, the Insurance Ombudsman Bureau (IOB) set up in 1981 and the Office of the Building Societies Ombudsmen (BSO) set up in 1987. The study was based on a series of in-depth interviews with consumers who had contact with the ombudsmen and questionnaires sent to a representative sample of consumers whose cases had been completed.     **12–38**

Users of the scheme tend to be from older age groups and around 70 per cent are male. Complaints cover a wide range of issues, with complaints about mortgages being the single largest group for the Building Societies scheme and complaints about life assurance or pensions predominating in the work of the Insurance Ombudsman Bureau.     **12–39**

Many complainants considered the schemes to be slow. The average time taken by the IOB to resolve a complaint was 25 weeks, while the BSO on average took 52 weeks. In the case of the IOB 32 per cent of cases took between 26 and 52 weeks to resolve; the BSO took this time to resolve 30 per cent of its cases and a further 33 per cent took between 12 and 18 months.     **12–40**

---

[32]  These figures, which are taken from the annual reports of the ombudsman schemes, exclude the total number of enquiries received by the offices of the various schemes which run at many times the number of decisions. Significant proportions of these enquiries will not be within the terms of reference of the schemes. It should also be remembered that significant proportions of complaints that are within the terms of the schemes are resolved without formal reference to the ombudsman.

[33]  *Ombudsman Services: Consumers's views of the Office of the Building Societies Ombudsmen and the Insurance Ombudsman Bureau*, National Consumer Council, London, June 1993.

**12–41**    Under both schemes complainants may not use the ombudsman's services until they have exhausted the internal complaints system of the company concerned. The study reveals that there is much dissatisfaction with these procedures. They appear to be slow in many cases and not to have consumer confidence.

**12–42**    The ombudsmen themselves come out of the study much better than the internal complaints procedures. In terms of accessibility, the schemes are considered to be particularly approachable. As one might expect, perceptions of the fairness of the procedures were coloured by the outcome of the complainants' cases. Overall, only 36 per cent of those who used the IOB thought that the decision was fair and 40 per cent of those who went to the BSO. Not surprisingly approximately 80 per cent of those who won their cases thought that the procedures were fair whereas roughly 70 per cent of those who were unsuccessful thought the procedures unfair. However, an interesting sidelight on these comments comes in the answer to the question "would you go to the ombudsman again?" Almost all who had won their cases would use the schemes again, but it is significant that so would 40 per cent of those who were unsuccessful before the IOB and 52 per cent of those who did not succeed in a complaint brought to the BSO.

**12–43**    The general conclusion of the NCC report is that "Ombudsman schemes are a cheap and often informal alternative to the courts and...have the potential to offer advantages to consumers and producers alike". Nevertheless, the report suggests that there are a number of ways in which the schemes could be improved. Public awareness of the schemes, it argues, should be increased by more publicity about them, including the publication of anonymous details of cases and information about the number and type of cases relating to individual companies. To improve perceptions of fairness it is suggested that the IOB should routinely make the comments and submissions of insurance companies available to complainants. The creation of an independent organisation to oversee all the ombudsman schemes is also recommended.

**12–44**    Gaps in the terms of reference of the schemes have been an irritation to complainants and it is recommended that these be widened and that consumer organisations be consulted on this matter. Slowness in reaching decisions was a frequent criticism of the schemes and it is recommended that the ombudsmen might help to speed up cases by ensuring that time limits are strictly enforced and, possibly, by awarding additional compensation where there is unreasonable delay by member companies.

**12–45**    The Financial Services and Markets Bill presently before Parliament provides for the creation of a single Ombudsman scheme to be known as the Financial Services Ombudsman Scheme to handle financial services complaints. This will be set up by the Financial Services Authority which has been consulting about the details of the new scheme.[34]

The Scottish Legal Services Ombudsman operates in a different way from the Financial Services Ombudsmen. His task is not to receive complaints directly from aggrieved clients of solicitors and advocates but to review the way in which the professional bodies, the Law Society of Scotland and the Faculty of Advocates deal with complaints. Where the handling of a complaint is referred to him he cannot alter the decision. In 1997, 241 new cases were raised with the Ombudsman and in 1998, 212 of which all but one related to the Law Society.

**12–46**

### The Law Society of Scotland Complaints Procedure

As the Law Society's mechanisms do not easily fit into other categories they are discussed here. Aggrieved clients can complain to the Law Society where their complaint will be dealt with initially by the staff of the Client Relations and Complaints Office which receives about 1,000 complaints each year. Where these relate to professional negligence they cannot be dealt with but the complainant can be put in touch with a "troubleshooter" who is one of a panel of solicitors prepared to handle such actions. Complaints, which are competent, can, if relatively minor, be dealt with by the staff, and in this way a proportion of complaints are resolved by a form of conciliation. If not they are passed to the Complaints Committee composed mainly of solicitors but also comprising two lay representatives. One member is appointed reporting officer and investigates the complaint making a report to the committee containing a recommendation. If the complaint is upheld the committee has various sanctions including reprimand and, since the amendment of the Solicitors (Scotland) Act 1980 in 1990, the power to award compensation of up to £1,000.[35]

**12–47**

## OTHER METHODS OF OBTAINING REDRESS

Most methods of obtaining redress place the onus on the consumer to take action. There are various reasons why consumers

**12–48**

---

[34] See *Consumer Complaints and the new single ombudsman scheme: Financial Services Authority and Financial Services Ombudsman Scheme: a joint consultation paper*, FSA, November 1999.
[35] For the background to the system see Christie, "Complaints Against Solicitors" (1994) J.L.S.S. 43.

may not do so. They may not be aware of their rights; and, if they are, they may be inhibited by the cost of litigation or fears about going to the alien environment of a court. In addition, if the loss is small, it may not be thought worthwhile to seek redress although it is realised that the individual consumer is but one of a large number who has been the victim of a legal wrong. Professor Cappelletti in his major study of these problems has argued that:

> "It is necessary to abandon the individualistic, essentially laissez-faire, 19th century concept of litigation, a concept which awards the right to sue, if at all, solely to the subject personally aggrieved in his own narrowly-defined individual rights — for example, to the owner of a neighbouring property in a case of pollution or of a zoning violation. The new social, collective, 'diffuse' rights and interests can be protected only by new social, collective, 'diffuse' remedies and procedures. Indeed, the quest for these new remedies and procedures is, in my judgment, the most fascinating feature in the modem evolution of judicial law."[36]

**12–49**   Scots law has not gone far in the direction of meeting these concerns. There have been a number of steps in this direction and these are discussed below.

**12–50**   Where a consumer suffers loss which also results in a criminal conviction Part 4 of the Criminal Justice (Scotland) Act 1980 introduced a procedure designed to remove the need for separate civil proceedings. The criminal court may make a compensation order directing the offender to pay compensation to the victim. If made by a judge other than a stipendiary magistrate in the district court they are limited to level 4 on the standard scale, currently £2,500; and to £5,000 in summary proceedings if made by a sheriff or stipendiary magistrate.[37] In solemn proceedings there is no limit on the amount that may be awarded. Orders should take precedence over fines[38] but may not be made in respect of death or of injury, loss or damage due to an accident arising out of the presence of a motor vehicle on a road, except damage treated as caused by the convicted person's acts.[39]

**12–51**   Like the equivalent English scheme, the procedure is designed to apply to fairly clear cases where no great amount is at stake

---

[36] *Access to Justice* (Cappelleti ed.), Vol III, pp. 519-520.
[37] See the Criminal Procedure (Scotland) Act 1975, s.289B (amended by the Criminal justice Act 1991, s. 17(2)).
[38] Criminal Justice (Scotland) Act 1980, ss. 61 and 62.
[39] *ibid.* s. 58(2),(3).

and the compensation can be assessed easily and quickly. An obvious example in a consumer context where orders have been made is following a conviction under the Trade Descriptions Act 1968 for "clocking", *i.e.* turning back the odometer of a car. A weakness of the procedure, apart from an apparent unwillingness of some sheriffs to apply it in what seem to be appropriate circumstances, lies in the fact that there is no formal procedure for invoking it. The victim has no standing to make an application and much depends on the procurator fiscal raising the matter and having some evidence on which the sheriff can base a compensation order.

In earlier chapters we have already seen a number of examples of a government official having power to take action for the benefit of consumers as a whole. The procedure under Part III of the Fair Trading Act 1973 designed to allow the Director General of Fair Trading to curb persistent unfair conduct is an example. The Director General also has powers to seek an interdict to stop misleading advertisements under the Control of Misleading Advertisements Regulations 1988[40] and may also seek an interdict where he considers that a contract term is unfair.[41] This power has recently been extended to other bodies.[42] When the E.C. Injunctions Directive is implemented by the end of 2000 this technique will be considerably extended.[43] The Office of Fair Trading has also recognised the importance of this kind of action in making private law rights effective in its proposals for reforming unjust credit transactions. There it proposes that the Director General should have a power to seek a declarator from the courts that a particular type of credit bargain is unjust.[44] **12–52**

Beyond these examples there are few other methods by which one or a small number of persons may take action to benefit a larger class, or the public at large. An action by one individual may, incidentally, benefit a large number of other people as where one person who is affected by a nuisance obtains an interdict to put an end to it and thereby improves matters for all those living in the vicinity.[45] Scots law does have the *actio populinis* and the possibility of action by the Lord Advocate or a **12–53**

---

[40] S.I. 1988 No. 915, reg.5.
[41] The Unfair Terms in Consumer Contracts Regulations 1999 (S.I. 1999 No. 2083), reg. 10. See Chap. 10.
[42] See Chap. 10.
[43] See *Implementation of Directive 98/27/EC on Injunctions for the Protection of Consumers' Interests: A Consultation Paper*, DTI, February 2000.
[44] *Unjust Credit Transactions: A report by the Director General of Fair Trading on the provisions of sections 137-140 of the Consumer Credit Act 1974*, OFT, 1991, paras 5.22–5.29.
[45] An example is *Webster v. Lord Advocate*, 1985 S.L.T. 361.

local authority in certain circumstances, but these seem to have
fallen into disuse.[46]

**12–54**     Where a number of individuals are affected by the same wrong
it is possible to deal more efficiently with litigation by the use of
a test case or, if several actions have been raised, they may be
heard at the same time or may even be formally conjoined.
Beyond the special circumstances of unincorporated societies,
Scots civil procedure does not permit a representative action
such as is available in limited circumstances in England and
Wales. In the United States and some Commonwealth countries
a special procedure exists permitting one or more people to raise
an action on behalf of a larger number who have been affected
by the same wrong. A widely quoted example from California,
the *Yellow Cab Case*,[47] involved one pursuer taking action for
the benefit of all those who had been overcharged by a taxi
company. In the Canadian case of *Naken v. General Motors of
Canada Ltd*[48] four plaintiffs sued on behalf of all those who had
purchased new 1971 or 1972 Firenzas claiming $1,000 for each as
damages for misrepresentations contained in advertising.

**12–55**     The Scottish Consumer Council produced a report of a working party which it set up recommending the introduction of class
actions into the Scottish legal system.[49] The issue has been under
consideration by the Scottish Law Commission which has published a discussion document and associated report of a working
party on multi-party actions.[50] The discussion document reviews
experience in other jurisdictions and sets out proposals for the
introduction of class actions.

**12–56**     The Scottish Consumer Council's report and the Scottish Law
Commission's discussion document propose class actions but do
not devote much space to another type of action designed to
benefit large groups of people. These are sometimes known as
group or public interest actions. The principle of such actions is
similar to the powers of the Director General of Fair Trading
under the Control of Misleading Advertisements Regulations
1988[51] but are available to a wider range of organisations. Under
the French Loi Royer, for example, approved consumer organisations may take action to assert the rights of aggrieved

---

[46] See *Class Action in the Scottish Court*, Scottish Consumer Council, 1982,
Chap.2.
[47] *Daar v. Yellow Cab Co.*, 433 P.2d 732 (1967).
[48] [1983] 144 D.L.R. (3d) 385.
[49] See *Class Action in the Scottish Court*, Scottish Consumer Council, 1982.
[50] *Multi-Party Actions: Court Proceedings and Funding*, Scot. Law Com. Discussion Paper No.98 (1994); *Multi-Party Actions: Report by Working Party Set
Up by Scottish Law Commission*, June 1993, but published in 1994.
[51] S.I. 1988 No. 915.

consumers. The advantages of such actions were set out in *Class Actions in the Scottish Courts*:

> "It places power to initiate legal action where it properly lies, that is in the hands of consumer, through their associations. It overcomes the problem of title to sue. It would probably benefit the hard-pressed Office of Fair Trading itself by relieving pressure of business and it would be democratically appropriate to distribute the task of ensuring conformity to legal rules and policies ... and it would legitimate the Director-General's justifiable reluctance to invoke judicial proceedings otherwise than a as a very long long-stop without thereby creating the impression amongst those who deal in business that invocation of the court's power is a remote possibility with which they need not be concerned."[52]

As Cranston has pointed out, "Class actions are not a universal panacea for consumers".[53] Indeed, it must be remembered that redress procedures are only one aspect of consumer protection. It must be seen as part of an overall strategy involving the enforcement work of the Office of Fair Trading and trading standards departments. Just as important is the provision of advice and information for consumers. Without this they may never learn of their rights or be able to avail themselves of the redress procedures that exist. The importance of an integrated network of advice agencies has been emphasised by the Scottish Consumer Council.[54]

**12–57**

[52] *op. cit.* note 5 p. 303.
[53] Weidenfeld and Nicolson, *Consumer and the Law* (2nd ed., 1984), p. 98.
[54] See *Let the People Know: a report on local advice services in Scotland*, SCC, 1977; and *Following Our Advice: a review of advice services in Scotland*, SCC, 1988.

# INDEX